THE DEATH PENALTY

THE SEMINARS OF JACQUES DERRIDA

Edited by Geoffrey Bennington and Peggy Kamuf

The Death Penalty

VOLUME I

Jacques Derrida

Edited by Geoffrey Bennington, Marc Crépon,
and Thomas Dutoit

Translated by Peggy Kamuf

The University of Chicago Press ‡ CHICAGO AND LONDON

JACQUES DERRIDA (1930–2004) was director of studies at the École des hautes études en sciences sociales, Paris, and professor of humanities at the University of California, Irvine. He is the author of many books published by the University of Chicago Press, most recently, *The Beast and the Sovereign Volume I* and *The Beast and the Sovereign Volume II*. PEGGY KAMUF is the Marion Frances Chevalier Professor of French and Comparative Literature at the University of Southern California. She has written, edited, or translated many books, by Derrida and others, and is coeditor of the series of Derrida's seminars at the University of Chicago Press.

Publication of this book has been aided by a grant from the National Endowment for the Humanities.

The University of Chicago Press, Chicago 60637
The University of Chicago Press, Ltd., London
© 2014 by The University of Chicago
All rights reserved. Published 2014.
Printed in the United States of America

Originally published as *Séminaire: La peine de mort, Volume I (1999–2000)*. © 2012 Éditions Galilée.

23 22 21 20 19 18 17 16 15 14   1 2 3 4 5

ISBN-13: 978-0-226-14432-0 (cloth)
ISBN-13: 978-0-226-09068-9 (e-book)
DOI: 10.7208/chicago/9780226090689.001.0001

Library of Congress Cataloging-in-Publication Data

Derrida, Jacques, author.
[Séminaire La peine de mort. Selections. English]
The death penalty. Volume I / Jacques Derrida ; edited by Geoffrey Bennington, Marc Crépon, and Thomas Dutoit ; translated by Peggy Kamuf.
pages cm — (The seminars of Jacques Derrida)
"Originally published as Séminaire: La peine de mort, vol. 1 (1999–2000). © 2012 Éditions Galilée"—Title page verso.
Includes bibliographical references and index.
ISBN 978-0-226-14432-0 (cloth : alkaline paper)—
ISBN 978-0-226-09068-9 (e-book) 1. Capital punishment—Philosophy. I. Bennington, Geoffrey, editor. II. Crépon, M. (Marc), 1962– editor. III. Dutoit, Thomas, editor. IV. Kamuf, Peggy, 1947– translator. V. Title. VI. Series: Derrida, Jacques. Works. Selections. English. 2009.
HV8698.D4713 2014
364.6601 — dc23

2013016561

♾ This paper meets the requirements of ANSI/NISO z39.48-1992 (Permanence of Paper).

CONTENTS

When the decision was made to edit and publish Jacques Derrida's teaching lectures, there was little question that they would and should be translated into English. From early in his career, in 1968, and annually thereafter until 2003, Derrida regularly taught at US universities. It was his custom to repeat for his American audience the lectures delivered to his students in France the same year. Teaching first at Johns Hopkins and then at Yale, he read the lectures in French as they had been written. But from 1987, when he began teaching at the University of California, Irvine, Derrida undertook to lecture in English, improvising on-the-spot translations of his lectures. Recognizing that the greater part of his audience outside of France depended on translation was easier, however, than providing an ad libitum English version of his own elegant, complex, and idiomatic writing. In the circumstance, to his evident joy in teaching was often added a measure of suffering and regret for all that remained behind in the French original. It is to the memory of Derrida the teacher as well as to all his students past and still to come that we offer these English translations of "The Seminars of Jacques Derrida."

The volumes in this series are translations of the original French editions published by Éditions Galilée, Paris, and will in each case follow shortly the publication of the corresponding French volume. The scope of the project, and the basic editorial principles followed in establishing the text, are outlined in the "General Introduction to the French Edition," translated here. Editorial issues and decisions relating more specifically to this volume are addressed in an "Editorial Note." Editors' footnotes and other editorial interventions are all translated without modification, except in the case of footnoted citations of quoted material, which refer to extant English translations of the source as necessary. Additional translators' notes have been kept to a minimum. To facilitate scholarly reference, the page numbers of the French edition are printed in the margin on the line at which the new page begins.

Translating Derrida is a notoriously difficult enterprise, and while the translator of each volume assumes full responsibility for the integrity of the translation, as series editors we have also reviewed the translations and sought to ensure a standard of accuracy and consistency across the volumes. Toward this end, in the first phase of work on the series, we have called upon the advice of other experienced translators of Derrida's work into English and wish to thank them here: Pascale-Anne Brault, Michael Naas, Elizabeth Rottenberg, and David Wills, as well as all the other participants in the Derrida Seminars Translation Project workshops.

Geoffrey Bennington
Peggy Kamuf
DECEMBER 2012

GENERAL INTRODUCTION TO
THE FRENCH EDITION

The complete edition of Jacques Derrida's seminars and lectures will give the reader the chance of an unprecedented contact with the philosopher's teaching voice. This edition will constitute a new part of his oeuvre, to be distinguished from the books and other texts published during his lifetime or revised by him before his death, and with a clearly different status. It is not certain that Jacques Derrida would have published the seminars as they stand: probably he would have reorganized or rewritten them. Taken as a whole, but also in their relation to Derrida's philosophical oeuvre, these lectures and seminars will constitute an incomparable research tool and will, we believe, give a different experience of his thinking, here linked to his teaching, which was always, both in France and abroad, a truly vital resource of his writing.

The corpus we are preparing for publication is vast. From the beginning of his teaching career, Derrida was in the habit of completely writing out almost all his lectures and seminars. This means that we have at our disposal the equivalent of some fourteen thousand printed pages, or forty-three volumes, on the basis of one volume per academic year. This material can be classified according to a variety of criteria. First, according to the place where the teaching took place: the Sorbonne from 1960 to 1964; the École normale supérieure in the rue d'Ulm, from 1964 to 1984; the École des hautes etudes en sciences sociales (EHESS) from 1984 to 2003.[1] Then

1. We need to add the American places as well: from fall 1968 to 1974 at the Johns Hopkins University, then as visiting professor in the humanities from 1975 to 1986 at Yale University, where he gave each year, in the fall or spring semester, a regular seminar. From 1987 to 2003, Derrida taught regularly at the University of California, Irvine, and at the New School for Social Research, the Cardozo Law School, and New York University (1992–2003). This American teaching (which, with a few exceptions, repeated the EHESS seminar) was given at first in French, but after 1987 most often

according to the type of teaching: classes with a very variable number of sessions (from one to fifteen) up until 1964; what he always called "seminars" thereafter. Finally—and no doubt most relevantly for the editorial work—according to the tools used: we have handwritten sessions from 1960 to 1970; typescripts, with manuscript annotations and corrections, from 1970 to 1988; electronic files and printouts from 1988 to 2003.

Derrida's seminars, which already had their own style and already attracted a broad and numerous following at the rue d'Ulm (where the choice of subjects and authors, if not the way they were treated, was constrained by the program of the Agrégation),[2] take on their definitive character at the EHESS where, on Wednesdays from 5:00 p.m. to 7:00 p.m., a dozen times a year, Jacques Derrida, sometimes improvising a little, would read before a large audience the text of his seminar, entirely written out for each session as the year proceeded. (Add to that a few improvised sessions, sometimes around a reading, and a few discussion sessions.) Henceforth free in his choice of subjects, Derrida launched research projects over periods of several years, which link together in explicit, coherent, and gripping fashion. The great question of philosophical nationality and nationalism (1984–88) leads to that of the "Politics of Friendship" (1988–91), and then to the long series of "Questions of Responsibility" (1991–2003), focusing successively on the Secret (1991–92), on Testimony (1992–95), Hostility and Hospitality (1995–97), Perjury and Pardon (1997–99) and the Death Penalty (1999–2001), with the final two years devoted to "The Beast and the Sovereign" (2001–3).

Derrida was in the habit of drawing on the abundant material of these seminars for the very numerous lectures he gave every year throughout the world, and often, via this route, parts of the seminars were reworked and published. Several of his books also find their point of departure in the work of the seminar: *Of Grammatology* (1967), for example, in large part develops sessions of the 1965–66 seminar on "Nature, Culture, Writing"; the seminar on "Hegel's Family" (1971–72) is picked up in *Glas* (1974). *Politics of Friendship* (1994) is explicitly presented as the expansion of the first session of the 1988–89 seminar, and there are traces in it of other sessions too. But in spite of these partial convergences and correspondences, the vast majority of the

---

in English: Derrida would improvise during the session an English version of his text, which he had previously annotated for this purpose.

2. [Translator's note:] The Agrégation is the notoriously competitive qualifying examination taken by prospective higher-level teachers in the secondary and university systems.

pages written from week to week for the seminar remain unpublished and will incomparably complement the work already published. Whenever a session was later published by Jacques Derrida, in modified form or not, we will give the reference. We do not consider it appropriate for the edition of the seminars themselves, as original material, to offer a comparative reading of those versions.

As we have already pointed out, the editorial work varies considerably according to the mode of production of the text. For the typewriter period, many handwritten amendments and annotations require a considerable effort of decipherment; the more so for the seminars entirely written in Derrida's handsome but difficult handwriting, which require laborious transcription. So we shall begin by publishing the seminars of the last twenty years, while beginning preparation of the rest. In all cases, our primary goal is to present the *text* of the seminar, as *written* by Derrida, *with a view to* speech, to reading aloud, and thus with some marks of anticipated orality and some familiar turns of phrase. It is not certain that Derrida would have published these seminars, although he occasionally expressed his intention of doing so,[3] but if he had taken up these texts for publication, he would probably have reworked them, as he always did, in the direction of a more written text. Obviously we have not taken it upon ourselves to do that work in his place. As we mentioned above, the reader may wish to compare the original version presented here with the few sessions published separately by Jacques Derrida himself.

Geoffrey Bennington
Marc Crépon
Marguerite Derrida
Thomas Dutoit
Peggy Kamuf
Michel Lisse
Marie-Louise Mallet
Ginette Michaud

---

3. See, for example, the foreword to *Politiques de l'amitié* (Paris: Galilée, 1994), p. 11; *Politics of Friendship*, trans. George Collins (London: Verso Books, 1997), p. vii.

The present volume edits the first of two years of a seminar that Jacques Derrida would devote to the subject of the death penalty, in 1999–2000 and 2000–2001. Presented integrally at the École des hautes études en sciences sociales (EHESS) in Paris, within the frame of its "Philosophy and Epistemology" program, this seminar was also the basis of teaching Derrida did in the United States: at the University of California, Irvine, during five weeks in spring 2000 and again in spring 2001, as well as at New York University, for three weeks in fall 2000 and fall 2001.

This seminar precedes immediately the one devoted to "The Beast and the Sovereign," which is already published.[1] It is part of the series begun in 1997–98 and continued in 1998–99 under the title "Perjury and Pardon," which itself belongs to a longer series, "Questions of Responsibility," begun in 1989 and ended in 2003, the last year Derrida taught.

The first year of this seminar did not have its own title, and it was not until the *EHESS Annual Report 2000–2001*, in the second year of this seminar, that the title was spelled out as "Questions of Responsibility (VIII: The Death Penalty)."[2]

1. *Séminaire La bête et le souverain*, vol. 1 (2001–2002) and vol. 2 (2002–2003), ed. Michel Lisse, Marie-Louise Mallet, and Ginette Michaud (Paris: Galilée, 2008 and 2010); *The Beast and the Sovereign*, vol. 1 (2001–2002) and vol. 2 (2002–2003), trans. Geoffrey Bennington (Chicago: University of Chicago Press, 2009 and 2011).

2. Reading the *Reports on Courses and Lectures* published by EHESS between 1996 and 2003, we remark that there is an error in the announcement for the seminar on the death penalty:

1996–97, "Questions of Responsibility (V. Hostility/Hospitality)"
1997–98, "Questions of Responsibility (VI. Perjury and Pardon)"
1998–99, "Questions of Responsibility (VII. Perjury and Pardon)"
1999–2000, "Questions of Responsibility (VII. Perjury and Pardon)"
2000–2001, "Questions of Responsibility (VIII. Death Penalty)"

The careful reader of the series represented by this two-year development on "the death penalty" will easily perceive each year's structure and
the way the total of twenty-two sessions is composed. It is not our task to
provide an interpretation or remarks as to details of this structure. However, the reader should have in mind already that the developments, or even
the areas or "themes" of the first volume are clearly distinct from those of
the seminar's second year. While a reading of the two together can reveal
some guiding threads, it should not mask the way in which Derrida dissociates the two years according to the different series or subseries that respec-
tively structure them, not to mention the corpus and the different disciplinary fields that vary from one year to the other. Derrida himself provides
some of these details at the beginning of the second year of his seminar,
as well as in the reports he wrote for the two years of the course. Thus we
invite the reader of this first volume not to finalize his "idea" of the death
penalty (or death penalties) according to Jacques Derrida so long as the second volume, which is different in many ways from the first, has not been
published.

15   Here is how Derrida summarized the 1999–2000 seminar that interests
us here:

> The problematic opened up under this title <"Perjury and Pardon"> these
> last two years led us to privilege this time the enormous question of the
> death penalty. This was necessary at least to the extent that so-called capital
> punishment puts into play, in the imminence of an irreversible sanction,
> along with what appears to be held to be unpardonable, the concepts of
> sovereignty (of the State or the head of State—right of life and death over
> the citizen), of the right to pardon, etc.
>   We studied the death penalty, at least in a preliminary manner, on the
> basis both of some great canonical examples (Socrates, Jesus, Hallaj, Joan of
> Arc) and of canonical texts, from the Bible to Camus or Badinter, via Bec-
> caria, Locke, Kant, Hugo—to whom we devoted many sessions—Genet,
> etc., and especially to post–World War II juridical texts. Indeed, a large
> number of international conventions recommend the end of cruel punish-
> ments and torture, including the death penalty, without ever making this
> an obligation for states, whose sovereignty had to be respected. We looked

---

2001–2002, "Questions of Responsibility (IX. The Beast and the Sovereign)"
2002–2003, "Questions of Responsibility (X. The Beast and the Sovereign)"
In fact, the title of the 1998–99 seminar is utilized again for 1999–2000, even though
the subject and the content had changed. An administrative error or oversight? In any
case, the numbering is also in error, VII is repeated, which throws off the numbering
of the following years.

at abolitionist movements, their logic and their rhetoric, and especially at the United States, the recent and even current history of which required much analysis—especially since the decision of the Supreme Court which, in 1972, judged unconstitutional the application of the death penalty ("cruel and unusual punishment"), up to the amplified and spectacular return to executions since 1977, and so on. We paid a great deal of attention to the exception of the United States.

Three problematic concepts dominated our questioning through the texts and examples we studied: *sovereignty*, *exception*, and *cruelty*. Another guiding question: why have abolitionism or condemnation of the death penalty, in its very principle, (almost) never, to date, found a properly philosophical place in the architectonic of a great philosophical discourse as such? How are we to interpret this highly significant fact?[3]

Several months earlier, he had written another description of the seminar, in English, for the American public to which he would be presenting it in the spring at the University of California, Irvine: *16*

DEATH PENALTY

In continuing the past years' seminars (Pardon and Perjury), we will take up this year, under the heading of the *unforgivable*, the question of capital punishment.

We will start by studying its history, its juridical and political dimensions, the present stakes of its abolishment (in the process of *mondialisation*, the becoming-worldwide, or "globalization," particularly in the United States). We will also analyze the "scene," the history of its visibility and of its "public" character generally, but also its representation in the arts of theater, painting, photography, cinema and of course, literature.

Intertwined in this first approach will be two guiding threads: the equivocal concepts of "cruelty" and of "exception," which play a determining role in juridical discourses (for and against the death penalty).

On the horizon—the big question of sovereignty in general, of sovereignty of the state in particular.[4]   *17*

The two years of this seminar include twenty-two separate sessions, of which there are twelve in the first year (1999–2000),[5] while the second year

3. *Annuaire de l'EHESS (1999–2000). Comptes-rendus des cours et conférences* (Paris: Éditions de l'EHESS, 2000), pp. 599–600.

4. A copy of this description in English is archived with the printed version of the seminar from which Derrida read to his English-speaking audience. It also contains a bibliography intended for the American students. Because the references it contains are given in various footnotes in the present volume, we do not reproduce it here.

5. In this first year, two sessions were divided between Derrida's prepared text and a student exposé: the fifth session, on January 26, 2000, and the eleventh session, on

(2000–2001) contains ten sessions. Both seminars were written by Derrida on the computer. Of the twelve sessions in this first year, the first is double, numbered 1 and 1 (continued),[6] which explains why the last session is numbered "eleventh." The entire set is unpublished, with the exception of this first double session, which was the basis of a lecture in Sofia, Bulgaria, followed by a publication titled "Peine de mort et souveraineté (pour une déconstruction de l'onto-théologie politique)" [Death penalty and sovereignty (for a deconstruction of political onto-theology)].[7]

For the present edition, we worked from different printed versions, which we designate as "typescript," as well as available electronic files. The printed set of the seminar for 1999–2000, deposited at the Institut Mémoires de l'Édition Contemporaine (IMEC, Caen), are found in three folders. A buff-colored folder contains sessions 2 through 7. On the first page of several sessions, Derrida has written "copy." There are no handwritten annotations on this set. A yellow folder contains sessions 1 and 1 (continued), and 8 through 11. Derrida has written "copy" on the first page of the first session. On the ninth session, he has corrected by hand several typos and indicated that he will present a part of this session at New York University. He has also corrected several typos on the printed copy of the tenth session. On the back of the last two pages of the ninth session (which are the photocopied pages of an American newspaper article), Derrida sketched a brief outline on the relation between bio-power according to Michel Foucault and the question of interest in the death penalty. We have not transcribed it because, first, we have not included an oral exposé that a student presented on the chapter "Right of Death and Power over Life" in Foucault's *History of Sexuality*, volume 1, *An Introduction*, and, second, it is only partially decipherable.

Finally, a blue folder contains a complete set of the seminar sessions, annotated by hand by Derrida, principally as he prepared the course for presentation in English at UC Irvine and NYU, and adapted certain parts as a lecture like the one given in Sofia. It is in this set that the photocopies of texts quoted in the seminar are included and annotated very clearly so as to find the precise passage and comment on it. It is thus above all on the basis of this copy that we worked.

Our editorial interventions in Derrida's typescript are as minimal as possible. As always, the seminar is entirely drafted, and Derrida carefully in-

March 22, 2000. We have not transcribed either the exposés or the discussion that followed them.

6. See below, "First Session, December 8, 1999," p. 28, n. 1.
7. In *Divinatio* 15 (Sofia) (Spring–Summer 2002): 13–38.

dicates on his typescript the source of the quotations that he will read out to the audience and comment on in detail. When he does not reproduce the text of quotations, he indicates very clearly where they begin and end with a system of cross-references between his typescript and the books or photocopies from the books from which they are extracted. When these bibliographic references had to be spelled out or completed, we did so on the basis of his own photocopies or the volumes consulted in his personal library. When the edition he used could not be found, we relied on the most authoritative editions.

19

We have footnoted significant handwritten additions that Derrida made in the margin of the typescript. When a grammatical correction seemed necessary, we signaled it either with angle brackets (< >) in the text or an explanatory footnote. Likewise, we have stayed close to this writing marked by its oral destination and thus, among other things, by a rhythm and temporality whose stylistic modalities affect the syntax of the sentence and the movement of the paragraph. We have occasionally made minimal adjustments to the punctuation. Concerned to preserve the orality of this writing, we have also reproduced all the didascalia that figure in the typescript, as well as the reminders he addressed to himself such as the "Read and comment on" that precede a quotation and often an improvised development during the session. Taken from audio recordings, these improvised comments have been integrated in footnotes each time they added substantially to the development under way.

Jacques Derrida's personal library on the death penalty is extensive; his annotations of books, scholarly articles, newspaper clippings but also of publications from Amnesty International attest to an abundant and varied documentation. In the study where he worked, these documents were prominently placed, next to those relating to different writing projects that occupied him during the same period—notably, *Touching—Jean-Luc Nancy*.[8]

Unlike certain other seminars that come before or after "The Death Penalty," very little of his own research devoted to the death penalty was published in France. Four years before the beginning of this seminar, however, he did write the preface to *Live from Death Row* by Mumia Abu-Jamal.[9] We have already mentioned that the only publication linked directly to the

20

---

8. Derrida, *Le Toucher, Jean-Luc Nancy* (Paris: Galilée, 2000); *Touching—Jean-Luc Nancy,* trans. Christine Irizarry (Stanford, CA: Stanford University Press, 2005).

9. Mumia Abu-Jamal, *En direct du couloir de la mort*, trans. J. Cohen, with a preface by Jacques Derrida (Paris: La Découverte, 1996); 7–13 for Derrida's preface.

seminar was of the lecture in Sofia, published in the journal *Divinatio*. One can nevertheless read Derrida's remarks in *For What Tomorrow* as a veritable synthesis of his seminar.[10]

During a stay in Hong Kong several days after September 11, 2001 (on a detour from a trip in China where he was not able to present his seminar openly given the taboo nature of the subject and the risks to which his hosts and friends would have been exposed),[11] Derrida ventured to discuss once again the theme of the death penalty. According to witness accounts by Chan-Fai Cheung and Kwok-Ying Lau (professors in the department of philosophy at the University of Hong Kong, who invited him), Derrida improvised for several hours on the conjoined questions of *mondialisation*, or globalization, and the death penalty.

We thank Marguerite Derrida, who opened her home to us and gave us access to Jacques Derrida's library and his working papers. Without her affectionate and attentive support, our work would never have been completed. We also thank Chan-Fai Cheung and Kwok-Ying Lau of the Chinese University of Hong Kong; François Bordes and José Ruiz-Funes of IMEC; our advance scouts, Michel Lisse, Marie-Louise Mallet, and Ginette Michaud, the editorial team of the preceding volumes of the "Beast and the Sovereign" seminar; Delmiro Rocha, Federico Rodriguez Gomez, and Beatriz Blanco, as well as Cristina de Peretti, for their help these last four years; the many participants in the Derrida Seminars Translation Project, directed by Peggy Kamuf; Eric Prenowitz for having given us access to his recordings of the seminar; and Patrice Théry and Dominique Perrin of the Centre Audiovisuel and Multimedia at the University of Lille 3 for the digital conversion of the audio files.

Geoffrey Bennington
Marc Crépon
Thomas Dutoit

10. J. Derrida and E. Roudinesco, *De quoi demain . . . Dialogue* (Paris: Fayard and Galilée, 2001); *For What Tomorrow . . . A Dialogue*, trans. Jeff Fort (Stanford, CA: Stanford University Press, 2004); chapter 8 is titled "Death Penalties."

11. For a summary of Derrida's several lectures and talks during this trip to China, see Ning Zhang, "Jacques Derrida's First Visit to China: A Summary of His Lectures and Seminars," *Dao: A Journal of Comparative Philosophy* 2, no. 1 (December 2002): 145.

December 8, 1999

What do you respond to someone who might come to you, at dawn, and say: "You know, the death penalty is what is proper to man"?

(Long silence)

As for me, I would first be tempted to answer him, too quickly: yes, you are right. Unless it is what is proper to God—or unless that comes down to the same thing. Then, resisting the temptation by virtue of another temptation—or in virtue of a counter-temptation—I would be tempted, upon reflection, not to respond too quickly and to let him wait—for many days and many nights. Until dawn.

(Long silence)

It is dawn, now, we are at dawn. In the first light of dawn. In the whiteness of dawn (*alba*). Before beginning, let us begin. We would begin.

We would begin by pretending to begin before the beginning.

As if, already, we wanted to delay the end, because this year, with the death penalty, it is indeed of the end that we are going to speak. It is indeed of an end, but of an end *decided*, by a verdict, of an end decreed by a judicial decree [*arrêtée par un arrêt de justice*], it is of a decided end that decidedly we are going to talk endlessly, but of an end decided by the other, which is not necessarily, a priori, the case of every end and every death, assuming at least, as concerns the decision this time, as concerns the essence of the decision, that it is ever decided otherwise than by the other. And assuming that the decision of which we are getting ready to speak, the death penalty, is not the very archetype of decision. Assuming, then, that anyone ever makes a decision that is his or hers, for himself or herself, his or her own proper decision. I have often expressed my doubts on this subject. The death penalty, as the sovereign decision of a power, reminds us perhaps, before anything else, that a sovereign decision is always the other's. Come from the other.

So we would pretend to begin not after the end, after the end of the death penalty, which is abolished today in only a limited number of nation-states

24

in the world, a growing number but still limited (ten years ago, it was a minority — fifty-eight; today it is a small majority), but to begin before the beginning, on the eve of the beginning, at dawn, in the early morning, as if I wanted to begin in a somewhat pathos-laden fashion (but who would dare conduct without pathos a seminar on the death penalty?) [as if I would prefer to begin, in a deliberately pathos-laden fashion] by leading you or keeping you with me, before beginning, at dawn, in this early morning of prisons, of all the places of detention in the world where those condemned to death are waiting for someone to come either to announce to them a sovereign pardon (that pardon [*grâce*] we often spoke of last year around the subject of forgiveness) or else to lead them away, a priest almost always being there (and I insist on this because today I will be speaking above all of political theology and of the religion of the death penalty, of the religion always present at the death penalty, of the death penalty as religion) [or else to lead them away, then,] toward one of those very numerous apparatuses for legally putting to death that men have ingeniously invented, throughout the history of humanity as history of techniques, techniques for policing and making war, military techniques but also medical, surgical, anesthesial techniques for administering so-called capital punishment. Along with the cruelty of which you are aware, and a cruelty, always the same, which you nevertheless know can range from the greatest brutality of slaughter to the most perverse refinement, from the most bloody or burning torture to the most denied, the most concealed, the most invisible, the most sublimely mechanized torture, invisibility and denial being never, and in no case, anything other than a piece of theatrical, spectacular, or even voyeuristic machinery. By definition, in essence, by vocation, there will never have been any invisibility for a legal putting to death, for an application of the death penalty; there has never been, on principle, a secret or invisible execution for this verdict. The spectacle and the spectator are required. The state, the polis, the whole of politics, the co-citizenry — itself or mediated through representation — must attend and attest, it must testify publicly that death was dealt or inflicted, it must *see die* the condemned one.

The state must and wants to *see die* the condemned one.

And moreover it is at that moment, in the instant at which the people having become the state or the nation-state *sees die* the condemned one that it best sees itself. It best sees itself, that is, it acknowledges and becomes aware of its absolute sovereignty and that it *sees itself* in the sense in French where "il se voit" can mean "it lets itself be seen" or "it gives itself to be seen."[1]

---

1. During the session, Derrida adds: "or else 'it sees itself.'"

Never is the state or the people or the community or the nation in its statist figure, never is the sovereignty of the state more *visible* in the gathering that founds it than when it makes itself into the *seer* and the *voyeur* [voyante *et* voyeuse] of the execution of an irrevocable and unpardoned verdict, of an *execution.* For this act of witnessing—the state as witness of the execution and witness of itself, of its own sovereignty, of its own almightiness—this act of witnessing must be visual: an eye witness. It thus never happens without a stage and lighting, that of the natural light of day or artificial lighting. In the course of history, the light of fire might have been added to it. Not always or only that of gunfire, of the condemned shot by a firing squad or by a single bullet to the base of the skull, but also sometimes the fire of the stake.

We have not yet begun, nothing has yet begun. We are in the early morning. It is dawn, the dawning of one knows not what, life or death, pardon or execution, the abolition or perpetuation of the death penalty, also the perpetration of the death penalty. Whatever we may think or say during this seminar, we have to think, we will have to think ceaselessly, taking ourselves there by way of the heart and the imagination, by the body as well, of the early morning of what is called an execution. At the dawn of the last day. 26

It is dawn, then. Early light, earliest light. Before the end, before even beginning, before the three blows are struck,[2] the actors and the places are ready, they are waiting for us in order to begin.

Just as, last year, we played without playing at the theater, we pretended to play at staging, as theatrically but also as nontheatrically as possible, [at staging] four men, statesmen or thinkers of the state, statesmen or churchmen, thinkers of the state or of the church or both (Hegel, Mandela, Tutu, Clinton: four Protestants of modern times—not one woman, no Catholic, no Orthodox, no Jew or Muslim),[3] well, this year, before beginning, and because the question of the theater will have to keep our attention even more and otherwise than in the scene without scene or stage without stage of forgiveness (the history of the relations between the death penalty and spec-

2. [Translator's note]: An allusion to the practice in French theaters where three blows are struck on the stage to signal the beginning of the performance.

3. This reference is to a development over several sessions of the seminar at EHESS "Perjury and Pardon" (second year, 1998–99) that Derrida wrote after returning from a trip to South Africa (session 1, December 2, 1998; session 2, December 9, 1998; and session 3, January 13, 1999). He published a part of this development with the title "Versöhnung, ubuntu, pardon : Quel genre?" in *Le genre humain* 43: *Vérité, réconciliation, réparation*, ed. Barbara Cassin, Olivier Cayla, and Philippe-Joseph Salazar (2004): 111–56. In a note accompanying the publication of this text, Derrida likewise points to the comparison with "the four witnesses" of the present seminar.

tacle, the *mise en scène*, the essential voyeurism that attaches to a putting to death that must be public because legal, this history of the theater of capital punishment would in itself deserve a whole seminar and it will interest us a lot, even if never enough), well, this year again I will begin, before beginning, by evoking, by convoking or resuscitating a few figures, great personalities, great characters[4] who will accompany us incessantly — whether or not we name them or see them. Once again they will be four; this time there will be no Protestant among them; they, masculine *and* feminine, will once again be four, but this time a woman will come to remind us of one of the sexual differences in this truth of the death penalty. (Recall the question that we were asking or quoting last year, from out of the South Africa of Antjie Krog, author of *Country of My Skull*, and of the women victims who testify or cannot testify before the Truth and Reconciliation Commission:[5] "Does truth have a gender?" or else, and it is the title of a chapter: "Truth Is a Woman.")[6]

What will be, this year, who will be these masculine and/or feminine "characters"? Those condemned to death, to be sure, or those who accompany them, a chorus of great condemned ones from our history, from the history of the Graeco-Abrahamic West, condemned ones who have illustrated, or even founded, by means of the scene, by means of the visibility and the time, by means of the duration of their putting to death, [who have illustrated, then,] the properly *theologico-political* meaning of what is called the "death penalty."

Each time the state, associated with a clerical or religious power in ways that must be examined, will have pronounced these verdicts and executed these great condemned ones that were then (there are four of them, once again), who were then (I will name them only one after the other when the time comes) first of all *Socrates*, of course, the first of the four. Socrates who, as you know — but we will come back to this — was reproached with having corrupted the youth by not believing in the gods of the city and by substituting for them new gods, as if his aim had been to found another religion and to think a new man. Reread the *Apology* and the *Crito*, you will see there that an essentially religious accusation is taken up by a state power, a power of the polis, a politics, a juridico-political authority, what one might

---

4. [Translator's note]: The word "characters" is in English in the original.

5. During the session, Derrida adds: "because, as women, they could not testify without repeating the violence of which they had been victims, and you remember that one of the chapters was titled . . ."

6. See Antjie Krog, *Country of My Skull* (Johannesburg: Random House, 1998).

call with terrible ambiguity a sovereign power as *executive* power. The *Apology* says it explicitly (24b–c): the *katēgoria*, the accusation lodged against Socrates, is to have done the wrong, to have been guilty, to have committed the injustice (*adikein*) of corrupting the youth and of (or for) having ceased to honor (*nomizein*) the gods (*theous*) of the city or the gods honored by the city—and especially of having substituted for them not simply new gods, as the translations often say, but new demons (*hetera de daimonia kaina*); and *daimonia* are doubtless often gods, divinities, but also sometimes, as in Homer, inferior gods or revenants, the souls of the dead; and the text does indeed make the distinction between gods and demons: Socrates did not honor the gods (*theous*) of the city and he introduced new demons (*hetera de daimonia kaina*). Thus, in its content the accusation is religious, properly theological, exegetical, even. Socrates is accused of heresy or blasphemy, of sacrilege or heterodoxy: he is misled about the gods; he is misled, or he misleads others, especially the youth, on the subject of the gods; he was mistaken about the gods or he has caused contempt and misunderstanding [*le mépris et la méprise*] concerning the gods of the city. But this accusation, this charge, this *katēgoria* of an essentially religious nature is taken up, as always—and we will be interested consistently in this recurrent, always recurrent articulation— by a state power, as sovereign, a state power whose sovereignty is itself essentially phantasmatico-theological and, like all sovereignty, is marked by the right of life and death over the citizen, by the power of deciding, laying down the law, judging, and *executing* the order at the same time as the condemned one. Even in nation-states that have abolished the death penalty, an abolition of the death penalty that is in no way equivalent to the abolition of the right to kill, for example, in war, well, these several nation-states of democratic modernity that have abolished the death penalty keep a sovereign right over the life of citizens whom they can send to war to kill or be killed in a space that is radically foreign to the space of internal legality, of the civil law where the death penalty may be either maintained or abolished.[7]

To return for a moment to Socrates and Plato and to the fundamentally religious character of the charge, the complaint, the incrimination, the

7. During the session, Derrida clarifies: "I say this briefly to indicate the direction. It is obvious that in my argumentation and in the pathos you will hear, my discourse is going to be abolitionist, obviously, you have already understood that, but this will not prevent me from posing critical or deconstructive questions about the abolitionist discourse, about the logic that supports at present the abolitionist discourse and that itself seems to me contestable."

criminalization, the inculpation taken up by the state, I refer you to Plato's *Laws* that justifies the death penalty in cases of *impiety* (*asebeia*), of stubborn impiety, of repeated offenses of impiety. I leave you to read closely these long and riveting pages in *Laws* (907d–909d). The city, the polis must proclaim to all that the impious must make amends and be converted to a pious life and that if they do not do so, if they show impiety (*asebeia*) in words or deeds, the first to witness this must denounce them to the magistrate who will call them before the appropriate tribunal. There follows the description of the types of impiety (including, and I note this because of the subject of our seminar, irreverence with regard to oaths [*horkous*]) and then the taxonomy of three types of prisons or houses of correction; I leave you to read this on your own, then. But in this long and rich passage, I note merely two or three indications.

1. *First indication:* To persist with this moment of dawn, I note that in the description of the punishments, it is said that the prisoner will receive no visit from citizens, with the exception of members of a certain *nocturnal council.* So, if you wish to know what this nocturnal council is (which I point to, then, because of dawn and religion, and soon the dawning of religions, if not the twilight of the gods), go to the place where the said nocturnal council is first defined by Plato, that is, not *Laws* (907–9), which I have just quoted and where the nocturnal council is certainly named, merely named, but further on, in *Laws* (951d–e), where the Athenian describes this nocturnal council, this nighttime *syllogos* as a place of gathering, an assembly where the young are mingled with the old but that, I quote, "shall be required to hold daily sessions from daybreak until after sunrise" (951d).[8] This *syllogos* is neither a synagogue (explain)[9] nor a *sanhedrin.* This supreme council of the nation that was also a high court of justice (the one that sentenced Jesus and that we will speak of again), but[10] a *syllogos* (comment) will be comprised of priests and, among the priests (*tōn hiereōn*; this is literally a *hierarchy*, a sacred order or authority of priests who are in command), those who have received the highest distinctions and then, among the guardians of the law (*tōn nomophulakōn*), the ten oldest, then finally any minister of education, whoever has charge of the education of the youth (*tēs paideias pasēs epime-*

8. Plato, *The Collected Dialogues,* ed. Edith Hamilton and Huntington Cairns (Princeton, NJ: Bollingen Series, Princeton University Press, 1961), p. 1497. The *Laws* is translated by A. E. Taylor.

9. During the session, Derrida adds: "A synagogue is a place where one goes together; the *syllogos* is a place where one discusses together."

10. As such in the typescript.

lētēs), whether he be currently in office or whether he has been in the past. (Imagine the equivalent of the nocturnal council in France today: Lustiger, the Head Rabbi, the Head Mufti, Allègre, his predecessors and company.)[11] So, this great *syllogos*, this great pedagogico-confessional council meets *at dawn*. And it alone is entitled to visit the prisoner. First indication.

2. *Second indication:* The council, the *syllogos*, receives visitors, consultants, observers, experts returning from abroad where they went to study the customs and laws of other countries. Well, if one of them comes back spoiled or corrupted, if he continues to make a display of his false wisdom, to refer willy-nilly to foreign models and if he does not obey the magistrate, "he shall have sentence of death (*tethnatō*) . . . if the court convicts him of illicit interference in any matter of education or legislation (*peri tēn paideian kai tous nomous*)" (*Laws* 952d).[12] Once the court of justice has proved that he is intervening wrongly, on behalf of the foreigner, in the formation of the youth and the formation of the laws, he is punished with death. So there is the definition and the theatrical scene of this nocturnal council that can decide life and death and that alone can visit prisoners. If now we leave book 12 of the *Laws*, where the status, the composition, and the jurisdictions of this dawn council are defined, and go back to book 10 with which I started, one finds the legitimation of the death penalty in the listing of all the punishments, all the modes and places of incarceration. When someone has made licentious comments about the gods, the sacrifices, or oaths, for example, or encouraged belief in corruptible gods and thus been guilty of a crime of impiety, irreligiosity, he is locked up in a house of correction, in a *sōphronistērion*, a sophronistery, literally, a place of wising up [*d'assagissement*], a house of correction or reformatory as a place of wising up, a place where one is supposed to acquire or recover *sōphrosunē*, wisdom, wisdom in the more precise sense of moderation, temperance, self- control, health of mind or heart. The point is to be put under surveillance so as to become "wise" once again, with that wisdom or *sagesse* (*sōphrosunē*) that has the sense given in French to the word *sage*, of the child who is *sage*, that is, not unruly, disciplined. The *sophronistery* is a disciplinary institution. One is locked up there for at least five years. There, during this time, no citizen can

31

---

11. At the time of the seminar, Cardinal Jean-Marie Lustiger (1926–2007) was archbishop of Paris; Claude Allègre was minister of national education from June 1997 to March 2000.

12. [Translator's note]: In this quotation, Derrida has significantly modified the published French translation by substituting *d'ingérance illicite* [rendered here as "illicit interference"] for *de s'immiscer* ["interfering"; A. E. Taylor translates: "meddling"].

visit the guilty one, with the exception precisely of the members of the noc-turnal council (*tou nukterinou syllogou*) who will come to see him to admon-ish him and — here is the most important point — to save his soul, for the salvation of his soul (*tēs psychēs sōtēria homilountes*). This soteriological func-tion is essential: one must first attempt to amend, save, rehabilitate the soul of the condemned one, and this soteriological mission, this work of saving or salvation is confided, assigned, by statute, to the nocturnal council, to those who alone have visiting rights, in the sophronistery, in the house of correc-tion, in the wising-up institution. Now, if (and here we come already upon our theme of forgiveness and repentance) after this soteriological attempt, the condemned one saves himself, if he repents, if he comes to see the error of his ways and wises up again, if he rehabilitates himself, then he will have the right to live among virtuous people; if not, if he incurs the same sentence a second time, if he commits the offense again and does not repent, he will be punished by death (*thanatōi zēmiousthō*). If he does not repent and mend his ways, then he is unforgivable and the sanction for the unforgivable, for the inexpiable, is the death penalty. Expiation of the inexpiable. But what I wish to underscore already, because this will become an organizing theme of our reflection, is that the death penalty, that is, the legal and legitimate sentencing, is distinct from murder or from putting to death outside the law, from assassination in some sense, in that it treats the condemned one as a subject of rights, a subject of the law, as human being, with the dignity that this still supposes. Here, in a logic that we will continue to find up to Kant and many others, but in Kant par excellence, access to the death penalty is an access to the dignity of human reason, and to the dignity of a man who, unlike beasts, is a subject of the law who raises himself above natural life. That is why, in this logic, in the *logos* of this *syllogos*, the death penalty marks the access to what is proper to man and to the dignity of reason or of hu-man *logos* and *nomos*. All of this, death included, supposedly testifies to the rationality of laws (*logos* and *nomos*) and not to natural or bestial savagery, with the consequence that even if the one condemned to death is deprived of life or of the right to life, he or she has the right to rights and, thus, in a certain way to honor and to a burial place. For, in this logic, in this obscure syllogistics, in the syllogism of this council or of this nocturnal *Syllogos*, there is something worse than the death sentence. This is the case of those guilty ones who are like beasts, who are no longer men and no longer have even the right to be condemned to death, no longer the right to a burial place, and no longer a right to visits by the nocturnal council. Here it is better to be content with reading an extraordinary passage from *Laws* (909b–d). It follows immediately the reference to the death penalty, the penalty deserved

by those who do not repent, the penalty destined, assigned to those who are not rehabilitated, the penalty set aside for those who thus remain as incorrigible as they are unforgivable. In the passage I am going to read, you will discover that there is something worse than the death penalty: there is a punishment more terrifying still because more inhuman, more ahuman than the death penalty, which remains a thing of reason and the law, a thing worthy of reason and the law (*logos* and *nomos*). The criterion of the distinc-   33
tion between the death penalty and what is supposedly still worse than the death penalty, this line of demarcation between the bad and the worst, is not determined by what precedes death, nor is it in the instant of death; it is not in the present of the event of death itself; it is not in death but in the corpse; it is in what follows death and happens to the corpse. For here it is the right to burial that marks the difference between man and beast, between the man condemned to death who still has a right to burial, to men's honor, and the one who no longer deserves even the name of man and who therefore does not deserve even the death penalty. I underscore this point heavily because later we are going to come upon the idea again that the death penalty is a sign of the access to the dignity of man, something that is proper to man who must, through his law, be able to raise himself above life (which beasts cannot do), this idea of the death penalty as condition of human law and of human dignity, one might almost say of the nobility of man, in particular in Kant's argument when he justifies the death penalty, and more than that, when he sees in it even the ultimate justification of the *jus*, of justice and of law. There would be no human *jus*, no law, and no justice in a system that excluded the death penalty. (Read *Laws* 909b–d)

> These distinctions once recognized, the law shall direct the judge to com-
> mit those whose fault is due to folly apart from viciousness of temper or
> disposition to the house of correction for a term of not less than five years.
> Throughout this period they shall have no communication with any citizen
> except the members of the nocturnal council, who shall visit them with a
> view to admonition and their soul's salvation. When the term of confine-
> ment has expired, if the prisoner is deemed to have returned to his right
> mind, he shall dwell with the right-minded, but if not, and he be condemned
> a second time on the same charge, he shall suffer the penalty of death. As
> for those who add the character of a beast of prey to their atheism or belief
> in divine indifference or venality, those who in their contempt of mankind
> bewitch so many of the living by the pretense of evoking the dead and the   34
> promise of winning over the gods by the supposed sorceries of prayer, sac-
> rifice, and incantations, and thus do their best for lucre to ruin individuals,
> whole families, and communities, the law shall direct the court to sentence

a culprit convicted of belonging to this class to incarceration in the central prison, where no free citizen whatsoever shall have access to him, and where he shall receive from the turnkeys the strict rations prescribed by the curators of the laws. At death he shall be cast out beyond the borders without burial, and if any free citizen has a hand in his burial, he shall be liable to a prosecution for impiety at the suit of any who cares to take proceedings. But should he leave children fit to be citizens, the guardians of orphans shall provide for them also, no worse than for other orphans, from the date of the father's conviction. (909a–d)

(Pick up again here)

Forgive me for recalling now at the outset, on the occasion of the example of Socrates and once and for all, a few massively obvious facts, notably the *two* most massive and, at least apparently, the crudest among them. These two obvious facts are going to hold my attention a certain while but do not forget that it is upon the occasion and in the margin of the *Socrates case*, of the first of our four exemplary or prototypical characters, that we take this long detour — after which we will let the three other exemplary condemned ones come or come back in our direction.

What, then, are these two massively obvious facts?

On the one hand, the struggles under way (for a long time now and in an accelerated fashion over the past few decades, since the end of World War II) for the universal abolition of the death penalty (struggles that we will study at least in their main outlines and international juridical sequences, for they have often taken the form of universal declarations and recommendations by international communities), these abolitionist struggles do not concern putting to death or killing in general, for example in wartime, but only the death penalty as legal apparatus of the domestic politics of a nation-state supposed to be sovereign. It is always legal to kill a foreign enemy in the context of declared war even for a country that has abolished the death penalty (and in this regard we will have to ask ourselves what defines an enemy, a stranger, a state of war — civil war or not; the criteria have always been difficult to determine and are becoming so more and more).

On the other hand, secondly, up until certain recent and limited phenomena of legal abolition of the death penalty in a strict sense in a still limited number of countries, well, nation-states of Abrahamic culture, the nation-states in which an Abrahamic religion (Jewish, Christian, or Islamic) was dominant, either because it was the state religion, the official and constitutional religion, or because it was simply the dominant religion in the civil society, well, these nation-states, up until certain recent and limited phenomena of abolitionism, found no contradiction between the death penalty and the commandment "Thou shalt not kill" (about which Lévinas says that, although sixth on the list, it is in fact the first, the fundamental commandment and the archi-foundation of ethics, the very essence of ethics and the first meaning that the Face signifies to me), these nation-states of Abrahamic culture saw no more contradiction between this "thou shalt not kill" (thus, apparently, this absolute right to life, this prohibition against putting to death) and the death penalty, no more contradiction in truth than God himself seemed to find there when, after having thus (in Exodus 20:1–17) prescribed "thou shalt not kill," he ordered Moses to set out before the children of Israel what is translated as the "judgments." What do these so-called judgments say specifically, right after the ten commandments? Well, in substance, that one must condemn to death, and put to death, all those who transgress one or the other of these ten commandments. As you might guess, there are delicate and decisive points of semantics and thus of translation here, we are coming to that, but I quote first Dhorme's translation in the Pléiade edition, which translated the sixth commandment as "tu ne tueras point";[13] in German (Luther's translation modernized and revised): "Du sollst nicht töten"; in English (King James Version): "thou shalt not kill." Chouraqui translates differently, and we will come to that in a moment so as to situate a crucial difference between two ways of inflicting death or putting to death or taking away life. Well, when God, after the Ten Commandments, and thus after this "thou shalt not kill," orders Moses to set out before the children of Israel a list of *judgments* (and it is indeed a matter of judgments, from the Hebrew word *michpat*, which has to do with justice, judgment, jurisprudence, law: God prescribes to his people or his nation, to the children of Israel, a constitution, a law, a jurisprudence, and in particular a penal law, a penal code — all the translations mark this fact, in French, in Dhorme and in Chouraqui, it is "jugements"), <when> God, then, orders Moses to set out these "judgments" before the children of Israel: "Voici les jugements que tu exposeras devant eux"(Dhorme); "Voici les jugements que tu mettras en face d'eux" (Chouraqui);[14] in English (King James): "Now these are the judgments which thou shalt set before them"; in German, the reference to the law, to penal justice is even more explicit: "Dies sind die Rechtsordnungen die du ihnen vorlegen sollst," among these judgments, in what is literally a penal code, a series of principles or rules for determining legal sentences, well, there are quite a few death sentences,

36

13. *La Bible. Ancien Testament*, trans. Édouard Dhorme (Paris: Gallimard, Bibliothèque de la Pléiade, 1956), pp. 235ff.

14. *La Bible*, trans. André Chouraqui (Paris: Desclée de Brouwer, 1985), p. 153.

precisely [*justement*], condemnations to death. God literally prescribes to condemn to death, to subject to the death penalty all those who transgress particular prohibitions set down by the Ten Commandments, in particular the "thou shalt not kill." I quote first the French translation by Dhorme and I defer temporarily that by Chouraqui, which will help us in a moment to see things more clearly here.[15] Among the judgments that God orders to be made known to the children of Israel, there are the following, which I select because they carry death penalties:

37

> He that smiteth a man, so that he die, shall be surely put to death. And if a man lie not in wait [thus whose deed is not premeditated, if I follow correctly], but God deliver him into his hand; then I will appoint thee a place whither he shall flee. But if a man come presumptuously upon his neighbour, to slay him with guile; thou shalt take him from mine altar, that he may die. And he that smiteth his father, or his mother, shall be surely put to death. And he that stealeth a man, and selleth him, or if he be found in his hand, he shall surely be put to death. And he that curseth his father, or his mother, shall surely be put to death. (21:12–17)[16]

In English, still in the King James Version, the equivalent of the French "il sera mis à mort" is "he shall be surely put to death," or for the para-sacrificial motif of "Si pourtant un homme attaque son prochain pour le tuer par ruse, d'auprès de mon autel tu pourras le prendre pour qu'il meure": "thou shalt take him from my altar, that he may die." In German (still Luther's translation revised and modernized), it is each time for whoever did this or that "der soll des Todes sterben," or in the para-sacrificial scene: "so sollst du ihn von meinem Altar wegreissen, dass man ihn töte."

So, how can God tell Moses to order the children of Israel "thou shalt not kill" and in the next moment, in an immediately consecutive and apparently inconsistent fashion, "you will deliver up to death whoever does not obey these commandments"?[17] How can he decree a penal code, a law that looks like a flagrant offense against the ethic of the Ten Commandments? Natu-

15. [Translator's note]: The King James Version has been substituted here for the French translation by Dhorme, which causes some redundancy later when Derrida remarks in particular on the English translation.

16. Dhorme's translation reads: "Quiconque frappe un homme et celui-ci meurt, sera mis à mort. Mais celui qui n'a pas guetté et à la main de qui l'Elohim a fourni l'occasion, je te fixerai un lieu où il pourra se réfugier. Si pourtant un homme attaque son prochain pour le tuer par ruse, d'auprès de mon autel tu pourras le prendre pour qu'il meure. Et celui qui frappe son père ou sa mère sera mis à mort. Celui qui ravit un homme et le vend, si on le trouve en sa main, il sera mis à mort. Celui qui maudit son père ou sa mère sera mis à mort."

17. Derrida is here condensing the verses he has just quoted, Exodus 21:12–17.

rally, I am limiting myself for the moment to this first, very initial example, of Exodus, because if one began to study the death penalty in the Bible we would need an interminable seminar. Well, it's because, as you suspect and no doubt have already understood, the death penalty, the juridical order (*Rechtsordnung*), the judgment, the verdict that sentences death does not refer to the same death, <to> the same putting to death as the one in question in the "thou shalt not kill." One must insist on this, on this difference between two deaths, both so as to discern the specificity of the *death penalty*, which by law ought to be something other than a simple *murder*, and because in the modernity of the abolitionist movement that we will be studying, reference is often made to a right to life as a human right that, even as it seems to refer implicitly to the biblical "thou shalt not kill," exceeds or disregards what it is in this biblical text that in no way concerns either the absolute right to life or even a simple opposition between life and death, but first of all a distinction between two ways of putting to death [*donner la mort*], the one prohibited by the "thou shalt not kill," the other prescribed by the penal code that God dictates to his people through the intermediary of Moses. And the words are not the same; God chooses his words carefully, if I can say that, and that is why Chouraqui's translation interests us here. Chouraqui translates the sixth commandment not by "tu ne tueras pas" [thou shalt not kill] but by "tu n'assassineras pas" [thou shalt not murder] (20:13), as if one had to recall here that the important thing is not the difference between life and death, between the fact of letting live or of taking life, but the modality, the unjustifiable quality of the aggression or the violence, the criminality of that which violates life, but not the fact of attacking life. And as for the judgments, the *Rechtsordnungen*, Chouraqui translates them, as close as possible to the letter and the repetition of the Hebrew, by "mourra, il mourra": "Frappeur d'homme qui meurt, mourra, il mourra . . ." [Striker of man who dies, will die, he will die]; "Qu'un homme prémédite contre son compagnon de le tuer par ruse, de mon autel, tu le prendras pour qu'il meure" [If a man premeditates against his companion to kill him by ruse, from my altar you will take him so that he will die]; "Frappeur de son père, de sa mère, mourra, il mourra" [Striker of his father, of his mother, will die, he will die]; "Voleur d'homme et qui le vend, trouvé en sa main, mourra, il mourra" [Thief of man and who sells him, found in his hand, will die, he will die]; "Maudisseur de son père, de sa mère, mourra, il mourra" [Curser of his father, of his mother, will die, he will die] (21:12–17).[18]

18. During the session, Derrida adds the following commentary: "This death is not a murder. A subtle but essential distinction that naturally will continue to traverse the whole history of law and of the death penalty."

38

39   The two deaths, the two puttings to death apparently have no relation, or so little relation, they are so heterogeneous that there would be no contradiction in *proscribing* the one while *prescribing* the other, in saying "thou shalt not kill" in the sense of "thou shalt not murder" and then saying, ordering that whoever murders shall be punished with death. No relation of affinity, in this logic, between murder and the death penalty, between murder outside the law and the legal death penalty. The difference that counts here is not between life and death but between two ways of putting to death. One death, that of the death penalty, reinstates the law or the commandment that the other death (murder) will have violated. This divine logic will be, moreover, the very one that inspired sometimes literally the most canonical philosophical discourses in favor of the death penalty, as we will see in studying them, I hope, more closely later. Furthermore, all the great thinkers of the Renaissance and the Reformation referred to the Bible. Grotius did so explicitly. Hobbes and Locke justified the death penalty for murderers, as Kant will do later, we are coming to that. Locke in his *Second Treatise of Government* says:

> *Political Power* then I take to be *a Right* of making Laws with Penalties of Death, and consequently all less Penalties, for the Regulating and Preserving of Property, and of employing the force of the Community, in the Execution of such Laws, and in the defence of the Common-wealth from Foreign Injury, and all this only for the Publick Good.[19]

Rousseau, in *The Social Contract*, also justifies the death penalty according to a logic that is more or less analogous (only analogous perhaps) in a very beautiful, very complex chapter that I hope to read closely with you later; it is chapter 5 of book 2 of *The Social Contract*, titled "On the Right of Life and Death," a chapter that not fortuitously comes just after the chapters
40   on *sovereignty*. In the course of a tricky, nuanced, uneasy, even awkward argumentation, from which I excerpt only, for the moment, the following proposition, Rousseau approves the death penalty in these terms:

> The death penalty inflicted on criminals may be seen from much the same point of view [the point of view he has just recalled, that of the state "whose prince says: 'It is expedient for the state that you should die,' and the citizen "must then die since it is only on this condition that he has lived in security until then and since his life is no longer just the bounty of nature but a

19. John Locke, *Two Treatises of Government*, ed. Peter Laslett (Cambridge: Cambridge University Press, 1988), p. 268. During the session, Derrida adds the following commentary: "Thus, the sovereignty of the state is first of all the right of death, the right to exercise the death penalty."

gift received conditionally from the state"]:[20] so as not to be the victim of a murderer, one consents to die if one becomes a murderer.[21] Far from throwing one's own life away, one thinks only of assuring it, and we should not presume that any of the contracting parties premeditates getting himself hanged.[22]

This is an extraordinary sentence in many ways, not least because it inscribes the death penalty in a calculating, calculated contract: I want my life to be safe and assured, I must therefore promise to lose it in exchange for this assurance if I should ever threaten or make an attempt on the life of another. A rational and contractual exchange, a total social contract and circular economy that, moreover, rests ingenuously on the principle of the preservation of life, on an instinct of preservation about which Rousseau says with an equal measure of prudence and imprudence that it may be "presumed," namely, that one may presume that none of the contracting parties premeditates getting himself hanged! Oh really? Really? For if this were the way it was, if no one dreamed of getting hanged or risking getting hanged, well, there would never be any murders or a death penalty. It is true that Rousseau is more meticulous in his expression, for he says "presume" that no one "*premeditates* getting himself hanged."[23] We will quickly see how gingerly one must take such a presumption, and without even invok-

41

20. During the session, Derrida pursues his commentary: "In other words, the citizen receives his life from the state, and therefore has no right over his life. His life is lent to him in some sense; life is a conditional gift of the state. An extraordinary formulation, isn't it! Life is no longer merely a bounty of nature, but a conditional gift of the state. The state retains a right of life and death over the citizen to whom it has lent his life, a conditional gift."

21. Another addition made during the session: "Insurance contract: if you want your life to be protected, then you must accept that if you kill, you will be killed."

22. Jean-Jacques Rousseau, *Du contrat social*, in *Œuvres complètes*, ed. Bernard Gagnebin and Marcel Raymond (Paris: Gallimard, Bibliothèque de la Pléiade, 1964), p. 376; *The Social Contract*, trans. Maurice Cranston (New York: Penguin Books, 1968), pp. 78–79 [translation modified; hereafter, modifications to published translations will not be signaled. I have supplied the translations of all quotations from works for which there is no extant translation].

23. During the session, Derrida continues: "So one cannot exclude that there are parties to the contract who do not exclude that it is their desire to get themselves hanged. It is true that Rousseau is even more meticulous in his formulation, for he says 'presume' that anyone 'premeditates getting himself hanged.' It is possible, he presumes, thus it is a hypothesis; it is possible that people unconsciously want to get themselves hanged, that's it [*inaudible*: ... criminal ... that means ...] *prendre et pendre* [to take and to hang]. But what Rousseau excludes is that they premeditate it, that is, consciously, that they calculate in advance, etc."

ing some notion of a death drive. Moreover, Rousseau himself does nothing more than nervously proliferate reservations, folds, and regrets in this
chapter that I hold to be one of the most tormented and most interesting
in *The Social Contract* (I hope to have the chance to come back to it so as to
read it with you word by word as it deserves). Provisionally, then, I outline
the *reservations* that Rousseau sets out at the very moment he is upholding
the principle of the death penalty, and apparently according to the biblical
tradition of the murderer who deserves to die.

1. *First reservation*: he makes of the death penalty a verdict that does not
fall under civil law but in fact under the law of war, as if in civil law there
were no place for capital punishment. The law of war because the wrongdoer, by attacking social law, becomes a traitor to the fatherland; he is no
longer a member of the state and becomes, in Rousseau's words, a "public
enemy": "for such an enemy is not a legal entity, he is simply a man: and
therefore the law of war is to kill the vanquished one" (377). This is a way
of expelling the death penalty from the internal civil penal law; one could
even say it is a way of abolishing it a priori by not admitting it into the law
except as a law of war. This gesture is all the more strange in that the question of "foreign policy" and notably of the law of war is excluded from *The
Social Contract* or treated by way of preterition, deferred until later in the
last paragraph of the conclusion (seven lines on this "new object that is too
vast for my short-sightedness: I should have kept my eyes trained on what
is ever closer to me") (470).

2. *Second reservation*: Rousseau dissociates, he is ready to dissociate — and
this is an unheard-of gesture in the tradition — the exercise of sovereignty
and the exercise of sentencing, of any sentencing even; he recognizes that
the sentencing of a criminal is not the general act of the sovereign but a
particular act; and then he adds, in a very embarrassed way:

> But, it will be said, the sentencing of a criminal is a particular act. Agreed:
> thus this sentencing does not belong to the sovereign; it is a right that he can
> confer without being able to exercise it himself. All my ideas hold together,
> but I cannot set them out all at once! (376) [Comment][24]

3. *Third reservation* : the guilty party can always be rehabilitated or ame-
liorated, and the idea of an exemplarity of punishment is unjustifiable (this
is a way for Rousseau to oppose in advance the most tenacious argument

---

24. No commentary during the session. All the reminders to "Comment" having
been verified on the session recordings, we will no longer specify those that were not
followed up.

in favor of the death penalty: exemplarity, the efficacity of the example). Nonetheless, despite this objection and this reservation, Rousseau upholds the principle of the death penalty in cases where a danger is in principle irreducible, which leads back to the example of the public enemy and of the law of war. He writes: "There is no man so bad that he cannot be made good for something. One has no right to put to death, even as an example, except whoever cannot be preserved without danger" (377).

These *three reservations* complicate in a singular manner and overdetermine the fundamental point (the affirmation of the legitimacy of the death penalty) enough to torment Rousseau who concludes the final paragraph on the right of pardon (a right that does belong to the sovereign and toward which Rousseau does not seem very favorable) [he concludes, then, the paragraph on the right to sovereign pardon] and the chapter "On the Right of Life and Death" with these words from the heart and with this signature of confession: "But I feel my heart stirring [that is, against my objection to the state's right of pardon] and restraining my pen: let us leave the discussion of these questions to the just man who has never erred and who has himself never had need of a pardon" (ibid.). (Guilt, confession, auto-biographical signature, not politico-juridical meta-theory — to be compared to the incidental remark: "All my ideas hold together, but I cannot set them out all at once.")[25]

To the long and still open list of those who legitimate the death penalty for murderers, as God does in Exodus, one could also add, just to remain in France, Diderot and Montesquieu (but we will come back to this history), Diderot who said (I cannot find the reference again, it will come back): "It is natural that the laws ordered the murder of murderers,"[26] or Montesquieu

43

25. In the margin of the typescript, Derrida writes: "(No philosophy against the death penalty)." During the session, he develops this parenthetical note in the following way: "After he had said a moment earlier, 'All my ideas hold together, but I cannot set them out all at once,' he explains: 'I have erred like everyone, only he who has not erred has the right to speak.' In other words, there is no metalanguage, no political, politico-juridical theory. Only someone who is above all suspicion has the right to speak and no one is above all suspicion. He thus mixes the confessional signature with this discourse on the death penalty."

26. Derrida might have found the sentence attributed to Diderot in his copy of William Schabas, *The Abolition of the Death Penalty in International Law* (Cambridge: Cambridge University Press, 1997), p. 4. Schabas quotes this sentence in French, and in a note he specifies: "Quoted in Jacques Goulet, *Robespierre, la peine de mort et la Terreur* (Bordeaux: Le Castor Astral, 1983), p. 13."

who, in *The Spirit of the Laws*, more reserved, more restrictive in the enumeration of death penalty cases, was nevertheless not an abolitionist, like the
44 great Beccaria whom we will speak of again, who wanted to substitute life imprisonment for the death penalty, and succeeded in convincing Voltaire, Jefferson, Paine, Lafayette, and even Robespierre who, before changing his mind, one must recall, argued abolitionist theses without success when the Penal Code was being drafted in 1791. Later, he demanded the execution of Louis XVI, described as a "criminal toward humanity,"[27] a turnaround that Thomas Paine deemed a betrayal of the abolitionist ideal that he had at first shared with Robespierre. It is also true that the abolitionist spirit had not vanished from the Revolution because the Convention, after the execution of Robespierre and during its last session, decreed, I quote: "Dating from the day of the general proclamation of peace, the death penalty will be abolished in the French Republic" (4 Brumaire, Year VI).[28] One would have to wait almost two centuries for this "day" and this "date" ["Dating from the day of the general proclamation of peace"] for the death penalty to be abolished in France (September–October 1981 — no execution since September 17, 1977). Two centuries is an infinity of eternities, and it is a fraction of a second in the history of humanity. All and nothing.

I point to these several examples only in order to give you a first small idea of the torturous complexity of this history, but especially in order to follow the inheritance or the tradition of the logic of the "judgments" that in Exodus followed on the Ten Commandments. But before leaving this context, which is a sequence in the course of which I allowed myself, then, to recall from the outset, and once and for all, a few massively obvious facts, notably the *two* most massive and, at least apparently, the crudest among them — before leaving this context, then, I note as well that in this same passage from Exodus, right after the Ten Commandments and before the
45 "judgments," there was that striking and very revealing moment, you remember it no doubt, when the people, the children of Israel, having heard the Ten Commandments but not yet the "judgments," [the children of Israel] want to hear no more. They do not want to hear God anymore. At least they do not want to lend an ear directly to the divine speech; they do not want to listen to God any longer, as if they were expecting the worst,

27. The reference is to the speech Robespierre delivered December 3, 1792, at the Convention, demanding in the name of the Montagnards the execution of Louis XVI.

28. Quoted by Jean Imbert, *La peine de mort*, 3rd. ed. (Paris: Presses Universitaires de France, 1999), p. 161.

which also awaited them, in fact, and they ask Moses to talk with them, because they will listen to Moses, whereas the word of God, if they hear it directly, without intermediary, risks bringing about their death, of putting them to death. As if (you are going to hear the text in a moment), as if, when God has just told them, among other commandments, "thou shalt not kill," but before he draws its legal and in a certain way jurisprudential consequence, that whoever kills will die, that whoever murders will be punished by death, as if God risked bringing about their death with his own voice, just after having told them "thou shalt not kill." As if the children of Israel felt, had the presentiment that the voice of God carried a sinister message, announced the news of death, the threat of death, of the death penalty, at the very moment in which he has just prohibited killing. It is the same law, the ethical law, "thou shalt not kill," that commands the juridical, or penal, law, the death penalty for the criminal who transgresses the ethical law. They have the presentiment that God is on the verge of inventing not killing but the death penalty — and the Jews, the children of Israel, are terrified by this divine word that elects them, that chooses them by uttering in their direction, addressing them, by getting ready to utter the first threat of the first death penalty in the world, on man's earth. This transition, this trance that then seizes hold of the children of Israel is extraordinary. They see the death penalty coming, they see it coming from God. I will read two translations of it. It is right after the last of the Ten Commandments (Exodus 20:18–21; King James Version):[29]

> And all the people saw the thunderings, and the lightnings, and the noise of the trumpet, and the mountain smoking: and when the people saw it, they removed, and stood afar off. And they said unto Moses, Speak thou with us, and we will hear [as if they could not, could no longer hear God himself, immediately, up close]: but let not God speak with us, lest we die. And Moses said unto the people, Fear not: for God is come to prove you, and that his fear may be before your faces, that ye sin not. And the people stood afar off, and Moses drew near unto the thick darkness where God was. And the LORD said unto Moses, Thus thou shalt say unto the children of Israel, etc. (20:18–22)

46

And soon it will be the list of "judgments" (the penal code and the death penalty). Another translation, that of Chouraqui:

> All the people see the voices, the torches,
> the voice of the shofar, the smoking mountain.

29. [Translator's note]: Here Derrida in fact reads the French translation by Dhorme.

The people see. They move and hold themselves far off.

They say to Moshe: "Speak, you, with us and we will hear you [As if they could not hear God, a God too fearsome and threatening who, after having told them "do not kill," was going to threaten them with death, with the death penalty that he premeditated inventing].

Let Elohim not speak with us [as if they were saying: let him be quiet, this God, be quiet, don't speak to us any more, you, you, Moses, tell him to be quiet and let him be content to tell you what he wants us to know].

Let Elohim not speak with us so that we do not die!"

Moshe says to the people: "Do not tremble.

Yes, it is in order to test you [same word, "test," as is used later for Abraham and the sacrifice of Isaac] that Elohim has come,

and in order that his trembling be upon your faces,

so that you do not err."

The people hold themselves far off.

Moshe goes toward the cloud, there where Elohim is. (20:18–22)[30]

(Mark a moment of silence)

47   Remember where we are coming from. Remember that it is the case of our first condemned one, the Greek, Socrates, that led us here. Now, among all the notes that are consonant or that resonate in an analogous fashion between such different and apparently incommensurable scenes as that of the Decalogue and the trial of Socrates, there is this one: denunciation of a cult of false gods, of bad gods. On the one side, Socrates is accused of having introduced new gods, on the other Yahweh's condemnation of the adoration of idols, of gods sculpted in stone, of images and of Elohims made of silver and gold, is made to precede, begin, and follow the Ten Commandments.

Naturally, among all the exegetical resources and hermeneutical models that could be brought to bear on such an account, some might be tempted to decipher in it a historical revelation, others a mythology lending an allegorico-narrative form to the birth of the law as birth of the death penalty; still others might be tempted to decipher through the weave of the narrative (revealed or mythological) a fabulous historical staging of the very structure of absolute law as founded on the death penalty, on the threat of

30. [Translator's note]: Chouraqui's translation reads as follows: "Tout le peuple voit les voix, les torches, / la voix du shophar, la montagne fumante. / Le peuple voit. Ils se meuvent et se tiennent au loin. / Ils disent à Moshè: 'Parle, toi, avec nous et nous entendrons. / Qu'Élohim ne parle pas avec nous. / Qu'Élohim ne parle pas avec nous pour que nous ne mourions pas!' / Moshè dit au peuple: 'Ne frémissez pas. / Oui, c'est pour vous éprouver qu'Élohim est venu, / et pour que son frémissement soit sur vos faces, / afin que vous ne fautiez pas.' / Le peuple se tient au loin. / Moshè avance vers le nuage, là où est l'Élohim."

the price to be paid for killing, namely, the death penalty, at the origin of the social contract or the contract of the nation-state, at the origin of any sovereignty, any community, or any genealogy, any people.

I have just recalled the analogy with the *Socrates case*, thus, the first one, but there will also be the *Jesus case*. I say each time the *case* as a reminder that it is a question of a judicial dispute, of a trial, and of penal law (moreover, the whole of American constitutional jurisprudence, which we will talk about again, particularly on the subject of the death penalty, the death penalty instated, then abolished, then reinstated, suspended, reapplied, in the legislation of one state or in another, and so forth, this jurisprudential history can be scanned through the history of law around "cases," "case X versus Y," that each time mark a date of decision—for example, by those Supreme Courts—decisions that set jurisprudential precedents). I say *case*, then, to recall this judicial dimension and these trials but also because "case" is the fall, the headlong descent, or even decapitation that brings down the head or the life or the body that falls, that drops, on the ground, beneath the scaffold or on the cross. There will, then, be the *Jesus case* on the subject of which one can carry out again the same demonstration: religious accusation taken up by a sovereignty or a political power of execution, of course. Socrates and Jesus, then, but also Joan of Arc (1431: same pattern, to which we will return again and again: religious incrimination at the service *of* or served *by* a political sovereignty capable of carrying out the execution: alliance between religion and the state). These three, Socrates, Jesus, Joan, are far from being the only or the first, of course, still less the last, but they are great emblematic figures with which, at the dawn of this seminar, I would like to begin before beginning. This time, there are no longer or not yet any Protestants; there is a Greek who is more or less pagan, prey to "new demons," Socrates; there is a woman who is very Christian but not Protestant, and there is a kind of Jew named Jesus, before Pauline Christianity.

The fourth one, my "Muslim," if one may say that, could be Hallaj, between the time of Jesus and that of Joan of Arc, which would allow us to reconnect with the texts of Massignon that we studied a few years ago in the seminar on hospitality,[31] and first of all on what Massignon called the hospitality of Abraham. In his 1914 preface to his great book *La passion de*

48

---

31. Second year of the seminar at EHESS in 1996–97, titled "Hospitalité" (1995–97): session 4, January 8, 1997; session 5, February 12, 1997; and session 8, May 7, 1997. Sessions 4 and 5 have been published in J. Derrida and Anne Dufourmantelle, *De l'hospitalité* (Paris: Calmann-Lévy, 1997); *Of Hospitality: Anne Dufourmantelle Invites Jacques Derrida to Respond*, trans. Rachel Bowlby (Stanford, CA: Stanford University Press, 2000).

Hallâj, martyr mystique de l'Islam,[32] Massignon recalls that, if one can believe Islamic legend (in Arab, Persian, Turkish, Hindu, and Malay poets), Hallaj is held to be "the perfect lover of God"—he will also be called "God's fool"—condemned to the gallows (hanging accompanied by torture) for having cried out, as if in a state of drunkenness, "I am the truth." Literally Christlike words, words of a Christ who is not content to say, as Socrates often did, that he is merely *seeking* truth, but that he *is* the truth. "I am the truth": Jesus does not merely invoke the truth at every turn in the four Gospels. In the Gospel of John, he says to Thomas (14:6): "I am the way, the truth, and the life: no man cometh unto the Father, but by me" ("Ego sum via, et veritas, et vita. Nemo venit ad Patrem, nisi per me"; "ego eimi è odos kai è aletheia kai è zoé; oudeis erkhetai pro ton patera ei me di'emou").[33]

49

So Hallaj was condemned to the gallows for having been intoxicated to the point of ecstasy and crying out "I am the truth" and crying it out again from the height of the gallows: "Anâ'l-haqq (here I am, the Truth)," which likely did not displease Massignon the great Christian, who recounts how, in 922 CE—and this is the point that is important for me here—in the history of the Abbasid Caliphate in Baghdad, Hallaj was the "victim" (victim is Massignon's word) of a great *political* trial provoked by his *public* preaching. This *political* and thoroughly *theologico-political* trial set all the Islamic forces of the period against each other: Imamite, Sunni, *fuqahâ*, and Sufi.

In order, then: Socrates, Jesus, Hallaj (922), Joan of Arc (1431). Each time a complaint, an accusation, a religious incrimination aimed at a blaspheming offense against some divine sacredness, a religious incrimination that is invested, taken up, incarnated, incorporated, put into effect, enforced,[34] applied by a sovereign political power, which thereby signals its sovereignty, its sovereign right over souls and bodies, and which in truth defines its sovereignty by this right and by this power: over the life and death of subjects. This is how the essence of sovereign power, as political but first of all theologico-political power, presents itself, represents itself as the right to decree and to execute a death penalty. Or to pardon arbitrarily, sovereignly.

If one wants to ask oneself "What is the death penalty?" or "What is the

---

32. Louis Massignon, *La passion de Hallâj, martyr mystique de l'Islam* (Paris : Gallimard, 1975); *The Passion of al-Hallāj: Mystic and Martyr of Islam*, trans. Herbert Mason (Princeton, NJ: Princeton University Press, 1982).

33. Derrida quotes the New Testament in Greek and Latin from *Novum Testamentum, Graece et Latine*, ed. Eberhard Nestle (London: United Bible Societies, n.d.).

34. [Translator's note]: The word "enforced" is in English in the original.

essence and the meaning of the death penalty?" it will indeed be necessary to reconstitute this history and this horizon of sovereignty as the hyphen in the theologico-political. An enormous history, the whole history that at the moment we are only touching on or glimpsing. It is not even certain that   50
the concept of *history* and the concept of *horizon* resist a deconstruction of the scaffolding of these scaffolds. By scaffolding, I mean the construction, the architecture to be deconstructed, as well as the speculation, the calculation, the market, but also the speculative idealism that provides its supports. History, the concept of history is perhaps linked, in its very possibility, in its scaffolding, to the Abrahamic and above all the Christian history of sovereignty, and thus of the possibility of the death penalty as theologico-political violence. Deconstruction is perhaps always, ultimately, through the deconstruction of carno-phallogocentrism, the deconstruction of this historical scaffolding of the death penalty, of the history of this scaffold or of history as scaffolding of this scaffold. Deconstruction, what is called by that name, is perhaps, *perhaps* the deconstruction of the death penalty, of the logocentric, logonomocentric scaffolding in which the death penalty is inscribed or prescribed. The concept of theologico-political violence is still confused, obscure, rather undifferentiated (despite the hyphen we see being clearly and undeniably inscribed in the four great examples, in the four great paradigmatic "cases" that I have just so quickly evoked: trial with thematic religious content and execution, putting to death by a state-political agency, law itself, the juridical, beginning with the "judgments" and the code of Exodus, the juridical, then, always assuring the mediation between the theological and the political); this relatively crude but already sufficiently determined concept of the theologico-political, the theologico-juridico-political will demand from us an interminable analysis. An analysis in the course of which we must not suppose that we already know what "theologico-political" means and that we have then only to apply this general concept to a particular case or phenomenon named "death penalty." No. Perhaps one must do just the reverse. One must perhaps proceed in the opposite direction, that is, attempt to think the theologico-political in its possibility beginning from the death penalty. One would then ask oneself: "What is the theologico-political?" And the   51
answer would take shape thus: the theologico-political is a system, an apparatus of sovereignty in which the death penalty is necessarily inscribed. There is theologico-political wherever there is death penalty.

This interminable analysis, this deconstruction could begin, at least in a very preliminary way today, by taking up the following feature, the following complication. In the four *cases* there is this other common feature, which we have not yet emphasized and which is all the more remarkable in that the contexts and the religions and the state structures are dissimilar and very distant in each one of them (Athens, Jerusalem, Baghdad, Rouen). It is that the point was not to condemn or execute in the name of the reason of state, the security of the city or the state, here allied or complicit with the religious authority, [the point was not to put to death], despite appearances and despite allegations or denials, an enemy of the state or still less an enemy of God. The point in all four cases was to put to death a speech, the body of a speech that claimed to be but the presentation of a divine speech to which the clerical-state authorities, the double power of the churches and the states, the twinned and conjugated power of the church and the state remained deaf—and intended very well to hear and understand nothing. All four of them, Socrates, Jesus, Hallaj, and Joan of Arc, said in sum that they heard voices, the voice of God, and that they were in this regard the truth. "I am the truth" said Jesus and Hallaj literally. Joan said literally that she heard voices. Jesus and Hallaj also bore the same witness, for by each saying "I am the truth," they meant to say, sometimes literally, I am the witness, I can testify to a truth greater than I and than you, which comes into me but into me from the beyond (I underscore this transcendence, and more precisely this word "beyond" for obvious and general reasons, but <also> for more literal, or even literary reasons that will be specified later on). They are killed perhaps because people are afraid to hear directly, immediately, the voice of God, like the children of Israel I was speaking about a moment ago. They are killed perhaps because they are felt to be bearers of death insofar as they say they bear the voice of God. This testimonial or even martyrological relation with the transcendence of a voice speaking from the beyond is too obvious in the case of Jesus, Hallaj, and Joan, but it is also true of Socrates, already, who not only claimed to speak and to question only in the name of truth, but who also said he bore within a daimon and received signs from God. This word "daimon " is important for us here, with all its Graeco-Christian ambivalence, Greek first of all, because the daimon is both divine and inferior to the divinity of the God (*theos*); it means both the soul of the dead and the revenant but also fate, the singular destiny, a kind of election, and often, in the bad sense, the unfortunate destiny, death; and in Christian language, in the Greek of the Gospels, in Matthew, Mark, and Luke, the daimon is always taken in the bad sense, as the bad spirit, the demonic, the spirit of evil. Thus in this unstable and equivocal value of the daimon, we have *both* the motif of the transcendent and sanctifying divinity *and* the motif of the evil demonic, of the evil genius, good and evil, the cursed and the sanctifiable. We will see these two sacred values crop up constantly in the scene of the condemnation to death and in the sacred figure (cursed and sanctified) of the one condemned to death. Now, to return to Socrates, precisely in the famous passage of the *Apology* (40a–b), he says that he, too, regularly hears the voice of his daimon. And what happens in this precise moment of the scene? Well, he announces to his judges that he is going to tell them how he interprets what is happening to him, the accident that is happening to him: his *casus*, his case, in some sense, this accident that is going to cause his fall. This accident is a "marvelous," miraculous (*thaumasion*) thing. And what is *thaumasion* here, what is astonishing, extraordinary, miraculous in this case, is that the voice of his daimon, the divinatory (mantic) power of his demonic god who usually, customarily speaks in him and warns him (*hē gar eiōthuia moi mantikē hē tou daimoniou*) so as to guide him in the most ordinary things of life, well, this mantic power of his daimon, this time, when he seems to be exposed to the worst, to the supreme misfortune (*eskhata kakōn*: the most extreme of ills, death) well, his daimon has fallen silent, has dropped him, it is as if he has let him fall—it is also that—as if his *case*, his *casus*, his god has not restrained him from presenting himself at the tribunal and from accepting the verdict. Socrates says: "Yet neither when I left home this morning, nor when I was taking my place here in the court, nor at any point in any part of my speech did the divine sign oppose me [I am quoting the translation of *theou sēmeion*: no sign of God held me back]."[35]

After which, read what follows, Socrates interprets this sudden silence of his god or his demon and the good reasons the god might have had to keep silent, and to drop him, to let him speak so as to accept his death from the laws of the city. And, I would say too elliptically, it is all of philosophy, Platonic philosophy, perhaps philosophy *tout court* that finds its place in this silence of the daimon, at the moment of the condemnation of Socrates. I will not compare this silence of the god of Socrates with the scene in which the children of Israel ask to hear Yahweh no more, but only his human mediator, Moses, at the moment of the establishment of the "judgments" and the sentences of penal law, but the temptation to do so would be strong indeed.

So what I would like to make clear with this reminder is that in the theologico-political structure we are talking about, and in the trait of this hyphen [*trait d'union*], the alliance of the theologico-political is not made against some *non*-theologico-political, against some atheologico-political; it is not opposed, in a simply antagonistic or oppositional or dialectical scene, to something that would be neither theological nor political; it attempts—

53

---

35. Plato, *Socrates' Defense (Apology)*, 40 b, trans. Hugh Tredennick, in *Collected Dialogues*.

either or, or both at once — to make immanent once again a transcendence, the reference to a transcendence, by signifying to the condemned ones, to the four condemned ones that they have no right to say they are bearers of God's word, that they are committing a crime, or even perjury and blasphemy, by claiming to hear voices come from beyond, and that it is necessary to bring them back to earth, to the laws of the city or the church or the clergy or some terrestrial organization — and this is politics or the state — or else, and this amounts to the same thing, by accusing them of profaning, blaspheming, abusing, perjuring, abjuring when they claim an immediate and personal contact with a beyond that ought to remain transcendent and inaccessible, an inaccessibility of which the church, the *sanhedrin*, or the Greek priests or the nocturnal council are the guardians and the only guarantors. This condemnation is issued, then, both *in the name of* transcendence and *against* transcendence. And this complication has the effect that what is condemned, in all four cases, what sees itself theologico-politically condemned is not the non-theologico-political but another political theology that is visibly promised or announced or demanded or attested to by the four who are condemned to death. All four have a theological and political message, another message. Later we will see to what extent today — at a moment when, by contrast with what was happening still in 1989, ten years ago, when only fifty-eight countries had abolished the death penalty for all crimes, today, then, when, conversely, the 105 countries that have put an end to the death penalty are now in the majority, even though there are still seventy-two countries that apply the death penalty — well, we will see to what extent the positions of the churches, the Christian churches and notably the Catholic church, are ambiguous or contradictory depending on which authority represents them (the Council of Christian Churches, for example, declared in 1991 its hostility to the death penalty, whereas the "universal catechism" signed by the pope justifies this penalty for what are called "cases of extreme gravity," thereby following the tradition illustrated notoriously, among so many others, by a Saint Thomas Aquinas who was an eloquent and fervent proponent of the death penalty for heretics, those counterfeiters of the faith who, like counterfeiters in general punished with death by secular princes, must also be "rightly killed").[36]

All four of them, I was saying, have a theological and political message, another message. And, by way of supplementary complication, we will find the essential part of this other message, in the history that is thereby opened

36. Saint Thomas Aquinas, *Summa Theologica*, quoted by Jean Imbert, *La peine de mort*, p. 21.

and already parsed out, across the whole cultural, political, juridical, and religious history of the death penalty, on the two sides, *both on the side* of those
who, from very early on, then in another manner in modernity, have fought
against the death penalty, *and on the side* of those who have upheld the principle of the death penalty, sometimes only the principle but sometimes also
its cruelest implementation. This will not simplify our readings, our interpretations, our work. But we are not here to simplify. We are here — permit
me to recall this because it is essential and decisive at this point — neither
in a courtroom or on a witness stand, nor in a place of worship, nor in a
parliament, nor in print, radio, or televised news. And neither are we in a
real theater. To exclude all of these places, to exit from all of these places,
without exception, is the first condition for *thinking* the death penalty. And
thus for hoping to change it in some way.

December 8, 1999 (continued)[1]

Socrates, Jesus, Hallaj, Joan of Arc: war, sometimes armed war, not between the theologico-political and its other but between at least two histories and two versions of the theologico-political. That is to say, also of sovereignty.

But, still before beginning, still at the dawn of the seminar on the quasi theater of the death penalty, I wish to bring in someone else here — not onto the stage or into the witness box, because I have just said that this is neither a courtroom nor a true theater, but right *here*. I would like to bring back *here* the ghost of Jean Genet, the great poet and playwright, the great witness and man of the theater of our time, the fascinated analyst (and this fascination will be one of our themes), the fascinated analyst of that legal murder called the execution of a death penalty, the great witness or actor, the great theatrical character who is equally fascinated — to the point of merging them or reminding us of their profound resemblance, or even of their essential collusion — with the weapon of the crime and the weapon of the capital punishment that for him is another crime, another kind of crime. And it is through him that we are really going to approach *here* our beginning, that we are going to begin to begin. Or pretend to begin.

For several reasons, which belong to very different orders. The first one counts less, for it is merely personal, autobiographical, as they say. The first

58

1. The first session of December 8, 1999, exists in two electronic files ("1" and "1 continued"), and on the hard copy from which Derrida read, there is reference to two separate copies. In fact, on December 8, 1999, Derrida was unable to present this part, "1 continued," in its entirety at the first session. He stopped a little further on, after the sentence: "Moreover, *The Miracle of the Rose* (1946, right after *Our Lady of the Flowers),* whose first page we will also read in a moment, is also a song to, I quote, 'death on the scaffold that is our glory'" (see below, p. 34). On December 15, 1999, Derrida began his second session with the paragraph where he ended on December 8. It is only in the third session that he was able to make up for this "delay." There is thus a disjunction between the recordings of the first three sessions and the typescript.

time that, as a child, before the last world war, I learned from the press in Algiers that something like the death sentence existed, that the condemned one was made to wait, and that he was made to wait and to hope for the sovereign presidential pardon, and that one morning, at dawn, one proceeded to decapitate him, well, the one condemned to death was named Weidmann. I can still see his image, the image of his photograph in *L'Echo d'Alger*. Now, Weidmann is the first word, the first word and the first proper name in *Our Lady of the Flowers* by Jean Genet, a book that was published right after the last world war—the end of the *worldwide* war after which there arose a vast, increasingly *worldwide* movement—and this is why I always underscore the word "worldwide" [*mondial*][2]—and numerous worldwide declarations with universal pretentions against the death penalty: appeals, declarations, or decisions condemning condemnation to death, and finally heard here, for example in Europe, and not there, in other parts of the world, in particular, in the United States. So, a fragment of *Our Lady of the Flowers* was published right after the worldwide war, in 1944, and the whole text in 1948, almost forty years, then, before the abolition of the death penalty in France: *Our Lady of the Flowers*, a book in which the imaginary hero, Our Lady, is sentenced to capital punishment; I say the imaginary hero because the first name and the first word of the book, Weidmann, whose name and face I saw appear in the newspapers of my childhood, Weidmann is the name of a real-life character, as they say, who was guillotined, and whose name echoed in everyone's ears in France, all the way to Algeria, which was then part of France.

I am going to read this passage from Genet in a moment. You will notice other motifs, which will be yet other reasons, so many reasons to quote it. One concerns the theatricality and the fascination with the spectacle, with the immediate or deferred spectacle, in the press (the written, or today the cinematographic press); the other concerns the Christlike allegory or metonymy, which, in our Abrahamic culture, makes of the one condemned to death a kind of repetition or parody, a comedy of Christ's Passion, an imitation of Jesus Christ.

Before reading this incipit of the book, I propose another reason for beginning in this fashion, in short with literature. Why, on the death penalty, begin with literature? Not only in order to revisit those large veins that are

59

2. [Translator's note]: Indeed, Derrida very often insists, for some of the reasons detailed here, on using the term *mondialisation* when he is speaking of what is also referred to in French as *globalisation*. The former term will be included in brackets in the text when appropriate.

"literature and death," "literature and the right to death," or the trail of countless literary or poetic works that put crime and punishment, and that punishment called the death penalty, to work or onstage. There is all of that, of course, and we will think about it, but I believe I have a more pointed hypothesis concerning what it is that can link, associate, or dissociate the history of literature and the history of the death penalty. This hypothesis will be put to the test slowly and in a discontinuous, careful, and uneasy fashion, no doubt, but in its major features it would come down to this: if the history of the general possibility, of the largest territory of the general conditions of possibility of epic, poetic, or belle-lettristic productions (not of literature in the strict and modern sense) supposes or goes hand in hand with the legitimacy or the legality of the death penalty, well then, on the contrary, the short, strict, and modern history of the institution named literature in Europe over the last three or four centuries is contemporary with and indissociable from a contestation of the death penalty, an abolitionist struggle that, to be sure, is uneven, heterogeneous, discontinuous, but irreversible and tending toward the worldwide as conjoined history, once again, of literature and rights, and of the right to literature. A desacralization that, in a complex and contradictory fashion, as in the history of the pardon or forgiveness, breaks with the scene and the authority of Exodus and of divine punishment. I leave this hypothesis here in its crudest and most risky

60   formulation. We will have the chance to discuss and come back to it. To support this hypothesis, I will not draw an argument from the fact that a good number of the most eloquent and committed abolitionist discourses, in what I call literary modernity, that is, in literature in the strict sense, were put forward by writers and poets, for example, Shelley, Hugo, Camus. These are merely indications from which I will draw no argument (all the more so in that there are also counterexamples, such as Wordsworth who wrote in favor of the death penalty). But these indications deserve to be pointed out as indications first, and then we will attempt to approach these texts.

Here then is the first page of *Our Lady of the Flowers*; it begins with a proper name (this is not the only example in Genet: *The Screens* began without a sentence, with the crying out of a name that is both proper and common noun: "Rose! Warda").[3] Here it is "Weidmann." That is the first name on a list of famous condemned ones who are celebrated, sung, commemorated, one has to say *glorified* by the narrator, glorified because it is a matter of a certain "glory" (you are going to hear the word "glory" resonate, that is,

3. Jean Genet, *Les paravents* (Paris: L'Arbalète, 1961), p. 13.

the word of a luminous radiance, a lustrum, an aura, a halo, a Christlike light provided, above their head, by their execution, sometimes by their decapitation, by their very decollation). Weidmann, first word, first name of the book, is also the moment of an apparition, a vision. Genet or the narrator has the vision of these men condemned to death, and this vision is the vision of a spectacular spectacle, of an apparition that is both theatrical and spectral—and Genet played a lot, you know, with specters in his theater ("Weidmann appeared before you" are the first four words of the book)—and while reading this list of those who died on the field of honor of capital punishment, of these martyrs and these saints, I will underscore certain Christlike features, perversely Christlike, but with a perversity that both reveals and betrays perhaps what could be called a Christian *perversity*. "I am the truth, I am the way, the truth, and the life: no man cometh unto the Father, but by me." Here then is the first sentence:

> Weidmann appeared before you in a five o'clock edition [thus apparition in the media, vision that is already tele-vision, in a newspaper photograph, the theatrical and the mediatic become one in this apparition, which is also an issue [*parution*] of the newspaper coinciding with a court appearance [*comparution*]: no death penalty without the phenomenality of an appearance], his head swaddled in white bandages [*bandelettes*], a nun [*religieuse*], or again a wounded pilot, fallen into the rye one September day like the day when the world came to know the name of Our Lady of the Flowers.[4]

I pause for a moment on this first sentence. I have to say that I remember this photograph myself. But that is not the important thing. What counts is not only the word *religieuse* that makes directly explicit the venerable sacredness of this apparition, this vision, the sacralization that immediately takes hold of this murderer condemned to death, in his public, theatrical, and fascinating image. Immediately one is in the sacred element of an appearing seized by religiosity, by religious solemnity. But more precisely, what counts is the analogy with Christ, as if *Our Lady of the Flowers*, as if the book that bears this title were a fifth apocryphal Gospel according to John/Jean (Genet), the analogy with Christ, then, in memory of Christ, an analogy that is marked by those "white bandages" that swaddle someone, a man who, because he is swaddled—the word sufficiently connotes it—is like a newborn babe, a little Jesus (we will come upon the name Jesus three pages later), but still more precisely "white bandages" that literally recall

61

4. Jean Genet, *Notre-Dame-des-Fleurs*, in *Œuvres complètes*, vol. 2 (Paris: Gallimard, 1951), p. 9; *Our Lady of the Flowers*, trans. Bernard Frechtman (New York: Grove Press, 1963), p. 61.

the "linen cloths" with which the body of Jesus is wrapped according to, this time, the authentic Gospel of John (19:40).[5] What does John's text say, I mean first of all John the Evangelist? This, after the description of the torture inflicted on those who had been crucified with Jesus and whose legs were broken. Jesus was already dead, his legs were not broken, but a soldier pierced his side with a spear and blood and water flowed from the wound.

62

> And after this [writes John], Joseph of Arimathaea, being a disciple of Jesus, but secretly for fear of the Jews, besought Pilate that he might take away the body of Jesus: and Pilate gave him leave. He came therefore, and took the body of Jesus. [So Pilate, representative of the Roman state, will have had in this whole process the role of the power that, despite a certain reticence to accede to the religious demand of the community and the *sanhedrin*, takes charge, while washing his hands of it, of organizing the death, the execution of the punishment, and the responsibility for the body; the text continues.] And there came also Nicodemus, which at the first came to Jesus by night, and brought a mixture of myrrh and aloes, about a hundred pound weight. Then took they the body of Jesus, and wound it in linen clothes with the spices (*elabon oun to sōma tou iēsou kai edēsan auto othoniois* [*othonion*, is a piece of linen, a strip or shred of cloth or a veil] *meta tōn arōmatōn*; in Latin: *Acceperunt ergo corpus Jesu, et ligaverunt illud linteis cum aromatibus* [*linteum* is also a cloth of linen, a veil, a fabric, a woven cloth]). (John 19:38–40)

Othonion or *linteum*, then, which in French is most often translated *bandelettes* because in fact in Jewish custom one bandages [*bande*] the corpse by rolling it up, surrounding it with strips that resemble bandages for the wounded or swaddling clothes for infants. By choosing the word *bandelettes* to describe Weidmann's face, which, then, I myself saw in the newspapers surrounded by strips or wrappers that were not linen cloths or *bandelettes*, this John/Jean (here Genet) seems to me to be pointing with a Christological sign toward John the Evangelist (or toward Luke who uses the same words for the same scene), and this seems significant in many respects. Not only because in a general, massive, and constitutive fashion, the whole book *Our Lady of the Flowers* (or even all of Genet's literature) is immersed in the

63 Gospels, in the spirit of the Good News, and plays with Christian notations and connotations, however perverse or iconoclast they may be — the work is a performance of anti-Christian Christian iconoclasm, of perjury and abjuration fascinated with the very thing that it makes literature of the way one says to make a mockery of — but more precisely, more locally, because

---

5. [Translator's note]: In French, there is a literal repetition of the Gospel's term "bandelettes" in Genet's phrase "bandelettes blanches."

the book *Our Lady of the Flowers* sings the passion of those condemned to death (you know that there is a long poem by Genet titled "Le condamné à mort" [The one condemned to death], also published in 1945, which follows *Our Lady of the Flowers* in Genet's *Œuvres complètes* and which is dedicated to Genet's friend, Maurice Pilorge, sentenced, says Genet, "to have his head cut off. He was executed March 17, 1939, in Saint-Brieuc"; this poem, "Le condamné à mort," tenderly and amorously names, in its poetico-slang usage, "my sweet Jesus" in its penultimate stanza:

> Ce n'est pas ce matin que l'on me guillotine.
> Je peux dormir tranquille. A l'étage au-dessus
> Mon mignon paresseux, ma perle, mon Jésus,
> S'éveille. Il va cogner de sa dure bottine
> A mon crâne tondu.)[6]

> [*It's not this morning that I'll be guillotined.*
> *I can sleep easy. On the floor above*
> *My lazy little one, my pearl, my sweet Jesus,*
> *Is waking up. He is going to knock with his hard boot*
> *On my shaved skull.*]

What is more, it also happens that *Our Lady of the Flowers* (likewise dedicated to Maurice Pilorge: "Without Maurice Pilorge, whose death is still poisoning my life, I would never have written this book. I dedicate it to his memory") [*Our Lady of the Flowers*] plays, mimes, simulates in a serious manner a kind of chant of mourning and resurrection that describes but also poetically provokes, produces, performs, and glorifies the *elevation*, the *ascension* of the victims of the scaffold (not the *Ascenseur pour l'échafaud*,[7] the famous film with a score by Miles Davis — I mention this before beginning because black Americans are today the primary victims of what remains of the death penalty in the so-called Western world, the demo-Christian world; not the *Ascenseur pour l'échafaud*, the elevator to the gallows, but the Christlike ascension, the elevation, after the gallows and a quasi resurrection, a quasi salvation, a poetico-literary quasi redemption after the gallows).

64

To be better convinced of this, one must follow, here too, the metonymy and the quotation of the *bandelettes*, or bandages. That is why I am insisting on them. The bandages envelop, attach, they tie but also become detached: they become untied from the body proper. If we pay attention, in

6. Jean Genet, "Le condamné à mort," in *Œuvres complètes*, vol. 2, p. 219.
7. Louis Malle, *Ascenseur pour l'échafaud* [*Elevator to the Gallows*], 1958.

the Gospels, to the theater of the bandages, we see them, at least *twice*, signify, at the moment they are seen for themselves, alone, untied, detached,
far from the body, on the ground, not in use, [signify] the end of death, if
I can say that, the resurrection of the body that has arisen from death and
stood up, elevated, lifted into life, upward. The bandages signify death, the
condemnation to death; when they fall away, out of use, undone, untied,
untying, they signal, they signify, like a detached signifier, that the dead one
is resuscitated, insurrectioned, insurresuscitated[8] if I can say that, once again
elevated, raised up, erected by a miracle, a divine miracle or a poetic miracle.
Moreover, *Miracle of the Rose* (1946, right after *Our Lady of the Flowers*),
whose first page we will also read in a moment, is also a song to, I quote,
"death on the scaffold that is our glory."[9]

    Two examples, then, from the Gospels, of the scene of the bandages. First,
the Passion (sentencing to death, crucifixion, and entombment). It is the
passage that I read a moment ago (John 19:40): "Then took they the body
of Jesus, and wound it in linen cloths with the spices, as the manner of the
Jews is to bury" (Jesus is buried like a Jew and that is why earlier, in my classification of the paradigmatic characters in our theater of the death penalty,
I defined him, for the record, as a kind of Jew). But here is the second moment and the second example, the second apparition of the bandages. The
bandages do indeed *appear*; they are there all of a sudden; they leap into the
light: it is a *phenomenon* that seems to signify, that makes a sign as in a vision.
The time of this phenomenon of the bandages, their moment in the story
and in the process is very remarkable (and if we had the leisure to do so, if
it were the subject of the seminar, we would meditate on this time of the
bandages as the lodging made ready for literature, for an ascension without
ascension, an elevation without elevation, an imminent but not yet accomplished resurrection, etc.). It is because, as you will hear, these bandages, the
second apparition of the bandages, the untied bandages, abandoned near
Christ's tomb, are going to signify that Christ is not dead, that he is *no longer*
dead: he will have been dead; to be sure, he died, but he is not yet resuscitated, not yet elevated: he is still there, standing on the ground, looking at
the others, and first of all Mary; he looks at her looking at his absence; he

    8. [Translator's note]: In the typescript: *insuressuscité*.

    9. Jean Genet, *Miracle de la rose*, in *Œuvres complètes*, vol. 2, p. 23; *Miracle of the Rose*,
trans. Bernard Frechtman (New York: Grove Press, 1966), pp. 1–2. On December 8,
1999, Derrida ended the first session here for lack of time. He began the second session,
on December 15, by repeating this paragraph starting from "The bandages envelop,
attach, they tie but also become detached: they become untied from the body proper."

is looking at her see him neither dead nor alive, and above all, it is right before the *noli me tangere* ("touch me not" [unique example; comment on touch, Jesus touching touched, except in John 20:17]).[10] I am going to read this well-known passage and draw your attention, among other things, to the moment in which Mary's tears, upon seeing the bandages, bespeak the mourning that is not done, that cannot set to work, because what Mary weeps for then, when faced with the bandages, is not only the death of Jesus buried but the *disappearance* of his unburied body. Not only has Jesus died; this one who has been condemned to death is first of all one who has *disappeared*, his corpse has disappeared (which is the first meaning of the untied bandages). The one condemned to death has not only been executed, the deceased has disappeared, without burial place, and the sorrow is worse, more inconsolable; it is the sorrow of the woman unable to weep over the body of the beloved, unable to do, as one says, her work of mourning. A little like Antigone whom we were talking about a few years ago and who weeps less for the death, in that case, of her father rather than her son, than for the absence of a localizable burial place—and who thus weeps for not being able to weep her mourning in front of a body, a present corpse.[11] This also recalls the text of *Laws* that I read a little while ago on the deprivation of burial.[12] In the case of Christ, of this moment in the Gospel, there is a burial place, but it comes down to a kind of absence of burial place, because there is also a cenotaph, an empty tomb and bandages that signal the absence of the body. At that moment, when Mary complains to the angels while standing before the bandages that she no longer knows where "they laid" the body of Jesus, one could say, without too much pathos, that she prefigures the misfortune and complaint and the anger of all the women, mothers, daughters, and sisters of the "disappeared" of our time who, whether in the streets of Chile, Argentina, or in South Africa, also accuse and denounce those who did worse than torture and kill their men, because

66

10. During the session, Derrida adds the following commentary: "I remark in passing that this is a unique example; that, on the subject of touching in the Gospels, Jesus is sometimes represented as a touching Jesus, a touching Messiah, that is, as healing by touching with his hand (he heals blind men; he heals the paralyzed by touching), sometimes as someone who is touched, whose garment must be touched. So, he is touching and touched. You have a thousand references in the Gospels, but the only occurrence where it is said *"noli me tangere* (touch me not)" is found precisely after the scene that we are examining here, that is, in John 20:17."

11. Second year of the seminar at EHESS titled "Hospitality," 1995–97. On Antigone, see Derrida and Dufourmantelle, *De l'hospitalité*, pp. 71 ff; *Of Hospitality*, pp. 75 ff.

12. See above, "First Session, December 8, 1999," pp. 8–10.

they also made them *disappear*, a disappearance that sometimes seems worse than death.

I read now straight through the passage from John 20:1–18:

1 The first day of the week cometh Mary Magdalene early, when it was yet dark, unto the sepulchre, and seeth the stone taken away from the sepulchre.

2 Then she runneth, and cometh to Simon Peter, and to the other disciple, whom Jesus loved, and saith unto them, They have taken away the Lord out of the sepulchre, and we know not where they have laid him.

3 Peter therefore went forth, and that other disciple, and came to the sepulchre.

4 So they ran both together: and the other disciple did outrun Peter, and came first to the sepulchre.

5 And he stooping down, and looking in, saw the linen clothes lying; yet went he not in.

6 Then cometh Simon Peter following him, and went into the sepulchre, and seeth the linen clothes lie,

7 And the napkin, that was about his head, not lying with the linen clothes, but wrapped together in a place by itself.

8 Then went in also that other disciple, which came first to the sepulchre, and he saw, and believed.

9 For as yet they knew not the scripture, that he must rise again from the dead.

10 Then the disciples went away again unto their own home.

11 But Mary stood without at the sepulchre weeping: and as she wept, she stooped down, and looked into the sepulchre,

12 And seeth two angels in white sitting, the one at the head, and the other at the feet, where the body of Jesus had lain.

13 And they say unto her, Woman, why weepest thou? She saith unto them, Because they have taken away my Lord, and I know not where they have laid him.

14 And when she had thus said, she turned herself back, and saw Jesus standing, and knew not that it was Jesus.

15 Jesus saith unto her, Woman, why weepest thou? whom seekest thou? She, supposing him to be the gardener, saith unto him, Sir, if thou have borne him hence, tell me where thou hast laid him, and I will take him away.

16 Jesus saith unto her, Mary. She turned herself, and saith unto him, Rabboni; which is to say, Master.

17 Jesus saith unto her, Touch me not; for I am not yet ascended to my Father: but go to my brethren, and say unto them, I ascend unto my Father, and your Father; and to my God, and your God.

18 Mary Magdalene came and told the disciples that she had seen the Lord, and that he had spoken these things unto her.

How does this singular instant, Christ's being-there without being-there, this *Dasein* that is not a *Da-sein,* this *Fort/Da-sein* of Christ who is dead but not dead, who is living dead [*mort vivant*], who is resuscitated but not yet risen, who is here without being here, here but there, over there (*fort, jenseits*), who is already beyond without yet being beyond, in the beyond, how is this moment, this singular time that does not belong to the ordinary unfolding of time, how is this time without time signified both in death as condemnation to death (as death penalty), in the death of the one condemned to death, but also in the discourse or the narrative, in ordinary public or mediatic speech, and first of all in literature, and here for example in Genet's text, in its poetic time as the very time that links, in a "story" (what Genet is going to call a "story," a "not always artificial" story) [that links, then] the one condemned to death to the Evangelist, to the speech of the one who bears the news, who moreover is going to ask to be forgiven? I am going to read some excerpts—it would be necessary to read or reread everything; you should do that—from a long passage up to the point we encounter, besides the "forgive me," a sentence that says of the condemned one (Weidmann) that he is also *beyond*, further than that, like Christ once the bandages were unwound.

Read and comment on *Notre Dame des Fleurs*, 9–10, then 12–13.

68

Weidmann appeared before you in a five o'clock edition, his head swaddled in white bandages, a nun, or again a wounded pilot fallen into the rye one September day like the day when the world came to know the name of Our Lady of the Flowers. His handsome face, multiplied by the machines, swept down upon Paris and all of France, to the depths of the most out-of-the-way village, in castles and cabins, revealing to the mirthless bourgeois that their daily lives are grazed by enchanting murderers, cunningly elevated even into their sleep, which they will cross by some back stairway that, by not creaking, is their accomplice. Beneath his picture burst the dawn of his crimes: murder one, murder two, murder three, up to six, bespeaking his secret glory and preparing his future glory.

A little earlier, the Negro Angel Sun had killed his mistress.

A little later, the soldier Maurice Pilorge killed his lover, Escudero, to rob him of not even a thousand francs, then, for his twentieth birthday, they cut off his head while, you will recall, he thumbed his nose at the enraged executioner.

Finally, a young ensign, still a child, committed treason for treason's sake: he was shot. And it is in honor of their crimes that I am writing my book.

It was only in bits and pieces that I learned of this wonderful blossoming of dark and lovely flowers: one was revealed to me by a scrap of newspaper; another was casually alluded to by my lawyer; another was mentioned, almost sung, by the prisoners — their song became fantastic and funereal (a *De Profundis*), as much so as the plaints which they sing in the evening, as the voice which crosses the cells and reaches me blurred, hopeless, altered. At the end of each phrase it breaks, and that crack makes it so sweet that it seems borne by the music of angels, which horrifies me, for angels fill me with horror, being, I imagine, neither mind nor matter, white, filmy, and frightening, like the translucent bodies of ghosts. . . .

So, with the help of my unknown lovers, I am going to write a story. My heroes are they, pasted on the wall, they and I who am here, locked up. As you read on, the characters, and Divine too, and Culafroy, will fall from the wall onto my pages like dead leaves, to fertilize my tale. As for their death, need I tell you about it? For all of them it will be the death of the one who, when he learned of his from the jury, merely mumbled in a Rhenish accent: "I'm already beyond that" (Weidmann).

This story may not always seem artificial, and despite myself you may recognize in it the voice of blood: that's because in my darkness I shall have happened to strike at some door with my forehead, freeing an anguished memory that had been haunting me since the world began. Forgive me for it. This book aims to be only a small fragment of my inner life. . . .

Divine died yesterday in a pool of her vomited blood which was so red that, as she expired, she had the supreme illusion that this blood was the visible equivalent of the black hole which a gutted violin, seen in a judge's office in the midst of a hodge-podge of pieces of evidence, revealed with dramatic insistence, as does a Jesus the gilded chancre where gleams His flaming Sacred Heart. So much for the divine aspect of her death. The other aspect, ours, because of those streams of blood that had been shed on her nightshirt and sheets (for the sun had set poignantly, not nastily, on the bloody sheets in her bed), makes her death tantamount to a murder.

Divine died holy and murdered — by consumption. (9–14; 61–67)

70   Read next the beginning of *Miracle de la Rose*, 223–224.

While the boy I was at fifteen twined in his hammock around a friend (if the rigors of life make us seek out a friendly presence, I think it is the rigors of prison that can drive us toward each other in bursts of love without which we could not live; unhappiness is the enchanted potion), he knew that his final form dwelt behind them and that the convict with his thirty-year sentence was the fulfillment of himself, the last transformation, which death would make permanent. And Fontevrault still gleams (though it is a very soft and faded brilliance) with the lights emitted in its darkest heart, the dungeon, by Harcamone, who was sentenced to death.

When I left La Santé Prison for Fontevrault, I already knew that Harcamone was there, awaiting execution. Upon my arrival I was therefore gripped by the mystery of one of my fellow inmates at Mettray who had been able to pursue the adventure all of us sought to its sharpest peak: the death on the scaffold that is our glory. Harcamone had "succeeded." And as this success was not of an earthly order, like fortune or honors, his achievement filled me with amazement and admiration (even the simplest achievement is miraculous), but also inspired the fear that overwhelms the witness of some magical operation. Harcamone's crimes might have meant nothing to my soul had I not known him at close range, but my love of beauty desired so ardently that my life be crowned with a violent, or rather bloody death, and my aspiration to a saintliness of muted brilliance preventing it from being heroic by men's standards made me secretly choose decapitation, which has the virtue of being reproved, of reproving the death that it gives and of illuminating its beneficiary with a glory more somber and gentle than the dancing, floating flame of velvet at great funerals; and Harcamone's crimes and death revealed to me — as if by taking it apart — the mechanism of that glory when finally attained. Such glory is not human. No one has ever heard of an executed one whose execution alone haloed him as the saints of the church and the glories of the age are haloed, yet we know that the purest of those who received that death felt placed, within themselves and on their severed head, the amazing and secret crown, studded with jewels wrested from the darkness of the heart. Each of them knew that the moment his head fell into the basket of sawdust and was lifted out by the ears by an assistant whose role seems to me strange indeed, his heart would be gathered up by fingers gloved with modesty and carried off in a youngster's bosom, adorned like a spring festival. It was thus a heavenly glory to which I aspired, and Harcamone had attained it before me, quietly, as the result of murdering a little girl and, fifteen years later, a Fontevrault guard. (223–24; 1–3)

71

Now, we begin. My transition between this long epigraph and our real beginning might be Genet's "forgive me for it" or more precisely the forgiveness requested by whoever says "I," let's say the "narrator" of *Our Lady of the Flowers*.

First of all, the question of the title. This year, beneath the title "Questions of Responsibility VII: Pardon and Perjury,"[13] we are thus inscribing a subtitle, namely "The Death Penalty."

13. Derrida here reverses the order in the title of his seminar "Perjury and Pardon."

As if up until now, in sum, we had been speaking about something else.

But nothing is less certain. For each time that, in our meditation on forgiveness, we deemed it necessary to set out from the unforgiven or the unforgivable, from the irreversible or the irreparable, each time as well that we spoke of some sur-viving [*du sur-vivre*], that is, of what leaves one defenseless in the face of the injury of a death that has already taken place, as well as of victims who could no longer testify or from whom it was no longer possible to ask forgiveness, we were speaking of death, of course, but also, as wherever it is a question of forgiveness, of *judgment*, of the judgment of an injury or a wrong.

Once again, the fact remains that every death and even every inflicted death is not the sentence or the application of a death penalty. And we must keep in mind in a vigilant manner that every death dealt, every murder, every crime against the living, every homicide even, does not necessarily correspond to what is strictly called a "death penalty," to the concept, to the supposed juridical concept of the death penalty, even if one can as a next step contest the juridical purity, the legitimacy, or even the legality of the death penalty. The concept of death penalty *presents itself*, in any case, as a concept of law, the concept of a sanction exercised by law in a state of law, even if one may then contest the well-foundedness of this self-presentation.

In past years, we spoke less of the death of the accused and more of the death of victims, of those who, as if they were dead, were sometimes deprived by violence even of the right of speech or the possibility of bearing witness and thus of being present enough at a possible request for forgiveness (as for example those South African women who were denied even the possibility of testifying to the violence or rapes they suffered, because the testimony and the exhibition of the wounds would have constituted another violence, a repetition of the worst: bearing witness itself, and the scene of forgiveness or reconciliation was itself a violence, another trauma).[14] We thus spoke of death inflicted on the innocent, on the presumed innocent, as the unpardonable or as the horizon of the unpardonable itself, but we did not speak of death inflicted by law on the guilty, on the accused or the presumed guilty, even if when we dealt, at some length, with the right of pardon, we were thinking especially of the sovereign's right to grant or refuse life to one condemned to death. Naturally we will return to all of this at length.

Why and how, by what right, then, would we now inscribe this question of the death penalty under the title of *pardon* and *perjury*?

The question of the title is always, at bottom, likewise a juridical question, the question of right and the question of the capital, of the chief or the

14. See above, "First Session, December 8, 1999," p. 3, n. 3.

head [*chef*], of the chapter, of what comes first or as a heading [*en tête*]. A text or a discourse without title is not only an outlaw discourse but a headless discourse, with neither head nor tail, a decapitated discourse. Without playing on words I recall that the death penalty, which in principle is distinguished, which tends to be conceptually distinguished, in law, from any murder, any crime, any natural vengeance through its reference by law to the law, through its supposed legality, through its state-juridical essence, the death penalty, then, is here and there called "capital punishment," in English for example. In German, one doesn't speak of capital punishment (rather of *Todesstrafe*) even if there is the expression of capital crime (*Kapitalverbrechen*), often in order to designate crimes sanctioned or punishable by capital punishment.

The death penalty is called *here and there*, I said, "capital punishment." Here and there means that it is not the case everywhere, according to the history and the geography of cultures and laws. Where one says "capital punishment" for the death penalty, capital execution is what costs the condemned one his head, literally or figuratively. And when I say "literally or figuratively," once again I am reinscribing without delay the question of the death penalty in a history, in the history of the law and of the technologies for legally putting to death, which we will have to examine as closely as possible. Within the legal procedure of execution, putting to death has not always involved attacking the head, decapitating, practicing decollation, hanging, or strangulation of the condemned one, or again by a firing squad aiming at the condemned one's face. In the United States (whose example I take without delay so as to announce that this seminar will be massively turned in the direction of the United States in the year 2000, that is, in the direction of one of the very rare, or even the only and the last large country of so-called European culture,[15] and with a so-called democratic constitution, that maintains—in conditions that we will examine more closely, and in defiance of numerous international conventions that we will also study—the principle of the death penalty and its massive, even growing, application, after a turbulent history, on this subject, from 1972, when the death penalty was judged unconstitutional, to 1976, when the Supreme Court reversed itself on this judgment and when thirty-eight states reinstated the death penalty and twenty-eight began once again to apply it, etc.), well, in the United States, the execution of "capital punishment" shows a great variety, a great technological refinement in cruelty or barbarity, but no longer goes directly, always, and literally after the head, whether one is talking about "decapitation" or hanging (the modality, said to be more or less cruel, of

73

74

15. During the session, Derrida adds: "predominantly Christian."

the application of the death penalty is today in the United States a more spectacular and heated debate than the debate over the death penalty itself, as if the essential thing were to maintain, or not, a human "ecology," a good and tolerable death penalty). But naturally, in the figurative sense, and the trope counts here, execution always attacks the head, the central seat of the cerebral and nervous systems, the presumed seat of consciousness and personality: the sign of this is that everywhere a prohibition is observed against executing a sentence on someone who is out of his head, as they say. The condemned man must be "normal," "responsible" and undergo punishment in full consciousness. He must die awake. In France, before the death penalty was abolished in 1981, in the course of a historical sequence, which was moreover as European as it was French (and to which we will return as well), it happened that a condemned man was revived and snatched back from the brink of suicide so that he could undergo his capital punishment in full lucidity, with, if I may say so, his head on straight. Under the heading of all these historical and rhetorical reservations concerning the expression "capital punishment," and before returning, then, to my question of the title, namely, of what comes by law at the head, first and foremost [*au premier chef*], in the place of the capital in some fashion (and in both senses of "capital") of a discourse, a chapter, or a seminar so as to define its status and its identity, under the heading of these historical reservations, I would like to begin by reading a few passages and first of all the opening two pages of Foucault's *Discipline and Punish* (1975). I choose to read them by way of overture for numerous reasons. First of all because it is a rich and important book, a very precious one for us, which I recommend you read or reread in its entirety. Even though he does not name Genet, his last chapter, "The Carceral," is devoted to Mettray, the disciplinary colony, the sophronistery, which resembles at once, Foucault recalls, the "cloister, prison, school, regiment"[16] and which, as you know, occupied such an important place in the life and work of Genet. Next because Foucault describes, in the first part of the book titled "Torture," instances of putting to death, executions of the death penalty accompanied by tortures that were both spectacular (and we will come back often, in countless ways, to the *spectacle* and the history of the scene, the theatricality, even today the cinematic theatricality of execution).[17] Foucault's book is not a book on the death penalty, but it is a

75

16. Michel Foucault, *Surveiller et punir. Naissance de la prison* (Paris: Collection Tel, Gallimard, 1993), p. 343; *Discipline and Punish: The Birth of the Prison*, trans. Alan Sheridan (New York: Vintage, 1977), p. 293.

17. The typescript does not complete this construction of "both . . . and."

book that deals among other things with the historical transformation of the spectacle, with the organized visibility of punishment, with what I will call, even though this is not Foucault's expression, the *seeing-punish* [voir-punir], a *seeing-punish* essential to punishment, to the right to punish as right to see-punish(ed), or even as duty-to-see-punish(ed) [*devoir de voir-punir*], one of Foucault's historical theses being that at the beginning of the nineteenth century, what "gets erased" is, I quote, "the great spectacle of physical punishment; the tortured body is avoided; the staging of suffering is excluded from the punishment. The age of punitive sobriety begins" (21). I am not so sure of this, but perhaps there is here a technical, tele-technical, or even televisual complication of seeing, or even a virtualization of visual perception to which we will return. Beccaria, in his famous book *On Crimes and Punishments* (1764), which is taken to be (rightly or wrongly, we will debate this) the first great abolitionist text written by a jurist, Beccaria who admired Rousseau but criticized *The Social Contract*, which had just appeared two years earlier, on the question of the death penalty, Beccaria proposed to replace the death penalty (except in two exceptional cases, we will come to this) by a life sentence of hard labor (we will see why) and had already written: "For most people, the death penalty becomes a spectacle."[18] According to Foucault, the guillotine had already marked an important stage in what he takes to be a process of erasure, I would say of de-spectacularization, since it reduces death to a "visible but instantaneous event . . . almost without touching the body" (14). But Foucault quotes the ordinance of 1670 that, up until the Revolution, "regulated the general forms of penal practice." (Read *Surveiller et punir*, 41)

76

> The ordinance of 1670 regulated the general forms of penal practice up to the Revolution. It laid down the following hierarchy of penalties: "Death, judicial torture pending proof, penal servitude, flogging, *amende honorable*, banishment." A high proportion of physical punishment. Customs, the nature of the crimes, the status of the condemned accounted for still more variations. "Capital punishment comprises many kinds of death: some prisoners may be condemned to be hanged, others to having their hands cut off or their tongues cut out or pierced and then to be hanged; others, for more serious crimes, to be broken alive and to die on the wheel, after having their limbs broken; others to be broken until they die a natural death, others to be

18. Cesare Beccaria, *Des délits et des peines*, with preface by Robert Badinter (Paris: Flammarion, 1991), 129; *On Crimes and Punishments and Other Writings*, ed. Aaron Thomas, trans. Aaron Thomas and Jeremy Parzen (Toronto: University of Toronto Press, 2008), p. 53.

strangled and then broken, others to be burnt alive, others to be burnt after first being strangled; others to be drawn by four horses, others to have their heads cut off, and others to have their heads broken." (32)

I will next read again the very first pages of the book. They describe an execution according to the rule of this ordinance and still in 1757 on the eve of the Revolution. I will interrupt my reading at the words "Pardon, Lord" so as to mark clearly the transition with the subject of last year's seminar. (Read *Surveiller et punir*, 9–10)

On 2 March 1757 Damiens the regicide was condemned "to make the *amende honorable* before the main door of the Church of Paris" where he was to be "taken and conveyed in a cart, wearing nothing but a shirt, holding a torch of burning wax weighing two pounds"; then, "in the said cart, to the Place de Grève, where, on a scaffold that will be erected there, the flesh will be torn from his breasts, arms, thighs and calves with red-hot pincers, his right hand, holding the knife with which he committed the said parricide, burnt with sulphur, and, on those places where the flesh will be torn away, poured molten lead, boiling oil, burning resin, wax and sulphur melted together and then his body drawn and quartered by four horses and his limbs and body consumed by fire, reduced to ashes and his ashes thrown to the winds."

"Finally, he was quartered," recounts the *Gazette d'Amsterdam* of 1 April 1757. "This last operation was very long, because the horses used were not accustomed to drawing; consequently, instead of four, six were needed; and when that did not suffice, they were forced, in order to cut off the wretch's thighs, to sever the sinews and hack at the joints. . . .

"It is said that, though he was always a great swearer, no blasphemy escaped his lips; but the excessive pain made him utter horrible cries, and he often repeated: 'My God, have pity on me! Jesus, help me!' The spectators were all edified by the solicitude of the parish priest of St Paul's who despite his great age did not spare himself in offering consolation to the patient."

Bouton, an officer on the watch, left us his account: "The sulphur was lit, but the flame was so poor that only the top skin of the hand was burnt, and that only slightly. Then the executioner, his sleeves rolled up, took the steel pincers, which had been especially made for the occasion, and which were about a foot and a half long, and pulled first at the calf of the right leg, then at the thigh, and from there at the two fleshy parts of the right arm; then at the breasts. Though a strong, sturdy fellow, this executioner found it so difficult to tear away the pieces of flesh that he set about the same spot two or three times, twisting the pincers as he did so, and what he took away formed at each part a wound about the size of a six-pound crown piece.

"After these tearings with the pincers, Damiens, who cried out profusely, though without swearing, raised his head and looked at himself; the same executioner dipped an iron spoon in the pot containing the boiling potion, which he poured liberally over each wound. Then the ropes that were to be harnessed to the horses were attached with cords to the patient's body; the horses were then harnessed and placed alongside the arms and legs, one at each limb.

"Monsieur Le Breton, the clerk of the court, went up to the patient several times and asked him if he had anything to say. He said he had not; at each moment, he cried out, as the damned in hell are supposed to cry out, 'Pardon, my God! Pardon, Lord.' Despite all this pain, he raised his head from time to time and looked at himself boldly. The cords had been tied so tightly by the men who pulled the ends that they caused him indescribable pain. Monsieur le Breton went up to him again and asked him if he had anything to say; he said no. Several confessors went up to him and spoke to him at length; he willingly kissed the crucifix that was held out to him; he opened his lips and repeated: 'Pardon, Lord.'" (3–4)

Question of the capital title, therefore. Why inscribe a seminar on the death penalty within or under the title of a seminar on pardon and perjury?

For a very first reason, which seems to go without saying. Even though we insisted a great deal, in past years, on the fact that pardon and forgiveness, unlike perjury, was foreign to the juridical space, heterogeneous to penal logic (despite certain structural and essential complications, such as for example the right of pardon, which grounded the law by means of the sovereign exception that it marked in that law, I will not return to this), well, despite this radical heterogeneity between the semantics of forgiveness or pardon and the semantics of right and penal justice, one cannot help but think that the death penalty (as a legal device, as a penal sanction administered by the state according to the order of a state of law, by which the death penalty *claims* to be — I repeat and emphasize this — *claims* to be something altogether other, in its concept, its aim, its allegation, altogether other than a murder, a crime, or a putting to death in general), well, one cannot help but think that the death penalty, inasmuch as it puts an end, irreversibly, along with the life of the accused, to any prospect of revision, reparation, redemption, even repentance, at least on earth and for someone living, the death penalty signifies that the crime it sanctions remains forever, on men's earth and in men's society, un-forgivable. To be sure, a victim can forgive, in his or her heart, an accused condemned to death and executed, but society — or the juridical apparatus — that condemns to death and proceeds to execution, or even the head of state or the governor who, having at his disposal the right of pardon or the right to clemency,[19] refuses it to the condemned

---

19. [Translator's note]: The phrase "right to clemency" is in English in the original.

79 one, this society, this social hierarchy thus represented no longer forgives. It all happens as if these powers decreed that the imputed crime must remain forever unforgiven: the death penalty signifies in this regard the inexpiable or the unpardonable, the irreversibly unpardoned. Pardon, the power to pardon is returned to God. "Pardon, Lord."[20]

20. At the end of this first session, Derrida recommended several readings in more than one language. We reproduce that list here:

Old Testament, Exodus 20; the Gospels; *The Killing State: Capital Punishment in Law, Politics, and Culture*, ed. Austin Sarat, Oxford University Press, 1999; Sister Helen Prejean, C.S.J., *Dead Man Walking: An Eyewitness Account of the Death Penalty in the United States*, Vintage Books, 1994 (includes a valuable bibliography); Michel Foucault, *Surveiller et Punir: Naissance de la prison*, Gallimard 1975, Tel Gallimard, 1999; *Discipline and Punish: The Birth of the Prison*, trans. A. Sheridan, Vintage Books, 1977; Cesare Beccaria, *Dei deletti et delle penne*, 1765; *On Crimes and Punishment*, trans. D. Young, New York: Hackett Publishing, 1986; *Des délits et des peines*, GF Flammarion, préface de Robert Badinter; W. Benjamin, "Critique of Violence"; *The Death Penalty in America, Current Controversies*, ed. Hugo Adam Bedau, Oxford University Press, 1996; William Schabas, *The Abolition of the Death Penalty in International Law*, Cambridge University Press (1993) 1997; Albert Camus, "Réflexions sur la guillotine," in *Réflexions sur la peine capitale*, ed. Arthur Koestler, Paris: Pluriel, 1979; "Reflections on the Guillotine," in *Resistance, Rebellion, and Death*, Vintage Books, 1974 ("In tomorrow's united Europe . . . the solemn abolition of the death penalty should be Article One of the European Code that we all are hoping for," [176]); Victor Hugo, *Écrits sur la peine de mort*, Avignon: Actes Sud, 1979; Death penalty: "the special and eternal sign of barbarity"; Kant, *The Metaphysics of Morals*, First Part, "Doctrine of Right," Public Right, General Remark E; Part Two, first section, §36; Jean Genet, *Notre Dame des Fleurs*, "Le condamné à mort," *Le miracle de la rose*, in *Œuvres Complètes*, Gallimard, 1951; Robert Badinter, *L'Exécution*, Grasset Fasquelle, 1973, Le livre de poche, 1998; Percy Bysshe Shelley, "On the Punishment of Death"; William Wordsworth, "Sonnets upon the Punishment of Death, in Series" [Composed 1839–40; published December 1841 (*Quarterly Review*, 1842)]; Herman Melville, *Billy Budd*; Le Collège de Sociologie (1937–39), NRF, Gallimard, 1979 (1938–39: P. Klossowski's Lecture, "Le marquis de Sade et la Révolution," p. 367; and R. Caillois's Lecture, "Sociologie du bourreau," p. 367 ff); Joan of Arc, Sacco and Vanzetti, the Rosenbergs; J. Derrida, *Demeure, Athènes*; Mumia Abu-Jamal . . . (my preface); Bible (references in Schabas, p. 3 notes 13,14); Jean Imbert, *La peine de mort*, PUF, 1989; J-J. Rousseau, *Le contrat social*, livre 2, ch. 5. "Du droit de vie et de mort"; Peter Linebaugh, "Politics of the Death Penalty (Gruesome Gertie at the Buckle of the Bible Belt)," in *New Left Review*, no. 209, 1995; Carl Schmitt, *Théologie politique*, trans. fr. Gallimard, 1988 (*Politische Theologie, Vier Kapitel zur Lehre von der Souveränität*, 1922, 2ème édition 1934).

December 15, 1999

What is an exception?

More than once, last year, we insisted on the character of absolute *exception* that pardon must maintain, a pardon worthy of the name, a pardon that is always unforeseeable and irreducible to statement as well as to contract, to determinative judgment, to the law, therefore, a pardon always outside the law, always heterogeneous to order, to norm, to rule, or to calculation, to the rule of calculation, to economic as well as juridical calculation. Every pardon worthy of that name, if there ever is any, must be *exceptional*, should be exceptional, that is in short the law of the pardon: it must be lawless and exceptional, above the laws or outside the laws.

The question then remains: what is an exception? Can one pose this question? Is there an essence of exception, an adequate concept of this supposed essence?

One may have one's doubts, and yet we commonly use this word, as if it had an assured semantic unity. We regularly act as if we know what an exception is or, likewise, what an exception is not, as if we had a valid criterion with which to identify an exception or the exceptionality of an exception, the rule, in short, of the exception, the rule for discerning between the exceptional <and> the non-exceptional—which seems, however, absurd or a contradiction in terms. And yet, people commonly speak of the exception, the exception to the rule, the exception that confirms the rule; there is even a law or laws of exception, exceptional tribunals, and so forth.

I wager that this problematic of the exception will stay with us from here on out, and that it will no doubt be the most reliable articulation between the questions of pardon, perjury, and death penalty. That is at least what I would like to begin to show today or tomorrow, next time, in the year 2000, through or after a certain detour.

For, having reached this point of my introduction, I wondered which guiding thread to privilege so as to orient myself in the thicket of problems and the immense overgrown archive of the death penalty. The conceptual delimitation is already a formidable prerequisite. It is easy, too easy perhaps, even if one must indeed begin there, to recall that the death penalty is a juridical concept that, insofar as it belongs to penal law, that is, to a set of calculable rules and prescriptions, is distinct from singular murder, from individual acts of vengeance and implies, by right and thus in principle, the intervention of a third party, of an arbitrating authority that is foreign or superior to the parties to a dispute, thus par excellence and at least virtually, the authority of a state, of an institution of the juridico-statist, juridico-political type, or even a reason of state, a rationality, a *logos* with general or universal claims, a juridical reason rising above the parties, particular interest, and passion, the *pathos*, the pathological, of individual affect. The effect of coldness, of frozen insensitivity that often seizes hold of us when faced with the discourse, with the process of judgment, or with the ritual of execution of the death penalty, this effect of cadaverous coldness or rigor as in rigor mortis is also or first of all the manifestation of this power or of this claim to the power of reason: it is the allegation of an imperturbable rationality rising above the heart, above immediate passion, and above the individual relations between men of flesh and blood; it is thus this alliance between reason, universal rationality, and the machine, the machinality of its operation. All discourses that legitimate the death penalty are first of all discourses of state rationality having a universal claim and structure; they are theorems of state right, of the machine of state. In the rationalist space thus defined or alleged, it is understandable that very often, if not always and typically, the abolitionist objection to the death penalty is tempted to oppose the cold machinelike, mediatized, technologized, mechanized reason, and its rather police-like and virile appearance, with immediate feeling, the heart, affectivity, and its rather feminine appearance, with the horror that the *cruelty* of execution inspires.

We will see that this motif of *cruelty* plays a large role in the schema of the abolitionist argument, in its logic and its rhetoric, notably, in a complex manner, in the United States, as if the principle of the death penalty were less in question than the cruelty of its application, to the point that if one could find a means of attenuating or even of causing cruelty to *disappear* (in the double sense of this word "disappear," in the sense of canceling and the sense of making invisible, insensible, non-phenomenal, non-appearing, in the sense of "dissimulate"), if, then, one could make cruelty disappear from the scene, then the death penalty, the principle of the death penalty, could be maintained: all it would take would be to make the death penalty insensible, anesthetized, to anesthetize both the condemned and the actors and spectators. The anesthesic, anesthetic, or anesthesial logic that thus poses the general philosophical problem of the relations between sensibility and reason, the heart and reason (in its most unlimited vein, up to the most refined zones of the Kantian or Husserlian philosophical problematic of a transcendental aesthetic, a theory of pure sensibility), this anesthesial logic of certain abolitionist discourses does in fact enter into, if only by appearing to oppose them, the axiomatics of the right to the death penalty that poses or supposes the rationality of the death penalty. This anesthesial logic of abolitionism can often play into the logic that maintains the principle of the death penalty. We are going to verify this. The anesthesial argument does not contest this rationality; it pleads merely for a less cruel, less painful application of the said rationality. We are going to see in a moment or at some later point what the national or international juridical deployment of this anesthesial logic leads to in our modernity. It is this logic that allows people, for example in the United States, to be in favor of the death penalty on the condition that it be administered by lethal injection and not by gas chamber, hanging, firing squad, or electric chair. Whence the new cinematographic staging of spectacle that is becoming a genre today, such as, for example, the film titled, I seem to recall, *True Crime*,[1] which is typical in this regard: a journalist, suspecting a judicial error that had led to a death sentence, conducts, not out of a taste for justice but out of the journalist's passion for information, a meticulous counter-inquiry — which takes up the whole film, which is the film — and ends up proving the innocence of the accused, thus judicial error, and is able to produce the proof at the very second when, the execution already under way, the lethal liquid having begun to penetrate the veins of the condemned man, one might almost say of the patient, a condemned man already anesthetized; the phone call from the governor, awakened by the journalist from his sleep, interrupts the execution in process, saves the innocent condemned one (a white man moreover whereas the true guilty one turns out as if by chance to be a black man),[2] with all the suspense that you can imagine of the cinematic exploitation, which shows all the operations, all the moments of the progression of the fluid, the phone call at the last second, for there is always a telephone today that links, like an umbilical cord of life or death, the place of execution to the executive power of the sovereign, here that of the governor who can grant a pardon or interrupt the execution up to the last instant, up to the instant of death. As a result, in numerous films or books of this kind, which

84

1. Clint Eastwood, *True Crime*, Warner Brothers, 1999.
2. In fact, the man wrongly accused in the film is also black.

are apparently moved by the just cause of a horrified opposition to the death penalty, what is exhibited are the remains of cruelty in the most medically refined modes of putting to death and what is exploited is the voyeuristic and ambiguous enjoyment of the spectator, the filmgoer who trembles up to the last second as he or she sees the liquid flow into the veins of the condemned. This argument against the cruelty rather than against the principle of the death penalty is both strong and weak, strong because it moves and thus motivates, provides a good psychological motivation for the abolition of the death penalty; but it is weak because it concerns only the modality of application, not the principle of the death penalty, and it becomes impotent in the face of what claims to be an incremental softening, an anesthesia that tends toward the general, or even a humanization of the death penalty that would spare the cruelty to both the condemned one and the witnesses, all the while maintaining the principle of capital punishment.

85

Hence the infinitely ambiguous, sometimes hypocritical role played by this appeal to emotion in the face of cruelty. It plays this role both in the best rhetoric of countless arguments against the death penalty and, in a manner that is finally more decisive because still more equivocal, in the texts of laws[3] that will have played a major role in the ongoing history of the abolition of the death penalty. I will take several examples of these two uses, in a way that is partly justified and partly arbitrary because there are so many others one might choose.

I take the first example because we are in France, in a country that, through parliamentary means, abolished the death penalty fewer than twenty years ago, although the majority of public opinion as measured by polls was and no doubt still remains in favor of the death penalty, and would vote for it if a referendum were organized or if European legislation authorized it, a double possibility that is henceforth excluded in principle. I take this first example, then, from what is closest to us and from someone who was a great attorney and then minister of justice, the fervent and efficacious proponent of abolition, Robert Badinter. Not only did Robert Badinter's eloquence move all the representatives and all of France when, presenting to parliament the bill abolishing the death penalty, he evoked in concrete terms its horror and cruelty. He is also the author, among other books, of a narrative titled L'Exécution [The Execution] (1973). I underscore the date 1973 for a reason that will become clear in a moment. In this book, then, Badinter recounts the sentencing to death and execution of two condemned men: Buffet, a former legionnaire, and Bontems, a former paratrooper, Buffet who was defended

86

3. During the session, Derrida adds: "worldwide and international."

by Thierry Lévy and Bontems by Badinter.[4] At the time, they were called the Clairvaux killers, accused of having acted in concert. This was one of the problematic dimensions of the indictment: whether or not one could dissociate the two indictments and the two accused parties, accused of having acted in concert, during an assault and a hostage-taking, when they killed a guard and a nurse whom they had taken hostage. Badinter, who wanted to save his client, Bontems, based his hope and his argument for the defense on this possible dissociation of the two accused men, Buffet and Bontems.

> If [Badinter writes] we could establish in the course of the arguments that Bontems had not wielded the knife, not only would he no longer appear like a hostage killer, but his opposition to Buffet would dissociate him from the latter. From that moment, one could permit oneself to harbor every hope. Even the talionic law could not be brought to bear: whoever has not killed must not be killed. So, we would save Bontems's head.[5]

His head because it is a matter of the guillotine. "Even the talionic law," says Badinter, which suggests that he does not subscribe to the talionic law, but that as a lawyer he is putting himself in the situation where the dominant opinion, and first of all that of a jury of the people, does believe in it, and one has to remove every chance of their making use of this bad logic. Before coming to the points that I want to underscore, concerning, let's say, the argument or the logic of cruelty, I draw your attention to several features in this book (which I ask you to read) that come to resonate or are consonant with what I was arguing last week. You recall that, while reading a passage from *The Social Contract*, "On the Right to Life and to Death," I expressed my perplexity, in truth some profound doubts, about what Rousseau prudently said one may "presume" or not "presume," namely that, I quote again, "we should not presume that any of the contracting parties premeditates getting himself hanged [*il n'est pas à présumer qu'aucun des contractants prémédite alors de se faire pendre*]."[6] What Rousseau says one should not presume is that a citizen entering into the *social contract* and into, in short, this insurance contract, into what assures security and life, cannot premeditate his own death; he cannot, if you wish to translate it thus, be suicidal or subject to the death drive, a death drive turned on himself. Now, one of the motifs that frequently recurs in Badinter's book is that one of the two ac-

87

4. At times Derrida writes "Bontemps" instead of "Bontems" including in quotations from Badinter. We have corrected the spelling.
5. Robert Badinter, *L'Exécution* (Paris: Grasset, 1973; LGF, Le Livre de Poche, 1976), p. 47.
6. See above, "First Session, December 8, 1999," pp. 14ff.

cused men, not the one he is defending, Bontems, but the other, Buffet, was motivated by such a suicidal drive; he wanted to be punished by death and he thus risked dragging down with him into death his accomplice, the one who allegedly had not killed with his own hand and did not want to die. I am going to read a passage where you will see the story of an oath and thus of non-perjury, of loyalty toward sworn faith grafted onto this question of the death drive. (Read *L'Exécution*, 89–91)

> For Buffet, death was now the surest means of avoiding prison, this carceral universe that he scorned and hated. The death instinct possessed Buffet, led him, carried him toward the guillotine. It exerted an obvious fascination on him. Buffet had always cut his victims' throats. The symbolic alliance of the knife with death was plunged deep within him. Now the immense shining blade of the guillotine was right there, nearby, looming above him, shutting out his horizon. It seemed to have been waiting for him for all eternity, at least for the eternity that is life for each of us. After the razor, the dagger with which he had killed, the big knife was in turn going to slash his throat with a clean cut. This was the secret and expected apotheosis.
>
> But there was the one he called his comrade. This word for the former legionnaire must have had its full meaning, expressing the indissoluble link between men who had seen combat together. A comrade does not betray you. A comrade does not leave you alone. Solitude is treason. Especially when one has sworn to conquer or die, together. It was a simple given that, even if obligated, even if forced, a comrade would go all the way when he was the comrade of Claude Buffet. This word alone, frequently repeated, cracked like a whip in the rare moments when Buffet let himself be carried away by a kind of murderous, terrifying rage whose object was Bontems.
>
> Looking at the two of them, I thought that they must have exchanged a juvenile and tragic oath. I imagined the former legionnaire Buffet and the former paratrooper Bontems whispering: "Failure or success, together all the way. — Swear it. — I swear it." For Buffet such a commitment could only have had an absolute value. It mattered little what had really been each one's role. Bontems had to keep his word to Buffet — even if he hadn't killed, even if he still had a chance of saving his head. That is what Buffet was saying, when standing up, in a metallic voice, he shouted: "What I cannot bear is that my comrade is shirking his responsibility." By "responsibility," his judges understood "responsibility before the law," and so powerful was Buffet's fascination, they saw in Bontems a coward who was running away and in Buffet a man who had the courage of his crimes. This logical interpretation overlaid Buffet's obsessions and rantings. Bontems had to take responsibility, but vis-à-vis him, Buffet. Bontems had to uphold to the end the promise solemnly exchanged between them and that bound them in a common destiny. For Buffet, the thought that Bontems might shirk his

88

duty to him at the last minute and prefer living to dying with him, after the failure of their tragic undertaking, was at moments unbearable for him. Then indifference and detachment seemed to overtake him entirely. He became once again the stranger — the spectator. (89–91).

The other feature I wanted already to underscore concerns the date of the book and the trial, the execution. It is 1972, a historic date of virtually worldwide dimension because it is during the trial itself, but too late, after Badinter's defense, that the Supreme Court of the United States (June 29, 1972) rules in favor of the abolition of the death penalty — or at least upholds a legal ruling that will be translated, with some equivocations that I will get to, as a de facto, if not de jure, *abolition* of the death penalty. An abolition that will not last — we'll return to this — because in 1977, the death penalty will be *practically* reinstated. The abolition of the death penalty will have survived, if one can say that, for only five years in the United States. But it is true that on June 29, 1972, by a vote of five to four, the smallest possible majority, the Supreme Court declared (and here is the argument I nickname the cruelty argument in this theater of cruelty constituted by the history of the death penalty, history as history of the death penalty) [the Supreme Court declared, then] that in the three specific cases it was reviewing (a rape in Texas, a rape and a murder in Georgia), that in these three cases — the Supreme Court rules on cases and its rulings have a generalizable jurisprudential value — the court did not abolish the death penalty; it declared that in these three typical cases, the death penalty is "cruel and unusual punishment," which would violate the Eighth and Fourteenth amendments to the Constitution. In other words, the court did not rule on the principle of the death sentence, but on the cruelty of its execution (this is the famous ruling in *Furman v. Georgia* to which we will return). The ambiguity of this decision, which is all the more fragile in that it was obtained by a one-vote majority (five justices against the four appointed by Nixon), this ambiguity explains the fragility, precariousness, and brief duration of this judicial precedent. Given that this 1972 decision had been prepared and awaited for five years, with the result that, between 1967 and 1972, all executions had been suspended in the United States, the last, in 1967 precisely, having been that of a man who had killed his wife and children in Colorado and was asphyxiated in a gas chamber; given also that, after 1972, this quasi abolition lasted until 1977, the date on which certain states, which are sometimes called "killing states," revised their laws so as to make the death penalty and its execution supposedly less "cruel" and therefore compatible with the Eighth and Fourteenth amendments (less cruel, less arbitrary, and

89

less discriminatory laws); given, finally, that the same Supreme Court later
validated these laws revised in 1976 (*Gregg v. Georgia*), well, the practical
abolition of the death penalty, or at least the general suspension of its application, lasted only ten years (1967–77), and ten years later again, in 1987,
90   the Supreme Court reaffirmed the constitutionality of the death penalty in
the case of a black man who had killed a police officer. Aggravating things
further, and still by a vote of five to four, the same Supreme Court ruled in
1989 that henceforth nothing stood in the way of the execution of death sentences for those between sixteen and eighteen years old (who were minors at
the time of the crime) or the mentally handicapped (a possibility which had
before then been excluded and posed all the problems that you can imagine,
to which we will also return). The example that Jean Imbert cites, among
other things, is one in which this law retroactively justified the execution (by
electric chair) in Virginia of a thirty-seven-year-old black farm worker even
though psychiatric experts had given him a mental age of eight.[7] One must
also recall, since we have arrived at this chapter of the recent history of the
United States, that in 1986 the same court allowed black plaintiffs to contest the exclusion of blacks from a jury. Amnesty International, which has
never relented in denouncing the United States in this regard, speaks of a
"horrible lottery" because for the same crime a black man is ten times more
likely to receive a death penalty than a white woman in Florida, Texas,
Georgia, or California. One should also know that in a recent poll, 79 percent of Americans declared that they were in favor of the death penalty. In
1981, a member of the Senate or the House of Representatives, I can't recall
which one, declared: "Our function is to obey the will of the voters," and the
Supreme Court referred in 1989 to "the absence of national consensus" in its
refusal to exclude the mentally handicapped from the sanction of the death
penalty.[8] Thus, if one compares this situation with the French situation,
where a majority of parliamentary representatives (including right-wing
representatives, one of whom was Chirac,[9] for example) voted in 1981 for
an abolition that they knew would go against the majority of public opinion
if it had been consulted by means of a poll or a referendum, well, we have
here two concepts or two implementations of democratic representation.
Must a representative *represent* in the sense of *reflect* or *reproduce* the present
91   state of constituent opinion or else does he or she have the responsibility to

7. Imbert, *La peine de mort.*
8. Ibid., p. 114.
9. [Translator's note]: Jacques Chirac, a leader of the right-wing Gaullist party
who would later be elected to two terms as president of the French Republic, in 1995
and 2002.

guide, through reflection and decision, a still shapeable and ill-formed or ill-informed opinion? And although this immense problem takes us beyond the field of penal law and the death penalty, it is not insignificant that this difference shows up in such a striking and clear manner on the subject of the death penalty. This question, let's say, of parliamentary democracy (this question of the *demos* between democracy and demagogy) must not, especially on the subject of the death penalty, be circumscribed within the limits of the nation-state. It is always, as we will see, some international pressure in the guise of universality or the universality of human rights that induces, directly or not, national decisions. Even in France, the vote of the French parliament was already inflected by the fact that, in the European Union then being formed, the death penalty was abolished or on the way toward progressive abolition, in an irreversible trend.

Before leaving the United States in order to situate the date of a certain historical chiasmus, namely that in 1972, when Badinter wrote *The Execution*, the death penalty was still in force in France and had just been abolished in the United States, whereas fewer than ten years later, it will have been abolished in France and reinstated in the United States; before leaving the United States, then, a few more factual details: at present, thirty-eight of the fifty states in the United States maintain the death penalty for murder with aggravating circumstances. Death is administered, depending on the state, by electric chair, lethal injection, gas chamber, hanging, or firing squad. Of the thirty-eight states that reinstated the death penalty in 1977, not all of them carry it out, only (if one can say that) twenty-seven do so, but the number of executions tends to increase (electric chair in 1990 in Arkansas, where Clinton — a hard-liner on this question — was the merciless[10] governor; lethal injection in Wyoming in 1992, gas chamber in Arizona and California in 1992).[11] In twenty years, from 1977 to 1997, there were 385 executions (averaging about twenty each year, the majority being poor blacks, a proportion that is repeated in the more than three thousand prisoners condemned to death who are waiting on death rows.[12] An approximate comparative statistic would give us the corresponding image of five executions a year in France).[13]

I return now to *The Execution* and to the historical chiasmus, to the con-

92

10. [Translator's note]: The word "merciless" is in English in the original

11. The closing parenthesis has been added.

12. [Translator's note]: Here and throughout, the phrase "death rows" or "death row" is in English in the original.

13. [Translator's note]: This figure is proportional to the French population of fifty million. By contrast, between 1960 and 1981, the year capital punishment was abolished in France, there were fewer than twenty-five executions carried out in France.

tretemps of "too soon" or "too late": too soon too late: essential anachronism of the death penalty. In 1972, Badinter had just concluded his defense an hour earlier when he was told that the death penalty had just been abolished in the United States and that—once again, because what happens in the United States has singular repercussions throughout the world—nothing would ever be as it was before. And you will see in the lines I am going to read the importance of the public space, of the new public space marked by radio, by the both powerful and powerless international media, of the globalization [*mondialisation*] already under way, of a globalization that is so unequal and heterogeneous in this debate. That is why I insist on it. (Read *L'Exécution*, 158–60)

> Upon entering the courtroom, two journalists surrounded me in a great state of excitement. "Did you hear the news?" I stared at them without understanding. "The United States Supreme Court just abolished the death penalty. The radio just announced it." I looked at the large clock. Less than an hour had passed since the end of arguments. Had I known the news an hour earlier, what closing argument might the defense have been able to draw from it! Now it was too late. The jury was closed up in its delibera-tions, as if cut off from the world. In my exasperation, I thought of taking a transistor radio and putting it in front of the closed window of the room where the jury was convened and turning it up loud at the news hour. Per-haps this news reaching the jurors unexpectedly and almost by breaking and entering would seem to them a sign of destiny, the indication that the death penalty was but the remnant of an age that elsewhere had ended and that could also end in France. But I quickly assessed the difficulties and the risks of such an undertaking that might, on the contrary, exasperate the court. After all, we were in Troyes, and it was the Clairvaux murderers who were being tried. The United States Supreme Court was very far away at that moment. I went back to the defense bench. I thought of Bontems, of what he must be feeling. I too could do nothing but sit and wait.
>
> 93   It didn't take long, moreover. Much quicker than I anticipated. The bell rang and right away, almost hastily, the court came back in. Everyone re-turned to his seat, in a disorder that was still going on when the judge, turn-ing toward us, ordered the accused men to be brought back in. I looked at each juror, with all my might, trying to intercept a look, to establish a com-munication, a sign. I was met with only closed faces. A kind of void made it-self felt around us, and I felt it in myself. The reading of the responses to the questions posed began. To the fourth question, which was the decisive one for us, the judge paused: "Is Bontems guilty of having, in the same circum-stances of time and place, killed [*donné la mort*] Mrs. . . . ?" *Response*: "NO by a majority of votes." A sigh rose in the room. A journalist friend smiled

at me. Bontems had saved his head. The judge continued: "Did Buffet kill Mrs. . . . ?" "YES." "Is Bontems the accomplice of Buffet?" "YES." "Are there any attenuating circumstances for Buffet? "NO." Buffet was sentenced to death. "Are there any attenuating circumstances for Bontems?" And the response came: "NO by a majority of votes." It was the death penalty. Already the judge was announcing it. From the back of the room, all around the court, through the open windows, the applause mounted with cries of "bravo!" The judge was outraged in vain. The mob shouted with joy and hate mixed together. I turned around toward Bontems. I grabbed his hand and told him in a restrained voice, with all the force that I could muster: "Bontems, you will be pardoned. They acknowledge that you didn't kill. You will be pardoned. For sure. The president of the republic will pardon you, for sure." Philippe Lemaire was already giving him instructions for filing his appeal. He smiled at us again, differently, and said: "Since you tell me so, I have faith . . ." I shook his hand again. The police were already taking him away. Philippe went out as well to talk with him some more. As for me, I stayed there, in the tumult. They had agreed with us; they admitted that he had not killed. But they had condemned to death this man who, they admitted, hadn't killed. I kept my eyes fixed on my papers, my notes, as useless as I was. I didn't want to see those faces. (158–60)

Let us return now to the motif of cruelty that is significant for us both because of its importance and the equivocation it will introduce, as we will constantly confirm, in the history of the law and in the history of the death penalty (in particular because, we will come back to this again, it is the cruelty of execution that is denounced both in the decisions of the Supreme Court and in a number of very ambiguous international declarations that encouraged abolition without really naming or denouncing the principle of the death penalty, the cruelty of execution being simply a case of "torture." So torture is denounced but not putting to death).[14] As I continue the reading of *The Execution* but also later of Badinter's speech to parliament, I want to privilege this logic or this rhetoric of cruelty, of the theater of cruelty by bringing it out in certain passages (among so many possible ones) where the motif of cruelty crosses with certain other motifs that we have already begun to interrogate, or even to put back onstage. Dawn, theater, and then fascination, and then the coldness of the machine, and then, to begin, the paradox of anesthesia.

I begin with the latter (the paradox of anesthesia) and you will see how it already follows the rhythm of nighttime up until dawn. Here is a paragraph

94

14. The closing parenthesis has been added.

that describes how the point was to anesthetize the condemned man, but to anesthetize him, to put him to sleep or to let him sleep, even to help him sleep, only up to the point at which he had to stay awake and alert, having his head on straight when he is about to lose it. (Read *L'Exécution*, 198)

> At La Santé Prison, the chief warden who greeted me every morning with a ritual "Sleep well, *maître?*"[15] out of sympathy or irony or perhaps both, found, as did the guards, that time passed slowly. He said to me each day while escorting me back down the corridor: "It's tough for them." Buffet used to walk until dawn. Then he would fall asleep from exhaustion. No doubt, the animal in him was not resigned to the death that he expected and demanded. Bontems, on the contrary, would go to bed at dusk, gaining several hours of sleep thanks to the sleeping pills that the doctor authorized (in small doses, to avoid a suicide attempt). He would awake well before dawn. Lying in bed, he would smoke one cigarette after another. Day would finally come, sometimes he would go back to sleep. (198)

95

That this whole theater of cruelty is put under the sign of fascination, of *fascinatio*, that is, <of> what is going to tie voyeurism, the scopic drive, the desire for drama to the charm, the enchantment that chains the spectator to the spectacle (*fascio* means to tense, tie, attach, and *fasciola* is the wrapping [*bandelette*], the ribbon, the strip, or the bandage for wrapping a leg), what links the voyeur-spectator to the *fascinum*, which means at once the charm, the enchantment, and the virile sex; that this whole theater is an experience of fascination is often literally signaled by *The Execution*. You recall Badinter saying that the guillotine exerted an "obvious fascination" on Buffet (89). These are the words with which Badinter describes the attraction exerted on Buffet's vision by the prospect of his own castration-decapitation or decollation. He is fascinated by what is going to cut off his head, by what is going to cut him off from his head, by the machine that is going to erect him making his head fall, and he desires this machine, the blade of the guillotine, which is essentially the same as his knife. (But it is Bontems who will cry out at the last moment addressing the attorney general: "So, you got a hard-on! [*tu bandes!*]" [216]. And one must connect this logic of erection to decapitation since people say that it is often organically linked to the experience of hanging for men.) In the passage I read a moment ago, Badinter spoke of the "symbolic alliance of the knife with death [Buffet's own as well as his victim's: he is his own victim] that was plunged deep within him" (89). Much earlier, Badinter admits his own fascination, and once again the word is his, with judicial theater; I underscore the word "fascination" and

15. [Translator's note]: A customary title and form of address for barristers.

the word "theater," along with the spectacle entailed by theater, to be sure, but also the religious sacredness it entails; and in this regard the example of medieval mystery plays, as a community experience of religious theater and of the Christian Passion or Incarnation, does not come up by chance, as you will hear. One should comment on every word on this page (35) of *The Execution* but let it suffice to tie together the threads I have just drawn out (theater of cruelty, fascination, spectacle, medieval Christian mystery play); it is the very literality of this passage where the next paragraph, which I am coming to, opens onto the void, all of a sudden, of this same theater. (Read *L'Exécution*, 35–36)

96

> For the last twenty years, since I became a lawyer, the places where justice is meted out have fascinated me [*exercent sur moi une fascination*]. In the provinces, abroad, where others go to visit museums, cathedrals, or antique dealers, I never fail to go to the courthouse. I mingle with the public in the back of courtrooms where the most banal cases, the smallest offenses are being tried. I listen, I breathe it in, I attempt to grasp the meaning of this particular justice [*cette justice-là*]. When I am not an actor in it, to see justice at work is, for me, a privileged spectacle. One learns more about a country, about a civilization, about its people, by seeing played out the eternal judicial tragicomedy than in any other place, be it in the square on market day. I sit there, attentive, entertained and vaguely anxious, no doubt a little like the medieval onlooker watching a mystery play. I sense that there is a deeper reality playing out behind the ritual, the formalities, the remarks of the adversaries, that what is being presented to us is a kind of failed incarnation, always failed, of an essential demand, of an indestructible hope: Justice. Even the deserted courts, the empty spectators' galleries are for me like abandoned churches, uninhabited castles where steps resound and where one instinctively lowers one's voice. History has kept no trace of the dramas that have happened there, but something of them still remains, invisible and weighty, in those walls.
>
> In Troyes, however, to my surprise, I felt none of that upon entering the courthouse. (35–36)

We could follow another trace of this word and this logic of fascination in Badinter's own argument, much earlier, almost ten years before his speech to the National Assembly, because, having remarked Buffet's fascination for his own execution, and first of all his own, Badinter's, fascination for the religious theater of the court of justice, what he also fears is that executions, far from discouraging with the example that they might present, exert in a perverse fashion (all fascination being in itself at bottom a virtual involvement with perversity or perversion) [exert in a perverse fashion] a fascination on

97

potential criminals, on hostage-takers who would like, in sum, to imitate Buffet and Bontems. The logic of fascination would finally be the best argument against the supposed exemplarity of the punishment or rather, the counterargument as to the perversion of the alleged exemplarity itself: the *bad example* risks becoming, as an effect of the law of fascination, the *good example*, the example to be followed, on the contrary, the one that criminals are going to want to imitate in order to resemble the one condemned to death. A kind of perversion of the Imitation of Christ. Which Genet said and also showed with a different concern in mind. The one condemned to death thus becomes a fascinating saint, a fascinating hero, a fascinating martyr. I read. (Read *L'Exécution*, 207–8)

> I knew that Bontems wanted to live. Each of his remarks showed that he still belonged to this life, that he was not tired of it, that as miserable as it was, it was still his life, still life. They were going to kill an animal that wanted to live, that was capable of living. Why? There was really no reason. The hostages had died, to be sure, not by his hand, but still by his fault. Was that sufficient reason for him to be killed in turn? Would the guard's wife and the nurse's husband be less unhappy tomorrow when Bontems was dead, decapitated? Was this the remedy, presuming that there was one? And tomorrow, would all those who dreamed in prison of taking hostages, would they, upon learning the news of the execution, abandon their plans? Come on! On the contrary, the deaths of Buffet and Bontems would exert a secret fascination on them that would urge them on in their undertakings. Hardly a few weeks had passed since the verdict in Troyes, and at Fresnes prison a prisoner had grabbed a nurse in the hospital and, scalpel in hand, threatened to cut her throat if he wasn't set free straightaway. The poor woman was saved only by the intervention of a prisoner who knocked the maniac senseless. Nice illustration of the exemplarity of punishment! (207–8)

But since we are talking about the theater of cruelty and since we intend to remain as close as possible to these two motifs — theater and cruelty, and theater of cruelty at Dawn — let us see how these different thematic threads (notations and connotations) are interwoven in the logic that is also a defense lawyer's rhetoric arguing already, in the course of a singular trial, against the death penalty in general, or rather for the abolition of the death penalty, almost ten years before he did so as a minister before the National Assembly,[16] and here knotting these threads in a film, in a narrative sequence of a reasoned, reasoning story, the status of which hesitates between,

16. Robert Badinter was minister of justice under President François Mitterrand from June 1981 to February 1986.

on the one hand, diary, chronicle, or autobiographical testimony and, on the other, the literary work of art. Which was also, in a wholly different way, of course, the status of the two books by Genet that we evoked and in which the proper names of real, historical persons, of men condemned to death who were in fact executed, did not reduce to silence, did not neutralize the fictional and poetic lyricism of a literary work. Well, Badinter knows very well how to let a touch of cruelty prevail over his whole narrative and, while denouncing or accusing the cruelty one finds everywhere, how to associate it, with artful effects of rhetoric, to the machination, the implacable, merciless machinism of a cold, icy, heartless reason. Hard and cold like a machine, like a guillotine, like an instrument that is not even still a tool (as the knife or axe could be), but a machine: the guillotine. Cruelty is hard because it is cold, because it has no heart. This association of coldness with cruelty is inscribed by Badinter in all the book's connotations (that I don't have the time to study with a magnifying glass from this point of view, but in which you would find for example a meteorology in accord with the book's climate and the landscape of the ongoing experience). For example, the rain is cold and cruel, and it makes the streets "inhospitable." (Read *L'Exécution*, 183–84)

99

> The gladiator has fallen onto the sand of the arena. He is caught in the leaded net of the retiary. The mob, standing in the bleachers of the circus, calls out for death. All faces turn toward Caesar. The heavily ringed hand is raised. A great silence falls. If Caesar chooses to turn his thumb toward the ground, who, finally, will have killed the gladiator: the brute with his sword already raised? The mob that wants his blood? Or Caesar, alone, from the front of his loge?
>
> It was raining that morning as well. A cold, cruel rain, a Parisian autumn rain that makes the streets inhospitable. People were hurrying, heads tucked into their shoulders, as if they were ready to push you aside to reach shelter more quickly. Philippe and I were going back up Faubourg Saint-Honoré, our arms linked, under the same umbrella. Going past a store window, I saw our reflection. We had the appearance and faces of mourners at a funeral, all dressed up in navy blue, under the large black umbrella. I picked up the pace. (183–84)

The freezing rain will fall on this film until the end, until the final lines of the book, after the execution. The words "cold" and even *glace* punctuate the last page and the last notations of the book. The lawyer leaves the scene of the guillotine, and the book, and he writes:

> I thought it was very cold. . . . My wife was driving slowly [all the notations concerning the presence of his wife in this book mark the counterpoint of

gentleness, softness, *douceur* ("my wife was driving *doucement*"), the counterpoint of gentleness and the heart, of *private* life (wife, family) opposed
to the cold and virile hardness of the citizen, of this heartless *politics* and
this heartless *public*—for the public is also the accused in this indictment,
as well as the politicking president. There would be a lot to say about this
sexual opposition as concerns the death penalty, to say and to complicate
or overdetermine]. My wife was driving slowly [*doucement*]. Like me, the
100   streets were empty. I wiped the window [*glace*] with my glove. There was
nothing more to be done, to be said. It was over, that's it, finished, the *affaire
Bontems*. (220).

This is the last word of the book, a proper name as name of an "affair." Bontems, last word, last name of this victim of a murder, last word
of the book, Bontems will have been murdered by the machine of the law
in these *times of bad weather* [temps de mauvais temps]. All of that is untranslatable into the landscape of another language, not only because of the
proper name, Bontems, and the homonymy between *temps* and *temps* (time
and weather,[17] the times that make history and the weather that prevails in
the story), but also untranslatable because the guillotine is French, like the
French Revolution and the Universal Declaration of the Rights of Man and
the Citizen, and because France still maintains the death penalty in 1972,
when it is being abolished elsewhere. Even in the United States. The bad
tems[18] that survives Bontems, the coldness of the rain, the cruel and heartless coldness of the sky above this urban landscape, this city, this capital of
capital punishment, this polis and this police, this politics (for this comes
after the refusal to pardon by a president who is concerned about his politics, we'll come to this), this icy and inhuman coldness of techno-politics is
theatrically incarnated, if I may say that, or rather dis-incarnated, incarnated as dis-incarnated by the personless personage that is the guillotine,
the spectacle of the persona that is the guillotine erected on the stage and in
the courtyard. Badinter describes its theatrical apparition as that of a stage
character, a terrifying persona, the cruel simulacrum of someone who is no
one, precisely, but who, resembling no one, still resembles a person. The
guillotine, this very French invention that carried off the proper name of its
inventor, Doctor Guillotin, into a common, patented noun, into the act of an
impersonal verb (to guillotine) come to enlarge the vocabulary and syntax
of the French language—the guillotine is no one. At once inhuman and
superhuman, almost divine. And there is something like religiosity in the

17. [Translator's note]: "Time" and "weather" are in English in the original.
18. As written in the typescript.

climate of this guillotine rising up toward the sky beneath the sky.[19] Listen.   *101*
(Read *L'Exécution*, 212)

> I entered the courtyard. The guillotine was there.
>
> I didn't expect it to be there in front of me right away. I had imagined that it would be hidden somewhere, in a tucked away courtyard. But that was it all right, just as I had seen it, just as we all have, in so many old photographs and prints. I was surprised, however, by the uprights, very tall, very slender, that stood out against the window behind it. By contrast, the body of the machine seemed to me rather small, like a small chest. But, as it was, with its two long, thin arms outstretched, it expressed death so well that it seemed to be death itself become thing, materialized, in that bare space. This impression was further reinforced by the huge black canopy, stretched like an awning or a circus tent over the whole courtyard. In this way it hid the guillotine from looks that, from above, would have been able to gaze down on it. This canopy hiding the sky transformed the courtyard into a sort of enormous room where the guillotine stood alone like an idol or an evil altar. Assistants bustled around it. The symbol was also a machine. And this mechanical, utilitarian aspect, confounded with the death that it expressed so powerfully, made the guillotine vile and terrible.
>
> I passed alongside it, refusing to slow down or speed up, to contemplate it or to avoid it. (212)

You noticed the arms of the guillotine. You noticed what in these arms signified death ("But, as it was, with its two long, thin arms outstretched, it expressed death so well . . ."). I wonder, then, to what extent Badinter intentionally calculated this effect and thus the meaning he would have given it (but really it little matters) when, five pages later, describing in some sense   *102* the religious, Christian, or even Christlike apparatus of this film, this scene, and this theatrical act, he also names the arms of Christ or the crucifix. Listen. (Read *L'Exécution*, 217–18)

> In a sort of side aisle, the chaplain had put up an altar. Christ stretched his arms toward the bars. Two wardens were stationed, each to one side of the desk covered with the altar cloth, standing back a little, a strange presence in that moment. The chaplain was waiting for Bontems. He led him to the back, behind the altar. We stopped. Bontems was very close to the priest. No

---

19. During the session, Derrida refers to a web site (www.guillotine.net) maintained by the Swede Eija-Riitta Eklöf, better known on the Internet by the name "Madame Guillotine," "creator of a monumental site, very well documented, and lavishly illustrated, devoted to the history of the guillotine in every country where it was used" (Yves Eudes, "www.guillotine.net," *Le Monde*, December 14, 1999, 34). This site no longer exists today.

doubt he was confessing. Now the priest was speaking to him. Everything was silent. I turned around. There were prison guards, policemen, other officers of the law, and the executioner who had kept his hat on. So had the priest, whose lips were moving and who doubtless was saying the Prayer for the Dying. And there were others as well. I looked at them. All of them, and I too no doubt, displayed a kind of grimace. The electrical light hardened their features even more. They all had, in that moment, the mugs of murderers. Only the priest and Bontems, who was receiving absolution, still had human faces. Crime had, physically, changed sides. (217–18)

As concerns this great question of the judicial and penal theater, and not just of the Christian theater as question of sovereignty, and of a sovereignty that is sometimes the presumed sovereignty of the people, of the jury of the people, at other times of the sovereign as head of state who has at his disposal, as ultimate recourse, the right of pardon (and we have here the whole history of sovereignty that is as Christian as the history of the right of pardon, pardon, *merci*, mercy[20] being in a prevalent manner a Christian thing), as concerns this space of theater as space of sovereignty, I would be tempted to bring to the surface or to see at the surface one dimension of it in Badinter's book, and literally at least in *two places*—that I am going to privilege for reasons you will recognize right away as we go.

103   1. The first place because a same sequence, which goes from an allusion to Shakespeare to an allusion to the trial of Socrates, names the Dawn, with a capital *D*, which is consonant with what I was saying about the Dawn last week, without knowing that I was going to find this capitalized Dawn in *The Execution*. As for the allusion to Shakespeare, it interests me not only because of theater, but for a supplementary reason that I will specify in a moment after I read the passage. The words you are going to hear are not only or first of all those of Badinter himself, but those of his master and teacher, the great lawyer Henry Torrès to whom the book is dedicated and whose figure haunts it throughout, as that of the teacher who formed the young Robert Badinter and inspired in him an infinite admiration and gratitude, which are constantly reiterated in the book. Now, according to the remarks recounted or reconstituted by Badinter, the old master tells him one day that he loves the judicial democracy of the jury of the people as something out of Shakespeare. He has the impression of living something out of Shakespeare, he says. He then names *King Lear*, but for my part I think of another play, I will say a word about it in a moment. (Read *L'Exécution*, 107–9)

20. [Translator's note]: "Mercy" is in English in the original.

The French do not like civil servants, and they seldom like policemen. Nor do they like lawyers, it is true. They are Latins, not Anglo-Saxons. They do not worship the law and all that is connected to it. But the French do love eloquence. So a lawyer's chances were good in front of jurors. But woe to the lawyer who bores them.

"However, on the day that Vichy decided to be done with this ridiculous judicial democracy, with this all-powerfulness of the people represented by the jurors, when it decided that such a scandal had also to be straightened out, in the name of efficiency and authority, and that from then on magistrates would sit with the jurors, would deliberate with them and vote with them, everything changed. The great age of the lawyer came to an end along with the jurors' anxiety. Now the Grand Vizir is always present at their side to show them the way and to restore them to reason as well. But how beautiful it was, this justice agreeing sometimes to be unreasonable, because men always are. In the past, my boy, whenever I was about to argue in criminal court before the jurors, all alone in front of me, I had the impression of living something out of Shakespeare. Now, looking at them, seated obediently in a semi-circle around the magistrate in red and black robes, like good students around their teacher, I feel like I'm playing a part in a play by Dumas the younger, where everything is reasonable, even passions, even whores. Of course, sometimes I am completely mistaken. You don't play King Lear for years to turn into Duval's father overnight . . ." And then my teacher would sigh and feign melancholy, until his powerful character would cause him to call out loudly for champagne, like a thirsty Cossack, to raise a toast to the jury. "To those who throughout history have been worthy of both condemning Socrates to death and acquitting Mme Caillaux, thus proving over two thousand years that a philosopher on the loose is more dangerous for the city than a bitch in prison." I will never know why my teacher hated Mme Caillaux so much, but I knew about his passion for Socrates, whose *Apology* he readily recited, the most beautiful defense ever delivered.

At the moment, we were far from Socrates, from the *Apology* and the jurors of Athens. Except on one essential point. Those men and women, jurors of Dawn, also enjoyed that incredible power: they had to decide the fate of two men. (107–9)[21]

21. [Translator's note]: Ever since Napoleon, the French judicial system had restricted eligibility for jury service in criminal trials (civil cases are tried without juries) to certain professions. In 1941, however, under the Vichy regime, this limited popular participation on juries was further limited. Since then, French criminal court juries consist of a mixed panel of lay jury members chosen at random and professional magistrates. The reference to "Dumas the younger" is to Alexandre Dumas fils, author of

Those who have followed this seminar on forgiveness for the last three years may be reminded by this allusion to Shakespeare of the long analysis we devoted to *The Merchant of Venice*, and in particular to the concern there with pardon, "the quality of mercy," in the great speech by Portia who wants to convince the Jew Shylock to forgive the debt in exchange for which he will be pardoned by the very Christian Doge of Venice.[22] In Portia's extraordinary tirade, to which I cannot return but that ends with "Mercy seasons justice," there was also—and this will be the only point I'll recall—the rain, the rain was already falling, another rain, a good rain this time, a "gentle rain," not a cruel rain, that fell from the sky like divine grace and a double benediction, for the one who receives it and the one who gives it:

> The quality of mercy is not strain'd,
> It droppeth as the gentle rain from heaven
> Upon the place beneath: it is twice blessed:
> It blesseth him that gives and him that takes. (4, 1)

2. Second place. We have just reconnected with the question of grace or pardon and thus with exception, which I said would be my first guiding thread, joined to the motif of cruelty, for this first trajectory. Badinter (who has since often declared himself, as concerns another problem—that of parity[23]—to be in favor of a certain logic of sovereignty) here seems to be wary of the recourse to pardon in this machine of the death penalty. The passage I am going to read is situated in the narrative just before the lawyers for the accused, who have already been sentenced to death, are received by the president of the republic at the time, [Georges] Pompidou (whose strat-

---

the popular 1852 play *La dame aux camélias* in which Georges Duval is the disapproving father of the heroine's lover. Henriette Caillaux was the accused in a highly publicized trial in 1914 during which she was acquitted for the murder of a journalist who had written damning exposés of her husband's dealings as minister of finance.

22. Seminar "Perjury and Pardon," (first year, 1997–98), session of November 26, 1997; see also J. Derrida, "Qu'est-ce qu'une traduction 'relevante'?," in *Cahiers de L'Herne: Jacques Derrida*, ed. Marie-Louise Mallet and Ginette Michaud (Paris: L'Herne, 2004), pp. 561–76; "What Is a 'Relevant' Translation?," trans. Lawrence Venuti, *Critical Inquiry* 27 (Winter 2001): 174–200.

23. [Translator's note]: "Parity" here refers to the movement in France to ensure women equal representation in political offices. At the time of the seminar, *la parité* was being hotly debated and would bring about an amendment to the constitution a few months later, in June 1999. For an idea of Derrida's own position in the debate, see Derrida and Elisabeth Roudinesco, *For What Tomorrow . . . : A Dialogue*, trans. Jeff Fort (Stanford, CA: Stanford University Press, 2004), chapter 2.

egy is often analyzed in uncompromising terms by Badinter in this book), whose decision for or against a presidential pardon is not yet known. In fact, we now know that he refused to pardon Buffet and Bontems even though he did pardon Touvier in the name of what he himself called "national reconciliation."[24]

Here is the passage from Badinter, before the visit to the Elysée Palace where the two lawyers will try to convince the sovereign or cause him to relent. (Read *L'Exécution*, 181–84)

> I was asking myself about the right of pardon. It seemed to me to contain a   *106*
> tricky ambiguity, one of those historical mystifications riddled with received
> ideas, with archetypes that distort our sensibilities. Obviously, the right of
> pardon is an advantage for the condemned. It gives him another chance to
> counter the injustice or the harshness of the judges. But for the sovereign
> who exercises it, what does this right over the life or death of others imply?
>
> The president pardons the condemned; destined to the guillotine, the lat-
> ter gets away at the last moment. Suspense. Extreme anxiety. Relief. Bravo.
> The clemency of the prince has worked. He emerges magnified, without a
> doubt. For there is no example one can cite in which, time having passed,
> history has ever reproached the prince for being merciful.
>
> Or, say, the prince refuses the pardon. The sentence of death is carried
> out. Apparently the prince has merely let stand the people's justice. It is
> the criminal court that condemned to death, not the prince. By not forbid-
> ding the execution, he does not contradict the decision handed down. On
> the contrary, he satisfies popular sentiment as expressed by the jury. The
> prince can say: "I did not want this. It is they who so decided. If they did
> not want this man to die, it was up to them to say so. But they have chosen.
> Let them bear responsibility for their choice before their fellow men. I wash
> my hands of it." In this way the right of pardon magnifies the one who uses
> it in the eyes of history. It often makes the one who refuses it popular. Strict
> or merciful, the prince wins every time.
>
> But what does the right of pardon imply in reality? Judges and juries do
> not in fact condemn the accused to die by guillotine. They simply offer the
> prince the possibility of this execution. They set the alternative before the
> prince: let live or put to death. It is up to him to choose. Still more precisely,
> the court does not condemn to death. It proposes to the prince that he have
> the condemned put to death. The prince alone decides in the final analysis.

24. [Translator's note]: Paul Touvier was a head of militia intelligence under the no-
torious Gestapo officer Klaus Barbie during the Nazi occupation of France. Sentenced
to death in absentia after the war, he was pardoned by President Georges Pompidou in
1971, but in 1973 was indicted again, this time for crimes against humanity, and finally
tried in 1994, when he was sentenced to life imprisonment. He died in prison in 1996.

It is in this way that he is responsible and totally responsible since he can do anything, just as he pleases, whatever he wants without being accountable to anyone but himself. Since he has at his disposal *sovereignly*, absolutely, the life of that man. No doubt he would not have it at his disposal if it were not offered to him. But that man thrown at the prince, in chains, already rejected by the people and their judges, so that the prince might do with him whatever he wants: this reality, this responsibility, the prince cannot refuse.

We must not try to get out of this. There is no sentencing to death in justice. Only a death wish that moves from the criminal court up toward the prince. It is up to him to hear it or refuse to hear it. He is the almighty one. (181–84; Derrida's emphasis)

107

Next time, we will take up again these two interwoven motifs of the same theater of cruelty and of sovereignty, on the one hand, the cruelty of anesthetizing (the cruelty invoked in an equivocal fashion by all the international declarations that for several decades have seemed to oppose the death penalty without doing so) and, on the other hand, the logic of exception as logic of sovereignty (it is thus that Schmitt, whom we will talk about again, defines the sovereignty of the sovereign: as the decision in or of the situation of exception), but also of exception as the margin or exteriority that is equally allowed *both* by all the discourses favorable to *and* by all the discourses hostile to the death penalty. Both of them equally. The great Beccaria himself, the first great thinker of abolitionist law, was in favor of the abolition of this capital punishment *except in exceptional cases.*

Thus the great question of the state will be revived again. For if capital punishment is distinct from murder, from crime, from assassination, or from vengeance because universal reason, the third party, the anonymity or the neutrality of state law intervenes, the question remains as to where the state begins. Perhaps, like the claims of law and justice, the state is already present in the seemingly most savage and singular, or even the most secret crime, when such a murder claims — and perhaps always so claims — *to do its own justice* [se faire justice].[25] What is one saying when one claims *to do one's own or to do oneself justice?* And where does a murder begin?

These are questions that will still await us (until January 12 of the year 2000).

25. During the session, Derrida adds: "When a singular murder claims to do its own justice, already the third party, the witness, the state is summoned into the wings: the state is already there, perhaps."

Perhaps you still remember, it was last century, the *two guiding threads* that I had proposed to privilege and knot together, to interweave around the immense corpus and through the dense history of the death penalty as theater of cruelty. These two guiding threads, not the bandages we have also talked about, were, *on the one hand*, cruelty, precisely, and *on the other hand*, the paradoxical logic, the unthinkable logic of the *exception*.

Cruelty and exception. Our two questions then became: what is cruelty? And what is the exception? Does one have the right to ask the question, what is? with respect to them? With respect to them, which is to say, for us, with respect to that which links them here indissociably, irreversibly, namely, what we call the death penalty, the question, itself enigmatic, of the death penalty. To think the tie between cruelty and exception, one would have to set out from this *exceptionally cruel* thing that is the death penalty.

Before even letting ourselves be pursued by this question, by the machinic and armed apparatus of these questions that descend on us even before we have asked them (What is and what does cruelty mean? What is and what does exception mean?), allow me on this date to mark precisely, and without convention, in what way they are questions of the millennium and questions of the century, questions of the historic passage at which we have arrived. Not only because the history of the death penalty has been irreversibly linked, as we will repeatedly verify, with the contradictions of Christianity, of the Gospels, and of Christian political theology, thus with the contradictions inscribed in a sort of Christian calendar, if not a Christian datebook. We will verify this very precisely. But also because we are at a unique moment in this history, at a moment when, often while basing itself on an equivocal thinking of cruelty (the reference, *on the one hand*, to red blood and, *on the other hand*, to the radical malice of evil for evil's sake, of the "making suffer just to make suffer," which are two very distinct semantic features of what is called cruelty), we are, then, I was saying, 110 at a unique moment in this history, at a moment when, often while basing itself on this equivocal thinking of cruelty, as we will see, the pressure of an unprecedented international movement has, over the course of the last ten years, just won over a majority of nations in the world to the abolition of the death penalty, while a minority of powerful nations resist it (including one nation that is, let us say, predominantly Christian democratic, the United States, and the other, China, potentially one of the most powerful states and at present one of the most populous in the world, although non-Christian — but whose leader has just publicly celebrated the passage to the year 2000, just as his country takes large steps to enter a worldwide market dominated by laws and a philosophy of international law that are European and Romano-Christian), while a minority of very powerful states, then, still resist and will likely resist abolitionist pressure for a long time.

A unique moment, an unprecedented passage in the history of what is called humanity and of so-called human rights. Is the tendency of this movement irreversible and destined to win out, ineluctably, to pursue its course all the way to its end with the inevitability of a machine that nothing can stop? Even if one hopes so, not only is nothing less certain, but the question of what the universal abolition of the death penalty would mean, an abolition accepted by all states and all the laws in the world, will remain intact. What would then be abolished? Which death? Which putting to death? What is death, in this case (next time we will see the extent to which the question remains altogether new and in the process of deconstruction). And which machine will have then run its course?

For emblematic reasons, so as to signal both toward the unique moment we are living, if one may say that (unique even if it was preceded by more or less two centuries of rumbling on an ageless terrain), and toward the machine that I have just named, the machine without which a death penalty cannot be conceived, but also toward that machine called today the computer, e-mail, the Internet, and the threat of all those Y2K bugs that has just been averted as of this date, to begin I will refer to at least *three facts or three indications*.

These three *signals* tie the unicity of this worldwide moment in the history of the death penalty to the machine in general, to what is represented by microcomputing and the computer in general. I am not alluding directly to methods of execution (neither to lethal injection, for example, which is by far the dominant mode in the United States and must put into operation today means for acting at a distance and microcomputing, nor to e-mail, which can sometimes relay the telephone connecting the governor to the team of

executioners, doctors, and lawyers). No, after having recalled the website
on the guillotine that I mentioned last time, I wanted to tell you that there
exists (I thank Olivier Morel for giving me the address) a website, thus a
worldwide site, on the death penalty (www.smu.edu/-deathpen).[1] A worldwide site although visibly American in origin, and from a university, and
in the abolitionist spirit. As always, let us not forget, it is also in the United
States that one finds, at least in this domain, the most vigilant and the best
informed forces of protest, however much in the minority and powerless
they may be. You can access this site. I will leave several copies of a recent
page on the subject at your disposal. Opening with a sentence from a text by
Camus ("Reflections on the Guillotine"), to which I will return at length,[2] it
lists the following facts as of December 15, 1999, at 6:00 a.m.: ninety-seven
executions in the United States in 1999, which means an average of more
than eight executions per month or two per week, almost all by lethal injection, with the exception of one by gas chamber and two by electric chair
("Old Sparky").[3] You may have read in a recent article, which was very well
informed and very well written, in *Le Monde* (January 11, 2000), that the
two chambers of the Florida legislature have just voted to replace the electric
chair with lethal injection.[4] As the author of the article, Sylvie Kaufmann,
points out, Florida is a state where the proportion of blacks sentenced to
death is comparable to that throughout the country: blacks are 12.5 percent
of the population and 35 percent of the 368 currently sentenced to death.
Bush, governor of Florida, son of the former president and brother of the
present candidate for the White House who is governor of Texas, which is

112

1. This address ceased being valid in 2005, but the page in question, regularly up-
dated by Rick Halperin, still exists: http://people.smu.edu/rhalperi/. One can still consult the page that Derrida would have seen in September 1999: http://web.archive.org
/web/19991003124916/www.smu.edu/-deathpen/.

2. See below, "Tenth Session, March 15, 2000," pp. 247ff.

3. During the session, Derrida adds the following commentary: "You remember that
it was called 'Old Sparky' because it sent out sparks like fireworks; one can compare
this play, this ludic relation to the name 'Old Sparky' to the way in which in France the
guillotine was referred to as The Widow. There is a need to laugh, to deride the killing
machine."

4. During the session, Derrida reads the sidebar published in *Le Monde* on January 11, 2000: "George W. Bush, son of the former president, governor of Texas, fervent
proponent of the death penalty and candidate for the Republican nomination, vows to
raise 'an army of compassion across America.' Already, thanks to his brother, Jeb Bush,
governor of the state, those condemned to die in Florida will have the choice between
the electric chair, a 'cruel punishment,' and lethal injection."

the state holding the record for executions over the last twenty years, Bush of Florida, then, has promised to create a commission on the subject but, like Clinton, he has also proposed to accelerate appeal procedures, thereby shortening delays of executions, which has aroused enthusiasm on one side and indignation on the other. We learn in the same article that Benetton, in a gesture that I find basically sympathetic and respectable — as it did earlier for AIDS — and despite its promotional ambiguity, is launching a worldwide abolitionist advertising campaign that consists of a series of photos showing twenty-six prisoners sentenced to death (with the agreement of the lawyers, prisoners, and the penal authorities).

113

I underscore these statistics concerning the mode of execution of the punishment (injection rather than gas chamber, electric chair, hanging, etc.) because it is a matter precisely of one of the aspects of our question of cruelty. I remind you again that when, in 1972, the Supreme Court by a vote of five to four did not abolish — as one says too often — the principle of the death penalty, but ruled that its application violated the Eighth and Fourteenth amendments, that is, that it inflicted in a discriminatory fashion "unusual and cruel punishment,"⁵ it was, then, a certain argument about cruelty, about the excess of cruelty that had won out — once again not against the principle and the possibility of the death penalty but against the technical modalities of its implementation, of its physical execution — an argument about cruelty (I will say a word about discrimination in a moment) whose weakness, or even hypocrisy, which consists of avoiding the real "question of the death penalty," the question of principle raised by the death penalty, allowed a good number of states several years later to begin executions once again on the pretext that these methods were less cruel and barbaric in the way they were implemented. Lethal injection is seen as indeed less cruel than hanging, electrocution, or the gas chamber, in particular because it is, if not *euthanasic* — the source of a beautiful and good death — at least *anesthetizing*: before the injection that reaches the centers of the brain deemed vital (later we will come to the question of the criterion allowing one to declare death, that someone is dead, and it is not an easy question today,⁶ whether

5. [Translator's note]: In English in the original. Derrida on occasion, as here, inverts the order of the phrase as it occurs in the Eighth Amendment to the US Constitution.

6. See below, "Ninth Session, March 1/8, 2000, pp. 237ff. Derrida adds during the session: "You will see in reading certain texts from the past, the present, or the recent past that sometimes putting to death takes different forms and takes time [*inaudible*], a time and gives rise to blunders of such a kind that the question of knowing when death comes about is both a grave and a difficult one."

or not one is talking about "capital punishment"): [before the injection that   *114*
reaches the centers of the brain deemed vital], in the United States an anesthetizing pre-injection is administered, the condemned one is anesthetized
before being killed (which leaves a few more minutes for the telephone call
announcing the governor's possible pardon, as is shown in certain films that
make the most of this moment of anesthesia to heighten the suspense). And
it is thus, with this anesthetic consideration, that one gets around the constitutional objection of "cruel and unusual punishment."

This year, on the eve of the jubilee, of the second millennium of the
Christian era, will thus have been the year in which the number of executions reached its highest record in the United States since 1976, date of the
"reinstatement," if one may say that, of the death penalty, or at least the
resumption of executions. Since 1976, then, there have been 597 executions,
the majority by lethal injection (439), whereas 142 of those sentenced went
to the electric chair, 11 to the gas chamber, 3 were hung, and 2 were shot. If
we now colored the map of the United States so as to transpose the sinister
record of this last year and the sum of the last twenty-five years of the second
millennium of the Christian calendar and if we colored the states red or
rather black according to the density of executions, the result of this operation (which no one has done but that I imagined right away) would make
evident in a spectacular way the sociohistorical and political distribution of
this state, if I can say that, of the Union. Why States of the Union? Because
the map would divide the United States according to the border that is close
to resembling (I say prudently "is close to resembling," I do not say it strictly
reproduces), like a scar or a still open wound, is close to resembling, give or
take a few divergences, that of the Civil War — that is, the war over abolition, this time the abolition of slavery. The states that kill the most are *all*
southern states with large black populations. Far out ahead is Texas (198 out
of 597), then comes Virginia (73), then Florida (44), then Missouri (41), Louisiana (25). Louisiana in 1982 is the setting of the testimonial novel by Sister
Helen Prejean, *Dead Man Walking* (1993), which caused such a stir and from
which a film was made (I also advise reading this book to which I hope to   *115*
return). It ends with the execution of Patrick Sonnier, the accused (with an
accomplice — and once again, as in Badinter's *Execution*, one of the un-
knowns in the trial has to do with this crime committed by the two together,
with the terrifying difficulty of evaluating the singular responsibility or
guilt of each of the two accomplices) and with a scene during which the condemned man asks for forgiveness. I read and translate very quickly a few
lines that form the book's conclusion. (Read *Dead Man Walking*, 244–45)

We pray the sorrowful mysteries. Jesus agonizing before he is led to execution. Jesus afraid. Jesus sweating blood. . . .

Lloyd LeBlanc has told me that he would have been content with imprisonment for Patrick Sonnier. He went to the execution, he says, not for revenge, but hoping for an apology. Patrick Sonnier had not disappointed him. Before sitting in the electric chair he had said, "Mr. LeBlanc, I want to ask your forgiveness for what me and Eddie done," and Lloyd LeBlanc had nodded his head, signaling a forgiveness he had already given. He says that when he arrived with the sheriff's deputies there in the cane field to identify his son, he had knelt by his boy — "laying down there with his two little eyes sticking out like bullets" — and prayed the Our Father. And when he came to the words: "Forgive us our trespasses as we forgive those who trespass against us," he had not halted or equivocated, and he said, "Whoever did this, I forgive them." But he acknowledges that it's a struggle to overcome the feelings of bitterness and revenge that well up, especially as he remembers David's birthday year by year and loses him all over again: David at twenty, David at twenty-five, David getting married, David standing at the back door with his little ones clustered around his knees, grown-up David, a man like himself, whom he will never know. Forgiveness is never going to be easy. Each day must be prayed for and struggled for and won.[7]

I return to my map colored in black. After Louisiana comes South Carolina (23), Arkansas (of which Clinton was the merciless governor: 21), Arizona (19). To the majority of the states in the South, one must add, with around the relatively small number of twelve executions, a few northern states with a large black population such as Illinois, or eastern states such as Pennsylvania or Delaware. This index is enough to remind us that one can understand nothing about the situation of the United States faced with the death penalty without taking into account a great number of historical factors, the history of the federal state, the history of racism, the history of slavery, and the long, interminable struggle for civil rights and the equality of blacks, the Civil War, the still critical relation of the states to the central government and federal authority, the ethics of so-called self-defense that overarms the population to a degree unknown in any other country in the world, a feeling of explosive insecurity unknown in Europe, against the background of social and racial inequality, etc.; and I am deliberately leaving aside the enormous religious question, the enormous question of Christianity, that I will formalize later taking as a pretext reflections by Hugo and Camus on the death penalty, in order to enlarge and displace them some-

7. Helen Prejean, C.S.J., *Dead Man Walking* (New York: Vintage Books, 1993), pp. 244–45.

what.[8] To put succinctly what I will develop later, the question would be the following: is the growing and perhaps irreversible force of the abolitionist movement a Christian force (in which case the countries that maintain the death penalty would betray both the cause and the spirit of Christianity; they would represent a vestige of pagan or pre-Christian barbarity) or else, on the contrary, is the force of the abolitionist movement linked (this is Camus's thesis) to the progression of an atheist humanism or of a secularization that no longer wants to accept a death penalty that trusts in the justice of   *117* heaven after death and thus, within this logic, it would not be difficult to understand that the death penalty is maintained and resistance to abolitionism remains invincible in a country, the United States, so strongly marked at the heart of its culture and its political institutions by religion and especially by the Christian religion? As you can imagine, we will have to complicate this schema, since the conflict here does not oppose Christianity to its other, but rather two experiences, two interpretations, and two instances of the Christian Passion, the Gospels, and the church. But we must not avoid the question of the relations between religion and the death penalty, of course, or the question of the relations between Christianity, Christianities, and the other monotheisms in this regard.

One of my pretexts for citing all these data (which are, moreover, necessary and significant in themselves) was my desire to call your attention to the fact that the accelerating worldwide debate on the subject of the death penalty (the European Parliament is about to examine and no doubt approve a motion calling for the abolition of the death penalty on earth, a motion that will doubtless be brought soon before the UN — just as I believed I myself had a duty to demand this solemnly a little more than a month ago during a session at UNESCO [the text of which will be published in *Regards* at the end of the month][9] — and this would be the first time that the European Parliament and the UN do so, for until now a large number of international declarations and conventions, which I will discuss, skirted the question by taking aim above all at the cruelty of the death penalty as torture; they condemned torture rather than the death penalty, which is always respected as an exception, but we will come back to this), the worldwide debate and the accelerating worldwide actions against the death penalty pass indispens-

8. For Hugo, see below, the whole "Fourth Session, January 19, 2000," pp. 97ff., and for Camus, see below, "Tenth Session, March 15, 2000, pp. 243ff.

9. On December 6, 1999, at the headquarters of UNESCO in Paris, in the context of "Twenty-First Century Conversation," Derrida delivered a speech titled "Mondialisation, la paix et la cosmopolitique," published in *Regards*, February 1, 2000.

118 ably through the Web, which thus becomes the web of an international and transnational movement. This confirms that only and always by limiting the sovereignty of states will the death penalty be put in question (last time I recalled that even in France, and again in Greece later than in France, the abolition by the state of the death penalty was already obeying transnational pressure and a moral then juridical obligation of the Europe that was then being formed).

It is, then, on the stage of the Web, it is online[10] that things are said; it is there henceforth that things are known and it is there that they call out to one another across state-national borders. Not only as regards the general principle of the death penalty but in the struggle to save individuals condemned to death in another country. For example (and if I take examples, it is not so as to transform this seminar into a militant activist cell but to let you *know* — and knowledge is the thing and the mission and the ethic of a seminar — to inform you and let you know what is happening in the world today, in the world in the process of globalization [*mondialisation*], as they say — and I hold this debate on capital punishment to be one of the best entry points, along with the debate on capital, period, for whoever wonders what this confused concept of *mondialisation* means [and I say, as always, *mondialisation* and not *globalisation* so as to recall the Christian memory of the notion of world (*monde*)]),[11] so, for example, I was saying, this letter and this document that I recently received, like many I receive because I modestly but clearly and publicly came forward, with others, with all those who throughout the world call for at least a review of the scandalously irregular trial that condemned to death Mumia Abu-Jamal seventeen years ago now.[12] We could come back to this in the discussions we will have at the end of this month.[13]

10. [Translator's note]: "Online" is in English in the original.

11. In the typescript this parenthesis is closed at the end of the paragraph.

12. See J. Derrida, "Lettre ouverte à Bill Clinton," in *Les Temps Modernes*, p. 582, February–March 1997, reprinted in Derrida, *Papier Machine* (Paris: Galilée, 2001). See as well J. Derrida, "Préface" to Mumia Abu-Jamal, *En direct du couloir de la mort*, trans. Jim Cohen (Paris: La Découverte, 1999); "Open Letter to Bill Clinton" and "For Mumia Abu-Jamal," trans. Elizabeth Rottenberg, in Derrida, *Negotiations: Interventions and Interviews, 1971–2001*, ed. Elizabeth Rottenberg (Stanford, CA: Stanford University Press, 2002).

13. During the session, Derrida remarks that "obviously on the Web, as people say, there are not only abolitionist networks. There is also, in the case of Mumia Abu-Jamal, those who are fighting to obtain at least a new trial, but there is also a site maintained by the Fraternal Order of Police of Philadelphia, which organizes the fight to put

By way of information, I repeat, and to cast a little more light on what is   *119*
happening in the world today, while commenting on them a little, I am going to read and translate (almost in their entirety, which will take some time,
but it is necessary, for every detail matters) this letter and this document (I
will also leave a few copies at your disposal, but you can make more copies
yourselves if you wish). (Read and comment on the letter and document
"Thomas Miller-El")[14]

5 October 1999

Dear M. Derrida,

I am writing to you as a representative of the Campaign for Thomas J.
Miller-El on a very pressing matter, and am writing to you of all people
because I believe that you may be willing and able to assist us.

Thomas J. Miller-El has been on Texas Death Row for 13 years since an
unfair trial in Dallas in 1986. His wife, Dorothy J. Miller-El, a victim of injustice also, is co-ordinating the campaign for her husband, a campaign that
aims to raise enough funds to obtain a fair trial <for> Thomas J. Miller-El.

Maybe you are already aware that the American justice system is unfortunately not always fair, not even when it comes to using the death penalty.
It has long been argued by researchers, attorneys and others that poor and
minorities are discriminated against in the application of the death penalty,
and there is a substantial risk of sentencing to death and executing innocent
people. More than 75 people have been released from death rows all over   *120*
the United States since the death penalty was reintroduced in 1976. [The
letter is here making allusion to the number of irregularities that have come
to light and been recognized. For example—but this is only one example
among many others—we know that in Chicago, a law professor had his
students examine the file of a death row inmate and they discovered so
many irregularities that a retrial was ordered and the prisoner released.
And the fact that one can count seventy-five people whose death penalty
verdicts were overturned points to the lack of certainty in the system's
framework.]

The people released from US death rows were fortunate enough that
somebody looked into their cases and saw to it that their cases were re-

---

Mumia Abu-Jamal to death and which has publicly called for a boycott of all those who
throughout the world have mobilized for Mumia Abu-Jamal." And he adds: "There is
a war. I am not sanctifying the Web."

14. Derrida specifies during the session that it is a letter he has received from (this is
the name of the group) "The Freedom and Life Campaign for Thomas J. Miller-El" in
Denmark. This letter and other documents in English are preserved with the typescript
of the seminar.

versed. These cases are testimony of the corruption and discrimination that unfortunately take place far too often.

You may want to consult the sources yourself, and a main one is the report made by congress members in 1993–94, *Innocence and the Death Penalty*, documenting a too fallible justice system and recommending a moratorium on executions. In 1997, the ABA repeated this call, but of no avail as of yet.

Having realized that justice does not come by itself through the judicial system, the international Freedom and Life Campaign for Thomas J. Miller-El has been working hard for several years to raise enough money to pay for a good attorney, whose case work will cost at least 75,000 dollars.

We therefore appeal to you, etc., etc.

I am going to summarize quickly the other document that came with the letter. What is interesting is that this enterprise, this network, this group fighting for a new trial and the release of Thomas Miller-El is called "Elohim Enterprises." This takes us back to what we began with this year.

121   On the occasion of President Clinton's visit in Denmark on July 12, 1997, the Campaign for Thomas J. Miller-El made the following announcement, which is related to the USA's violations of basic human rights, etc., etc.

[This is the case of Thomas J. Miller-El, but there are many others.] Thomas J. Miller-El is incarcerated on Texas Death Row, sentenced for robbery murder, which took place in Dallas in 1985. He is black, poor, and his trial was full of violations of his rights to a fair trial: he had been shot and seriously wounded during his arrest in Houston (where he had been during the robbery in Dallas [and Dallas is very far from Houston] according to his own and other people's testimony). [In other words, he was arrested hundreds of miles or kilometers from the scene of the crime] and was dragged into court more dead than alive. He was unable to attend fully to what was going on in court, couldn't communicate with his court appointed attorneys, and was all in all incompetent to participate in his own defense.

Thomas J. Miller-El's jury consisted of 11 white people and 1 black person, who in all likeliness was only accepted because he had previously stated that the death penalty was too easy as a punishment—Thomas J. Miller-El should instead be eaten alive by ants. One of Thomas J. Miller-El's appointed attorneys was running for Dallas County District Attorney, and a great part of the trial consisted of a political showdown between him and his rival candidate, the sitting District Attorney. Consequently, Thomas J. Miller-El's attorney was not interested in postponing the trial until Thomas was fully conscious for fear of giving the impression that he would not be tough on crime if Thomas J. Miller-El was acquitted. [I will not read the whole letter, but what follows are remarks about President Clinton's visit.]

[President Clinton] in 1995 agrees to cutting all federal funding to the national Resource Centers. The purpose of these legal aid agencies were [sic] to make certain that all death row inmates were properly represented in their appeals. . . . In May 1996, President Clinton signs into law another proposal, severely limiting the appeal process in death penalty cases, thereby accepting an even greater risk for executing innocent people. . . .

Before taking up again the question of cruelty from a different angle and with renewed effort, let us make clear the risks involved, up until now, in the equivocation, the always virtually equivocal use of this notion of cruelty — I deliberately say "notion" to avoid saying "concept" but also so as not to limit things to the word, the European word, the Latin-Roman word of cruelty. We have already seen, then, how the decision of the US Supreme Court, by referring only to "unusual and cruel punishments,"[15] allowed, after a first moment of surprise had passed, certain states to regroup and reinstate a death penalty that basically had never been abolished in its principle, only criticized for the so-called cruel modalities of its application, cruel, that is to say, painful for the sensibility and the imagination, in the sense of *aisthesis* or of *phantasia* or even of *phantasma*. These states had merely to practice or to allege the practice of a manner of putting to death that seemed to them to be anesthetized, anesthetizing, or even euthanasic (which lethal injection claims to be, hence its development over the last twenty-five years) in order to get around the Supreme Court ruling and reverse the tendency. But what happens thus in the United States[16] stands out against an international background to which we should pay the closest attention. For the past and for the future, because one has every reason to think that tomorrow the United States, China, and all the states that maintain and apply the death penalty are going to find themselves accused more and more by international law and, in their very sovereignty, put under increasing pressure. An external and internal pressure, symbolic first of all and then, perhaps one day, juridically mandated.

Now, if we look at what has happened in this regard, from the viewpoint of law, international conventions, and declarations over the last few decades, what does one observe? I draw my information here from various sources, but in particular from a monumental book, the definitive work, as one says, which I don't believe has been translated into French but rec-

15. [Translator's note]: In English and as such in the original.
16. During the session, Derrida adds: "My intent is not to hound the United States; rather I am interested in what is both exemplary and exceptional about this country."

ommend you read: William Schabas, *The Abolition of the Death Penalty in International Law*.[17]

What one sees at first glance is a constant strategy, *on the one hand*, to affirm the absolute right to life and to condemn torture and cruelty without, *on the other hand*, violating the sovereignty of states and without condemning the death penalty explicitly, absolutely, unconditionally, without exception — that is, without denying, without disputing in the least the right of sovereign states to maintain, in certain conditions, the principle of the death penalty. For example, from this viewpoint we should pay the most vigilant attention to the Universal Declaration of Human Rights, adopted, as you know, by the UN on December 10, 1948, and celebrated two years ago on its fiftieth anniversary. I insist on this: with such declarations, we are and we are not in the realm of Law. This declaration, to be sure, says what is right, it says what are rights, it is jurisdictional, but it is not a text of law; it does not have the force of law to the extent that no coercive force is placed at its service, even with regard to the states that officially subscribe to it. As Kant rightly says, there is no justice in the strict sense, in the legal sense, in the judicial sense, as long as there is no binding force, as long as commitments are not duties to which the subjects of the law are held on pain of punishment [*sous peine de peine*], precisely, on pain of being punished by the law if they should infringe it. One must be able to apply the law by force, one must be able to "enforce" it as one says so well in English, in order for it to be a law, in the full sense. From this point of view, even if a Universal Declaration of Human Rights were to condemn the death penalty (which it has not yet done, far from it, we are coming to that), it would have no ju-

124 ridical value. It would be simply a declaration of principle without juridical effect. The day when states consent to abandon sovereignty and to appear before an international criminal court that refers to a legal text condemning a state for putting to death a subject, only then will one be able to speak of a universal abolition of the death penalty. That is a long way off even if the apparent teleology of the movement under way seems *to tend* toward that end. In any case, it is necessary and interesting to see where the diverse international declarations or conventions are in this regard, even if they do not have the force of law. And I begin therefore, as I believe one must, with the Universal Declaration of Human Rights renewed in 1948 and with certain declarations that followed it and drew out its consequences. I select here

---

17. William Schabas, *The Abolition of the Death Penalty in International Law* (Cambridge: Grotius, 1993; revised 1997). [Translator's note]: Subsequently revised again in 2002; page references are to this latest edition.

what concerns the death penalty and this equivocal motif of cruelty. The Universal Declaration of Human Rights itself poses in article 3 that "Everyone has the right to life, liberty, and security of the person." No allusion at all to the death penalty. As Schabas remarks, all reference to a limitation on this right to life (thus, for example and par excellence, the death penalty) remains implicit. The same was true in the American declaration that had been adopted a few months earlier, in May 1948, titled American Declaration on the Rights and Duties of Man. But in the declarations that followed these two and that spelled out their premises and their consequences, namely the following three declarations: International Covenant on Civil and Political Rights (1976), the European Convention on Human Rights (1955), and the American Convention on Human Rights (1978), in all these declarations, then, it is a question of the death penalty, but it is never condemned in its principle; it is merely defined as an "exception" to the right to life. As Schabas says on a page in which the word "exception" is repeated regularly: "The death penalty is mentioned as a carefully worded exception to the right of life. In other words, from a normative standpoint, the right to life protects the individual against the death penalty unless otherwise provided as an implicit or express exception." Or again: "The European Convention on Human Rights is the only instrument to attempt an exhaustive list of exceptions to the right of life. Careful analysis shows that it is not in fact a thorough one. The self-defense exception is mentioned but not that of wartime" (7).[18] This is not only a key point but the focus of all the difficulties, of all the hypocrisies, and to which we will constantly return: What is a state of war? What is a civil war? And if the death penalty is abolished within a country in peacetime, what is going to define the enemy, the public enemy, as Rousseau says, and wartime? External war and civil war? I leave in reserve here what stands at the heart of the problem: not only the definition of the *exception*, of the state of exception, but of war and the state of war.

On this very difficult point, I often think of the example of what is called *la guerre d'Algérie* [the Algerian war], in the recent history of this country. It took place, as you know (some of you, perhaps still), between 1954 and 1962, during a period when the death penalty was not yet abolished in France. And besides all the terrible violence of which you are aware (war crimes and no doubt crimes against humanity, and so forth, whose archives are still waiting to be opened, studied, and their memory judged), there were death sentences according to the so-called legal procedures. Now imagine (and

125

126

18. [Translator's note]: The last two sentences are no longer included in the 2002 edition of Schabas's work.

this is not an unthinkable fiction) that during this period the death penalty had already been abolished in France, as it would be fewer than twenty years later. Well, since the official doctrine in France was that what was happening there was not a war but an operation of the police and of civil, internal, domestic security, there would have been no right to condemn anyone to death. The concept and the name of war, which alone allows one to kill legally the foreign enemy where, the death penalty having been abolished, one does not have the right to kill the citizen-enemy, this concept and this name of war, like the at times so unstable difference between civil war and national war, this is what makes the abolitionist discourse so fragile[19] when it banishes the death penalty at home and maintains the right to kill in war.[20] Between civil war and national or international war, there is the *war of partisans* whose concept Schmitt elaborated and which introduces, as he showed, great disorganization into the order of this polemological conceptuality. And history sometimes, not always, takes it upon itself to change fragile and precarious names, that is, of unmasking hypocrisies, removing the masks in this theater of nomination. You know that it was only less than a year ago, on June 10, 1999, that the French National Assembly decided to enter the term "war" into the official lexicon concerning Algeria. And if now one can officially speak of the "Algerian war," as was always done unofficially, this is not only out of a belated concern for "truth"; it is to satisfy a demand coming from the FNACA, the National Federation of Veterans of Algeria, <who> wanted to be granted the same status as veterans of 1914–18 and of 1940–45, a status that brings with it, along with some military honors, a certain number of benefits. I mention this by way of identifying clearly, along with the question of sovereignty, another great question which is indissociable from that of the death penalty: the question of war. What does "war" mean? What is a war? A civil war and a national war? What is a public enemy? As these questions are more open than ever, as the definition of the state of war is one of the definitions made more precarious than ever by what is happening today, from Iraq to Kosovo, from East Timor to Chechnya, all of this is part of the same upheaval [*séisme*].[21]

19. Derrida clarifies during the session that "despite all the sympathy I have for it, the abolitionist discourse is deconstructible in its current state."

20. During the session Derrida specifies: "presuming that one knows clearly where an enemy of the nation begins and can be found."

21. During the session, Derrida adds: "In *Politics of Friendship* I tried to repose this question of the enemy and partisan war by following Schmitt's text in a more critical and deconstructive fashion." See Derrida, *Politics of Friendship*, pp. 138–70. It is in chapter 6,

After having noted that the European Convention on Human Rights is the only one that attempts to list exceptions to the right to life, Schabas points out that the United Nations and the Inter-American systems[22] chose to avoid this approach and declared simply that life could not be taken away "arbitrarily," leaving the extent and the evaluation of such exceptions up to the freedom of the interpreter. But the three declarations set the death penalty apart on their list of exceptions as "the most striking exception to the right to life," thus, I would say, the absolute exception, the exception par excellence, the exception among exceptions. The European Convention even sets it visibly apart because it devotes a separate paragraph to it. As Schabas once again correctly notes, while "the other exceptions are logical and self-evident, there is something contradictory and incompatible about recognizing a right to life and at the same time permitting capital punishment. The drafters of the various instruments, intuitively, knew this" (7–8). Let us not hide from the fact that what they know and recognize in this way, whether intuitively or not, is that it was impossible to disallow exceptions, and this exception among exceptions, without putting in question the sovereignty of the state, which none of the declarations could or wanted to do.

For the sovereignty of the state is marked precisely by this power to decide, to judge, to rule, to interpret freely and sovereignly what is exceptional, what is the exception. Sovereignty is the right, the power authorized to decide what is exceptional, what is the the exception. Sovereignty is the absolute exception, the right to give oneself the right to the exception and to judge, to decide arbitrarily, sovereignly, on exceptionality. This is how, moreover — in a text I hope to return to — Carl Schmitt defines the sovereign, the sovereignty of the sovereign. At the beginning of his *Political Theology: Four Chapters on the Concept of Sovereignty* (1922–34), Schmitt writes (it is a famous sentence): "Sovereign is he who decides on the exception," a translation of "Souverän ist, wer über den Ausnahmezustand entscheidet."[23] Some have seen an ambiguity in the *über* (does it mean: the one who decides *on* the exceptional situation, *on what is* an exceptional situation and must be considered such, or else the one who decides, who makes decisions *in* an ex-

128

129

---

titled "Oath, Conjuration, Fraternization or the 'Armed' Question," that Derrida proposes the most explicit commentary of Carl Schmitt's *Theory of the Partisan*.

22. [Translator's note]: This is how Schabas refers to "the human rights system of the Organization of American States, encompassing the Western hemisphere" (311).

23. Carl Schmitt, *Politische Theologie: Vier Kapitel zur Lehre von der Souveränität* (Munich and Leipzig: Duncker & Humblot, 1922), p. 9; *Political Theology: Four Chapters on the Concept of Sovereignty*, trans. George Schwab (Chicago: University of Chicago Press, 1985), p. 5.

ceptional situation?).[24] One of Schmitt's French translators, Julien Freund, got around the difficulty by translating "décide *lors de* la situation exceptionnelle," that is, "decides *at the time of* the exceptional situation." But like J.-L. Schlegel, the current translator of these texts for Gallimard, I think the whole context clearly shows that it is a matter of the one who decides on *what is* an exceptional situation and who affirms or proves thereby that he is the sovereign. We will come back to this, but I invite you to read this whole chapter and everything that Schmitt says about this limit concept, the concept of exception, which is not a confused notion but what permits one to think decision in its purity. Schmitt notes, pointing to the obvious, that exception is, of course, what cannot be subsumed, what escapes by definition from all definition, from all general formulation, but in this way it reveals in its pure form, in its pure juridical formality, what the pure decision is, a decision that, in essence, can only be absolutely singular. This is why Schmitt claims that far from giving in to a romantic taste for irony and paradox, one must assert seriously that only the exception is interesting, more interesting than the so-called normal case in its generality. "The rule proves nothing," he says, "the exception proves everything" (15). The exception not only confirms the rule; the rule lives only by virtue of the exception. Schmitt quotes a Protestant theologian[25] (and from here on we are going to pick up again our Christian question of the death penalty and our political theology of sovereignty) who says:

> The exception explains the general and itself. And if one wants to study the general correctly, one only needs to look around for a true exception. It reveals everything more clearly than does the general. Endless talk about the general becomes boring; there are exceptions. If they cannot be explained, then the general also cannot be explained. The difficulty is usually not noticed because the general is not thought about with passion but with a comfortable superficiality. The exception, on the other hand, thinks the general with intense passion. (15)

130

In the debate that opposes him to other jurists, like Kelsen, for example, who wants to set aside radically the problem of sovereignty and has no use for the exceptional situation (18), Schmitt observes this, which is important for us here, namely, that in any case, whether or not one admits the abstract definition of sovereignty (a definition that is fundamentally, structurally theological, I will return to this in a moment; that is, sovereignty is

24. The closing parenthesis has been added.
25. The English translation of Schmitt's book specifies that the "Protestant theologian" whom Schmitt does not identify is Søren Kierkegaard (15).

the supreme power, the originary and not derived power of governing), whether or not one admits this definition, the controversy is not in general about the history of sovereignty, but about the concrete use, the concrete determination of the sovereign. (Which is why, moreover, Schmitt defines not sovereignty but the sovereign, and says "sovereign is he who decides on the exception," and not sovereignty consists in, etc.; he defines an individual and a singularity that is itself exceptional: there is no sovereignty, there is the sovereign; the sovereign, the sovereignty of the sovereign exists, but the sovereignty of the sovereign exists only insofar as the sovereign exists: the generality does not exist; this is the profound and, up to a certain point, consistent nominalism of this political theory, of this theory of the political that is also, indissociably, a political theory.) The controversy, then, is not about the general and abstract history of sovereignty but about the concrete determination of the sovereign, namely, the one who, in a conflict, decides on what constitutes the public interest, the interest of the state, security and public order — thus, public safety (the French expression *salut public* is in the text: it refers to a revolutionary situation;[26] it is always in the name of the *salut public* that one sentences to death someone who, basically, even if   *131* he has killed only one person, in a singular crime, is determined as a public enemy, a threat to society, order, and public security, public safety, *salut public*). In these pages, which I recommend you read, Schmitt analyzes all those states of exception in which the state has the right, the right to give itself the right to suspend right and law. Schmitt speaks of an "unlimited authority" that consists in the power to "suspend the entire existing order" (12). In this situation of exception, or of exceptional urgency, when the state deems that it is threatened in its existence, it has the right to subsist even if it does so by rolling back the law. Not that the exceptional situation signifies chaos or anarchy; on the contrary, according to Schmitt, an order subsists, a juridical order even if this new juridical order is in contradiction with the law:

> The existence of the state is undoubted proof of its superiority over the va-
> lidity of the legal norm. The decision frees itself from all normative ties and
> becomes in the true sense absolute [liberated, detached, without tie, untied,
> *absoluta*].[27] The state suspends the law in the exception on the basis of its
> right of self-preservation, as one would say. (12)

26. [Translator's note]: During the French Revolution, the Comité de salut public became the de facto seat of government especially during the Terror under the leadership of Robespierre.

27. During the session, Derrida adds the following commentary: "He means absoluta, that is, untied, detached, without tie. That's what sovereignty is. The decision

You can clearly sense how this logic, which is that of absolute sovereignty and the self-preservation of the political body, is going to authorize the absolute maintenance, *even though or because it is exceptional*, of the death penalty, in the name of the self-preservation of the sociopolitical body. This logic is very solid, and very logical. Schmitt uses several times a very strong expression that defines both the exception and sovereignty: law *suspends itself*, law has the right or grants the right to *suspend itself* (this is the structure of the right of pardon: law above the laws, right above rights). One has to start from the possibility of this self-suspension, of this interruption of itself by the law, in order to understand both the law and its foundation in the principle of sovereignty. And the indisputable force of this logic is that the source of the law, of *dictating the law* or of *making law* [*du* dire le droit *ou du* faire le droit], this performative source, this performative power before the performative that presupposes some convention, this power before convention cannot be juridical; it is the power of a decision that, in itself, does not come under the law and must remain, if not illegal, at least a-legal. In this sense every decision is revolutionary because it is an exception [*elle fait exception*] (hence the power of seduction that this great conservative Catholic theologian-jurist has over all extreme left-wing and extreme right-wing revolutionaries of the period).

Schmitt also translates this logic of the suspension of law in the production of law by a formula that is a play on words: "Die Autorität beweist, dass sie, um Recht zu schaffen, nicht Recht zu haben braucht," which, without following the published translation, I would translate as: "Authority demonstrates that in order to create the law [or right], it does not need to have the right" (comment).[28] It is the definition of sovereign authority as excep-

frees itself from any normative obligation. Therefore, there is no norm. And in fact, this logic is unimpeachable, hence Schmitt's force, even if one does not agree: because a decision, in order to be a decision, cannot conform to a norm. If, in deciding, I decide in conformity with a law or a norm, that is, a program, well, I apply a program, but I do not decide. Decision has no norm, in other words. And that is why a decision is always exceptional. It is always a transgression of norms. This logic is very strong."

28. Schmitt, *Politische Theologie*, p. 14. The French translation by Jean-Louis Schlegel reads: "L'autorité démontre que pour créer le droit il n'est nul besoin d'être dans son bon droit" (Schmitt, *Théologie politique* [Paris: Gallimard, 1988], p. 24.) Derrida revises this translation to read: "L'autorité démontre que pour créer le droit, elle n'a pas besoin d'en avoir le droit," and then he comments during the session: "This is authority. To create right, one does not need to have the right. What may appear shocking is that instituting law must be done from situations in which there is no law; therefore, it is from non-law that one creates law; therefore, one need not wait to have the right to create a right; therefore, one does not have to wait for a prior constitution to set down a new constitution."

tion and as decision: to create right and law, it does not have to be within its rights; it does not have to be fully within its rights. Schmitt often recalls, in order to praise and reaffirm it, moreover, the Christian genealogy of this definition of sovereign authority. See, for example, what he says about this again in 1969, in the second text titled *Political Theology II: The Myth of the Closure of Any Political Theology* (particularly on p. 73 of the translation), where he shows how the ancient Roman idea of *auctoritas* was renewed and transformed by the sovereignty of Christ and received a new meaning from it, the Roman pair of *auctoritas* and *potestas* yielding in the Christian realm the pair *ecclesia* and *imperium*; I don't have the time here to delve into these very valuable texts, but I refer you to them. Never forget, however, that despite his insistence on the state, on sovereignty as sovereignty of the state, Schmitt also says, more discreetly but in what I think is a very significant manner, that his theory is not so much a theory of the state as a theory of the political. The theory of the state presupposes the theory of the political, that is, the distinction between the friend and the enemy (thus, the public enemy; see *Politics of Friendship* where I attempted to, let us say, "deconstruct" this discourse). [The theory of the state presupposes the theory of the political, that is, the distinction between the friend and the enemy] even if the state is an eminent form of the political. As he recalls,[29] the systematic work connected to *Der Begriff des Politischen*[30] is a theory of the constitution (*Verfassungslehre*) and not a theory of the state. The discourse on sovereignty and on the exception is a discourse on this a-legal *position*, as I will call it, of the law that is the inaugural and founding act of a constitution. A constitution, the performative act that poses and imposes a constitution, is a pre-legal or a-legal creation of the law: law is suspended, de-posed by the act that poses it; it is de-posed in all senses of the term, deposited or laid down by being posed, and de-posed, that is, suspended; it is suspended, I will say, for this is not literally Schmitt's language, *from* and *at the* constitution [à la *constitution*]. It depends on the constitution even as it is suspended and therefore did <not> exist at the moment, on the date on which the constitution was constituted by a constituting act.

133

134

29. Carl Schmitt, *Political Theology II: The Myth of the Closure of Any Political Theology*, trans. Michael Hoelzl and Graham Ward (Cambridge: Polity Press, 2008), p. 45; Schmitt refers there to his text *Constitutional Theory*, trans. and ed. Jeffrey Seitzer (Durham, NC: Duke University Press, 2008).

30. During the session, Derrida translates this title as "Le concept du politique," which corresponds to the English title of this work by Schmitt: *The Concept of the Political*. The French translation is titled *La notion du politique*, trans. M.-L. Steinhauser (Paris: Calmann-Lévy, 1972).

Since we will soon have to come back to this great question of Christianity in the history of the death penalty and its abolition, since we will do this soon, at our next session, by rereading and problematizing, for example, texts by Hugo and Camus, I would like to remark the following, by way of anticipation and so as to try to tidy things up a bit in this historical space, but also so as to continue to tie, to weave together, these two motifs of cruelty and exception: Schmitt refers above all and solely to Christianity, to Christian theology when he says, as he so often does, that the concept of sovereignty refers first of all to the absolute power of God (for example, "Whether God alone is sovereign, that is, the one who acts as his acknowledged representative on earth, or the emperor, or prince, or the people, meaning those who identify themselves directly with the people, the question is always aimed at the question of sovereignty, at the application of the concept to a concrete situation" [10]), when he says again (at the beginning of chapter 3 titled "Political Theology"):

All significant concepts of the modern theory of the state are secularized theological concepts not only because of their historical development — in which they were transferred from theology to the theory of the state, whereby, for example, the omnipotent God became the omnipotent lawgiver — but also because of their systematic structure, the recognition of which is necessary for a sociological consideration of these concepts. The exception in jurisprudence is analogous to the miracle in theology. (36) (comment?)[31]

31. During the session, Derrida adds: "What does this mean? When he says that all concepts of the modern theory of the state are secularized theological concepts and that one must know this not only historically in a genesis or genealogy, but also systematically, that is, in the logical articulation of these concepts, in order to understand, it is not a matter of merely returning to the sources. To understand how this functions, the concepts of the political; to understand how together they form a system, one has to think them as theological concepts. Only the theological can account for them. And this means, as he himself says, that a sociological or historical or empirical analysis has no chance of understanding what is going on there. Only a theologian, only someone who understands the theological necessity of these concepts, can understand the law. One must be a theologian in order to be a thinker of the law, and this is indeed the case of Schmitt. One must be a thinking or informed theologian to understand modern politics, and therefore what sovereignty is, what the law is, what the state is, what jurisprudence is. And when he compares the exception to the miracle, what difference is there between this absolute exception when it is a matter in the law of the death penalty, of the exception to the right to life, and the miracle? None. The definition of the miracle is the exception. And the definition of the exception is the miracle, that is, the fact of transgressing or disobeying normality, the ordinary. A decision is always miraculous, a

I note in passing, until we can return to this later: when, as he does con-   135
stantly, Schmitt opposes thinkers of the Enlightenment or the Aufklärung
(those of the eighteenth century and those of today) whom he reproaches
for neglecting or for not needing a theory of the exception, or even of sovereignty, he is wrong, I believe, in at least one case, exceptionally, and from
the point of view that interests us; there is at least one notable exception to
this law and it is very significant for us. It is the case of Beccaria, man and
jurist of the Enlightenment, of the Illuminismo, admirer of Rousseau and
of Montesquieu, first great jurist-theoretician of the abolition of the death
penalty. Well, Beccaria himself, in his famous *On Crimes and Punishments*,
a work that concludes with praise of the Enlightenment and of education
and that urges the abolition of the death penalty in conditions we will study
later, Beccaria foresees a highly significant exception, the trace of which we
will discover in all the modern texts, the declarations and conventions that
I began by evoking. Beccaria declares at the beginning of chapter 28, "The   136
Death Penalty," that the death penalty cannot be a right, that it is an act of
war against a citizen whom one deems it necessary or useful to kill, and that,
therefore, if as a right and a punishment, as a judicial sanction, it is neither
just, nor useful, nor necessary (which he is going to endeavor to show), in
fact, as an exceptional act of war, it can be considered useful when the citizen, even though deprived of his freedom (imprisoned and imprisoned for
life, then) still had "such connections and such power that he endangers the
security of the nation even when deprived of his liberty, that is, when his
very existence can provoke a dangerous revolution in the established form
of government."[32]

Beccaria spells out his thinking, showing that in an exceptional situation,
one that threatens with disorder and chaos the very principle of the law, the
sovereignty of the state or of the nation, in that case, the death of a citizen
becomes necessary. But he is very careful at this point to say "the death of
a citizen" and not the principle of the death penalty. "The death of such a
citizen becomes necessary, then, when a nation is recovering or losing its liberty, or in time of anarchy, when disorder itself takes the place of laws" (52).
(This is the moment of the French Revolution: when Badinter comments on

---

decision, if there is any, a decision outside norms that invents its own law, that is absolutely singular, if there is any, is a miracle. There are no other concepts except that of
miracle with which to think what is extraordinary about a decision or an exception, and
consequently a revolution. This is what Schmitt reminds us of. One must be a theologian
in order to understand the modern theory of the state and, for example, the globalization
[*mondialisation*] under way."

32. Beccaria, *On Crimes and Punishments and Other Writings*, p. 52.

this passage, he notes that "already sketched in these lines is the procedure of the members of the Committee on Criminal Legislation of the Constituent Assembly, who will urge the abolition of the death penalty for common law crimes, but which will prefer to preserve it for political matters";[33] Badinter has devoted an article to this moment and gives the reference to it here.[34] We will return later to this difference between political crime and common law crime,[35] as regards the death penalty, notably in the USSR, where political crimes were also held to be more serious than crimes of so-called common law, presuming this distinction is ever possible and rigorous.)

137

On this point, Beccaria seems to agree with Schmitt because he takes into account those situations of exception where the state and the nation have to protect and preserve themselves against the absolute threat that weighs on their very existence. But whereas Schmitt sees in this exception an essential moment of law and an order, Beccaria, for his part, wants to maintain, precisely, this character of exception in an exceptional moment of anarchy, disorder, and chaos. But beneath this apparent disagreement, and even though Schmitt makes of exception the truth, the condition of possibility, if not the norm of sovereignty and of law, whereas Beccaria insists on the rule, the norm, the general normality that the exception cannot contradict except in a manner that is, precisely, exceptional and abnormal, [beneath this apparent disagreement] the two agree in wanting to guarantee sovereignty. Indeed, after having evoked the exception, the logic of war, of disorder, or of chaos, or even of the birth of freedom when the nation can put a citizen to death, Beccaria continues:

> But when the calm rule of law prevails, under a form of government that has the support of the nation, which is well-fortified both externally and internally by both force and opinion (which is perhaps more efficacious than force itself), and in which the power to rule is vested only in the true sovereign and wealth can buy only pleasures not authority, I do not see any

33. Robert Badinter, "Présence de Beccaria," preface to Beccaria, *Des délits et des peines*, trans. Maurice Chevallier (Paris: Flammarion, 1991), p. 24.

34. See Robert Badinter, "Beccaria, l'abolition de la peine de mort et la révolution française," *Revue de science criminelle* (1989): 245–46.

35. During the session, Derrida adds the following commentary: "This distinction is very fragile. Moreover, the case of Mumia Abu-Jamal demonstrates this. It is obvious that Mumia Abu-Jamal was sentenced apparently for a common law crime (he is alleged to have killed a policeman), but in fact, if he is being hounded, one knows quite well it is because he was a former militant in the Black Panthers and has a political past that makes him intolerable for a certain segment of American society; and this is why one may say he is a political prisoner. And he is often defended as a political prisoner."

need to destroy a citizen, unless his death were the only real way to deter others from committing crimes. And this is the second reason for believing the death penalty could be just and necessary. [In what follows he is going to endeavor to show that this is not at all the case.]

If centuries of experience, during which the ultimate punishment has never deterred men determined to harm society; if the example of the citizens of Rome or the twenty-year reign of the Empress Elizabeth of Moscovy . . . (52)

138

[I interrupt my quotation briefly for a detour and a few details: Elizabeth of Moscovy reigned after a coup d'état in 1741; she promised to undertake no capital execution and abolished the death penalty with two decrees, in 1753–54; later on we will approach the singular case of Russia and the USSR. I also recall briefly that, in 1996, three years ago therefore, the Russian Federation declared a moratorium on executions and announced that it would abolish the death penalty the following year — I am not sure if this was done — even as the preceding year, in 1995 then, former Communist countries such as Ukraine, Albania, Moldavia, and Bosnia and Herzegovina had abolished the death penalty, the same year as South Africa and Mauritius. Since I am listing statistics of this sort, I recall that since World War II, the acceleration of the abolitionist movement has not abated, notably between 1988 and 1996: in eight years, thirty-seven states abolished the death penalty, and in 1997, the majority of states, 108, as I think I have already mentioned, had abolished the death penalty, as against eighty-three that had not yet done so, including the Arab states of North Africa (whereas the rest of Africa, with the notable and glaring exception of Nigeria, has abolished the death penalty), the United States, of course, Cuba and the West Indies, China, Iraq, and Iran. Schabas asserts that Islamic law is "an insurmountable obstacle" to the abolition of the death penalty, even though, he wisely adds, it would not be fair to generalize from this and say that there is a link of cause and effect here (365); on the subject of Iran, you saw what happened at the end of the first week of January 2000, when between five and six thousand people gathered starting at two o'clock in the morning in Tehran to witness the hanging of a young seventeen- or eighteen-year-old man on the same site where he had killed one of the *bassidj* (militiamen mobilized to enforce compliance with the Islamic morals policy). The crowd shouted "Aafve, aafve," God's forgiveness, against a minority that shouted "vengeance." The Koranic law that has prevailed in Iran since the return of Khomeini in 1979 allows the victim's family to ask for capital punishment or to grant a pardon (problem "civil society and state," etc.; comment). In this case, for personal reasons or after having undergone more obscurely

139

political pressures, the father finally forgave him at the last moment while the young man had been waiting with the noose around his neck for a half hour. Without anesthesia, needless to say, that is a difference, the difference of anesthesia, in what Hugo calls, speaking thus of the death penalty, "the special and eternal sign of barbarity" (that is a difference, I was saying, the difference of anesthesia between these two enemies that are Iran and the United States). This episode might have featured and been analyzed in the book by Beccaria to which I return.]

> If centuries of experience, during which the ultimate punishment has never deterred men determined to harm society; if the example of the citizens of Rome or the twenty-year reign of the Empress Elizabeth of Moscovy, during which she gave the leaders of all peoples an illustrious example worth at least as much as many conquests bought with the blood of her country's sons — if none of this has convinced men, for whom the voice of reason is always suspect while the voice of authority is compelling, then it suffices to consult human nature in order to appreciate the truth of my assertion. (52)

Basically, upon hearing this declaration and in order to grasp the most interesting difference between a thinking of this type (a thinking of Enlightenment and Reason) and a thinking like Schmitt's, one could say that the latter attempts to think this "authority," this *auctoritas* and this *potestas*, this power of the constitutive authority of sovereignty and of its theological history, whereas Beccaria, by saying he prefers reason to authority, basically deprives himself of the means of understanding this logic of sovereignty to which he is nevertheless not opposed. He would like to reconcile reason and right or law, where Schmitt, in a manner that is just as rational and logical, recalls that the origin of the law, like the origin of reason, cannot be legal or rational, and this is the source of authority, its always exceptional source.

[Before concluding] here again are four framing perspectives. Two turn or return toward what we have just said; two are oriented by what awaits us in the next sessions.

1. *Europe, the French Revolution, and the sign of a possible progress of humanity*, as Kant used to say, Kant who was moreover in favor of maintaining the principle of the death penalty in the law, we will see how and why. Let us return to the time of the French Revolution, which essentially opened a debate on the death penalty that preoccupied the whole nineteenth century and of which Hugo, as we will hear, was one of the great abolitionist witnesses. I have already referred to the evolution of Robespierre, the converted abolitionist; but the Convention, in its last session, had nevertheless insisted on decreeing that, I quote once again:

Dating from the day of the general proclamation of peace, the death penalty will be abolished in the French Republic.

Extraordinary declaration, unprecedented commitment.

Even if the abolition of the death penalty in France happened only about two centuries later (on a certain scale, that is not very long), it is not unreasonable to consider that the revolutionaries, who wanted to export the Revolution and make peace, their public and republican peace in Europe, had registered the necessity of awaiting a *pax europeana* in conformity with their declaration of the rights of man before abolishing the death penalty in a pacified Europe whose security had been assured. Is this not what is happening? And is it not what confirms that the death penalty is not abolished for reasons of principle and of the unconditional right to life but (whence a fundamental, structural hypocrisy of the abolitionist discourse in its present state) wherever order, peace, and security allow it to be abolished, as Beccaria basically said when, treating the question of the exception (chaos, disorder, end, or birth of a nation), he added all the same, I quote him again:

> But when the calm rule of law prevails, under a form of government that has the support of the nation, which is well-fortified both externally and internally by both force and opinion (which is perhaps more efficacious than force itself), and in which the power to rule is vested only in the true sovereign and wealth can buy only pleasures not authority, I do not see any need to destroy a citizen . . . (127)[36]

2. Hyperbole or raising the stakes of cruelty. On the subject of cruelty, which we have barely begun to speak about, it is necessary to remark one of the numerous equivocations or complexities in the thought of Beccaria, this great model or this great initiator, this great patron of abolitionism. On the one hand, he clearly denounces the cruelty of the death penalty and the cruelty of punishment in general, which, he says, has consequences that are disastrous and contrary to the proposed aim (punishment is disproportionate and leads to impunity): "If the laws are truly cruel," he says, "they must be changed or fatal impunity will arise from the laws themselves" (51); or again, "The death penalty is not useful because of the example of cruelty that it gives to men" (55). Beccaria thus reverses the argument of exemplarity that we will talk a

141

36. Derrida spells out during the session: "Is this not the Europe of today? But this marks in some way the foundation without foundation of the abolition of the death penalty. If the abolition of the death penalty is conditioned by peace and security, externally and internally, it is not abolished for reasons of principle. Basically, it is no longer really needed, whereas there are countries like the United States and China that still need it."

lot about later. Far from setting the good example that would deter potential criminals, the cruelty of the death penalty is a bad example that encourages "blood letting," like war. By condemning to death, far from discouraging for example murderers, their cruelty is encouraged by the example.

And yet, when he proposes to replace the death penalty by life imprisonment, Beccaria seems not to realize that his best argument is the reference to the cruelty of "perpetual penal servitude," concerning which he says calmly that it is more dissuasive than the death penalty because more dreadful than death. Basically the death penalty may not be cruel enough. One has to find something crueler, perpetual penal servitude, with chains and beatings. (In Alabama, chain gangs with leg irons have been reinstated.) I leave you to appreciate this passage; it will show you that Beccaria's first concern is not a "principle," a compassionate goodness (moreover, he is rather opposed to the right to pardon, see the end of the book), or the right to life; it is a concern for effectiveness in the maintenance of order. And for that, he raises the stakes in calling for cruelty — while omitting the word:

> Therefore [he says], the intensity of perpetual penal servitude, substituted for the death penalty, has all that is necessary to deter even the most determined mind. Indeed, I would say that it has even more: a great many men look upon death with a calm and steady gaze, some out of fanaticism, some out of vanity (which almost always accompanies man beyond the grave [a very interesting remark!]),[37] and some out of a final and desperate attempt either to live no longer or to escape from poverty. But neither fanaticism nor vanity survives in fetters or chains, under the cudgel and the yoke, or in an iron cage; and the desperate finds that his woes are just beginning, rather than ending. (53–54)[38]

37. During the session, Derrida expands his interpolation thus: "Finally, this goes very far, we saw a few examples while reading Badinter: the death penalty can seduce. There is some of that in Genet as well. There are those who desire it. And this is what Beccaria is wary of. There are those who may love it. And not only in life but in the afterlife, those who want to remain, who will beyond the grave, a feeling that accompanies men beyond the grave. This is very powerful. So, this is the risk that the death penalty encourages, that there are those who may cultivate this, who may not only let themselves be fascinated, but do everything necessary to take maximum pleasure from [*jouir de*] the death penalty, in the present and in the future. Not in the future of what may happen to them when they are killed, but after death. So, one must not give them this bonus of immortality, of afterlife."

38. During the session, Derrida adds: "This is the hero of abolitionism. Life imprisonment, suffering has only begun, it is hell. It is not death, it is hell. This is the logic of the great abolitionist, who is admired and respected by many, myself included I must say; I have a certain respect for Beccaria, but finally one must still look at it closely. For Badinter, Beccaria is his great man ; for Victor Hugo, as well ; for the abolitionists, Beccaria is the prophet."

3. *The double bind[39] of the laws, in universal declarations.* Next week, we will return to the worldwide declarations and conventions of the last decades that I mentioned at the beginning. I take or recognize only two reference points that show the equivocal interweaving of a logic of exception and a logic of cruelty. For example, the International Covenant on Civil and Political Rights in its article 6 declares that "Every human being has the inherent right to life,"[40] but allows nevertheless the right in principle to maintain the death penalty, and merely accompanies this right with conditions such as (in section 4 of the same article) "Anyone sentenced to death shall have the right to seek pardon and commutation of the sentence. Amnesty, pardon or commutation of the sentence of death *may be* granted in all cases" (ibid.). (I underscore this sublime "may be," the hypocritical or equivocal caution of which—where the point is to respect the sovereignty of states and create no obligations for anyone—becomes even more readable in section 6 of article 6: "Nothing in this article shall be invoked to delay or to prevent the abolition of capital punishment by any State Party to the present Covenant.")[41] [Comment on the hypocrisy: I don't forbid your maintaining the death penalty, but don't go drawing the conclusion from there that I forbid your abolishing it!][42]

Article 7 of the same text deals with cruelty: "No one shall be subjected to torture or to cruel, inhuman or degrading treatment or punishment. In particular, no one shall be subjected without his free consent to medical or scientific experimentation." (The vast question of man and animal: what is cruelty?). Section 5 of article 6 prohibits the death penalty for crimes committed by persons younger than eighteen and prohibits the execution of pregnant women.

Finally, and still by way of anticipation, this explicit formulation of the logic of the exception, of the "save," in the Convention for the Protection of Hu-

144

39. [Translator's note]: In English in the original.

40. Quoted in Schabas, *The Abolition of the Death Penalty*, p. 312, as are the succeeding quotations from the International Covenant on Civil and Political Rights.

41. The closing parenthesis has been added.

42. During the session, Derrida comments: "What has just been said about the right to life and the right to seek pardon cannot be invoked by any signatory state so as not to abolish the death penalty. They imagine cases where a member state says: you provided for exceptions, so we don't have to abolish the death penalty. They anticipate the perverse use that could be made of their own article. But they do nothing to avoid it in a categorical manner. I translate thus: I don't forbid your maintaining the death penalty, but don't go drawing the conclusion from there that I forbid your abolishing it!"

man Rights and Fundamental Freedoms (European Convention on Human Rights, 1953, ratified by thirty-one countries as of 1996), article 2:1: "Everyone's right to life shall be protected by law. No one shall be deprived of his life intentionally *save* in the execution of a sentence of a court following his conviction of a crime for which this penalty is provided by law." (Comment: no death penalty or at least no execution without a death penalty having been legally imposed in cases provided for by the law. Save if a death penalty has been legally imposed in cases provided for by the law. No illegal death penalty, in sum; no death penalty *save* in the (exceptional!) cases where it is deserved or provided for by law!)[43]

4. Finally, fourth and last point, which we will approach directly next week: *what is cruelty?* What is the *meaning* of cruelty? Is it *blood*, a history of blood, as the etymology seems to indicate (*cruor* is red blood, blood that flows)? And does one put an end to cruelty on the day that one no longer makes blood flow? Or else does cruelty point toward a radical evil, an evil for evil's sake, a suffering inflicted so as to make suffer, with or without blood? What of Christianity in this history of cruelty, in this history of red blood or in this history of cruelty without blood, beyond blood? What is cruelty: blood, or evil for evil's sake? And what is death? These are questions that we will elaborate in the course of or in the margin of readings of Hugo (*Writings on the Death Penalty* and we will follow there, among others, the red thread of red blood, of the red color in his admirable texts on the guillotine) and readings of Camus ("Reflections on the Guillotine").

The interpretation of Christianity is different in these two great French abolitionists who see red when they hear speak of the death penalty, and we will try, for our part, to see things more clearly.

---

43. During the session, Derrida adds: "In other words, I paraphrase, everyone's life is protected by the law; no one may be deprived of his or her life, save in cases where the execution of a court sentence is provided for by law. No death penalty, or at least no execution, save if a death penalty has been legally handed down in cases provided for by law. Other than that, absolute right to life. No illegal death penalty, in sum; no death penalty *save* in (exceptional!) cases where it is deserved or provided for by law!"

January 19, 2000
Right to Life, Right to Death

I vote for the pure, simple, and definitive abolition of the death penalty.

You know who dared to say this: it was, of course, the immense Victor Hugo.

We are going to continue today — but differently, changing our references and rhythm a little — with what we began to elaborate last time by interweaving the two motifs or the two logics of *cruelty* on the one hand and *sovereign exception* on the other, all the while analyzing the current situation in the ongoing struggle for abolition, with the role of new media (Internet, etc.) and the strategy of texts on human rights, the right to life, and on the theological origins of the concepts of modern politics, notably of sovereignty (with reference to Schmitt).

The history of law and the history of so-called communications technologies, the joint history of the juridical or judicial machine and of the informative or informational machine were and remain, then, the irreducible element of our questioning.

On September 15, 1848, speaking from the podium of the Constituent Assembly,[1] Victor Hugo proclaimed, or rather declared without clamoring (because it is said that his written eloquence did not have a powerful voice at its command, contrary to what one might think when reading him, since his writing voice is powerful, powerful in essence, if one can say that, it is deployed in the genre and style of oratorical power, and I would distinguish the writing voice from the voice *tout court*, that of the classroom, for

148

1. [Translator's note]: As in 1789, in 1848 after the February Revolution a representative body called the Assemblée constituante or simply La Constituante, was formed to write a constitution for the Second French Republic. I have retained the French terminology, although a closer historical equivalent and translation would be "Constitutional Convention."

example, or of parliament, and let's never forget that there was no micro-phone at the time; one must always think about these technical conditions that program and structure the space, the space and time of so-called public speech), Victor Hugo was announcing, then, in his powerful and powerless voice:

I vote for the pure, simple, and definitive abolition of the death penalty.

It is a simple sentence, it carries, it is direct, it states in the first per-son a vote, that is to say, a voice.[2] It says "my voice, my vote," a vote that counts, it is that of "Victor Hugo, I myself" but it counts as one vote, which is and is not a voice-vote among others, the voice-vote of just anyone, a voice-vote at once singular and universal that always claims to speak in the name of the universal, of universal rights (but above all French rights, we will get to that). But a vote that refuses all equivocation, all hypocrisy, all complications, all detours, all moratoria, all exceptions, even any guilty nuance: "I vote for the pure, simple, and definitive abolition of the death penalty."

Later we will read the brief speech that this sentence concludes and signs.[3] It is the last sentence of an *intervention*, as we say, at the Constituent Assembly. Because let us not forget that this parliamentary assembly is a constituting one.

The year 1848 was exactly one century before a Universal Declaration of Human Rights, debated and adopted by the UN, about which the least one could say is that, if it was taking a certain step in the direction of a possible or final abolition of the death penalty, it was careful not to progress too far and too quickly or too directly straight ahead; it stopped on the verge of decision, at the instant of deciding on such an abolition, of voting in favor of such an abolition; on the contrary, it proliferated impure, complicated, and provisional gestures. It protected itself with adjournments, as we are going to spell out once again.

All of which leads us to think that, besides the intrinsic, dare I say *vi-tal* interest of this question of the death penalty, well, its history is itself a guiding thread, a red thread that is indispensable today for the reading and interpretation of a history of universal law, of a history of international or cosmopolitical law, of what the law can mean, the so-called natural law and the historical law, the historicity of the law, the historicity of relations

2. [Translator's note:] The frequent repetitions throughout this paragraph of *voix* could all be translated as either "voice" or "vote."

3. Victor Hugo, *Écrits sur la peine de mort* (Arles: Actes Sud, 1979), p. 71.

between penal or criminal law and other laws, the relation between national and international law, the essential historicity of this relation, of what could be called a *progress* (or not), a *telos* or not in this history, following the indications or signs, as Kant says, of a *possibility* of progress in the history of humanity, of the relations of adequation or inadequation between justice and law, and above all the question of man or the human, of human rights and of what ultimately a human is, of what is proper to the human—for example, if one distinguishes it from both the animal and God, from other animals and from gods. The question then of the right to life as a human right and of this single living being that is called man or the human person. Inviolability of human life, Hugo will say countless times.

Because, of course, beyond the conceptual limits that ought to define the death penalty and thus distinguish it from death *tout court*, from so-called natural death and from murder and suicide, from all the many ways of inflicting death or committing suicide [*de donner ou de se donner la mort*], with all of the distinctions with which we began, beyond these necessary but always precarious and problematic conceptual limits, one must ask oneself what it is *to die* (not only in the sense in which, according to Heidegger, only *Dasein* dies, only *Dasein* has, if I can say this, the right and the possibility of dying, whereas the animal stops living or perishes [*crève*] but never dies—cf. *Sein und Zeit, Unterwegs zur Sprache,* and my short book, *Aporias,* where I quote and analyze these texts,[4]—but also in the sense in which one must ask oneself as well what are the so-called objective criteria for death, for the state of death, and later we will get to some terrifying examples of executions that never end, and some effects of this question for the application of the death penalty).[5]

If, then,1848, the date of this declaration by Hugo to the Constituent Assembly, precedes by one century a new Declaration of Human Rights (1948) that asserts the right to life (article 3: "Everyone has the right to life, liberty and security of the person"—I underline "person" again for reasons that will, I think, continue to be clarified), still without proposing and even less prescribing the abolition of the death penalty, we must, therefore, before returning to these modern declarations and the meaning of their limits, take the measure of what Hugo says, of its literality on this date, and of its philosophical, metaphysical, religious, or historical implications.

150

4. Jacques Derrida, *Apories, mourir—s'attendre aux "limites de la vérité"* (Paris: Galilée, 1996); *Aporias: Dying—Awaiting (one another) at "the limits of truth,"* trans. Thomas Dutoit (Stanford, CA: Stanford University Press, 1993).

5. The closing parenthesis has been moved here; in the typescript, the parenthesis closes after "where I quote and analyze these texts."

This declaration is far from being the only one, on Hugo's part, and it was brief. But I begin with it because it was made, statutorily, on the floor of a legislative body and of a Constituent Assembly of a revolutionary kind, in an assembly conscious of its inaugural, founding, instituting power. It is a Constituent Assembly. It is a bit as if the point were to reconnect with the time of the French Revolution and in memory of the last session of the Convention, which, I again remind you, after the execution of Robespierre, had decreed:

> Dating from the day of the general proclamation of peace, the death penalty will be abolished in the French Republic.

In this speech, however, and as he does in so many other texts on the death penalty, Victor Hugo is going to make use several times of a word, "inviolability," more precisely "the inviolability of human life," which, on the one hand, will split off [*tranchera*], if I may use such a cutting word in this theater of the guillotine that is the whole of the French history of the death penalty, will split off, then, from that decisive moment of the French Revolution which decided, precisely, that, in the case of the king, human life was not inviolable, that the body of the king was no longer inviolable or sacrosanct, and that the <case of the> king could be judged either like that of any citizen who is a traitor to the nation (like all those who would be guillotined from then on), or like that of a public enemy, who is not even a citizen but a foreigner in wartime.

(Here we would have to reread all the texts, those of Robespierre or of Saint-Just in particular, but also—and unfortunately we will not be able to do this—reconsider from the perspective of our problematic of the death penalty everything that concerns the origins, the end, and the limits of the Terror, its place in the French Revolution and therefore the reality and the figure of the guillotine; we will do so, at best, only indirectly. About the unheard-of event that was the death of Louis XVI, which had no precedent other than the decapitation of a king of England [and with notable differences], I will say, without playing too much on words, that by dividing in this way the body of the king in two, the head on one side, the body on the other, this unprecedented event was destined at least to put an end to what Kantorowicz calls the *double body of the king*, the king's two bodies, the empirical and carnal, mortal body, on one side, and the body of the glorious, sovereign, and immortal function, on the other.[6] In this logic of the king's

6. See Ernst Kantorowicz, *The King's Two Bodies: A Study in Mediaeval Political Theology* (Princeton, NJ: Princeton University Press, 1970).

two bodies, when the mortal body dies, one can say *long live the king!* and replace him within the body of the function by the body of another king, who is another and the same, but immortal. Well, by dividing in two the body of Louis Capet beneath the blade of the guillotine, the revolutionaries, in this paradoxical arithmetic of bodies, were reducing it to a single body at the moment of splitting it up like that: there remained only a single body; there was then only the body of a mortal cut in two; and it is true that, in this single body in two parts, one could still see, according to the interpretations of the indictments,

A. *either* a simple citizen traitor to the nation, an internal public enemy who deserved to be judged as just one citizen among others, which certain arguments of the accusation maintained,

B. *or* a noncitizen, a foreign public enemy who deserved to be eliminated as such in an act of war.)

In any case, by taking a position for the inviolability of life, and I specify of *human* life, because this is the point — we are coming to it — that concentrates all the difficulty; (it is not about the inviolability of the living being, of the life of the living being in general, but of human life, of the human person, so that the border in question, and the place of the problem, is not the opposition life/death, <between> life and its contrary, but <between> human life and its other, we will return to this at length, notably with the modern question or complication of the voluntary termination of pregnancy [*IVG*][7] and of abortion), by taking a position for the inviolability of human life, Hugo is at the same time a revolutionary and someone who, even as he realizes one aim of the French Revolution, contradicts all the same a practice of the same Revolution, breaks with it, with the principle of Terror. Hugo proposes in sum a revolution within the Revolution, a revolution that contradicts the Revolution of 1789 in order to confirm it.

In this way, asserting the inviolability of human life, he also heralds the principle of the right to life that will be posed one hundred years later in the 1948 Declaration of Human Rights. And Hugo is aware of the historicity of his appeal. He is aware of both the brutal and decisive interruption, the rupture of continuity, the irruption, the absolute surprise, that his declarative gesture constitutes, but also of the historical memory that he reawakens, that he brutally yanks from its slumber, and of the future that he heralds. The very rhetoric of address or of apostrophe is marked by it, very artfully.

Apropos of this art and of that which (I alluded to it at the outset) ties

152

7. [Translator's note:] *IVG* stands for *interruption volontaire de grossesse*, "voluntary interruption of pregnancy," which is the legal designation of abortion in France.

literature to the abolition of the death penalty, no less and infinitely more than to the right to death, Hugo on several occasions asserts the right of the writer to defy or to change the law.

Thus, before returning to this text that, on September 15, 1848, one century before the Declaration of Human Rights, so solemnly says "I vote for the pure, simple, and definitive abolition of the death penalty," in the name of the inviolability of human life, I would like to take a (rather long) detour by way of literature and by way of the question of literature on Christian soil, on French Christian soil, even. And therefore also a detour by way of the figure of the writer or even of the intellectual in this history of France, of Christian France.

Hugo is conscious of the role both of historical responsibility and especially the responsibility of literature and the writer in this history, and marks it at least twice. Once was during his exile, in 1862, in a letter to M. Bost, a pastor in Geneva, where the death penalty was about to be debated (Hugo was already famous in Europe as a defender of the abolitionist cause and he was asked to *intervene* everywhere in Europe that a debate was being initiated on the death penalty). In this letter, where he speaks again of the inviolability of human life ("among these questions, the gravest of all, the inviolability of human life, is the order of the day. It is the death penalty that is in question" [186–87]), Hugo does not merely recall the role of writers in this debate. He assigns or grants them a signal responsibility; it falls to those who write literature to call people back to the inviolability of human life and to the respect for justice beyond the law; to them, par excellence, falls the task of transforming the law in the direction of a justice that is more than juridical. He writes, for example, in the past and in the future:

> Writers of the eighteenth century *destroyed* torture; writers of the nineteenth, I have no doubt, *will destroy* the death penalty.

[This word "destroy," used with insistence and deliberately twice, signifies clearly that it is a question of something other than a simple legislative decision or even of an institutional or constitutional, constituting, act: it is a question, I don't dare say of deconstructing but in any case of destroying, of attacking, through writing, by speaking and by writing publicly, it is a question of attacking the foundations or the presuppositions alleged by the law or by public opinion wherever the bases of this law or the underpinnings of this public opinion, this *doxa*, or this orthodoxy uphold the death penalty; it is a question of *destroying* the discursive and other mechanisms, the supports, phantasms, and opinions, the drives, the conscious or semiconscious or unconscious representations, that work to legitimate the death penalty; and this presupposes a certain type of writing, of public speech, and a certain type of treatment of language (national and international) that has a privileged tie to what in Europe is called literature, as well as to those citizens who have more or less broken with citizenship, who are sometimes ready, as you are going to hear in a moment, to engage in certain acts of civil disobedience, to those citizens of the world who are called writers. I pick up my quotation again, but I am going to proceed by constantly inserting texts into each other.]

> Writers of the eighteenth century destroyed torture; writers of the nine-teenth, I have no doubt, will destroy the death penalty. They have already brought about the suppression of the practices of cutting off hands and the branding iron [*le fer* rouge;[8] I underline this "red," you are going to see it reappear everywhere as the color of blood and of shame: the cruelty of *cruor*]; they have brought about the abrogation of civil death; and they have suggested the admirable expedient of extenuating circumstances. "It is atro-cious books like *The Last Day of a Condemned Man*," said the assemblyman Salverte, "that are responsible for the detestable introduction of attenuating circumstances."

[This is, then, the accusation made by this assemblyman Salverte as to the detrimental influence exerted by, according to him, *The Last Day of a Condemned Man*, a book by the young Hugo dating from 1829 (Victor Hugo was then twenty-seven, remember this age; later we will hear an older Hugo identify with his son who was being prosecuted for standing up, like his father, against the death penalty), *The Last Day of a Condemned Man*, a book by the young Hugo that three years later will be preceded by a long preface, which constitutes no doubt the first, the longest, and the richest, the most eloquent of Hugo's manifestos against the death penalty. Every-thing is already in place there: the principle of the inviolability of human life, expressly formulated, one of the many expressions of praise for Becca-ria, a refutation of the argument of exemplarity, accusations of cruelty and barbarity, an abundant *mise en scène* of red blood, and already (but we will return to all this, the text is placed at the beginning of the volume of Hugo's *Writings on the Death Penalty*), already, a Christian or rather Christological axiomatics whose ambiguity we will analyze.] Hugo continues: {155}

> *Extenuating circumstances in the law are the wedge in the oak. Let us seize the divine hammer, strike the wedge relentlessly, strike great blows of truth, and we will shatter the chopping block.* (189; emphases added)

8. [Translator's note]: Literally, the red iron.

This simple sentence says a lot. It is full of sap and verve. And it is very effective, as always with Hugo. It does what he wants, it says what he wants to say. But also perhaps a bit more, and this then is what interests us most. It says and does at least four things.

First, it suggests that it is writers who, before abolishing the death penalty or "destroying" it, have imposed the concept of extenuating circumstances. Not innocence, but the means of exculpation by sheltering from the blind hardness of the law, by attenuating the punishment.

Second, by means of an image, it leads one to think that this concept of extenuating circumstances was inserted into an oak that had to be cut down, a large tree, an old and sturdy tree, and that, in the long process which will lead up to cutting down this tree and to the abolition of the death penalty, one had to start from premises, with levers, with the insertion of wedges. And for this, one needs knowledge, one must be a good woodcutter, a good worker with thought and language, a good historian, a good sociologist, a good analyst. It is long-term labor in which the writer-destroyer has to aim well and know where to strike, with his wedge, with the cutting and incisive instrument of his writing.

156   *Third*, this tree, the oak that must be cut down, is not a good tree, it is not the good oak of liberty or the good oak under which the justice of Saint Louis is meted out; quite on the contrary, it is a bad oak, namely, the tree from which will be hewn a piece of the death machine, the chopping block, that is, the proper place of decapitation, the place where heads must fall.

Fourth, as you have noticed, if the writing of the writer inserts the wedge into the oak, if the writer then seizes the hammer and strikes great blows of truth to shatter the chopping block, the hammer he uses is called a "divine hammer." In other words, the end of the death penalty, the order to put an end to the death penalty, the abolitionist instrument must be divine; it acts out of respect for God and for Christ (albeit against the church and the Inquisition). For a Christ who is the truth, who says "I am the life and the truth." With great blows of truth: it suffices to recall the truth, to recall the truth *to oneself*, to call oneself back to truth in order to strike the blows that will one day cut down this bad oak.

We will verify this repeatedly: Hugo's abolitionism is profoundly Christian, Christlike, evangelical. Whether it is a matter here of profound faith or of rhetorical flourish or, as I believe to be the case, somewhere between the two, a matter of moral conscience or of a discourse of moral conscience, of an inner conviction [*for intérieur*] that can be cultivated as an authority only in a Christian space, of an idea of man, of "human life," of the inviolability of life as human life that is fundamentally heir to and the elementary off-

spring of a Christian family, a holy family, it remains that it is in the name
of God and of a Christian God that the death penalty is going to be opposed.

And again in 1862, in the letter where Hugo states the mission and the
exemplary responsibility and therefore the painful privilege of the writer,
he knows and he admits that the road will be long, but he never misses an
opportunity to remind one of the role of writing, of *his* own writings, of the
already international journey (last time we were talking about the Web;
well there was already international communication, already all the way to
America, fairly rapid *interventions* — this is already Hugo's word — of writers). I read what follows. (Read Hugo's *Écrits*, 189–91)   *157*

> Slowly, I agree. It will take time, to be sure. Nevertheless, let us not be
> discouraged. Our efforts, even the smallest ones, are not always useless. I
> have just recalled the incident at Charleroi; here is another. Eight years ago,
> in Guernsey, in 1854, a man named Tapner was sentenced to the gallows;
> I intervened, an appeal for pardon was signed by six hundred notables of
> the island, the man was hanged; now, listen: a few European newspapers
> that printed the letter I wrote to the citizens of Guernsey to prevent the
> execution made their way to America in time for this letter to be reprinted
> usefully by American newspapers; they were going to hang a man in Que-
> bec, a certain Julien; the people of Canada rightly considered the letter I
> had written to the people of Guernsey to be addressed to them and, by a
> providential counter-blow, this letter saved — permit me to say so — not
> Tapner whom it intended, but Julien whom it did not intend. I cite the facts;
> why? Because they prove the necessity of persistence. Alas, the executioner's
> sword also persists.
>
> The statistics of the guillotine and the scaffold maintain their hideous
> levels; the number of legal murders has not decreased in any country. For
> the last ten years even, the sense of morality having declined, execution
> has regained favor, and it is back on the rise again. As a small people, you
> in your sole city of Geneva have seen two guillotines erected in eighteen
> months. In fact, having killed Vary, why not kill Elcy? In Spain, there is
> the garrot; in Russia, death by caning. In Rome, because the church is hor-
> rified by blood, the condemned is bludgeoned, *ammazzato*. England, where
> a woman reigns, has just hanged a woman. (189–91)

As for this responsibility of the writer, which is already, as we have just
seen, international or cosmopolitical, as for his or her mission that consists
in overcoming or transforming nation-state law, Hugo does not hesitate to
call it also a right. In the passage I am going to read, he speaks of the writer's
right, a right no less sacred than the legislator's. Sacred, that is to say, in sum,   *158*
divine or of divine right, a sovereign right. Because if you pay attention,

you will see how it is a right that has or grants the right not to let oneself be limited by existing law. It is a right that gives the right to go beyond right and sometimes to engage in and commit oneself to what, during the same period in the United States, certain writer-citizens were also elaborating under the name "civil disobedience"[9] to current legislation in the name of a higher law or justice.

Well, what about this responsibility of the writer, this right above right? Before even formulating them explicitly, as you will hear in the speech he delivered before the Criminal Court of the Seine when his son, Charles Hugo, was prosecuted there precisely for having "offended the law" by writing against the death penalty, Hugo claims this responsibility and unconditional right of the writer for himself, for him the father. And he presents himself ironically but with conviction as the real guilty party, the one who is really responsible, he the father, he the model, he the writer. And he does so by declaring once more the inviolability of life, his condemnation of the law of blood for blood in the name of a fidelity to Christ, in other words — and this is the crux of his demonstration — by asserting divine law above human law. The death penalty is too human; abolition is divine. It is the logic of this hierarchy that, later in the same speech, will ensure in a consistent manner the sanctity of the writer's right. Obviously it is a very noble gesture, but also overdetermined and ambiguous, the scene of a claim of paternity by this father who says he is reincarnated in his son when he accuses himself of the son's fault, when he presents himself ironically but seriously as the real guilty party, that is, as the real hero, the real author of the fault that consists of speaking out against the death penalty, the real and the first, the first in the order of generation, the first to take the side of life, of the right to life, he, the father, but in the same blow when he reminds one, as he never fails to do, of his virtues as a father — and that this fight against the death penalty is his fight, that it is he the writer who has always been recognized all over the world as the hero of abolitionism; he does not tire of saying, in sum: I am the father reincarnated in the son, it is I who must be judged. And it is then, as if fortuitously and I imagine entirely unconsciously, with the gesture of a rhetorician, a lawyer, or a prosecutor, so as to remind the jurors that they risk repeating, like vulgar Romans or vulgar Jews, the gesture of putting Christ to death, that he points Christ out to the jurors and invokes the crucifixion of Jesus the son of God. He is, thus, both the father incarnated in Jesus, the father defending his son, who has been tried and is about to be sentenced, but he is also the Son, the true reincarnated victim

159

9. [Translator's note]: In English in the original.

of God made man, Father and son at once, two in one body. Naturally, as you are going to hear, the idea of comparing, still less of identifying the family of God and Christ with his own family is doubtless far from his conscious intention. And if he points to Christ it is so as to move the jurors and to show them how men, how the human law of barbaric Romans or Jews, condemned to death the incarnation of divine law. But he says more than he means to say: you will appreciate his use of the word "family," a use that he believes is ironic and biting, but which I believe exceeds his own thought when he blinds himself to the family drama that he thinks he is directing whereas doubtless he is its noble, unconscious, narcissistic, and naïve pawn.

Like all fathers and like all sons, as such. I read. (Read and comment on 96–97)

For, and since I have been led to the subject, I must say to you, gentlemen of the jury, so that you will understand the depths of my emotion, the real guilty party in this affair, if there is a guilty party, is not my son, it is I. (*Prolonged stirring*)

The real guilty party, I insist, is I, I who, for the last twenty-five years, have fought in every way against irreparable punishments! I who, for the last twenty-five years, have defended at every opportunity the inviolability of human life!

I committed this crime, defending the inviolability of human life, well before my son, much more than my son. I give myself up, Mr. Attorney General! I committed it with full aggravating circumstances! With premeditation, with tenacity, and repeatedly! (*Renewed stirring*)

Yes, I declare it: against this vestige of savage punishment, this old and unintelligent talionic law, this law of blood for blood, I have fought all my life — all my life, gentlemen of the jury! — and, so long as a breath remains in my body, I will fight it with all my strength as a writer, with all my acts and all my votes as a legislator, I declare it (*Mr. Victor Hugo extends his arm and points to the figure of Christ at the back of the room, above the judge's bench*) before the victim of the death penalty who is there, who watches us and hears us! I swear before that gallows, where, two thousand years ago, as an eternal lesson to the generations, human law nailed divine law! (*Profound and inexpressible emotion*)

160

What my son wrote, he wrote, I repeat, because I inspired it in him since childhood, because at the same time as he is my son by blood, he is my son by spirit, because he wants to continue the tradition of his father. To continue the tradition of his father! Now that is a strange crime, for which I am amazed that anyone is prosecuted! It was up to the exclusive defenders of the family to show us this novelty! (*Laughter*) (96–97)

The ground has thus been prepared to advance the following three theses. I believe them to be indissociable within the logic and the rhetoric of all Hugo's writings on the death penalty. And if I insist on this, it is because their system, their systemic articulation, is proper not only to Hugo, or even only to the nineteenth century; we are constantly going to come upon signs of it again still today, even if Hugo lent them, obviously, an exemplary voice, or even a voice of genius, in any case a generic voice. With genius, but also with the sense of father-son generation, he assured and inaugurated the law of their genre.

What then are these three theses or axioms?

A. *On the one hand*, writers, the filiation of writers, and here, of great French writers, the chain of the generations of men-writers in French literature, from Voltaire to Chateaubriand and to Hugo, institute the responsibility and give themselves the *sacred* right to make the law above the laws, to make themselves the representatives of eternal justice above law and thus of divine justice. But to make the law, to invent a new law, here, is simply to appeal to a divine law, to a divine justice that has *already* spoken, a law older than they and more ancient than men, a law that must be *invented* but in the sense of being discovered or found, the way one speaks of the invention of the body of Christ to mean the discovery of his unlocatable body; the writer, therefore, does not perform new laws; he does not invent or produce a new code of law except by listening, by knowing how to listen in his heart to a divine law that already speaks and that men, and sometimes churches, have muffled, hidden, buried, or silenced.

B. *On the other hand*, and secondly, this divine and Christlike justice must on occasion — and we could find many examples of this — be turned back against the church when, along with the state, the church betrays this eternal and Christian justice (here the Inquisition is the best example of the church's guilt).

C. *Finally, thirdly*, just as one condemns a certain church, or even a certain political theology in the name of Christ, one condemns the guillotine or revolutionary terror in the name of true fidelity to the spirit of the French Revolution: the borderline of this right to literature thus runs through Christianity; it marks the divide between a good and a bad Christianity, between a Christianity that is faithful and one that is unfaithful to itself; likewise, this borderline, this line of demarcation, runs between several figures of the French Revolution.

I am indeed speaking of the French Revolution, of the Revolution of France. For it must be underscored here that these three arguments, however distinct they may appear to be, are united in the body of France, of the history of France, in the history of French literature and its great men, in the history of the state and of politics, in the history of the French church. For in the course of the same session during the trial of his son, the father dared to say, as he rose up against the spectacle offered by this law and this trial, that France was no longer France, but Mongolia or Tibet. This was when, faced with the public's emotional outburst, the judge threatened to clear the room, whereupon Hugo continues in the sequence I am going to read and comment on. (Read and comment on 98–101)

Very well, then! Let us close the courtroom, close the schools, no more prog- *162* ress is possible, call us Mogol or Thibet [*sic*], we are no longer a civilized nation! Yes, it will be done all the sooner, tell us that we are in Asia, that long ago there used to be a country that was called France, but that this country no longer exists, and that you have replaced it by something which is no longer a monarchy, I agree, but which is certainly not the republic! (*Renewed laughter*)

JUDGE: I make my observation once again. The public is reminded to be silent; otherwise, I will be forced to clear the room.

Mr. VICTOR HUGO, *continuing*: But let us see, let us look at the facts, let us compare the wording of the indictment with the reality.

Gentlemen of the jury, in Spain, the Inquisition was law. Well! It must be said that people failed to respect the Inquisition. In France, torture was the law. Well! Once again, it must be said that people failed to respect torture. Cutting off the hand was the law. People failed . . . I failed to respect the blade! The branding iron [*le fer rouge*] was the law. People failed to respect the branding iron! The guillotine is the law. Well! It is true, I agree, people fail to respect the guillotine! (*Stirring*)

Do you know why, Mr. Attorney General? I am going to tell you. It is because people want to throw the guillotine into that abyss of execration into which the branding iron, the severed hand, torture, and the Inquisition have already fallen, to the applause of humankind! It is because people want to chase from the august and luminous sanctuary of justice that sinister figure who alone is enough to fill it with horror and darkness, the executioner! (*Profound reaction*)

Oh! And because we want this, we are undermining society! Oh, yes, it is true! We are very dangerous men, we want to do away with the guillotine! It is monstrous!

Gentlemen of the jury, you are *sovereign* [emphasis added] citizens of a free nation and, without distorting this debate, one may, one must speak to you as one does to politicians. Well! Think about it and, since we are traversing a period of revolution, draw the consequences of what I am going to say to you. If Louis XVI had abolished the death penalty, as he had abolished torture, his head would not have fallen. Ninety-three would not have been armed with the blade.[10] There would be one less bloody page in history, the lugubrious date of January 21 would not exist. Who then, in the presence of public conscience, standing before France, standing before the civilized world, who then would have dared to erect the scaffold for the king, for the man about whom one could have said: It is he who tore it down! (*Prolonged disturbance*)

163

The editor of *L'Événement* is accused of having failed to respect the laws! Of having failed to respect the death penalty! Gentlemen, let us rise a little higher than a debatable text, let us rise all the way to the very basis of all legislation, all the way to man's inner conviction [*for intérieur*]. When Servan, who was all the same Attorney General at the time, when Servan branded the criminal law of his time with this memorable rebuke: "Our penal laws open all doors to the accuser, and close almost all of them to the accused"; when Voltaire described the judges of Calas in these terms: *Oh! Do not speak to me of those judges, who are part monkey and part tiger!* (*Laughter*); when Chateaubriand, in *Le Conservateur*, called the law of the double vote a *stupid and guilty law*; when Royer-Collard, right in the Chamber of Deputies, apropos of I no longer know which law of censorship, launched his famous cry: *If you pass this law, I swear to disobey it*; when these legislators, these magistrates, these philosophers, these great minds, these men, some illustrious, some venerable, spoke thus, what were they doing? Were they failing to respect the law, the local and temporary law? It is possible; Mr. Attorney General says so, I do not know. But what I do know is that they were the religious echoes of the law of laws, of universal conscience! Were they offending justice, the justice of their time, transitory and fallible justice? I have no idea; but what I do know, is that they proclaimed eternal justice. (*General show of agreement*)

It is true that today, as one has done us the favor of saying in the very heart of the National Assembly, there would be prosecutions against the atheist Voltaire, the immoral Molière, the obscene La Fontaine, the demagogue Jean-Jacques Rousseau! (*Laughter*). That is what some people think, that is what is admitted, that is where we are! You will appreciate it, gentlemen of the jury!

Gentlemen of the jury, this right to criticize the law, to criticize it severely, in particular and above all penal law, which can so easily take on the stamp of barbaric customs, this right to criticize, which is set alongside the

10. [Translator's note]: "Ninety-Three" or "Quatre-vingt-treize" refers to the onset of the Terror, which began in June 1793 and lasted until July 1794, after its leaders, Robespierre and Saint-Just, were guillotined. *Quatre-vingt-treize* is also the title of Hugo's last work of fiction, published in 1874. The trial of Charles Hugo took place in 1850. In the next sentence, "January 21" refers to the date of the execution by guillotine of Louis XVI in 1793.

duty to improve, like the candle flame alongside the work to be done, this right of the writer, no less sacred than the right of the legislator, this necessary right, this imprescriptible right, you will recognize with your verdict, you will acquit the accused. (98–101)

End of this detour. You remember that when I was about to underscore how the very rhetoric of address or apostrophe was marked by it, with great art, in the declaration to vote ("I vote for the pure, simple, and definitive abolition of the death penalty"), I began this detour on the subject of the writer and of the right of literature not as a right to death (as has been said, otherwise, since Blanchot), but as right to life, right beyond right, and right to the abolition of the death penalty.

Since I have just alluded to this famous text by Blanchot, "La Littérature et le droit à la mort" in *La part du feu* ["Literature and the Right to Death" in *The Work of Fire*], I recommend you reread it, particularly from the viewpoint of this seminar and what we are saying today, around the pages that deal with the Revolution and the Terror, Saint-Just, and Robespierre. In a certain way, one could read these pages in a very uneasy or even critical manner as a terrifying document from a certain period of French literature, very French literature, and of the best, the most fascinating, the most fascinated, but also the most equivocal political thinking of literature. One could also read this document (and I am going to do so) as the counterpoint, but in the name of literature itself, to the inviolable right to life and as the Hegelian-Mallarmean obverse of Hugo's abolitionism. This is certainly not—I agree and I even insist—the only possible reading of this other great text to which a whole seminar would have to be devoted. The fact remains that, for the moment and in a partial and provisional way, one can note at least this: in that text, at that time (1949 when it was collected in *La part du feu*, but first published in *Critique* in January 1948—once again, 1948, the date of the Universal Declaration of Human Rights, exactly one century after Hugo's abolitionist text and vote that we are now pondering), Blanchot inscribes literature not only under the sign of revolution, which he has always done, of two revolutions, from the extreme right to the extreme left, but more precisely here of the French Revolution and in its period of Terror.

Literature contemplates itself in revolution, it finds its justification there, and if it has been called Terror [the word is Paulhan's],[11] this is because its

11. [Translator's note]: The allusion is to Jean Paulhan's influential 1941 essay, *Les fleurs de Tarbes, ou la Terreur dans les lettres*.

165   ideal is indeed that historical moment in which "life bears death and maintains itself in death itself" [quotation from Hegel] so as to gain from death
the possibility and the truth of speech. This is the "question" that seeks to
realize itself in literature and that is its being.[12]

With this, Blanchot does not want to recall merely, as he is also doing in
the double wake of Hegel and Mallarmé, the negative or annihilating force
of nomination, the essential link between language and death, language and
murder, language that annihilates the existence of the thing (and not only
in the famous example from Mallarmé, so often evoked by Blanchot, of the
"I say a flower" and of the "flower absent from every bouquet";[13] although
in the passage we are reading the flower is a woman and Blanchot twice
chooses the metonymic example of the woman, of the flower woman, to
illustrate this putting to death by nomination—and as you have seen me
following for a little while the thread of sexual differences in this history of
French literature and the death penalty, this example should be added to
the same file: why, like Joan of Arc, is it a woman who is here exemplarily
put to death by the act of nomination and by the simple fact of speaking?)
("I say, 'This woman,' and she is immediately available to me, I push her
away, I bring her close, she is everything I want her to be . . ." and further
on the same page [322], "I say: 'This woman.' Hölderlin, Mallarmé and, in
general, all those whose poetry takes as its theme the essence of poetry have
seen the act of naming as disturbing and marvelous. The word gives me
what it signifies, but first it suppresses it. To be able to say: 'This woman,' I
must somehow take her flesh and blood reality away from her, cause her to
be absent, annihilate her. The word gives me the being, but it gives it to me
deprived of being" [322].)

It is not only this annihilating power of the name that inscribes literature under the sign of revolutionary terror. More precisely, at least for this
Blanchot, at least at this time, in 1948, it is the literal alliance of literature
166   with Terror as a guillotining machine; it is also the reference to the Sadian
version [*instance*] of the Revolution. The Sadian version, which is to say,
that of an absolute cruelty, a radical perversion. Is it insignificant that, on
the facing page, right before the two allusions to the "I say: 'This woman'"
and the "I must . . . annihilate her," one sees loom up the figure of Sade

12. Maurice Blanchot, "La Littérature et le droit à la mort," in *La part du feu* (Paris:
Gallimard, 1949) p. 324; "Literature and the Right to Death," in *The Work of Fire*, trans.
Lydia Davis (Stanford, CA: Stanford University Press, 1995), p. 321.

13. [Translator's note]: The quotations are from Stéphane Mallarmé's famous prose
poem "Crise de vers."

during the revolutionary Terror? Blanchot had already evoked the Terror, Robespierre, Saint-Just; he had just said, I quote,

> It is the Terror and the revolution — not the war — that taught us this. The writer recognizes himself in the Revolution. It attracts him because it is the time during which literature becomes history [Same thing as Hugo, but the opposite, like death and life, comment].[14] Revolution is its truth [Revolution is the truth of literature]. Any writer who, by the very fact of writing, is not induced to think: I am the revolution, only freedom makes me write, is not really writing. (321).

Right after that, so as to illustrate, but with an irreplaceable example, this universal but also historical truth, Blanchot causes the figure of Sade during the Revolution to loom up, and you will see reappear, this time valorized, affirmed, even extolled, the motifs and the words of "sovereignty in death" (read also Bataille from this point of view), the words "cruelty" and "madness" and even, again valorized, reaffirmed, or even extolled — the very opposite of what Hugo and every abolitionist do[15] — the motif and word of "blood." I read. (Read *La part du feu*, 324)

> In 1793, there is a man who identifies himself completely with revolution and the Reign of Terror. He is an aristocrat fond of the battlements of his medieval castle, a tolerant man, rather shy and obsequiously polite: but he writes, all he does is write, and it does not matter that freedom lands him back in the Bastille from which it had plucked him, he is the one who understands freedom best, because he understands that it is a time when the most insane passions can turn into political realities, a time when they have the right to be seen, and are the law. He is also the man for whom death is the greatest passion and the ultimate platitude, who cuts off people's heads the way you cut a head of cabbage, with such indifference that nothing is more unreal than the death he inflicts, and yet no one is more acutely aware that death is sovereign, that freedom is death. Sade is the writer par excellence, he combines all the writer's contradictions. Alone: of all men he is the most alone, and yet at the same time a public figure and an important political personage; forever locked up and yet absolutely free, theoretician and symbol of absolute freedom. He writes a vast body of work, and that work exists for no one. Unknown: but what he represents has an immedi-

167

---

14. During the session, Derrida adds: "So, the writer loves revolution because, during revolution, literature becomes history. He says the same thing as Hugo, but the opposite, doesn't he! Namely, that the writer makes history, to the extent we have determined. He says the same thing, but he says the opposite, since Hugo says it on the side of life, and Blanchot on the side of death."

15. In the typescript: "does."

ate significance for everyone. He is nothing more than a writer, and he figures life raised to the level of passion, a passion become cruelty and madness. He turns the oddest, the most hidden, the most unreasonable kind of feeling into a universal affirmation, the reality of a public discourse, which when turned over to history, becomes a legitimate explanation of man's general condition. He is, finally, negation itself: his oeuvre is nothing but the work of negation, his experience the movement of a dogged negation, driven to blood, denying others, denying God, denying nature, and within this circle in which it turns endlessly, reveling in itself as absolute sovereignty. (321)

Although Blanchot does not praise the death penalty as such, the logic of his discourse on literature as right to death, even if one cannot consider it to be a thesis he argues for but above all an analysis of what literature is or of what it attempts to be, even if he basically analyzes literature's temptation as its truth (and moreover he uses the word "temptation," and the whole page I am now going to quote analyzes or describes an essential *temptation* of literature, a temptation that is constitutive of the project of writing literature — which can, thus, always leave Blanchot the option of saying that he is analyzing this temptation, describing it, stating it, thinking its essential movement without thoroughly giving into it himself, etc.; he is analyzing a temptation without necessarily subscribing to every aspect of it), the fact remains that the link between literature and the revolutionary Terror that condemns to death is clearly posed, and even if it is unwarranted to conclude that Maurice Blanchot is *for* a literature in solidarity with the death penalty, the tone and the movement of his text forbid concluding the contrary or saying that Blanchot is against the death penalty during this period, and that he has no sympathy or inclination toward this literary temptation that he describes so well. On this page, I would underscore, among other things, the sensitivity to the Theater of the Revolution as a theater of cruelty and as "Last Act," the words are his, as last judgment, both apocalyptic and eschatological, in sum. (Read and comment on *La part du feu*, 321–23)

> But there is another temptation.
> Let us recognize in the writer the movement that goes without pausing, and almost without transition, from nothing to everything. Let us see in him that negation which is not satisfied with the unreality in which it exists, because it wants to realize itself and can do so only by negating something real, more real than words, more true than the isolated individual at its disposal: it therefore keeps urging him toward a worldly life and a public existence in order to induce him to conceive how, even as he writes, he can become that very existence. It is at this point that he encounters those decisive moments in history when everything seems put in question, when

law, faith, the state, the world above, the world of the past—everything
sinks effortlessly, without work, into nothingness. The man knows that he
has not stepped out of history, but history is now the void, the void become
real; it is *absolute* freedom become event. Such periods are called Revolution. At that moment, freedom aspires to be realized in the *immediate* form
of the *everything* is possible, everything can be done. A fabulous moment,
from which the one who has experienced it can never completely recover,
since he has experienced history as his own history and his own freedom
as universal freedom. Fabulous moments indeed: in them, fable speaks;
in them the speech of fable becomes action. That they should tempt the
writer, nothing is more justified. Revolutionary action is in every respect
analogous to action as embodied in literature: the passage from nothing to
everything, the affirmation of the absolute as event, and of every event as
absolute. Revolutionary action explodes with the same force and the same
facility as the writer who has only to align a few words in order to change
the world. It also has the same demand for purity, and the certainty that
everything it does has absolute value, that it is not just any action in relation to some desirable and respectable end, but the ultimate end, the Last
Act. This last act is freedom, and the only choice left is between freedom
and nothing. That is why, at that point, the only tolerable slogan [*parole*]
is: freedom or death. Thus the Terror arises. No man is any longer an individual working at a specific task, acting here and only now: he is universal
freedom, which knows neither elsewhere nor tomorrow, neither work nor
oeuvre. In such moments, there is nothing left for anyone to do, because
everything is done. No one has the right to a private life any longer, everything is public, and the most guilty man is the suspect, the one who has a
secret, who keeps a thought, an intimacy to himself alone. And, finally, no
one has a right to his life any longer, to his actually separate and physically
distinct existence. This is the meaning of Terror. Every citizen has a right
to death, so to speak: death is not a sentence passed on him, it is the essence
of his right; he is not suppressed as guilty, but he needs death so that he can
proclaim himself a citizen, and it is in the disappearance of death that freedom causes him to be born. In this way, the French Revolution has a more
manifest meaning than all other revolutions. Death under the Terror is not
simply punishment for seditionaries, but, as the unavoidable, in some sense
desired lot of everyone, it appears to be the very operation of freedom in
free men. When the blade falls on Saint-Just and Robespierre, in some way
it touches no one. Robespierre's virtue, Saint-Just's severity are nothing but
their existence already suppressed, the anticipated presence of their death,
the decision to let freedom assert itself completely in them and, by virtue
of its universal character, negate in them the particular reality of their own
lives. Perhaps they did cause Terror to reign. But the Terror they embody
comes not from the death they inflict on others but from the death they
inflict on themselves. (319–20)

169

170   Whatever may be the originality of this post-Hegelian and post-Mallarmean discourse in 1948, it reproduces—across all the historical symptoms of the France of the period, which would deserve a long analysis—and without constituting an explicit thesis in favor of the death penalty, it reproduces, then, the argumentative core, the classic philosopheme of all the great right-wing philosophies that have favored the death penalty, such as the logical core of Kant's philosophy of right and of Hegelian philosophy. The dignity of man, his sovereignty, the sign that he accedes to universal right and rises above animality is that he rises above biological life, puts his life in play in the law, risks his life and thus affirms his sovereignty as subject or consciousness. A code of law that would refrain from inscribing the death penalty within it would not be a code of law; it would not be a human law, it would not be a law worthy of human dignity. It would not be a law. The very idea of law implies that something is worth more than life and that therefore life must not be sacred as such; it must be liable to be sacrificed for there to be law. And the idea of sacrifice is common as much to Kant, Hegel, as it is to Bataille and to this Blanchot, even when they are speaking of literature. Sacrifice is what raises, what raises itself above the egoism and the anxiety of individual life. Between law and death, between penal law and death penalty, there is a structural indissociability, a mutual, a priori dependence that is inscribed in the concept of law or right, human right, human law, as much as in the concept of death, of nonnatural death, thus of death as decided by a universal reason, a death that is given or that one gives oneself sovereignly. Right is both the right of literature and the right to death, as right to the death penalty.

In any case, it is striking to see this discourse on "Literature and the Right to Death" arise with so much force and authority, even originality, despite what it is reproducing, to see it arise exactly one century (1848–1948) after Hugo's vote for abolition, after and against Hugo's interpretation, which appears to be diametrically opposed, of literature and of writers in the service

171   of the right to life, of an inviolable right of human life that is one with the sacred right of writers who, sovereignly according to Hugo, can sometimes produce laws, destroy old laws and affirm the law above the law, above the law as law of death, as association between law and death, in the way Blanchot is thinking it, and especially above and against revolutionary Terror. This coincidence of dates is all the more remarkable in that 1948 is also the same year in which, in a humanist and confident style, an optimistic although cautious and calculating style, the Declaration of Human Rights in its turn proclaims the imprescriptible right to human life. It is certainly not a coincidence, even if the simultaneity in the same year may well be coincidental. It is indeed the simultaneity, the synchrony, the concurrence of two great discourses, of two great irreconcilable axiomatics (a humanism of the Enlightenment and its opposite) that divide and will continue for a long time to divide the world. And it is always around the idea of right, of human rights. For if one wants to sharpen the intention of Blanchot's text, and the singular, though frightening, terrifying, properly terrorizing beauty of its title, one must clearly understand that the right to death signifies the right to accede to death (to think it, to open oneself to it, to cross its limit) both by exposing oneself to losing it, or even by giving it to oneself [*en se la donnant*] (suicide) and by giving it [*en la donnant*] in putting to death or inflicting the death penalty. It is the right to kill oneself, to be killed, or to kill: to accede to death by exceeding natural life, biological or so-called animal life. Death is not natural. And this right that is the condition of literature, the condition in the sense of the element, the *situation* of literature, this right is not a right among others. It is both the right that gives birth to literature as such, but also the law that gives birth to the law itself. There is no law or right that would not be or imply a right to death. Literature is what would think this right of right, this right to right, and this revolutionary right poses the right to literature.

But I would be unjust, and I do not want to be unjust, I would be unjust if at this point I abandoned the reading and the terrible diagnosis aimed at or against this text, which is typical of the Blanchot of this period. To be sure, I believe this reading is correct and necessary (and one must endlessly recall the properly terrifying and sinister resonances and connotations of this terrorist, terrorizing thinking of literature, of this literature as Terror). But let us not in our turn go and make of this diagnosis or this interpretation a verdict beyond appeal. Let us not condemn it to death, to the death it demands. For in "Literature and the Right to Death" (which I invite you to reread closely and in all its rich complexity, beyond what I must take note of today), there is still something else, which could cause to tip over, all the way into its opposite, the analysis of this essence of literature as terror, by this writer [*littérateur*] of literaterror, as an originary temptation of literature. And these contrary motifs, to put it too hastily and very schematically, would be the following *three motifs*.

1. Literary language is contradictory, it is in contradiction: "Ordinary language is probably right, that is the price of tranquility. But literary language is made of uneasiness; it is also made of contradictions" (325).

2. Now, in the name and by virtue of these contradictions, death, the principle of death that we have just recognized, is also a principle of resurrection and salvation. Hence the figure, which is once more evangelical, of

172

Lazarus who in a certain way comes to cast a halo on the figures of Robes-pierre and Saint-Just. Lazarus was revived by Jesus (in the Gospel of John, 11:1–46, where moreover, we could find once again our precious bandages). When Jesus cried out in a loud voice: "'El'azar, come forth (*veni foras*)!' / The dead man came out, hands and feet tied by strips of cloth, / and his face surrounded with a shroud / Ieshoua' said to them: 'Untie him and let him go.'"[16] (All things considered, it's a little like what happens in *The Instant of My Death*, Blanchot's last book, where the narrator is condemned to death, almost executed, about to be shot, in fact already virtually shot and dead, he has already traversed life and death, the limit between life and death, when a miraculous Russian soldier [from the extreme left-wing Russian Revolution therefore] serving under the Nazis [from the extreme right-wing Nazi revolution, therefore, from the other totalitarianism] saves him and in a way revives him since he is already dead. *Veni foras*, he says to him, in effect: come out of there and save yourself). Well, in "Literature and the Right to Death," Blanchot twice refers in a very significant way to Lazarus as one whom literature or the Terror revives after having killed him or let him die. And here, the flower reappears in the place of the woman of a moment ago. (Read 329–30)

> Even if literature stopped there, it would have a strange and awkward task. But it does not stop there. It remembers the first name that would have been the murder Hegel speaks of. The "existant" was called out of its existence by the word, and became being. The *Lazarus, veni foras* summoned the dark, cadaverous reality from its primordial depths and, in exchange, gave it only the life of the mind. Language knows that its realm is day and not the intimacy of the unrevealed. . . .
>
> Whoever sees God dies. In speech what dies is what gives life to speech; speech is the life of that death; it is "the life that bears death and maintains itself in it." An admirable power. But something was there that is no longer there. Something has disappeared. How can I recover it, how can I turn around toward what exists *before*, if all my power consists of making it into what exists *after*? The language of literature is the search for this moment that precedes literature. Generally, it calls this moment existence; it wants the cat as it exists, the pebble in its *taking sides with the thing* [*son parti pris de chose*], not man in general, but this one, and in this one, what man rejects so as to say it, what is the foundation of speech and that speech excludes by speaking, the abyss, the Lazarus of the tomb and not Lazarus brought back to light again, the one who already smells bad, who is Evil, the lost Lazarus, and not the Lazarus saved and revived. *I say a flower!* But in the absence in which I mention it, through the oblivion to which I relegate the

16. *La Bible*, trans. André Chouraqui, p. 2087.

image it gives me, in the depths of this heavy word, itself looming up like an unknown thing, I passionately summon the darkness of this flower, of this perfume that passes through me and that I do not breathe in, this dust that fills me but that I do not see, this color that is trace and not light. How then can I hope to attain the thing I push away? My hope lies in the materiality of language, in the fact that words too are things, a nature, what is given to me and gives me more than I understand. A moment ago, the reality of words was an obstacle. Now, it is my only chance. (326–27)

174

3. Finally, let us not forget that, already in 1948, Blanchot speaks of dying only as an impossibility. The right to death always fails in the face of this impossibility. I refer you to all the passages that advance the affirmation, at least twice, of "death as the impossibility of dying." The phrase, the syntagm "the impossibility of dying," will return tirelessly, over a half century, in almost all Blanchot's works. Here you find it already: "And it [literature] is not death either, because it manifests existence without being, the existence that remains beneath existence, like an inexorable affirmation, without beginning or end, death as the impossibility of dying" (328); and the same affirmation is repeated eight pages later, this time in the first person, like the confession of one condemned to death who is never executed or pardoned: "As long as I live, I am a mortal man, but when I die, by ceasing to be a man, I also cease to be mortal, I am no longer capable of dying, and my impending death horrifies me because I see it as it is: no longer death but the impossibility of dying" (337).

Read what follows, the beautiful page on Kafka and the kabbalah, and finally the characteristic use of "without" (which I analyzed in the past)[17] in expressions such as "It [literature] expresses without expressing," or again "this death without death" that, in sum, defines the horizon without horizon of the responsibility without responsibility of the writer:

175

> The writer senses he is prey to an impersonal power that does not let him either live or die: the irresponsibility he cannot surmount becomes the translation of that death without death that awaits him at the edge of nothingness; literary immortality is the very movement by which the nausea of a survival that is not a survival, a death that puts an end to nothing, insinuates itself into the world, a world sapped by crude existence. (340)

Further on he will speak, within the same logic, of the *without* without contradiction, of a life that is not part of life, of a "derision of immortality,"

---

17. Jacques Derrida, "Pas" and "Survivre," in *Parages* (Paris: Galilée, 1986); *Parages*, ed. John P. Leavey, trans. John P. Leavey et al. (Stanford, CA: Stanford University Press, 2011).

of this "strange right" of literature that lives on ambiguity and responds and seduces by ambiguity ("nausea" and "ambiguity" are words of the period): "One of the ways it seduces us is by instilling the desire to clear it [ambiguity] up, a struggle that resembles the struggle against evil that Kafka talks about and that ends up in evil, 'like the struggle with women, which ends in bed'" (341). All of this signals clearly that literature, I quote, "is divided between these two slopes"; all of this also gives rise to a theory or a thinking of "resifting" [*ressassement*], of the "interminable resifting of words" (which I will leave you to analyze for yourselves) (332).

1848–1948. To conclude today, provisionally, I come back, then, to the declaration of September 15, 1848, a century before a Declaration of Human Rights that proclaims the right to life without abolishing the death penalty. I would like to read it so as to underscore the following features.

1. First of all, the surprise at the beginning of the session, the rhetorical skill of the orator who feigns surprise while making this question <of the death penalty> the first question on the agenda, but so as to indicate thereby *176* (and here the rhetoric is more than rhetoric) that it is the first question, the condition of conditions, the base and foundation of any constitution. One must begin, a constitution must begin by posing the inviolability of human life. But with the same blow, while surprising the constitutional representatives by posing this first question, strategically, like a strategist who catches the others out in their own game, in the game of their own belief, their credo, and their own presuppositions, namely, the right of property, Hugo poses the inviolability of human life as an *inalienable property*, as a right of property over one's own life, which is no less sacred than the inviolability of the domicile as right of property and thus the patrimonial right of the family; and this occurs in a movement that is once again a national-patriotic act which inscribes itself in the history of France, of France and this country here as responsible for universal civilization, for civilization, period. The abolition of the death penalty would be in this regard the first sign of civilization versus barbarity. I am now going to read and comment on these first paragraphs. (Read and comment on *Écrits* by Victor Hugo, 69)

> I regret that this question, perhaps the first among all questions, arrives in the middle of your deliberations almost without warning to surprise the unprepared speakers.
>
> As for me, I will say just a few words, but they will come from a deep and long-standing conviction.
>
> You have just consecrated the inviolability of the domicile; we are asking you to consecrate an even higher and holier inviolability, the inviolability of human life.

Gentlemen, a constitution, and especially a constitution made by France and for France, is necessarily a step forward in civilization. If it is not a step forward in civilization, it is nothing. (*Very good! Very good!*)

Well, think about it, what is the death penalty? The death penalty is the specific and eternal sign of barbarity. (*Stirring*) Everywhere the death penalty is generously doled out, barbarity is dominant; everywhere the death penalty is rare, civilization reigns. (*Loud stirring*) (75)

One of the many questions that will await us when we return to the modern universal declarations that pose the inviolability of the right to life of the human person is not only the link to the death penalty, but all the ruses and strategic complications which insist that, in the name of the same principle, especially Christian and almost always violent campaigns against the voluntary interruption of pregnancy and abortion in general, the "right-to-life" [*laissez-les-vivre*] movements come to be unleashed. It is always in the name of the right to life that these militants (most often Christians) claim to be fighting, and often violently; in the name of the right to life of the human person (with the consciousness of knowing what the human person is, when it begins, from what date of conception and gestation — and that is why I always insist on the fact that the right to life is always specified in law as right to human life, to the life of the human person). The fact that sociologically, statistically, historically, these militants are most often, notably in the United States, violent in their acts and speech, that they are in favor of the death penalty and think sometimes of killing abortion doctors, is but one of the signs we have to interrogate.

At the other end of life, if I can say that, at the moment not of birth but of death, there is also immense debate around the right to euthanasia, around the suffering, compassion, and/or the cruelty of the relation to the dying and around the determination of the state of death. I am merely citing and situating here these debates to which we will have to return (perhaps in the discussion next Wednesday).

2. Finally, in the second part of Hugo's speech on September 15, 1848, I would highlight what I propose to call the *teleo-theology* of the Revolution, namely, the conviction that there is historical progress to come. The abolition of the death penalty would be the last aim, the ineluctable telos, the irreversible movement of history, but of a history that is both made by men (and singularly by the virility of men [in *Politics of Friendship*, in a somewhat different context, I analyzed the profound virilism or androcentrism of Hugo's discourse][18] — *de viris illustribus* — by the illustrious men of French literature, as thinkers and writers of the French Revolution, as

18. Derrida, *Politics of Friendship*, pp. 263–69.

universal revolution in human rights) and guided by God, by divine provi-
dence. Consequently, this abolitionist discourse is a revolutionary theodicy,
a revolutionary Christian theodicy.

Read and comment on *Écrits*, 69–71.

177

Gentlemen, these facts are indisputable. The reduction of penal sentences
is a great and serious progress. The eighteenth century, and this is part of
its glory, abolished torture; the nineteenth century will abolish the death
penalty. (*Loud agreement. Yes! Yes!*)

You will not abolish it today, perhaps; but have no doubt that tomorrow you will abolish it, or your successors will abolish it. (*We will abolish
it!*—*Agitation*)

You write at the beginning of the preamble to your constitution: "In
the presence of God," and you would begin by robbing him, this God, of
the right that belongs only to him, the right of life and death. (*Very good!
Very good!*)

Gentlemen, there are three things that are God's and that do not belong to man: the irrevocable, the irreparable, the indissoluble. Woe to man
if he introduces them into his laws! (*Stirring*) soon or late <sic> they will
make society bend beneath their weight, they upset the necessary balance of
laws and customs, they deprive human justice of its proportions; and then it
comes to pass—think about this gentlemen—that law terrifies conscience.
(*Loud reaction*)

I came to this podium to say a single word to you, a decisive word in my
opinion; here it is. (*Listen! Listen!*)

After February, the people had a great idea: the day after the day on
which they burned down the throne, they wanted to burn down the scaffold. (*Very good!*—*Other voices: Very bad!*)

Those who were influencing the mind of the people were not then, I
regret it profoundly, equal to their great heart. (*On the left : very good!*) The
people were prevented from executing this sublime idea.

Well, in the first article of the constitution you are adopting, you have
just consecrated the people's first thought, you have overthrown the throne.
Now consecrate the other one, overthrow the scaffold. (*Applause on the left.
Protests on the right.*)

I vote for the pure, simple, and definitive abolition of the death penalty.
(75–76)

January 26, 2000[1]

While still knotting together the two guiding threads of *exception* and *cruelty*, we followed as carefully as possible, and as if on the threshold of our age, on this edge of what is becoming of the death penalty in the world, two texts that are as opposite, it would seem, as a speech by Hugo to the Constituent Assembly in September 1848 ("I vote for the pure, simple, and definitive abolition of the death penalty") and, one hundred years later, the same year as the last Declaration of Human Rights (so equivocal and silent on the death penalty, which is not simply the right to life), the powerful and powerfully ambiguous text by Blanchot "Literature and the Right to Death," constructed, like Hugo's speeches, on a reference to the Terror, here to Robespierre, Saint-Just, and Sade, but diametrically opposed to that of Hugo, of course, although contradictory in itself (we allowed for this deliberate contradiction) and more Christian (like Hugo's rhetoric and no doubt his thinking) than it appears, especially in the moment of the *veni foras* that Jesus says to Lazarus in the moment of the resurrection. We also underscored at the end of our session the Christian teleo-theological character of Hugo's interpretation of the history of humanity's progress toward the abolition of the death penalty, and his revolutionary theodicy as revolutionary Christian theodicy.

I do not intend to return to all of this and to the many detours that we were obliged to take. I remind you merely of the excursions we made in direction of the question of euthanasia and abortion, or even of contraception on the subject of the right to life (which is often invoked by the opponents of abortion or even of contraception who nevertheless are not always — far from it, if one may say that — opponents of the death penalty).

By way of anticipation, I note that when we later read Kant closely on the death penalty, when the time comes (and this will be necessary so as to

¹⁸⁰

---

1. The session began by a discussion with students.

recognize there what is certainly the purest ethico-juridico-rational formulation of the necessity of the death penalty and the most acute critique of
Beccaria, all that in the name of what Kant intends to demonstrate is the
categorical imperative of penal justice, namely that, according to talionic
law[2] [*jus talionis*], homicide — contrary to the law — must be punished by
death, since *homo noumenon* must raise himself above the *homo phaenomenon* who clings to life and to the motives of vital interest, to hypothetical
imperatives, etc. [Comment][3]),[4] well, when we later read Kant closely on
the death penalty, when the time comes, in passing we will find there some
strange assertions (notably in "The Doctrine of Right" in the *Metaphysics of
Morals*, part 2, section 1, remark E) concerning the case of what Kant calls
maternal infanticide (*infanticidium maternale*).

181　　Why is it that only maternal infanticide, along with homicide committed
in a duel, cannot or must not be punished by death? Maternal infanticide is
here understood as the putting to death of a child <born> out of wedlock
and it is meant to erase the shame of a maternity outside of marriage and
save, Kant says, the honor of the feminine sex. As in the case of the duel
(these are two ways of saving honor), this maternal infanticide is indeed a
homicide (*homicidium*), to be sure, it indeed puts to death a human being,
but it is nevertheless not a murder (*homicidium dolosum*): that is, a putting to
death, a killing that implies a wrong, some treachery (*dolos, dolus*), a crime of
malice, a malicious ruse, thus an evil [*un mal*], an evildoing [*une malignité*],
a cruelty in the sense of wanting-to-make-suffer. You recall that we began
to distinguish among cruelty as bloody violence, cruelty that spills blood
(*cruor*), cruelty as inflicted suffering that spills no blood, and cruelty as evildoing, as the will to make suffer for the sake of making suffer, as pleasure
taken in the suffering of another, in calculated suffering, in organized torture. Well, says Kant, such maternal infanticide, *homicidium* but not *homicidium dolosum*, must not be punished by death. One must not punish it by
death and apply the pure talionic law (*jus talionis*) to it not only because it

2. Derrida specifies, emphatically, "what *he* interprets as talionic law."

3. During the session, Derrida in fact adds the following commentary: "If one wants
to get beyond *homo phaenomenon*, the empirical attachment to life, one must raise oneself
by means of law above life and thus inscribe from the height of noumenal man the death
penalty in the law. This is a logic that we saw in Blanchot as well. There is no law without death penalty. That's it! The concept of law in itself would not be coherent without
a death penalty. One cannot think a code of law without death penalty. This is the logic
that runs from Kant to Blanchot in a certain way."

4. In the typescript, this parenthesis was closed above, after "the most acute critique
of Beccaria."

is a matter of saving sexual honor from an extramarital birth, but because the child born outside of marriage is born outside of the law (the law that is marriage, Kant says) and consequently also outside the protection of the law. And Kant has this extraordinary formulation:

> It [the child born outside of marriage and thus outside of law and thus outside the protection of the law] has, as it were, stolen into the commonwealth [*in das gemeine Wesen*] (like contraband merchandise [*wie verbotene Ware*]), so that the commonwealth can ignore its existence (since it was not right that it should have come to exist this way), and can therefore also ignore its annihilation [*eine Vernichtung*]; and no decree can remove the mother's shame when it becomes known that she gave birth without being married.[5]

This case, like the associated case of the duel, is very symptomatic of the logic that Kant puts to work or claims to see at work in the concept of law and penal law. Since the categorical imperative — that is, a pure imperative that, in its immanent and pure calculation free of any extrinsic calculation, of any hypothetical and phenomenal imperative of *homo phaenomenon* — must not take into account any interest, any empirical or sociopolitical end, since the categorical imperative of penal law is the talionic law, the equivalence of the crime and the punishment, thus of murder and the death penalty (we will later see how this works in Kant and why he criticizes Beccaria from this viewpoint), since, in addition, this civil penal law, that is, the law internal to the state, to the community as a commonwealth, implies that the crime, the criminal, and the victim are all subjects of the state, well, when a mother puts to death an illegitimate child that is not recognized by the state as a legal subject, in that case the act of putting to death is indeed a homicide but not a crime punishable by the law, and the state cannot, by punishing the mother, repair the damage or the shame. The victim is nothing and nobody, in a certain way. It is indeed a human being, and that is why there is *homicidium*, but this human being is not a citizen, not even the citizen of a foreign and enemy state, like a foreign soldier legitimately killed in combat by an act for which no soldier of my country will ever be punished, but sometimes on the contrary glorified. No, it is truly one of the two cases that undermines, but also perhaps lays bare, the legislation of the death penalty. And one must think about this example historically (it is not a matter only of abortion, which is still a supplementary dimen-

182

5. Immanuel Kant, *Die Metaphysik der Sitten*, in *Kant's Gesammelte Schriften*, vol. 6, ed. Preussischen Akademie der Wissenschaften (Berlin: G. Reimer, 1907), pp. 336 ff; "Doctrine of Right," in *The Metaphysics of Morals*, trans. and ed. Mary Gregor (Cambridge: Cambridge University Press, 1996), p. 109.

sion, and I don't know if Kant would have considered the embryo put to death to be a human person or its death a homicide): it was possible to put to death children already born. Even as he reasons firmly and steadily, Kant acknowledges some awkwardness and he does so at the beginning and the end of his argumentation—which concerns basically the impossibility or illegitimacy of dealing with homicides that do not affect legitimate citizens, or warriors who are citizens of other countries in wartime, but have to do with human beings who are killed to save honor. In the beginning Kant says that this double case (the duel and maternal infanticide) makes "doubtful" (*zweifelhaft*) the right of legislation to inflict the death penalty. And at the end, he goes further and declares that, in these two cases, justice is upset, it is put into great difficulty, an extreme confusion, a chaotic scramble (*ins Gedränge*). It finds itself caught up in an impossible double bind:[6]

A. *either* declare, in the name of the law, that the concept of honor (*Ehrbegriff*) is vain (but honor here, Kant says, is not an illusion or a whim <or> a mad folly, *Wahn*) and therefore punish with death (the infanticidal mother or the dueller), because honor is deemed, wrongly according to Kant, a vain illusion;

B. *or else* set aside the death penalty in the case of this homicide.

In the first case, the law would be too cruel (*grausam*: once again the question of the cruelty to be avoided), it would be excessively cruel in punishing the mother and the dueller who both wanted to save their honor.

In the second case, by shielding them from the death penalty, as Kant in bad conscience seems to want to do, it would be too "indulgent" (*nachsichtig*).

I call this a double bind because Kant himself sees there a knot (*Knoten*) to be untied. The solution of this knot (*Die Auflösung dieses Knotens*), says Kant, is that the categorical imperative of penal justice still remains (*der kategorische Imperative der Strafgerechtigkeit . . . bleibt*); and this categorical imperative of penal justice demands that any act of putting to death contrary to the law, the killing of another when it is contrary to the law (*die gesetzwidrige Tödtung eines Anderen*) must be punished by death; that is the absolute law, the categorical imperative, the principle that must remain (*bleiben*), and must remain always intact. But look, there are in fact times when legislation (*Gesetzgebung*), that is, in fact the civil constitution (*die bürgerliche Verfassung*) that conditions this legislation, remains barbaric and undeveloped (*barbarisch und unausgebildet*), that is, is responsible for or guilty of—this is its fault and its debt (*Schuld*)—the fact that incentives of honor in the people (*die Triebfedern der Ehre im Volk*) (subjectively [*subjectiv*]) are not

6. [Translator's note]: "Double bind" here and below in English in the original.

in accordance with the rules that conform objectively to their intention, to   *184*
their aim [*Absicht*], in such a way, concludes Kant, that at that particular
time, in that situation, the public justice arising from the state is an injustice
(*Ungerechtigkeit*) in relation to the justice emanating from the people (109).
In other words, there are times (and these times are empirical situations
even if they endure and are found everywhere) where the people obey subjective motives (for example, having children out of wedlock and having to
kill them, or else in a duel when, to retrieve his honor, an officer behaves,
like the infanticidal mother, in accord with the state of nature) [subjective
motives] that are in disagreement with the objective rules; well, this state
of fact or this state of nature, this residue of the state of nature translates a
lack of culture or a barbarity that is reflected in the disagreement between
the subjective and the objective, between the primitive desire or the state
of nature of the citizens and the law, with the result that the civil constitution which records or reflects this inadequation itself remains, to this extent
at least, barbaric or ignorant, still held back in the state of nature that it
should have surpassed. Hence the extraordinary rationality but also the stupid uselessness of this Kantian logic. If the categorical imperative — which
in any case remains (*bleibt*) — is one day to be in agreement with customs,
then culture, non-barbarity, and civilization are necessary, which is to say:
it would be necessary for women no longer to have children out of wedlock
and for there to be no more cause for dueling, for the sense of honor to be
respected in fact by morality; then the knot will be untied, there will be an
Auflösung dieses Knotens. In other words — and this is one of the great paradoxically interesting things about this Kantian position, which is as rigorous
as it is absurd — when the history of morality and of civil society will have
progressed to the point where there is no more discord between the subjective motives and the objective rules, then the categorical imperative that
presides over the death penalty will be fully coherent, with neither cruelty
nor indulgence, but of course, there will be no more need to sentence to
death. But while waiting for that to happen, in order to think the law, the
ideal and rational purity of the law, one must maintain the principle of the
categorical imperative, that is, the talionic law (a life for a life, a death for   *185*
a death) and inscribe the death penalty in the law, even if the ideal is to be
never obliged to pronounce it in a verdict. In any case, the possibility of
the death penalty, that is, of the law as what raises *homo noumenon* above
homo phaenomenon (above its empirical life), belongs to the structure of the
law. This logic implies that to seek to abolish the death penalty, as Beccaria
and so many others like Hugo sought, is to understand nothing about the
law and to put the attachment to phenomenal life above everything; it is to

understand nothing about what surpasses the value of life, and surpasses moreover all price (for the talionic law, at least as it is interpreted by Kant, does not set a price; it is not a commercial exchange; on the contrary, he places the categorical imperative beyond all exchange: no law will ever be founded on an unconditional love of life for its own sake, on the absolute refusal of any sacrifice of life).

I specify this point both in passing and with insistence so as to return in a moment to the question of literature that will continue to stay with us. I had suggested that there was nothing fortuitous in the fact that the cause of abolitionism has been linked in a visible and essential fashion to a certain time, a certain history, and even a certain essence of literature, finding even in the voice of certain writers who became its spokesmen more than an interpretation and various accents, finding there in truth an argumentation, a vital commitment, and an inspiration. Recall the texts by Hugo we read last week, and the whole history of "extenuating circumstances." But I hastened to add that the question remained ambiguous, as are *both* the cause of abolitionism in a certain form (and we began to undo, or even to deconstruct this ambiguity) *and* the cause of the death penalty, which can sometimes, in certain discourses, claim it is right, claim it is right in claiming to save both the dignity of man or what is proper to man and the "categorical imperative" of the law, and even — we got an idea of this, at least virtually, last week — the destiny of literature as right to death and as Terror. We have already said that if on one side there were Shelley, Hugo, and Camus and a few others who await us, there were also, on the other side, Wordsworth, that ambiguous text by Blanchot, etc., even Genet, for one cannot say that he condemns the death penalty when he sings of those condemned to death and recalls that they are the Christlike and fascinating heroes of prisoners, criminals, and evildoers. The death penalty can always, also, be reaffirmed and celebrated in the name of the literature and poetry linked to the possibility of evil, to the right to evil, to the right to death, to the right to death beyond life, to the Sadian tradition of cruelty that Blanchot spoke of, in short, to what might be called the flower of evil, the possibility of the poetic and of poetic blossoming that ties the tradition of the *Flowers of Evil* to *Our Lady of the Flowers,* evil being, in Baudelaire as much as in Genet, that which even in death (criminal death or death as punishment for the crime, the two being indissociable here) awakens to poetry and to literature, grants the right to literature, <both> defies a certain Christianity and confirms a certain Christianity, this contradiction within Christianity being the most constant law of all the discourses (all of them, without exception) we have analyzed and of those still awaiting us from both sides, from the two parties to this debate, if I can say that. It is in the name of a certain evangelical Christianity that the death penalty is condemned, a death penalty whose history is also linked, in the West, to the history of Christianity and the Christian church. I spoke of *evil*doers and the flowers of evil in order to introduce, in parentheses, a parenthesis of Baudelaire's — which I thank Jennifer Bajorek for having reminded me of last week — that comes to inscribe itself in the program, in a certain way, of the Kantian discourse that we have just glimpsed, namely, that the death penalty testifies to human dignity and the remarkable possibility that properly distinguishes man by allowing him to rise above life, and to do so by inscribing in his law the possibility of the death penalty, somewhat in the same way Blanchot says basically that law itself, the concept of law, presupposes death, as we heard, even if dying is impossible.

Well, what does Baudelaire say about the death penalty and abolitionism? And about Victor Hugo? One may, if one likes, consider that what I am going to read is one of Baudelaire's terrifying excesses or missteps, like that direct appeal for the extermination of the Jews that I previously quoted in this seminar and in *Given Time*, an appeal that had the intonation and used terms worthy of what this century would become famous for in the 1930s and '40s.[7] So, Baudelaire is in Belgium, and in the collection *Pauvre Belgique!* [*Poor Belgium!*] you can read these five sentences in parentheses whose essential philosophical argument, once extracted from the humorous and heated context and once reduced to its logical design, is that criticism of the death penalty, abolitionism in the name of the absolute right to life, is doubly guilty. (1) It signals a regression toward animality: to be attached to life for life's sake, to the right to life, is animalistic (and often in Baudelaire, this means feminine: the abolitionists, in sum, would be living beings who have a sickly sweet attachment to life like beasts or like women who place life above everything and fear death above all); and (2) the second way in which abolitionist discourse is guilty is, well, guilt itself, and here the suspicion takes on a Nietzschean cast: if these abolitionists are so compulsively passionate against the death penalty, Baudelaire clearly suggests, it is because they are afraid for their own skins, because they feel guilty and their tremulations are a confession; they confess, with the symptom of their abolitionism as it were, that they want to save their lives, that they tremble

187

7. Derrida is referring to his seminar at the École Normale Supérieure in 1977–78 titled "Donner le temps" and to the book *Donner le temps* (Paris: Galilée, 1991), pp. 166–67, n1; *Given Time: I. Counterfeit Money*, trans. Peggy Kamuf (Chicago: University of Chicago Press, 1992), p. 130, n14.

for themselves because at bottom, unconsciously, they feel guilty of a mortal sin, they want to save their skins. This latter polemical argument is, one must admit, quite strong. It links the juridical thematic of the death penalty to criminal drives that do not depend on being effectively carried out by passing into action (and, moreover, how many ways of killing can one count in our day-to-day, and night-to-night, lives that do not need to put anyone to death in a legal sense?). Who could deny that the fear of death or that the infinite protest against mortality and against one's own mortality, especially against what is held to be an unnatural death, is the mechanism driving all discourses on the right to life and the inviolable property of my life (we saw how Hugo put this mechanism of the proper in play in his speech to the Constituent Assembly — reminder?)?[8] How can one deny that abolitionist discourse is rooted in the evil of a finitude and of a fallible finitude? I want to abolish the death penalty because I am afraid of being condemned, afraid of dying but also because I know that <I> am always in the process of killing someone. I am sufficiently the victim and guilty of homicide to wish to be done with the death penalty, but this wish to be done with legal killing would testify, according to Baudelaire, to the fact that I am always calculating my salvation — as victim or guilty party, as guilty victim, and so forth. But what I want to note here about the parenthesis I am now going to read is, first of all, the dryness of the argumentation of a Kantian type: to make life for life's sake an inviolable principle, to fail to inscribe death in the law is unworthy of human dignity; it is a return to the state of nature and animality. Here then is what Baudelaire says at a time when the campaign for the abolition of the death penalty was spreading throughout Europe, when, in February 1865, a large abolitionist meeting was held in Milan, and when Hugo wrote letters to support the movement. Baudelaire's attack against Hugo, whom, as you will hear, he associates with Courbet, leads the editors of the Pléiade,[9] Crépet and Pichois, to say that, even though one cannot assert that Courbet was an abolitionist, in Baudelaire's view Hugo is the dominant figure in humanitarianism just as Courbet is in realism (I realize just now, returning to what I was saying about animal life, the right to life, and the woman, that Courbet painted the famous *Origin of the World*, a

8. During the session, Derrida added: "Hugo refers to it all the time, if you read the collection. What comes back all the time is the inviolability of the life of the human person. Life is what is proper to me, inviolable by definition. If one extends this logic to its limit, then even if you kill me, you cannot violate the properness or property of my life. It is as if the abolitionists were people who basically dreamed of eternity, who dreamed of remaining eternally the proprietors of their lives."

9. [Translator's note]: The authoritative edition of Baudelaire's complete works.

painting that shows both a woman's sex that is among the most realistic ever   *189*
done and the place of birth, of the right to life, and of the gift of life). Here
now is the passage, the parenthesis in question: Baudelaire has just, as always, dismissed back-to-back the clerical party and the revolutionary party,
the Belgian revolutionaries in particular who, he says, "believe every stupid
thing the French liberals throw out."[10] He then opens this parenthesis:

> (Abolition of the death penalty. Victor Hugo the dominant figure like
> Courbet . . .

[You see the scene, and the whole seminar that would be needed to comment
suitably on this sentence, to devote to the well-known relations, the so very
complex, filial, oedipal, and criminal relations, full of Baudelaire's admiration and resentment against father Hugo who dominates the media, Baudelaire speaking here as an avant-garde and censored poet might do today, one
who has been condemned, forbidden, and exiled in his turn—like Hugo,
moreover, although differently, Hugo who continues in spite of his exile
and from his exile to occupy and dominate the scene of the media, to defend
good causes and to get himself talked about in newspapers throughout the
world, and in the television studios of the period, with his right-thinking
eloquence, etc.[11] So as to understand Baudelaire's irritation and to illustrate
the situation, I read two letters from Hugo:

> To the President of the Liège meeting
>
> Hauteville-House, February 26, 1863
>
> Sir,
>
> Your letter of February 20 was delayed at sea and I received it only today.
> There is no longer enough time for me to attend your meeting on March 1.
> Please, therefore, convey to your friends my regrets and tell them how   *190*
> touched I am by their honorable invitation.
>   The abolition of the death penalty is from now on a certainty in civilized
> countries; human inviolability is the point of departure of all principles; the
> nineteenth century will have the honor of making this philosophical truth
> into a social reality and of having erased the bloodstain from the august
> forehead of civilization.

---

10. Charles Baudelaire, *Pauvre Belgique!* in *Œuvres complètes*, vol. 2 (Paris: Gallimard, Bibliothèque de la Pléiade, 1976), p. 899.

11. In the typescript, Derrida writes by hand after "etc.": "Read Hugo 212–13." We
transcribe here the two letters actually read out during the session, after which the text
of the typescript resumes.

Belgians, I wish you courage in your noble efforts; I am with you with all my heart.

I ask you, sir, to be my interpreter with the members of the Liège meeting, to whom I extend, as to yourself, my deep cordiality.

Then, another letter two weeks later:

To Van Lhoest, Editor-in-Chief, *La Gazette de Mons*

Hauteville-House, March 10, 1863.

Sir,

Your letter, which brings me such an eloquent appeal and the charming lines of your popular poet Mr. Clesse, is welcome.

Your goodwill exaggerates the part I have had, if any at all, in the magnificent movement of minds in favor of the abolition of the death penalty. When, as a humble servant of progress, I cried out: *Death to death!* I hoped for some small echo, but I found there was a large one, especially in Belgium, thanks to people's generosity; but it is the press, of which you are one of the megaphones, as well as people's assemblies like the one you are convening, that assure its success, and it is to them that it is owed.

After the meeting in Liège, the meeting in Mons, how wonderful; mobilization to bring down the scaffold is growing in Belgium, and will surely win over your parliament. It would be a supreme honor for the Belgian parliament to give the signal to other legislators and, in the presence of the applauding civilized world, to lay the first stone in the edifice of principles: the inviolability of human life.][12]

191   (Abolition of the death penalty. Victor Hugo is the dominant figure like Courbet. I am told that in Paris 30,000 petitioning for the abolition of the death penalty. That's 30,000 people who deserve it. You tremble, so you are already guilty. At least you are interested in the question. . . .

[This sentence, this "at least," is, precisely, very interesting. Moreover, in another fragment, a variant, Baudelaire had written: "Abolishers of the death penalty—very interested parties no doubt" (895). It means, once again in a very Nietzschean gesture, or even Freudian and symptomatologistic one, that the abolitionist passion must betray an interest; it must not be disinterested, and if the abolitionist is so interested, then necessarily [*fatalement*] it is in his interest; he is looking out for his interest: ruse of generosity or compassion for the other that as ruse of life or the animal signifies that a

---

12. Hugo, *Écrits sur la peine de mort*, pp. 212–13. The bracket closes the one opened above, p. 131 and concludes the addition made during the session.

beast is feeling threatened and guilty and is really only looking to save its life while pretending to save that of others; whereas on the contrary, in the logic of the categorical imperative of the penal law, in the Kantian sense whose logic is also at work since Baudelaire is going to speak in a moment of animality, it is in the name of absolute, endless disinterestedness that the death penalty is inscribed in the law. What would remain to be analyzed and psychoanalyzed here is the psychoanalyst or the Kantian or the neo-Kantian: an infinite circle of resentment in which the two postures or the two postulations can be interpreted as reactive movements of resentment. The defenders of the death penalty and the abolitionists would be waging a war of resentment against each other.]

I return to the parenthesis, which this time I will read to the end:

(Abolition of the death penalty. Victor Hugo is the dominant figure like Courbet. I am told that in Paris 30,000 are petitioning for the abolition of the death penalty. That's 30,000 people who deserve it. You tremble, so you are already guilty. At least you are interested in the question. The excessive love of life is a descent into animality.) (899) (Comment: *homo phaenomenon*, etc. . . .)[13]

192

This retrospective detour thus leads us back to this question of the "right to life" as it has been proclaimed from Hugo, who reaffirms or recalls, with the insistence you now recognize, the principle of "the inviolability of human life," up to the different declarations in our time, in particular the Declaration of Human Rights in 1948. If I wanted to quote Baudelaire, it is not, as you can well imagine, because I subscribe to what he says, quite the opposite, but because his mistrustful gesture strikes me as always and indefinitely necessary with respect to the hypocrisy and the symptomal ruses that conceal themselves, with respect to the concealment or the hypocrisy that animates and agitates the defenders of just causes Thus, before even returning to the ambiguity of Hugo's abolitionist rhetoric, I would like at least to begin to analyze the hypocrisy, the strategy of the double language that, on the subject of the death penalty, constructs or structures, in what is *here* an unconscious and symptomatic fashion and *there* a deliberately calculated fashion, the different well-intentioned declarations that I have already mentioned.

I recall first of all that the Eighth Amendment of the American Bill of Rights prohibits any "cruel and unusual punishment," which are terribly

---

13. During the session, Derrida comments: "Thus on the side of *homo phaenomenon* if one translates into Kantian terms."

vague words and notions, in consideration of which the Supreme Court caused all executions between 1972 and 1977 to be suspended, until one could claim to proceed with executions in agreement with this amendment; second, that the Universal Declaration of Human Rights (1948), after having mentioned in article 3 that "everyone has the right to life, liberty and the security of the person" (an article that I commented on the last time insisting on the word "person," I will not come back to this), affirms in article 7: "No one shall be subjected to torture or to cruel, inhuman or degrading treatment or punishment. In particular, no one shall be subjected without his free consent to medical or scientific experimentation" (qtd. in Schabas, 48).[14]

Now, given that in the interval between these two articles, article 3 and article 7, the one dealing with the right to life and the one on torture and "cruel and unusual punishment," one finds article 6 that allows for the death penalty, even if it sets conditions on it, as we will see, one has to conclude that, for the drafters and the signatory states of this declaration, it did not appear contradictory to make these two gestures simultaneously: *on the one hand*, to set down the right to life, to exclude torture and degrading punishments and, *on the other hand*, to allow for the legitimacy of the death penalty, even if one accompanied it with conditions, which moreover, as we will see, are not really conditions. In other words, in the internal and systematic logic of this declaration, it seems to go without saying that the death penalty, *on the one hand*, does not contradict the right to life and, *on the other*, in no way constitutes, as such, a cruel and degrading punishment.

I will now read and comment on article 6, that itself includes six sub-articles. (Read and comment on Schabas, 312)

ARTICLE 6

1. Every human being has the inherent right to life. This right shall be protected by law. No one shall be *arbitrarily* deprived of his life. [Arbitrarily. When it is not arbitrary, it is possible. "No one shall be arbitrarily deprived of his life."]

2. In countries which have not abolished the death penalty, sentence of death may be imposed only for the most serious crimes in accordance

14. Derrida mixes up here the International Covenant on Civil and Political Rights and the Universal Declaration of Human Rights. Article 3, which he has just quoted, is indeed from the declaration (which does not speak directly of the death penalty), but articles 6 and 7 on which he comments here come from the International Covenant. The latter was drafted between 1947 and 1954 and adopted by the General Assembly of the United Nations in 1966. We will signal in a note each time Derrida writes "declaration" in the place of "covenant."

with the law in force at the time of the commission of the crime and not
contrary to the provisions of the present Covenant and to the Convention on the Prevention and Punishment of the Crime of Genocide. This
penalty can only be carried out pursuant to a final judgement rendered
by a competent court.

3. When deprivation of life constitutes the crime of genocide, it is understood that nothing in this article shall authorize any State Party to the
   present Covenant to derogate in any way from any obligation assumed
   under the provisions of the Convention on the Prevention and Punishment of the Crime of Genocide.

4. Anyone sentenced to death shall have the right to seek pardon or commutation of the sentence. Amnesty, pardon or commutation of the sentence of death may be granted in all cases.

5. Sentence of death shall not be imposed for crimes committed by persons
   below eighteen years of age and shall not be carried out on pregnant
   women.

6. Nothing in this article shall be invoked to delay or to prevent the abolition of capital punishment by any State Party to the present Covenant.
   (Qtd. in Schabas, 380)

One must now further complicate the analysis of these texts and this
process, whether one is talking about the status of this declaration or the
procedural character, that is, the dynamic, evolving, and teleological character of these performative events.

As to the status of the declaration, as Schabas rightly notes with insistence, the Universal Declaration was not held to be a juridical instrument
or a written law or a treaty creating binding norms or binding obligations.
The states that signed and endorsed it did so, in a way in spirit, by moral
commitment, but if they did not uphold this commitment, they would not
be prosecuted under the law; they would not appear before an international
tribunal representing international law, before a penal court that not only
did not exist but had not even been projected at the time, as it has today.
Nevertheless, many jurists have since suggested that the declaration codi-
fied norms that, although they did not belong to the order of legislative
or constitutional law, were part of *customary* normativity in some way. Already, according to these jurists, it was customary law. The fact remains
that the drafters of the declaration were not thinking of such a customary
law because they were at work in a parallel manner on the elaboration of
another instrument, the project of a "covenant," an alliance, an agreement
whose aim was precisely to go beyond the declaration and create "bind-

195

ing obligations." In this respect, examining what are called the Working Group papers, to which Schabas pays a lot of attention, is quite revealing. We cannot read or analyze them here but you can do this for yourselves. The archive of these deliberations clearly shows that although there was no consensus that the declaration should take a position against the death penalty (too many states still opposed doing so), there was a consensus for considering that the death penalty be treated as an *exception* to the "right to life" and, at least in peacetime, as a "necessary evil." But the same papers also show clearly that article 3 (the right to life, to liberty, and to the security of the person) as well as the discussion of article 6 that we have just read brought out a widely shared conviction that all of this was aiming, for a time to come, at the final abolition of the death penalty. All of this was clearly going in the direction of a declaration that would explicitly recommend, one day, finally, the pure and simple abolition of the death penalty. It's just that this decision had not yet fully matured. It still has not done so, but after all, it has only been fifty years, an eternity for the dead, but a fraction of a thousandth of a second in the history of humanity. So the declaration of 1948 confirmed,[15] even as it still deferred things, the optimistic and teleological tendency that we recognized in Hugo. The abolitionist movement is irreversible and irresistible, however long it may take. An indication of this is the Second Optional [merely optional] Protocol to the International Covenant on Civil and Political Rights Aiming at the Abolition of the Death Penalty, which says clearly, without any possible equivocation (but under the heading of the optional) that "abolition of the death penalty contributes to enhancement of human dignity and progressive development of human rights," and again that it is a "progress in the enjoyment of the right to life" (qtd. in Schabas, 397).[16]

One should also note, so as to specify and illustrate these deliberations, that it was Eleanor Roosevelt — representing the United States; she played a large role in this whole affair — who opposed any reference to the death penalty in the declaration and was followed in this by the Soviet Union, France (<René> Cassin), Chile, and the United Kingdom.

In addition, the United States expressed reservations on the subject of the prohibition set on the execution for crimes committed before the age of eighteen. They accepted the prohibition of the execution of pregnant women, but not that concerning minors under age eighteen at the time of

196

---

15. In question here is the covenant and not the declaration.

16. This Second Optional Protocol was adopted by the the General Assembly of the United Nations in 1989.

the crime, and referring always to their own Constitution, the United States insisted on the necessity of interpreting the allusion to "cruel, inhuman or degrading treatment or punishment" in accordance with amendments 5, 8, and 14 of the US Bill of Rights. Which means, in short, that state sovereignty ought not to suffer from this declaration and that even the interpretation of what was meant by each article of the declaration[17] (for example, "cruel, inhuman or degrading") was left up to each country, taking into account its constitution, laws, and cultural norms. It must be noted that these American reservations provoked a general outcry and many European countries officially objected to them. For example, France, Belgium, Denmark, Finland, Germany, Italy, The Netherlands, Portugal, Spain, and Sweden.

197

Next time we will return once more to France and to Victor Hugo so as to attempt to clarify both this question of cruelty where it still has, but not only, the color of blood and the figure of the guillotine (the conjoined history, then, of red blood and the guillotine, but also the confluence of human blood and the blood of Christ's Passion, which should lead us into the great ambiguity of Christianity, within and beyond Hugo's exemplary text). It will also be the question, this time, not only of literature but also of philosophy, for we will wonder how Hugo's Christian reference, as fundamental as it is for his abolitionist discourse, can find agreement with the reference not to a historical right but to a natural one, how it can harmonize with a foundation in the principle of the inviolability of human life in natural law. We will begin no doubt with the letter that Hugo wrote, after the Commune, in 1871, to the attorney for the political prisoners who had been condemned to death, where he conveyed his agreement even as he specified this:

> The question that you see as a man of the law, I see as a philosopher. The problem that you elucidate perfectly, and with an eloquent logic, from the point of view of the written law, is illuminated for me in an even higher and more complete light by natural law. At a certain level, natural law cannot be distinguished from social law. (250)

17. This sentence is referring to the covenant and not the declaration.

February 2, 2000

(very slowly)

Today we are going to talk about the telephone.

We are going to talk on the telephone.

Hello, is that you? Hello, it's me, can you talk? Where are you? The way one asks today when using a cell phone. Where are you? Where are you calling from? That's the question. Where are you calling from? I'm on the road. Which road?

That's the question. Who calls from where? Who calls whom from the road, in this story, in what is a story, and on which road? Who asks if he can talk to whom?

When one does not want a seminar on the death penalty to be merely a seminar on the death penalty; when one would like to avoid its being just another discourse, and a discourse of good conscience, among people who, like us after all, will never be or believe they will never be executioners carrying out the sentence, or sentenced to death, or even the defense attorneys or prosecutors of those sentenced to death, or the governors or heads of state who wield the right of pardon, one must at least do everything one can to come as close as possible, in one's body, to those for whom the death penalty is the death penalty, effectively, in an effective way, concretely, undeniably, and cruelly threatening, in the absolute imminence of execution, and sometimes in the suspension of an imminence that can appear infinitely brief or last interminably (in the United States, this can go on, as in the case of Mumia Abu-Jamal, for up to eighteen years at least, eighteen years day after day and night after night). One must never stop thinking about this instant of execution, when there is no more beyond, or when the beyond remains the beyond, either the beyond of what awaits us after death, God or nothing, salvation or nothing, or the beyond from which the pardon [*grâce*] might still come, at the last second, the grace of the sovereign God or the sovereign pardon [*grâce*] of the governor to which the only link is the telephone line.[1] It's from the telephone that the life of the condemned one is today, but no doubt always has been, suspended.

It is of this telephone to the beyond that we are no doubt going to talk; it is on this telephone that we are going to talk and from which we will remain suspended, as we will each time that we attempt to think religion or the theologico-political apparatus of the death penalty. For example with Victor Hugo.

We return, then, once again to France and to Victor Hugo to attempt to specify both this question of cruelty where it still has, although no longer merely, the color of blood and the figure of the guillotine (the joint history, then, as I was saying the last time, of red blood and the guillotine, but also the confluence of human blood and the blood of Christ's Passion, which ought to lead us toward the great ambiguity of Christianity, in and beyond Hugo's exemplary text).

It will also be the question, this time, not only of literature but of philosophy. For we will ask ourselves how Hugo's Christian reference, as fundamental as it is for his abolitionist discourse, can be aligned with the reference to a law that is not historical but natural. How can this Christology harmonize with a grounding of the principle of the inviolability of human life in natural law, in a right to life that would claim to be natural, like the property of what we have that is most proper? Recall the letter that Hugo wrote, after the Commune, in 1871, to the attorney for the political prisoners condemned to death, in order to express his agreement, even as he spelled out the following—and here is the excerpt I read in conclusion last week:

> The question that you see as a man of law, I see as a philosopher. The problem that you elucidate perfectly, and with an eloquent logic, from the point of view of the written law, is illuminated for me in an even higher and more complete light by natural law. At a certain level, natural law cannot be distinguished from social law. (250)

201

We are going to make a big detour and take a long trip, today, before finally returning to this point of departure. How can Hugo ground his abolitionism in a natural law, an unwritten, non-positive, nonhistorical law— which cannot be distinguished from a social law—even as he constantly alleges all the same a kind of evangelical Christianity? Even as he points

---

1. [Translator's note]: In French, *grâce* is used both in the sense of divine grace and judicial or political pardon.

to the tortures of Christ? How can his permanent recourse to what he calls the inviolability of human life claim to ground itself both in a "natural" social law — natural, that is, ahistorical, unwritten, a law written only in the hearts of men and foreign to any historical revelation and, at the same time, then, in a Christian law? In other words, where does this law come from? From nature or from revelation? And let us not forget that the revelation in question is tied, in an essential way, to an incarnation and a sentencing to death of Jesus, which remains to be interpreted. How could an abolitionism ground itself on the example of a death sentence? And who, in the end, sentenced Jesus to death? The Jews? The Romans? Or God his father? How is one to organize this genealogical question, this genealogy of law? Of law in general, of penal law in particular, presuming that they can be distinguished here?

Starting from this, the reading we are going to attempt and the questions we are going to pose might, up to a certain point, be inscribed under the expanded sign of what Baudelaire calls, as you remember, *interest*.

What is an interest? The word itself is interesting, where it implies in Latin both the fact of finding oneself or of being in the middle, between, implicated in a space larger than oneself and, on the other hand, fiduciary calculation, surplus value, the search for a profit and a capitalization, in short, an economy — either monetary or psychological, the search for a greater well-being, for a greater good, one's own good or one's own well-being, an increase of enjoyment. What is an interest? What does it mean "to be interested," "to be interested in"?

Baudelaire speaks of the interest of the abolitionist discourse, that is, of what the abolitionists are interested in, of their unspoken or unspeakable motivations, motives they hide or hide from themselves behind the ethical, political, or juridical motives and principles that they advance. One does not need to subscribe to Baudelaire's theses or hypotheses to be interested in such interests, as in the interests and calculations, hidden or not, of the abolitionists and also of those who favor the death penalty.

The general question then becomes, who has an interest in what in this affair? Does one have the right to pose this question of *interest* or of fiduciary calculation when, on one side and the other, one claims to be looking in principle, and by principle, beyond calculation? Beyond all interest? To be sure, those in favor of the death penalty often put forward the argument of the deterrent example and thus the argument of a probabilistic calculation serving society's interests. But we have glimpsed and we will confirm still further based on Kant that the affirmation of the *principle* of the death *penalty*, as pure juridical rationality, of the *jus talionis* as "categori-

202

cal imperative" of penal justice, can be advanced without reference to the least phenomenal, empirical interest, for the body of society or the nation. As imperative of justice, it must even be detached from any interest of this kind. Conversely, or reciprocally, abolitionist discourse claims to be driven by a pure principle, by the concern with putting life above any other value, and human dignity above any market, any price (dignity is not a price, Kant himself said, and it is in the name of dignity (*Würde*), of the dignity of man that transcends price or the *Marktpreis* that both the Kantian proponents of the death penalty as well as the abolitionists speak.[2] Even when he speaks, with reference to the *jus talionis*, of moral compensation (*moralische Vergel-* *tung*), Kant does not introduce or claims not to introduce any phenomenal calculation, any arithmetic of penalties but only a pure equivalence between the absolute crime (*homicidium dolosum*) and the capital punishment, which deprives the murderer of the life of which he has deprived the victim. The *jus talionis* is not in principle, in law, a horrible vengeance, but the reference to an impersonal principle of reparative justice that, precisely, does not obey the subjective and egotistical and impassioned or impulse-driven interest of vengeance. No more than a tooth for a tooth, no more than an eye for an eye: this is the beginning of justice or right in talionic law).[3]   *203*

If we persisted in posing the question of interest in the two cases and to the two parties (abolitionist and anti-abolitionist), it would thus have the following form: what is the secret interest that drives these two discourses of absolute disinterest? What is the interest of these allegations of disinterest? And even—for you know that there is another resource in Kant, another concept of interest, what he calls an interest of pure reason that transcends empirical or pathological interest and has, by right, in principle, no relation with any phenomenal interest—so even, then, if we pressed our question to this point of radicality, what would be the unavowed interest behind *both* the alleged disinterest *and/or* the so-called pure interest of pure reason?

If I said that this is a Nietzschean-type question, it is because, as you know, one of the critiques of Kant by Nietzsche consists in rejecting the latter's allegation regarding the disinterested character of the experience of the beautiful. We are dealing here with a chiasmus since Nietzsche attacks Kant, attacks a Kantian-type gesture alleging the disinterest that supposedly raises itself above life, that supposedly sacrifices the living, whereas it is according to a Kantian logic that Baudelaire suspects the interest that motivates abolitionists concerned with the inviolability of life and of the

2. Kant, *The Metaphysics of Morals*, p. 105.
3. The closing parenthesis has been added.

right to human life. Let's leave this chiasmus there and return to Nietzsche for whom there is always an interest hidden beneath this alleged disinterest, in particular beneath aesthetic disinterest.

204   One could cite numerous texts of Nietzsche on this subject. I will refer you only to the Third Essay in the *Genealogy of Morals* because there he evokes, in the name of life, the law that produces a hostility to life, but a hostility to life that is also an interest *of* life, an overwhelming [*renversant*] interest of life. Speaking (in section 11 of the Third Essay) of the ascetic priest and of asceticism in general, Nietzsche describes what he calls a "necessity of the first order that again and again promotes the growth and prosperity of this [the ascetic's] *life-inimical* species (*diese* Lebensfeindliche *Spezies*)"[4] [Nietzsche underscores *Lebensfeindliche* because in question is a principle of death, in sum, a hostility to life, which is a movement that is both irreducibly necessary and immanent to life itself. It is life against life, life taking pleasure in life against life, counter-pleasuring in life (*contre-jouissant de la vie*). It is life that is hostile to life, that bears within itself this pathogenic or suicidal reactivity, this cruel violence toward itself, this self-flagellation, this self-punishment].[5] And continuing to underscore, Nietzsche adds:[6]

> It must indeed be in the *interest of life itself* that such a self-contradictory type [the ascetic] does not die out (*es muss wohl ein Interesse des Lebens selbst sein, dass ein solcher Typus des Selbstwiderspruchs nicht ausstirbt*; it must be an interest of life itself not to let perish such a type of self-contradiction, internal contradiction, contradiction turned against its own interest, against what is proper to it, in some way). (Ibid.)[7]

205   So hostility to life is inherent to life itself [*la vie même*], to the *itself* of life [*au* même *de la vie*], it is found right on life [*à même la vie*], and disinterest is still the symptom of a repressed interest. Nietzsche often uses the word

---

4. Friedrich Nietzsche, *Zur Genealogie der Moral*, in *Kritische Studien Ausgabe* (hereafter *KSA*), vol. 5 (Munich: Kritische Deutsche Taschenbuch Verlag, 1988), p. 363; *On the Genealogy of Morals,* trans. Walter Kaufmann and R. J. Hollingdale (New York: Vintage Books, 1989), p. 117; the closing quotation mark and parenthesis have been added.

5. The closing bracket has been added.

6. [Translator's note]: Derrida here announces "I quote first from a mediocre translation." The French translation in question is by Henri Albert, first published in 1900 and reissued in 1964 by Mercure de France.

7. During the session, Derrida here inserts the following commentary: "Such a type of self-contradiction cannot be allowed to die. Life has an interest in keeping the ascetic, where the ascetic or the ascetic type consists in contradicting itself, that is, of marking a life hostile to itself."

"repression," as you know. Since it would not be reasonable in the finite economy or strategy of this seminar to devote to Nietzsche all the room and the time that one nevertheless should, I will do no more than point you in *two directions*, still limiting myself to *The Genealogy of Morals*. These two intersecting directions would be those of *interest* and of *cruelty*, or even of the interest of cruelty, the interest in cruelty, *Grausamkeit*.

As for the notion and the word "interest," a little before what I have just quoted (in section 6 of the Third Essay), and still in order to attack Kant's discourse on disinterest and its legacy in Schopenhauer, Nietzsche contrasts Stendhal to them (he praises Stendhal everywhere, in particular in the preceding book *Beyond Good and Evil*, and in particular in the eighth part, section 254, a passage I choose because, although in it Nietzsche praises France as the "place of the most spiritual and sophisticated culture in Europe"[8] and although he recognizes in Henri Beyle an expert in *voluptate psychologica*, a "remarkable, anticipatory forerunner [who] ran with a Napoleonic tempo through *his* Europe, through several centuries of the European soul, as a pathfinder and discoverer of this soul. It took two generations to somehow *catch up* with him" (146), by contrast, at the beginning of the same passage, he sees a sign of France's decline into the stupidity and vulgarity of bourgeois democracy in the recent funeral of Victor Hugo during which, says Nietzsche, France indulged in "a veritable orgy of bad taste and vacuous self-satisfaction (*eine wahre Orgie des Ungeschmacks und zugleich der Selbstbewunderung gefeiert*)" (145; *KSA*, 198). Remember this motif of the festival; we will find it again elsewhere, when it is a question of a festival of cruelty, on the contrary). In section 6 of the Third Essay of the *Genealogy*, then, Nietzsche declares that in the famous Kantian definition of the beautiful, one detects a lack, the lack of a subtle self-experience (of a vigilant self-analysis, basically): *der Mangel an feinerer Selbst-Erfahrung*—and that this lack resembles a worm, a fat worm within the self, the fat worm of fundamental error. Recalling the animal is always essential, and for good reason, in these Nietzschean genealogies. What has the animal form of this fat worm of fundamental error (*Gestalt eines dicken Wurms von Grundirrtum*) is saying, as Kant does: "That is beautiful . . . which gives us pleasure *without interest* (*Schön ist, hat Kant gesagt, was* ohne interesse *gefällt*)" (104; *KSA*, 347). And Nietzsche exclaims: "Ohne Interesse!" "Without interest! Compare with this definition one framed by a genuine 'spectator' and artist (*ein wirklicher "Zu-*

206

8. Nietzsche, *Jenseits von Gut und Böse*, in *KSA*, vol. 5, p. 198; *Beyond Good and Evil: Prelude to a Philosophy of the Future*, ed. Rolf-Peter Horstmann and Judith Norman, trans. Judith Norman (Cambridge: Cambridge University Press, 2002), p. 145.

schauer": in quotation marks since, precisely, the artist is not an impotent or passive spectator; he takes pleasure)—Stendhal, who once called the beautiful *'une promesse de bonheur'*[9] [in French in Nietzsche's text; don't forget that the preceding essay, which concerns both debt and law, and punishment and cruelty—I am coming to that—begins with a kind of treatise on the promise]." The end of section 6 of the Third Essay takes up again Stendhal's formula but within a new development that would interest us more because it links the remark to the double motif of torture and sexuality. Nietzsche recalls that Schopenhauer insists on the "calming," soothing effect on the will (*Willenkalmierende*) of aesthetic feeling and of the beautiful. The beautiful would be, basically, an anesthetic, a sleeping pill, or rather a tranquilizer of the will. The aesthetic would be anesthetic. This is the point of view of the spectator to which Nietzsche opposes once again the point of view of the creative artist, and elsewhere the cruelty of the artist (*die Künstler-Grausamkeit*) and once again of Stendhal whose constitution is no less sensitive or sensual (*nicht weniger sinnliche*) but happier than Schopenhauer's, the Stendhal who said, precisely, that the beautiful promises happiness (this time in German: *das Schöne verspricht Glück*). For Stendhal, Nietzsche comments, what

207   counts is the "arousal of the will" "Erregung des Willens" (105; *KSA*, 349), that is, the complete opposite of insensitivity, anesthesia, or a tranquilized will. And at that point, Nietzsche reverses things: he accuses Schopenhauer of not having understood the true motive, true movement, and motivation of Kant whom he nevertheless claims to be following, the motivation hidden behind the motifs of disinterest that go well beyond the beautiful and that concern, basically, every categorical imperative (for the proper trait of a categorical imperative is to command beyond empirical or pathological interest in Kant's sense; and this should be true in particular of that categorical imperative of penal justice that, as we saw last week, the death penalty is, a death penalty that should then also be disinterested, according to Kant, pure of any calculation). So I was saying, at that point, Nietzsche reverses things. He accuses Schopenhauer of not having understood the true motive, true movement, and motivation of Kant whom he claims to be following, the motivation hidden behind the motifs of disinterest, namely that Kant does finally have an interest behind the alleged disinterest and it is "the greatest and most personal interest (*allerpersönlichsten Interesse*)," "that of a tortured man who gains release from his torture (*Interesse . . . des Torturierten, der von seiner Tortur loskommt*)" (105–6; *KSA*, 349).

Nietzsche's conclusion: the ascetic ideal that inspires Kant and Scho-

9. [Translator's note]: A promise of happiness.

penhauer consists in this: *von ein Tortur loskommen*, gaining release from torture. If one transposes this logic of an always hidden "personal" interest onto alleged disinterest, if one transposes this interested disinterest from aesthetics to penal law, one meets up again, down to the words themselves, with Baudelaire's denunciation, but this time turned back against a proponent of the death penalty as categorical imperative. In other words, the same argument, the same objection (your disinterest, your nobility of soul, your loftiness, your ethical pretension is a mask, the mask of an actor who hides interested calculation), this same unmasking of a masquerade can concern the Hugolian abolitionist for Baudelaire just as much as the Kantian or *208* Schopenhauerian "mortalist" (as one sometimes says, I believe in the juridical code) for Nietzsche. Just as much as the abolitionist, the proponents of the death penalty as categorical imperative are afraid for themselves; they seek to gain release from a sentencing or a threat of a verdict—and from the torture that this threat constitutes.

It would be necessary to link this filiation, this misunderstanding in the Kantian filiation of Schopenhauer and of his disinterested asceticism, to a theory of music that I would have liked to gloss, if I had the time, according to two motifs: *sovereignty* and the *telephone*. Sovereignty, which we are insisting on here for the reasons you know and that I will not recall; the telephone because there is a figure here of what I will call the technics of transcendence, and, what is more, the technics of this teleferic relation to the sovereignty of the absent other, of the absent God—we would find an illustration of this in the telephonic apparatus that, in the United States, links until the last moment the one sentenced to death whose execution is imminent, or even already under way, at the stage of the anesthetizing injection, that links, then, the place of execution to the mouth and the ear of the sovereign governor, keeping it in tele-technic relation with the transcendent place of sovereignty, with the governor who holds the quasi-divine power of pardoning. Well, what does Nietzsche say about the sovereignty of music and the telephone apropos of Schopenhauer and then Wagner?

It is at the end of section 5 of the Third Essay of *The Genealogy of Morals*. Linking the ascetic ideal of disinterest to Wagner and then, or first of all, to Schopenhauer, he sees in the ascetic ideal a decisive influence of Kant on Schopenhauer and of Schopenhauer on Wagner when the latter, Wagner, changed in some sense his concept, his interpretation, his strategy of music. Up until then music was for Wagner a means, a medium, a "woman" Nietzsche even notes in quotation marks (*ein "Weib"*), a woman who, to be fruitful, increase, bear children, needed a goal, namely, a man, that is to say, she needed drama. Following Schopenhauer, Wagner then understood that

there were better things to do in *majorem musicae gloriam*, namely with "die
Souveränität der Musik" (sovereignty is underlined by Nietzsche, who thus
clearly signals that it is the divine omnipotence of music that governs this
conversion). The sovereignty of music is then related, like all sovereignty, to
the absolute power of the will, to the will as all powerful, to the sovereign essence, in short, of what is called the will (and this pure, absolute voluntarism
is also a Kantian legacy): pure will, sovereign music as pure will, not as a
representation or reflection of phenomena, an imitation of the phenomenality of phenomena (*Abbilder der Phänomenalität*), but as language of the will
(*Sprache* des *Willens*; Nietzsche underlines the "of," *des*: it is the language
of the will, subjective genitive, it is the will itself speaking of itself, music,
music speaking music to itself, that is its sovereignty). And you are going
to see how, moving from this language of music as language of the will to
the language of metaphysics, all of this speaking, in short, the same language, one moves from this sovereignty of willing to the telephone with the
transcendence of the absolute sovereign, the telephone call exchanged with
God, with the beyond, through the musician who is also an oracle, a priest,
a mouthpiece for the in-itself of things, a ventriloquist of God (*Bauchredner
Gottes*) who, on the telephone, "speaks metaphysics" (*er redete Metaphysik*,
speaks in metaphysics, speaks the language of metaphysics, speaks in the
language of metaphysics, *er redete Metaphysik*), and this metaphysical idiom
is a telephonic language, the telephonic language of the ascesis that rises
above sensible or sensual touch — or at least subtilizes it, by a ruse, to the
point of giving it back to itself [*se le rendre*] by telephone, to the point of
bringing [*se rendre*] the distant close to oneself, and the mediate immediate,
and the transcendent immanent by the grace of the telephone, of a telephone
that is the language of music, and of God speaking himself to himself, at
will. If the ascetic's ideal is deprived or deprives itself of the enjoyment of
the senses and the body, he still has the ability to take pleasure [*jouir*] on the
telephone, while speaking with God, with the sovereign beyond, with the
other sovereign, with the other as sovereign, in the language of metaphysics, by harmonizing himself with the language of metaphysics, by according
himself the language of metaphysics, of the metaphysics of the will on the
telephone, and at will.

As if the telephone then became portable and cellular.

Telephony is metaphysics; it is religious, sacrificial, asceticism itself, the
priesthood itself. But obviously, this ascetic renunciation renounces nothing;
it is yet another ruse of the ascetic in order to take pleasure; it is the pleasure
of the priest, who knows what he is talking about and how abstinence causes
desire to grow and intensify and sharpen, the pleasure of desire, enjoyment

[*jouissance*] as enjoyment right on [*à même*] desire. I read these few lines (section 5 of the Third Essay):

> He [Wagner] grasped all at once that with the Schopenhauerian theory and innovation *more* [mehr: underlined] could be done in *majorem musicae gloriam* [this more, don't forget, will be sovereignty on the telephone and at will in place of music as woman]—namely, with the theory of the *sovereignty* of music [*nämlich mit der* Souveränität *der Musik*: sovereignty underlined] as Schopenhauer conceived it: music set apart from all the other arts, the independent art as such (*die Unabhängige Kunst an sich*), *not* offering images (*Abbilder*) of phenomenality as the other arts did, but speaking rather the language of the will itself (*vielmehr die Sprache* des *Willens selbst redend*), directly out of the "abyss" (*unmittelbar aus dem "Abgrundes" heraus*) as its most authentic (*eigenste*), elemental (*ursprunglischste*), nonderivative revelation. With this extraordinary rise in the value of music which appeared to follow from Schopenhauer's philosophy, the value of *the musician* himself all at once went up in an unheard-of manner, too; from now on he became an oracle, a priest, indeed more than priest, a kind of mouthpiece of the "in-itself" [or of the essence] of things (*eine Art Mündstück des "An-sich" der Dinge*), a telephone from the beyond (*ein Telephon des Jenseits*)—henceforth he uttered not only music, this ventriloquist of God—he uttered metaphysics: no wonder he one day finally uttered *ascetic ideals.* (103; *KSA*, 346)

You notice that I am interpreting here texts of Nietzsche that are not concerned directly with and do not literally mention the death penalty, but that unmask an all-powerful interest hidden behind the discourse of disinterest of the Kantian type, which elsewhere, as we had begun to see, conditions the legal doctrine of the death penalty. What authorizes me to do this—besides the inseparable couple of interest and disinterest, the interest *in* disinterest, the interest taken in disinterest, the interest *of* disinterest—is the allusion to torture and punishment, and thus, I am coming to it now, to a logic of cruelty (torture, punishment), of the relations between the cruelty of life and the law, a logic that, as you know, governs in particular the whole preceding essay, the Second Essay in *The Genealogy of Morals*, on wrong or guilt (*Schuld*), bad conscience, and what resembles them. I invite you to reread everything that concerns the promise, memory, responsibility (*Verantwortlichkeit*), and especially the origin of the right to vengeance, punishment, penal law.

Since our question for the moment is also, what is cruelty? one sees unfold there a philosophy of cruelty, the philosophy of a cruelty that, in sum, has no contrary. There are to be sure differences among several modes or different degrees of intensity of cruelty, between an active cruelty and a reactive cruelty, but there is no opposition between cruelty and non-cruelty.

211

As a result, in this logic of the differential of cruelty rather than of the opposition between cruelty and non-cruelty, there is no true, original place
for a debate for or against the death penalty. Both postulations can find inspiration in Nietzsche's discourse. Life is — it owes it to itself to be — cruel
wherever it keeps itself, wherever it keeps the memory and even, I will add,
the truth of itself. This means, it seems to me, that in these pages where, as
you will hear, it is a question of torture, torment, terrible punishments, the
question of the death penalty does not have an original place; it is named
only once in a series of tortures or spectacles of cruelty. From these pages
can be drawn, equally well and as one wishes, an abolitionist doctrine or its
contrary. The death penalty, I repeat, has no originality; putting to death is
a degree of torture and a strategy in cruelty, which requires one to interpret
it in a non-juridical fashion, as it were, since this whole essay and this whole
book are genealogies of law and of penal law that go back to movements of
animal-human life that are prehistoric or in any case anterior to law, older
and more profound, more irreducible than law itself and always ready to
leave undeniable symptoms in the law itself. The cruelty of putting to death
is not a matter for law. And finally — here is the passage at which I wanted
to arrive, after a few preliminaries — Nietzsche is going to accuse Kant and
the categorical imperative of cruelty (*Grausamkeit*), a cruelty that does not
speak its name, a hypocritical cruelty that gives itself airs of keeping its
hands clean [*de n'y pas toucher*], a cruelty (I will insist on this before pick-
ing up again the trace of red blood in Hugo) that has the odor of blood and
torture, on a ground soaked in blood. In the same movement, Nietzsche
is going to name the pleasure taken from causing suffering. Beginning in
section 3 of this Second Essay, Nietzsche links the question of memory to
that of suffering. And, as with the telephone, the technical dimension is not
absent, it <is> even named. The question is: how to make a memory for the
man-animal (*Menschen-Tiere*) — and Nietzsche's point of departure consists
in not dissociating, not forgetting the beast in man — how to make him remember. A very old problem (*Uralte Problem*), Nietzsche notes, that has not
received very gentle, very mild (*Zarten*) answers. Nothing is more terrifying
and *unheimlich* in the prehistory of man than his *mnemotechnics*. (Nietzsche
underlines this word, *Mnemoteknik*, in order to underscore that archiviza-
tion and recollection engage the suffering body in a machine, in a technical
repetition.) It is thus indeed a history or rather a prehistory of cruelty: to
remember, to imprint the memory, one causes suffering, one must cause suffering; here is where the red appears, the red of fire before the red of blood:
a thing is applied with a red-hot iron to imprint it on the memory (and this
whole text is written according to the figure of impression, of the painful
inscription in the body: "Mann brennt etwas ein, damit es im Gedächtnis

212

bleibt," something is burned, something is made red hot by penetrating un-   *213*
til it draws blood so that it remains in memory). And Nietzsche specifies
what is then the universal law that he wants to recall here, the law that links
memory to pain, wound, trauma: "only that which never ceases to *hurt* stays
in the memory (*nur was nicht aufhört*, wehzutun, *bleibt im Gedächtnis* — and
Nietzsche underlines *wehzutun*)" (61; *KSA*, 295).

It is an entire reading of history and culture, of law and religion, that
Nietzsche submits to this natural and zoological principle of cruelty, of the
causing-to-hurt, causing-to-suffer so as to remember. With the result that
punishment is not first of all a juridical apparatus; it is a movement of life,
a writing of life so as to remember, to inscribe, imprint the past in its body.

Nietzsche goes so far as to say that wherever there is some gravity in the
life of men and peoples (for obviously this is also a biopsychology and a bio-
politics of peoples), wherever there is solemnity, celebration, festival in short
(*Feierlichkeit*: and I insist on this once more because the motif of the cruel
festival, of the theater of cruelty that is deployed during the tortures of punishment is at the heart of this essay, the festival as a serious thing, the most
serious thing there is; the values of *Ernst* and of *Feierlichkeit* go together:
one doesn't laugh at the festival, one isn't having fun [*on n'est pas à la fête*];
one suffers and causes suffering in order to take pleasure [*jouir*]), wherever
there is some solemn, ritual feast, wherever there is some secret or mystery (*Geheimnis*), well, there then remains or comes back (*nachwirkt*, says
Nietzsche underlining aftereffect, remainder effect) a remainder of the fear
(*Schrecklichkeit*) that formerly presided over all the acts of memory, promises, engagements, oaths. And in the passage I am going to read, you will see
all religions in general defined as systems of cruelty, *Systeme der Grausamkeit*, with the result that cruelty is no longer just one part among others of
the mechanism of psychobiology; it is the essence of life, insofar as it keeps
itself, insofar as, at the same time, it protects and keeps itself in memory in
its truth; and it can, of course, in sacrifice and death, lose itself in order to   *214*
keep itself. Life knows how to make itself suffer in order to keep itself, and
to keep itself from forgetting, to keep itself in memory. For all of this is, of
course, an interpretation of sacrificiality. (Read Second Essay, pp. 70–72 C)

> One might even say that wherever on earth solemnity, seriousness, mystery,
> and gloomy coloring still distinguish the life of man and a people, there *re-
> mains* something of the terror that formerly attended all promises, pledges,
> and vows on earth: the past, the longest, deepest, and sternest past, breathes
> upon us and rises up in us whenever we become "serious." Man could never
> do without blood, torture, and sacrifices when he felt the need to create a
> memory for himself; the most dreadful sacrifices and pledges (sacrifices of
> the first-born among them), the most hideous mutilations (castration, for

example), the cruelest rites of all the religious cults (and all religions are at the deepest level systems of cruelties) — all this has its origin in the instinct that realized that pain is the most powerful aid to mnemotechnics.

In a certain sense, the whole of asceticism belongs here: a few ideas are to be rendered inextinguishable, ever-present, unforgettable, "fixed," with the aim of hypnotizing the entire nervous and intellectual system with these "fixed ideas" — and ascetic procedures and modes of life are means of freeing these ideas from the competition of all other ideas, so as to make them "unforgettable." The worse man's memory has been, the more fearful has been the appearance of his customs; the severity of the penal code provides an especially significant measure of the degree of effort needed to overcome forgetfulness and to impose a few primitive demands of social existence as *present realities* upon these slaves of momentary affect and desire.

215
We Germans certainly do not regard ourselves as a particularly cruel and hardhearted people, still less as a particularly frivolous one, living only for the day; but one has only to look at our former codes of punishments to understand what effort it costs on this earth to breed a "nation of thinkers" (which is to say, *the* nation in Europe in which one still finds today the maximum of trust, seriousness, lack of taste, and matter-of-factness — and with these qualities one has the right to breed every kind of European mandarin). These Germans have employed fearful means to acquire a memory, so as to master their basic mob-instinct and its brutal coarseness. Consider the old German punishments; for example, stoning (the sagas already have millstones drop on the head of the guilty), breaking on the wheel (the most characteristic invention and specialty of the German genius in the realm of punishment!), piercing with stakes, tearing apart or trampling by horses ("quartering"), boiling of the criminal in oil or wine (still employed in the fourteenth and fifteenth centuries), the popular flaying alive ("cutting straps"), cutting flesh from the chest, and also the practice of smearing the wrongdoer with honey and leaving him in the blazing sun for flies. With the aid of such images and procedures one finally remembers five or six "I will not's," in regard to which one had given one's *promise* so as to participate in the advantages of society — and it was indeed with the aid of this kind of memory that one at last came "to reason"! Ah, reason, seriousness, mastery over the affects, the whole somber thing called reflection, all these prerogatives and showpieces of man: how dearly they have been bought! How much blood and cruelty lie at the bottom of all "good things"! (61–62)

All of this is, as always with Nietzsche, highly interesting. Interesting as the interest there always is in thinking about interest. The complication and the interest of the Nietzschean gesture, an interest that one can take in it even if one does not subscribe to his utterances or his conclusions, what makes Nietzsche so *interesting* (as he himself says, at the opening of *The*

Genealogy of Morals, that the English psychologists to whom he is indebted, to whom he wants to say "thank you"—do not forget this recognition of debt—are themselves interesting [*sie selbst sind interessant!*] and they are interesting because they are preoccupied with making apparent the "shameful part" of our internal world ["partie honteuse"[10] in French in the text to play on the figure and the sexual origin of this shame]) (24), what makes Nietzsche interesting, then, like the English psychologists to whom he is indebted and whom he thanks, whom he pays back with interest, what makes Nietzsche interesting there where he is interested, whether or not one agrees with what he says, is that he suspects and sniffs out the *partie honteuse*, the modestly hidden or negated interest, both in those who advocate interest and in those who allege disinterest, and among the latter both in the abolitionists and in the anti-abolitionists, for example in Kant, who attempts to raise the categorical imperative of the death penalty above the calculation of interest but in the name of another rationally and morally pure calculation, the principle of equivalence, the *jus talionis* between the crime and the punishment, between the injury and the price to be paid.

Nietzsche deems this idea of *equivalence* at once mad, unbelievable, inadmissible, and he wants to retrace its genealogy. In the course of the long and insistent geneses of punishment that he proposes and to which I must refer you, he comes back first to a psychology of primitive humanity that he claims has survived in us moderns. It is to this archeology of law and of the law of punishment that Nietzsche devotes himself, obviously. During the longest period of human history, one did not punish because one held the wrongdoer to be responsible (*verantwortlich*, section 4, 2 [64; *KSA*, 298]), one did not acknowledge that only the guilty one should be punished. In this primitive humanity, which survives in us, one punished the way one punishes children when driven by anger. But at a given moment this anger comes to be contained within certain limits; it comes to be repressed and modified by the idea that every injury has its equivalent (*Äquivalent*), and that it can be compensated in a calculable fashion (*abgezahlt werden könne*), be it through some pain that would affect the author of the injury. Nietzsche's archeo-genealogical question, which is in short the question of the origin of law, and of penal law, as origin of a calculation, a rule of calculation, Nietzsche's question is then: whence comes this bizarre, bizarre idea, this ancient, archaic (*uralte*) idea, this so very deeply rooted, perhaps indestructible idea, of a possible equivalence between injury and pain (*Schaden und Schmerz*)? Whence comes this strange hypothesis or presumption of

216

217

10. [Translator's note]: A dated expression for the genitalia.

an equivalence between two such incommensurable things? What can a wrong and a suffering have in common? Obviously Nietzsche's very legitimate question is that these are things of such heterogeneous quality that there cannot be, there should not be, any possible equivalence, any common measure between a wrong or an injury, on the one hand, and on the other, the suffering inflicted by a punishment. Nietzsche's response consists then in seeking the origin of this unbelievable equivalence, this unbelievable *jus talionis*, in which it is not possible to believe, to which it is not possible to grant the least credit, to seek the origin of this unbelievable and uncreditable equivalence and to find it in, precisely, credit, in commerce, exchange, sale, trafficking, and so forth. The origin of the legal subject, and notably of penal law, is commercial law; it is the law of commerce, debt, the market, the exchange between things, bodies, and monetary signs, with their general equivalent and their surplus value, their interest. This would mean, in sum, that what *makes us believe*, credulous as we are, what makes us believe in an equivalence between crime and punishment, at bottom, is belief itself; it is the fiduciary phenomenon of credit or faith (*Glauben*). The origin of the belief in equivalence, that is, in penal law, the origin of our belief in penal law, the origin of the credit we grant it or that in truth we believe we must grant it, is belief itself. It is because we believe (always in a dogmatic fashion, always in a credulous fashion); it is because we grant credit that we believe in some equivalence between crime and punishment. But this belief does not consist only in believing in what we believe to be or to be true, but in believing by posing, performatively, by inventing an equivalence that does not exist, that has never existed, and that will never exist between crime

218 and punishment, a convenient equivalence but a fictive one in short, which allows us both to believe and to exchange signs and things, signs and affects (elsewhere Nietzsche speaks of a semiotics of affects), which allows us to speak, to exchange things, words, signs, to commerce, in short, to engage in commerce, to contract loans and debts.

Nietzsche's astonishment is at its core very healthy and very trivial, very vital. Whom will one ever make believe, seriously, in what precisely we believe or pretend to believe, whom will one ever make believe what we affect to believe, namely that there exists some sort of common measure, some homogeneity, some homology, some common value, some equivalence, for example, between murder and the death penalty (but Nietzsche doesn't take this example; he speaks of punishment in general)? Whom will one ever make believe, seriously, in what we believe or feign to believe, in what we claim to believe, namely, that there exists some common measure between a homicide and the death of the criminal, between the presumed murder and the execution of the criminal, and that the one can measure up to the other, that the one can take the place of the other, that the one can surrender itself in place of the other, substitute for the other as its equivalent? At bottom, no one believes <it> or has ever believed it seriously. No one can believe in the very thing one pretends to believe and pretends to credit. The caustic force of the Nietzschean genealogy consists finally in saying something like this: at bottom, we do not believe; we do not believe even in what we believe or say we believe; we do not believe in what we pretend and affect to believe or to credit in order to make the market possible, to make commerce, contract, exchange, and finally language possible and thus a social contract, a law that is always first of all commercial law.

By pushing this logic as far as the example of the death penalty, which Nietzsche does not talk about directly or only very little, in this context where it is a question only of punishment in general, legal subjects, and penal law in general, [by pushing this logic as far as the example of the death penalty, then], we would say that the death penalty is an article of law or an article of faith of commercial law, the market, trafficking, what Nietzsche will call *Kauf, Verkauf, Tausch, Handel und Wandel.* 219

Nietzsche wonders, at the end of section 4 of the Second Essay:

> And whence did this . . . idea draw its power (*Macht*) — this idea of an equivalence between injury and pain (*die Idee einer Äquivalenz von Schaden und Schmerz*)? I have already divulged it: [it has drawn its power] in the contractual relationship (*in dem Vertrags-verhältnis*) between *creditor* and *debtor* (*Gläubiger und Schuldner*), which is as old as the idea of "legal subjects" (*Rechtssubjekte*) and in turn points back to the fundamental forms of buying, selling, barter, trade, and traffic (*Kauf, Verkauf, Tausch, Handel und Wandel*). (63)

What must be properly and well *analyzed* — I say *well analyzed* because it's a matter of analysis and thus of internal dissociation, element by element — what must be well analyzed in this logic of the Nietzschean argument, beyond even what Nietzsche himself says or means to say about it explicitly, is this strange and troubling, *unheimlich* concept of belief or credit, of the act of faith, of trusting, or rather this concept of the believer (*Gläubiger*), of the believing subject who does not believe, of the believing subject who is both believing, credulous, and yet who does not believe in what he believes he believes, and who thus divides his own belief, affects to believe, simulates belief, this simulacrum being in some way a part of belief itself, the fiction of this simulacrum belonging to the very structure of what we call credit or belief. To believe is this strange divided state or this strange divided movement, quasi-hypnotic, in which I am not myself, in which I do not know what I know, in which I do not do what I do, in which I doubt the very thing I believe or in which I believe. Believing, in sum, is not believing; to believe is not to believe. And the whole origin of religion, like that of society, culture, the contract in general, has to do with this nonbelief at the heart of believing. Skepsis, skepticism, incredulity, ēpokhē, all these suspensions of belief or of *doxa*, of the opining of opinion, of the "saying yes to," are not accidents that happen to believing; they are believing itself. Believing is its own contrary and thus it has no contrary.[11] Not to believe in it is not the contrary of believing, of trusting, of crediting, of having faith. This is the essence of the fiduciary and of interest. And the market, exchange, the social contract, the promise, the whole system of supposed equivalences that ground money, language, law as well as penal law; all of this presupposes this trafficking in the act of faith, in believing, which is also believing without believing as condition of trafficking. I was saying that this internal division, this properly analytic dissociation, this cleavage, this split of believing haunted by nonbelief is almost quasi-hypnotic, one might say spectral, quasi-hallucinatory, or unconscious.

This leads us little by little to a reevaluation of both Christianity's and Kant's categorical imperative, of the bloody or bloodthirsty cruelty of the categorical imperative.

I insist on these two points for obvious reasons, in particular because I would like to prepare a return to the ambiguous Christianity of Hugo's abolitionism and the questions it poses, while at the same time treating these questions in closest proximity to those of blood and cruelty.

In section 5 of the Second Essay, Nietzsche explores this process of the social contract, thus of the duty and debt that imply promise and memory. Now, promise and memory always entail harshness, cruelty, and violence (*Hartes, Grausames, Peinliches*). The debtor pledges himself, he gives a pledge to inspire trust in his promise, to consecrate the holiness of his promise (*die Heiligkeit seines Versprechens*); the debtor pledges to indemnify the creditor in case he does not pay, by giving the creditor something he possesses, for example his body, or his wife, or his freedom, or even his life (*oder auch sein Leben*), or even in certain religions, his eternal salvation, the salvation of his soul, up to and including his rest in the grave — as for ex-

11. During the session, Derrida adds: "This is the same logic as that of cruelty."

ample in Egypt where the corpse of the debtor continued to be pursued or persecuted by the creditor. And Nietzsche adds an example that makes one think of Shylock of whom we spoke a lot here last year or two years ago.[12] He writes:

> Above all, however, the creditor could inflict every kind of indignity and torture upon the body of the debtor; for example, cut from it as much as seemed commensurate with the size of the debt—and everywhere and from early times one had exact evaluations, *legal* evaluations, of the individual limbs and parts of the body from this point of view, some of them going into horrible and minute detail. I consider it as an advance, as evidence of a freer, more generous, *more Roman* conception of law when the Twelve Tables of Rome decreed it a matter of indifference how much or how little the creditor cut off in such cases: "*si plus minusve secuerunt, ne fraude esto.*" (64)[13]

But notice how Nietzsche interprets this progress, which is a progress in the evaluation of this famous "equivalence." In place of an advantage that compensates (as *Rückzahlung*, as equal and accountable compensation in return) in the form of something or someone, a wife, for example, or a good, a thing, a body, the creditor is granted a psychic reimbursement, as it were, psychic or symbolic. Instead of a thing, instead of something or someone, he will be given some pleasure, some enjoyment [*jouissance*], a feeling of well-being or of a greater well-being (*Wohlgefühl*), he will be given a pleasure that consists in the voluptuous pleasure of causing the other to suffer, and cruelly, the voluptuous pleasure, says Nietzsche in French, of "faire le mal pour le plaisir de le faire," that is, of doing harm for the pleasure of it [here is a definition of cruelty, the cruelty condemned by the declarations we have quoted, and that think they are doing justice to justice, doing right by the law, fully within the law, by authorizing one to punish, to be sure, thus to do harm, but not "for the pleasure of doing evil, of causing pain"]. I return to Nietzsche.[14] In place of some equivalent, something or someone, one grants in return, as payment, the pleasure of doing violence (*Genuss in der Vergewaltigung*), "la jouissance de faire violence," as the French translation has it; I would also say the pleasure taken, the enjoying [*le jouir*] that has to do with

222

---

12. First year of the EHESS seminar "Perjury and Pardon" (1997–99), the session of November 26, 1997.

13. During the session, Derrida provides a translation of the Latin quotation: "it is not wrong to take more or less."

14. A notation in the typescript reads: "I return to N. pick up from above."

exercising power (*Gewalt*), and here even with exercising one's sovereignty over the debtor — man or woman. This is the foundation of what Nietzsche in concluding section 5 calls a "right to cruelty (*Anrecht auf Grausamkeit*)": "The compensation (*Ausgleich*), then, consists in a warrant for (*Anweis*) and right to cruelty" (65; *KSA*, 300).

Since the spiritualizing ruse of this principle of equivalence (spiritualizing because it transforms, transmutes the payment of an external thing or good into a psychic enjoyment, an internal enjoyment: instead of something or someone, I receive in compensation, as payment of the debt, as redemption of the debt, the right to enjoy, the right to the pleasure of making the other suffer, the right to cruelty), since the spiritualizing ruse of this principle of equivalence is the origin of the social contract, of the law, and of religion, you see how Nietzsche might interpret Christianity and even Christ's sentencing to death (you remember that, at the beginning of the seminar, Christ was one of our four theatrical paradigms of the theologico-political dimension of the death penalty). Nietzsche, in sum, does not read the crucifixion as a simple sentencing to death by men or by a theologico-political power, or rather, he interprets this sentence of theologico-political origin as an extraordinary ruse of cruelty in the logic of debt and payment or redemption of the debt. What he calls the stroke of genius of Christianity (*Geniestreich des Christentums*) is that God sacrifices himself, condemns himself to death; he sacrifices himself in the person of his son to redeem man, to pay the debt or the guilt of man and the sinner, who is a debtor. That is the ultimate meaning, the unbelievable meaning of the Incarnation and the Passion. I say "unbelievable" because, concerning this commercial transaction of redemption of the debt of the other, our debt, by God, in the course of an execution, and the liquidation of the credit by the crucifixion, Nietzsche himself says: "Can one credit that?" (92; *KSA*, 331). So the sentencing to death of Jesus by God, who first of all refused to pardon him, like some common governor (for who else but God the father finally sentenced him to death, by abandoning him to the Jews and the Romans? And the bloody crucifixion might be compared to the infanticide, this time paternal, comparable to the maternal infanticide we were talking about the last time while reading Kant, and that shields the criminal, man or woman, from the death penalty; and in both cases there is an illegitimate child, born out of wedlock: Jesus is not a legitimate son), so the sentencing to death of Jesus by God, this Passion and this Crucifixion that will become a point of reference for abolitionists, Hugo in the lead, would be one such cruel transaction in the payment of the debt for a wrong or an irremissible debt, that is, unpayable and unpardonable. All of this is a priceless [*impayable*][15] story, a story of the payment of an unpayable debt and the forgiving of the unforgivable, the irremissible; but the stroke of genius of Christianity is to have opened a hyperbolic passage at the limit of spiritualization and thereby to have reversed or feigned to reverse the order of things by having it be the creditor himself who offers himself in sacrifice (via his Son) for the debtor, for the payment of the debtor's debt. And this is called love, the love that means that the creditor pays the debt, pays the debt to himself and says to the other in sum: I love you, I pay you what you owe me, I give you what you owe me, I give you what you do not have or else I forgive you your unpayable wrongs, your debts, your unfulfilled promises, your unpardonable perjuries. Christianity's priceless [*impayable*] stroke of genius, this reversal of the debt, this love, Nietzsche believes it is unbelievable and he wonders, in parentheses "can one credit that?": (*sollte man's glauben?* must one believe that, should one believe in it? Should one put faith in these unbelievable things on the subject of credit?).

224

Here are the several lines I have just glossed (read also what precedes them in section 21 of the Second Essay) and you are going to see the idea of eternal punishment, of the inexpiable, of the unforgivable link up with our problematic of the death sentence — which Nietzsche does not speak of explicitly under that name but which he is speaking of all the time in sum. For, in short, to condemn to death is either to refuse to forgive, to deem the crime inexpiable, or else — we will come back to this — to leave to God, in another world, the freedom and the sovereign power to forgive there where we, finite men, cannot do it. (Read and comment on *GM*, 111)

> ... until at last the irredeemable debt gives rise to the conception of irredeemable penance, the idea that it cannot be discharged ("*eternal* punishment"). Finally, however, they are turned back against the creditor, too: whether we think of the *causa prima* of man, the beginning of the human race, its primal ancestor who is from now on burdened with a curse ("Adam," "original sin," "unfreedom of the will"), or of nature from whose womb mankind arose and into whom the principle of evil is projected from now on ("the diabolizing of nature"), or of existence in general, which is now considered *worthless as such* (nihilistic withdrawal from it, a desire for nothingness or a desire for its antithesis, for a different mode of being,

15. [Translator's note]: Derrida is here flexing the adjective *impayable* between its more literal use, "unpayable," like a debt, and the figurative sense of "priceless" or "hilarious," as one might say of a very improbable story.

Buddhism and the like)—suddenly we stand before the paradoxical and horrifying expedient that afforded temporary relief for tormented humanity, that stroke of genius on the part of Christianity: God himself sacrifices himself for the guilt of mankind, God himself makes payment to himself, God as the only being who can redeem man from what has become unredeemable for man himself—the creditor sacrifices himself for his debtor, out of *love* (can one credit that?), out of love for his debtor! —(91–92)

225   Read as well the following section, section 22. There Nietzsche analyzes in very powerful terms this executioner that God is, this madness of the will that is psychical cruelty (*eine Art Willens-Wahnsinn in der seelischen Grausamkeit* [the will becomes mad, the will itself wills, it wills itself mad, it is mad to will itself mad, madness is not an accident or an affect; it is maddened by itself, mad about itself, intoxicated and mad with a madness of voluntary freedom, of pure will, thus of sovereignty, and even of good will; Kant is mad, and cruel, as you will hear in a moment]),[16] all of this transforming the earth itself into an insane asylum (*Die Erde war zu lange schon ein Irrenhaus*: the earth has been for too long already a madhouse!).

To do evil for the pleasure of doing evil, to take pleasure in it, to take even an infinite pleasure, at the very place where one does not know, here then is the cruel mechanism, the very definition of bloody cruelty that is supposedly at work in all these phenomena of belief, social contract, culture, religion, and especially morality; here is the "genealogy of morals": cruelty, the theater of cruelty, the history of cruelty, or rather the prehistory of history as cruelty. There is nothing surprising then if Kant, the greatest thinker of the purest morality in the history of humanity, but also the one who said, in *Religion within the Limits of Reason Alone*, that only Christianity was an intrinsically moral religion (see "Faith and Knowledge"),[17] there is nothing surprising in the fact that Nietzsche finds Kant "cruel" and that he finds a certain wreak of cruelty, a certain odor of cruelty in the categorical imperative. I indeed say "odor" of cruelty because that is Nietzsche's sensual register when he speaks about it: he sniffs; he smells the symptom with keen nostrils, the sensitive sense of smell of a genealogist animal; he smells blood, even if cruelty is

16. The closing parenthesis has been added.
17. J. Derrida, "Foi et savoir: Les deux sources de la 'religion' aux limites de la simple raison," in Derrida, Gianni Vattimo, et al., *La religion* (Paris: Le Seuil, 1996), pp. 9–86; Derrida, "Faith and Knowledge: The Two Sources of 'Religion' at the Limits of Reason Alone," trans. Samuel Weber, in Derrida, *Acts of Religion*, ed. Gil Anidjar (New York: Routledge, 2002), pp. 42–101.

not what Kant means to say, and even if the word *grausam* makes no reference, like *cruor*, *crudelis*, *crudelitas*, to blood, to flowing red blood (*cruor*);   226
but Nietzsche, on the other hand, in the same context, makes several literal
references to blood. Nietzsche smells the odor of cruelty (he smells it, he says
that the categorical imperative, the soul of Kantian morality, smells or even
stinks of cruelty: *der kategorische Imperativ riecht nach Grausamkeit*). Kant
stinks[18] (as one would say in English) of Christian cruelty.

This Nietzschean diagnosis (namely that Kantian morality is sick with
cruelty, that the categorical imperative is, stinks of cruelty) opens the way to
any thinking of "Kant with Sade" to cite Lacan's text, about which I will say
a word in a moment. First of all, because at issue is a diagnosis of a cruelty
that has no contrary because it is originary, and therefore the phenomenon
of non-cruelty, the appearance of non-cruelty would be but a dissimulated
cruelty, or even a bid to raise the level of cruelty. Originary cruelty, originary
sadism, we could treat this patiently only by questioning in particular the
Freud of *Three Essays*, of "Instincts and Their Vicissitudes," or of *Beyond the
Pleasure Principle*, "The Economic Problem of Masochism," notably when
he defines masochism as a sadism turned back against the self, either directly
or through the mediation of another. Before taking on the passive voice, the
verb "to make suffer" passes by way of the reflexive middle voice ("to make
oneself suffer"[19] whether by oneself or by the other). I will not get involved
here in the debate, which is moreover internal to Freud's thought itself,
concerning whether or not this masochism is originary qua sadism turned
back on itself, or on the subject of which comes first, sadism or masochism
("a sadist is always at the same time a masochist," says Freud already in
1905 in the *Three Essays*).[20] But since the question of death and sentencing
to death by the state is our subject, I will refer especially to *Beyond the Pleasure Principle* — where moreover Freud acknowledges that he has steered a
course "into the harbor of Schopenhauer's philosophy"[21] and where Nietz-   227
sche is implicitly very present; where moreover the motif of the "demonic"
is fundamental, as is what is said about the drive to dominate (domination,
Bemächtigung, *Bewältigung*, the specificity of which I underscored with

18. [Translator's note]: "Stinks" is in English in the original.
19. The closing quotation mark has been added.
20. Sigmund Freud, *Three Essays on the Theory of Sexuality*, trans. James Strachey,
(New York: Basic Books, 1962), p. 25.
21. Sigmund Freud, *Beyond the Pleasure Principle*, trans. James Strachey (New York:
W. W. Norton, 1961), p. 44.

great insistence in "To Speculate—on 'Freud'" in *The Post Card*, notably in its relation to love life and to the couple formed by sadomasochism).[22] In the same chapter of *Beyond the Pleasure Principle*, Freud evokes the possibility that erotic sadism is merely a death drive detached from the ego by the narcissistic libido, which can be directed only at the object, with the result that amorous possession tends toward the cruel destruction of the object; and when originary sadism remains pure of any mixture, we would then have this too familiar and indiscernible mixture of love/hate. But it is in the same chapter of *Beyond the Pleasure Principle* that there appears, to be sure as a figure, as a political metaphor of the organic, the image of the sacrifice of cells by the cellular state that, in certain illnesses, sends cells to their death so that it, the state, can survive.

This bid to raise the level of originary sadistic cruelty that has no contrary and that means that surpassing cruelty by an apparent non-cruelty would be merely a surpassing *in* cruelty, a surfeit of cruelty, finds its illustration, as concerns the death penalty, in the debate between, let us say, abolitionism (Beccaria) and non-abolitionism (Kant), given that, as we were saying, one can always interpret Beccaria's proposal as still more cruel than the still more cruel proposal of Kant, more cruel, then, than the death penalty, since Beccaria claims that the risk of a life sentence of hard labor will make the criminal suffer more and thus fear more than the threat of immediate death. What is more, Voltaire, even as he supported Beccaria, had already evoked this logic when he wrote in the article "On Murder" in his text *The Price of Justice and of Humanity* (1777). (Read Voltaire, 18)

228

> The damage must be repaired: death repairs nothing. One will say to you perhaps: "Mr. Beccaria is mistaken; his preference for painful and useful labor, which will last a lifetime, is founded on the opinion that such a long and ignominious punishment is more terrible than death, which is felt for only a moment. One will point out to you that, if he is right, then he is the cruel one and the judge who sentences to the gallows, to the wheel, to the flames, is the indulgent man." You will no doubt respond that it is not a matter of arguing which is the gentler punishment, but which is the more useful one.[23]

22. J. Derrida, *La carte postale: De Socrate à Freud et au-delà* (Paris: Flammarion, 1980), pp. 430 ff.; *The Post Card: From Socrates to Freud and Beyond*, trans. Alan Bass (Chicago: University of Chicago Press, 1987), pp. 402 ff.

23. Voltaire, "Du meurtre," *Prix de la justice et de l'humanité* (Paris: Éditions de L'Arche, 1999), p. 18.

Thus, one no longer knows who is more cruel or more sadistic, Beccaria or Kant, the one who opposes the death penalty or the one who maintains its principle. Here, then, in any case is what Nietzsche would teach us about the Sadian cruelty of the categorical imperative. If you wish to follow, both along this path and that of *Beyond the Pleasure Principle*, the consequence that Lacan draws in his fine text "Kant with Sade" (1963, reprinted in *Écrits*), I would advise you to read or reread this text, and, especially as concerns the death penalty, since that is our subject, in the passages where, as you recall Blanchot had done some fifteen years earlier (but his name does not appear a single time in *Écrits*, of course) in "Literature and the Right to Death," he thinks together Sade and Saint-Just, and the guillotine. ("Sade," says Lacan, "the former aristocrat, takes up Saint-Just right where one should. . . . Consequently, the revolution also wants the law to be free, so free that it must be a widow, the Widow *par excellence*, the one that sends your head to the basket if it so much as balks regarding the matter at hand."[24] On the next page, a more interesting and original suggestion of a "sadistic impotence" [665] that Sade would have "failed" to remark: "The fact that Sade failed to make [the remark] gives us pause for thought" [ibid.]. 229 The suggestion is discreetly taken up again at the end of the text: "I have forbidden myself to say a word about what Sade is missing here" [667], the next sentence unfortunately letting one think that for Lacan what is missed in this way should be sought in the vicinity of the mother, yet again, and of *Penisneid*.)[25] More interesting, for us in any case, especially when we seek to elucidate the double Christian root of both the death penalty and its abolition, is what Lacan notes for example in homage to Klossowski's *Sade mon prochain*. (Read Lacan, *Écrits*, 789, then possibly 781)

> My structural reference points make it easy to grasp that the Sadean fantasy is better situated among the stays of Christian ethics than elsewhere. . . .
>
> In my view, Sade does not have neighborly enough relations with his own malice to encounter his neighbor in it, a characteristic he shares with many people and with Freud, in particular. For this is indeed the only reason why beings, who are sometimes experienced, back away from the Christian commandment.
>
> We see what is, to my mind, the crucial test of this in Sade's rejection of

24. J. Lacan, "Kant avec Sade," in *Écrits* (Paris: Le Seuil, 1966), pp. 785–86; "Kant with Sade," in Lacan, *Écrits*, trans. Bruce Fink (New York: W. W. Norton, 2006), p. 663.

25. The closing parenthesis has been added.

the death penalty, the history of which would suffice to prove, if not its logic, at least that it is one of the correlates of Charity. (666–67)[26]

But let us listen to Kant himself illustrate it once more:

Suppose someone alleges that his lustful inclination is quite irresistible to him when he encounters the favored object and the opportunity. [Ask him] whether, if in front of the house where he finds this opportunity a gallows were erected on which he would be strung up immediately after gratifying his lust, he would not then conquer his inclination. One does not have to guess long what he would reply. But ask him whether, if his prince demanded, on the threat of the same prompt penalty of death, that he give false testimony against an honest man whom the prince would like to ruin under specious pretenses, he might consider it possible to overcome his love of life, however great it may be. He will perhaps not venture to assure us whether or not he would overcome that love, but he must concede without hesitation that doing so would be possible for him. He judges, therefore, that he can do something because he ought to do it, and he cognizes freedom within himself—the freedom with which otherwise, without the moral law, he would have remained unacquainted. (659)

230

These are the paths that Nietzsche opened when speaking of the— fundamentally Christian—cruelty of Kant, Nietzsche, the thinker that Lacan unwisely believed he could relegate to what he called, I no longer remember where, "cheap junk" [*la pacotille*]. Here then, finally, is what Nietzsche says of the categorical imperative: it is the passage at the beginning of section 6 of the Second Essay:

It was in *this* sphere then, the sphere of legal obligations, (*In diese Sphäre, im Obligationen-Rechte also*), that the moral conceptual world of "guilt," "conscience," "duty," "sacredness of duty" had its origin (*ihr Entstehungsherd*): its beginnings were, like the beginning of everything great on earth, soaked in blood thoroughly (*mit Blut begossen worden*) and for a long time. And might one not add that, fundamentally, this world has never since lost a certain odor of blood and torture (*einen gewissen Geruch von Blut und Folter*)? (Not even in good old Kant: the categorical imperative smells of cruelty.) (65; *KSA*, 300)

26. Derrida adds during the session: "In other words, Sade is opposed to the death penalty out of Christianity. I would have liked to quote another passage in the same volume where he refers to Kant, not to Kant's canonical text on the death penalty, to which we will return, but to a certain very interesting passage in the *Critique of Pure Reason*."

And then, re-posing, relaunching his question about the equivalent, the compensation for the debt by suffering, Nietzsche underscores not only the spiritualization, the internalization I was talking about a moment ago, but the bid to raise the stakes, the hyperbolic augmentation, the infinite disproportion, a pleasure of the "highest degree" that accompanies this law of cruelty: for a finite debt, in some sense, the compensation in psychic cruelty   *231* does not merely correspond but exceeds the correspondence by responding to it with a pleasure of cruelty that becomes infinite, in any case extreme, of the "highest degree." Hence the enigma of Christianity and of the infinite counter-pleasure in cruelty, the counter-pleasure that goes to the limit of itself—and one may suppose that it is a matter of cruelty right up to death, to the death that the living must endure by dying living in some sense, by dying in its lifetime [*en mourant de son vivant*], as I read somewhere:

> To ask it again: to what extent can suffering be equal or comparable (*Ausgleichung*) compensation for debts or guilt (*Schulden*)? To the extent that to *make* suffer [Nietzsche underlines *make*, *machen*, *leiden*-machen, not to suffer but to *make* suffer] was in the highest degree pleasurable [an extreme pleasure (*im höchsten Grade*)], to the extent that the injured party exchanged for the loss he had sustained, including the displeasure caused by the loss, an extraordinary counter-pleasure (*einen ausserordentlichen Gegengenuss*): that of *making* suffer (*das Leiden*-machen)—a genuine *festival* (*ein eigentliches* Fest; *Fest* is underlined, as is *machen*). (Ibid.)

And the important thing here is at the same time the festival, the spectacle, the jubilation, but especially that it be motivated by a counter-pleasure, the concept of counter-pleasure having here a specificity that is irreducible to that of pleasure.

Let me quickly read the lines that follow and leave you then to read the whole for yourselves. I quote only up to the point where, for once, Nietzsche names "capital executions" (*Hinrichtungen*).

> . . . *making* suffer—a genuine *festival*, something which, as aforesaid, was prized the more highly the more violently it contrasted with the rank and social standing of the creditor. This is offered only as a conjecture for the depths of such subterranean things are difficult to fathom, besides being painful; and whoever clumsily interposes the concept of "revenge" does not enhance his insight into the matter but further veils and darkens it (—for   *232* revenge merely leads us back to the same problem: "how can making suffer constitute a compensation?").
>
> It seems to me that the delicacy and even more the tartuffery of tame

domestic animals (which is to say modern men, which is to say us) resist a
really vivid comprehension of the degree to which *cruelty* constituted the
great festival pleasure of more primitive men and was indeed an ingredient
of almost every one of their pleasures; and how naïvely, how innocently
their thirst for cruelty manifested itself, how, as a matter of principle, they
posited "disinterested malice" (or, in Spinoza's words, *sympathia malevolens*)
as a *normal* quality of man — and thus as something to which the conscience
cordially *says Yes!* A more profound eye might perceive enough of this oldest
and most fundamental festival pleasure of man even in our time; in *Beyond
Good and Evil*, section 229 (and earlier in *The Dawn*, sections 18, 77, 113), I
pointed cautiously to the ever-increasing spiritualization and "deification"
of cruelty which permeates the entire history of higher culture (and in a
significant sense actually constitutes it). In any event, it is not long since
princely weddings and public festivals of the more magnificent kind were
unthinkable without executions, torturing, or perhaps an auto-da-fé, and
no noble household was without creatures upon whom one could heedlessly
vent one's malice and cruel jokes. (Consider, for instance, Don Quixote at
the court of the Duchess. Today we read *Don Quixote* with a bitter taste in
our mouths, almost with a feeling of torment, and would thus seem very
strange and incomprehensible to its author and his contemporaries: they
read it with the clearest conscience in the world as the most cheerful of
books, they laughed themselves almost to death over it). To see others suffer does one good, to make others suffer even more; this is a hard saying
but an ancient, mighty, human, all-too-human principle to which even the
apes might subscribe; for it has been said that in devising bizarre cruelties they anticipate man and are, as it were, his "prelude." Without cruelty
233 there is no festival: thus the longest and most ancient part of human history teaches — and in punishment there is so much that is *festive!* — (65–67;
KSA, 300–301)

In section 7 Nietzsche will speak again of the pleasure (*Lust*) that cruelty
procures, and further on, in section 13, he insists on the fact that punishment
is "indefinable (*undefinierbar*)." Indefinable because it has and it is a history,
and only what has no history is definable. He specifies in parentheses:

> Today it is impossible to say for certain *why* people are really punished: all
> concepts in which an entire process is semiotically (*semiotisch*) concentrated
> elude definition; only that which has no history is definable (*definierbar ist
> nur das, was keine Geschichte hat*). (80; KSA, 317)

The remark is very significant on the part of a genealogist who is basically proposing a genealogy of the source of punishment and cruelty rather
than a history, and who acknowledges that the historicity of punishment,

and of cruelty or counter-pleasure, eludes definition precisely by reason of their historicity.

See as well the whole Third Essay, in particular section 21 on "death-seeking mass deliria": "evviva la morte" (142).

This question of history and nature (of animal nature ultimately, of the nature of the living, of this *zoophysis* or of this zoo- or bio-physiology) brings us back, after this long circular detour, to what Hugo says about the unwritten law, natural law as social law, and to our initial question about the relations between this supposed natural law (namely, the so-called inviolability of human life or the "right to life") and the history of Christianity.

We will come back to it next time, as well as to this question of red blood, the guillotine, and cruelty in Hugo.

As for the motif of *interest*, one should not necessarily confine it, as Baudelaire does, as Nietzsche also does no doubt, although less narrowly, to the sphere of zoo-psychobiology, in the common sense of this term, to the conscious or unconscious motivations of an individual, whether he be an abolitionist or an anti-abolitionist. No doubt we must broaden this analytic of interest to the social or national or state body and ask ourselves what interest a state, a national state, or even a global state might have in maintaining or suspending capital punishment.

234

February 9, 2000

Economy. Might there be an economy of the death penalty?

And what could that mean?

If someone formulated the following sentence: "to abolish the death penalty is to economize [*faire l'économie de*] the death penalty," how would one interpret such a declaration?

Or again if someone said, in French, the European Union has from now on "classé"[1] the death penalty, how does one hear that?

Before attempting to respond to these questions and to the logic they put to work, let us form already the hypothesis that the stakes of this semantic and syntactic inquiry have to do no less with the words or the lexicon of "economy," "economize," or even of "class," "classify," and "classification" than those of the so-called death penalty. As if, fundamentally, one had to define "economy" or "class" and have access to the semantics of economy and class by beginning from the death penalty and punishment in general, rather than the reverse; this would be good common sense if one recalled that penalty (*poena, peine*) had first of all the trivially economic sense of ransom, repurchase, or redemption, of the punishment meant to pay for damage, to repair a wrong. Penalty is a payment and even if, with Nietzsche, one puts in question the projection or the posing of a general *equivalent* for the payment of a wrong, no one can dispute that the concept of "penalty," be it penalty as cruel suffering, has an economic sense of buying back or redemption in a market. And thus that a calculation, the calculation of a price, tends to be sought there. Whether or not this calculation is possible, whether it is conscious or unconscious, there is no penal law without this project of calculation, be it the calculation of the incalculable, with or without interest, with or without surplus value. And when I say conscious or unconscious calculation, it will always remain to be known (but I hold this knowledge

236

---

1. [Translator's note]: That is, to classify, close the file on, sort, arrange, label, rank.

to be impossible, by definition) if what appears incalculable cannot still be calculated by what we blithely call the unconscious.

But then the question of an economy of the death penalty risks losing or dividing its meaning, like a river that gets lost by dividing into a delta, as one says the Mississippi delta, the Nile delta, or the Rhône delta. The water rushes, with open arms, into the literal triangle of a Delta that forever divides its course (the water that gets lost like this will never again go back up toward the supposed uniqueness of a source, and the triangle is often a sea, when it is not oceanic). To economize the death penalty, is that to calculate its interest, the interest there is in saving it, or does economizing the death penalty mean, on the contrary, <learning> to economize the death penalty, learning to do without it, to abolish it? But is it ever abolished? Has one ever, forever, abolished the death penalty? Will one ever have abolished it forever? Is a law, a legal stipulation and stipulation of a state, enough for that? And then what is the economy of abolition? Is there an economy of economy? And is there an economy in thus filing away [*classer*] the death penalty in the past? And what if this economy were still an economy of class?

Let us leave these questions hanging over our heads; we'll see later where they fall. And if they fall, if they fall, as a sign of coherence or consistency, on their feet, or on their head or on whose head, and which head they cause once again to fall. If there is something cruel, with that cruelty of which we have already spoken so much, without being sure what it could mean, in particular in legal texts — if there is something cruel, it is perhaps, to begin with, the question itself, the putting into question as putting to the question that initiates torture and that threatens, in the course of an interrogation, in the course of a quest, an inquest, a requisition, an inquisition, a perquisition, to cause the subject in question to lose his or her head. Where does the cruelty of the questioning of a question begin and where does it end?

237

Let us then begin again.

To believe — not to be cruel.

If I tried to sum up in four to five words, for example "To believe — not to be cruel," the impossible questions that have imposed themselves on us, that have not failed to *impose themselves* on us even as we were trying to *pose* them, without ever managing precisely either to drop them or to pose them, I mean to master them in a formal, formalizable, and manipulable structure, I would say this: not, what is cruelty? (on the subject of which we saw that, along with that of the *exception*, this question, what is cruelty? this series of questions—where does cruelty begin? where does it end? does it ever begin or end?—governed the whole debate in modernity around the death penalty, on both sides of the front, the side of abolitionism and the side of mortalism or of death-dealing [*du morticole*]), not what is cruelty? then, but how am I cruel? how to be cruel? a question that becomes, once one takes cognizance of the fact, following Nietzsche, that cruelty has no contrary but only different ways, different modalities, different intensities, different values (active or reactive) of being cruel, only a differ*a*nce, with an *a*, in cruelty, a differ*a*nt cruelty—and the logic without logic of differ*a*nce is that of a paradoxical economy—a question that becomes, then, how *not* to be cruel? a question (how *not* to be cruel?) whose syntax itself allows two tonalities or two values: (1) that of *fatal misfortune* ("whatever I do, I can only be cruel") or (2) that of the *revolt of innocence* that refuses the fateful misfortune described by Nietzsche and still wonders, full of hope, how *not* to be cruel? what to do so as *not* to be cruel, *in view of not* being cruel, if I want to escape from the Nietzschean belief? How not to be cruel with the other but just as well with myself, given that, as you recall, masochism is supposedly merely a sadism turned round against the self, all this malice surrendering or condemning itself to the death from which it proceeds. Does this question itself, the strange question, how to be cruel? or just as well how *not* to be cruel? proceed from a place that is still protected by some innocence or some *immunity* or indemnity (the one who poses this question having to do so from a place still intact from any cruelty, any cruel contagion) or else is it already, already and always, contaminated, overtaken by the contagion of this cruelty that it comprehends in advance?

This impossible and unstable and contagious and endemic question of cruelty (*Grausamkeit*) is reinscribed, if you will be so good as to remember, in the hollow, that is, the *creux* of another question, that of belief [*croyance*], in the way we were trying to think it the last time, setting out from and going beyond Nietzsche: How to believe? How *not* to believe? given that believing and not-believing are no longer opposed, given that the one, believing, constitutes the other, non-believing, the *not-believing-in-it* of unbelief or incredulity in a hollow [*en creux*], resonating spectrally in the shell or the hollow of the other's ear, and given that every believing is ventriloquized, telephonically, if you will, by the skepsis or the *epokhē* of a *not-believing-in-it*, of an unbelievable or an incredible[2] that is anything but its contrary, but always a belief without belief, a cruelty without cruelty?

2. [Translator's note]: The word "incredible" is also in English in parentheses in the original.

Since these two words hollowed into each other, *en creux*—belief [*croyance*] and cruelty, the credited [*cru*, also crude] and the cruel, whether or not there is blood involved—referred first of all, in the texts we read and deliberately oriented in this direction, to Christian faith, in Kant and even in Sade, here we are again before the question of the death penalty and religion, before the question of Christian political theology and/or of the Gospels faced with the death penalty. We had begun to elaborate it.

To save time, then, I will not go back over any of the six long preceding sessions. The last time, at the end of a long detour, then of a circular return, through relays that I recall merely by way of their titles or common names, for example the telephone (cf. Avital Ronell, *The Telephone Book: Technology, Schizophrenia, Electric Speech*, p. 416),[3] and the technics of transcendence, musical sovereignty, the *interest of disinterest*, and especially cruelty, the festival of cruelty (a cruelty without contrary, only differences, a differant cruelty whose concept without opposition was as paradoxical as those two other concepts that we turned inside out, as it were, like gloves, the concept of interest and that of belief), the cruelty of the categorical imperative in general that smells of cruelty according to Nietzsche, the cruelty of the categorical imperative of the talionic law and of the death penalty in Kant, following this whole detour and every return, thus through Hugo, Baudelaire, Kant, Nietzsche, Sade, Blanchot, Lacan, we were coming back, between literature and philosophy, between law and religion, to the question that we were asking on the subject of this remark of Hugo's when he wrote to an abolitionist lawyer to whom he professed his agreement:

> The question that you see as a man of the law [Hugo was saying], I see as a philosopher. The problem that you elucidate perfectly, and with an eloquent logic, from the point of view of the written law, is illuminated for me in an even higher and more complete light by natural law. At a certain level, natural law cannot be distinguished from social law.[4]

How can Hugo, we were asking ourselves—a Hugo we have begun to read according to three different registers: that of his absolute singularity, to be sure, of *Victor* Hugo, also that of his historical singularity, and that of his paradigmatic exemplarity, in his argumentation for abolitionism—how can Hugo both ground his abolitionism in a natural law, an unwritten, non-positive, non-historical law—a philosophical law—that cannot be distin-

239

240

3. Avital Ronell, *The Telephone Book. Technology, Schizophrenia, Electric Speech* (Lincoln: University of Nebraska Press, 1989).

4. Hugo, *Écrits sur la peine de mort*, 250.

guished from a social law, even as he constantly alleges all the same a kind of evangelical Christianity? Even as he points to the tortures of Christ?

This is another way of posing and displacing the great Baudelairean or Nietzschean (in a moment we will say Marxian) question of *interest*, thus of economy, of the interest there is in decreeing or maintaining, even in inventing the death penalty, the interest there can be in contesting its law or in abolishing it. Speaking of this interest, I open here a parenthesis on current affairs. About two months ago, even before it was spread across our newspapers and our walls, I had alluded to the Benetton campaign against the death penalty:[5] enormous photographs of American prisoners sentenced to death, almost all of them black, who await their executions on death rows. I had said that, all things considered and without having too many illusions about the overdetermined interest of its initiator, it seemed to me that I should applaud this campaign that I found rather sympathetic. Whether or not one agrees to applaud it, one must nevertheless ask oneself what is presupposed by the interested calculation that presides over this campaign of worldwide publicity directed against the death sentence in a single country (if indeed that is, as I suppose, the case). The axiom of the campaign is that there is a capital of sympathy in the world for the abolition of the death penalty, a virtually acquired solidarity among those who oppose, in the United States and outside the United States, the American policy and practice of the death penalty. One must analyze this virtual or potential consensus that is being constituted or is constantly progressing: why are there more and more people in the world who do not tolerate capital executions whereas so many other cruelties and forms of pain and suffering are in fact deemed to be tolerable? If there were not a worldwide, irrepressible, irreversible, and unambiguous tendency here, the ad men of Benetton would not have pursued the idea of this campaign, however original, unusual, inventive, and well-intentioned it may be. And this virtually worldwide tendency of the abolitionist ethic espouses in some way the economic globalization [*mondialisation*] of the market. It is in a market moving toward globalization, which tends to get confused, despite powerful pockets of resistance, with the globalization of law and human rights, and with the abolition of capital punishment whose progress over the last ten years in a majority of states on earth we have followed, it is in this field of economico-juridico-political globalization that a European big businessman has an interest in launching his campaign, an economic interest, to be sure—and who takes risks (but finally there is little risk)—and an interest in disinterest itself, for even if he

241

5. See above, "Third Session: January 12, 2000," pp. 71–72.

lost money or credit here or there, he would earn it back elsewhere (as in the case of AIDS, another Benetton campaign theme, which, according to the mechanisms we are alluding to here, is another form of "death sentence," with all the quotation marks you wish, and of failure to come to the aid of a person in danger of death, effectively a crime, albeit passive, of which all the rich and European countries [abolitionist or not] are guilty with regard to the poor countries of the South, of Africa and Southeast Asia).[6]

In this great question of the right to life, of the declaration of the right to life as human right, what is the portion of natural right and the portion of legislative or historical or written right, the portion in a word of the history of law?

> The question that you see as a man of the law [Hugo was saying, then], I see as a philosopher. The problem that you elucidate perfectly, and with an eloquent logic, from the point of view of the written law, is illuminated for me in an even higher and more complete light by natural law. At a certain level, natural law cannot be distinguished from social law.

The sentences I have just quoted on "natural law" and what Hugo says he "sees as a philosopher," all of this is excerpted from a letter to a law- 242
yer dated November 1871, after the Commune. The end of this long letter (which I leave you to read) evokes the figure of Christ. It does so in a mode that is both ironic and desperate but rather significant. Christ appears as one of the possible saviors of a society, a nation, and a state on the road to ruin, but a savior who is missing, who does not respond to the call, who does not come out of his tomb after his sentencing to death. As yet no bandages next to the tomb. Hugo imagines a statesman trying to think the absolute disaster of France after the Commune. The statesman is "bent over his desk, his head in his hands, counting up terrible statistics, studying a torn map, measuring the defeats, the catastrophes, the retreats, the capitulations, the betrayals . . . the frightening future"; "musing in the face of so many abysses, he seeks help from the unknown . . . he calls for the Turgot needed by our finances, the Mirabeau needed by our Parliaments, the Aristides needed by our justice system, the Hannibal needed by our armies, the Christ needed by our society" (257–58).

It seems indeed that Christ does not belong, then, to the same series. The others, Turgot, Mirabeau, Aristides, Hannibal, have each one some competence, a know-how in a circumscribed domain (finance, parliament,

6. During the session, Derrida adds: "who are left to die miserably with their AIDS, no one bringing them help proportional to what we bring to Europeans who are ill."

justice, army). As for Christ, he is the savior of society, the savior of mankind, of social man, of social justice, of that "social right" that at the beginning of the letter Hugo nevertheless identifies with natural law or right.
Since Jesus is not there, not resurrected, since society has lost track of him,
the only resource, both sinister and laughable, without deus ex machina for
this national theater on the road to ruin, for this kingdom in which there is
something rotten, the only resource is the death sentence and burial:

> When he [this statesman] leans over the shadow and implores it to send
> him truth, wisdom, enlightenment, counsel, knowledge, genius; when in
> his thoughts he evokes the deus ex machina, the supreme captain of great
> shipwrecks, the healer of the people's wounds, the archangel of nations in
> distress, the savior, whom does he see appear? A gravedigger, with a shovel
> on his shoulder. (258)

243

One must hear these words in the atmosphere of an aftermath of the
Commune. Death sentences and executions are piling up. Hugo, who has
struggled his whole life in favor of abolition, and now that he is once again
in Paris, returned from exile, sees the disaster unfolding. Several days later,
November 28, he notes, in *Choses vues*, that a death penalty for political
crimes, which had been abolished in 1848, was being reinstated. We are going to come to this, to this abolition of the death penalty for political crimes.

What is a political death penalty? And how is one to distinguish in all
rigor between the enemy in general, the enemy from abroad (who can always be killed in war), and the public enemy (as Rousseau calls him in *The
Social Contract*, as you remember)? Then how to distinguish between the
public enemy as charged or convicted under common law and the public
enemy as charged with or convicted of political crimes? The brief moment
of the Commune, and what immediately followed its crushing defeat, is
rather difficult to identify in this respect. Was it a revolution? Was it the
experimental laboratory of a proletarian revolution that failed (you know
the texts of Marx who saw in the Commune the positive form of the Revolution of February 1848, which replaced the permanent army with the armed
populace and the national guard, deprived the police of its political attribu-
tions, opened up to an expansive and no longer repressive political form,
etc., emancipated labor, etc.) or else a civil war within the enclave or on the
border of a national war, and so forth? Who were the traitors and the public
enemies in this situation? Depending on the answer one gives to this type
of question, the significance of the death penalty, or rather the significance
of death itself, changes, and Marx himself notes in *The Eighteenth Brumaire*
that "the multiplicity of interpretations to which the Commune has been

subjected, and the multiplicity of *interests* which construed it in their favor,   *244*
show that it was a thoroughly expansive political form, while all previous
forms of government had been emphatically repressive."[7]

What is at stake in these difficult or even impossible distinctions (civil
war or revolution or internal discord, delinquency, or even treason, or even
proto-partisan war, which calls up the problematic of a Schmitt on the subject of a mutation of the political, etc.) is considerable, as we have already
said. One has often thought it possible, throughout history, to suspend or
even prohibit the political death penalty; sometimes, on the contrary, it has
been allowed to take precedence over the other. Hugo deplores the fact that,
after the Commune, the political death penalty is being reestablished after
having been abolished — I will come back to this later — during the Revolution of 1848. He writes:

> November 28, 1871. I have just learned that Rossel, Ferré, and a sergeant
> named Bourgeois, a prisoner whose name no one even knew, were shot
> this morning in Satory [not guillotined but shot, like soldiers convicted of
> desertion, treason, or mutiny]. They died steadfastly, Rossel attended by the
> Protestant pastor Passa, Bourgeois by the Catholic chaplain Pollet, Ferré
> without a priest.

[Whether or not there is a Christian priest, Protestant or Catholic, Hugo
notes that religion is convoked to attend these executions, to assist those
sentenced in their death; the question of religion is posed; that Hugo notes it
although he writes only three lines; that he reports only these facts, the presence of two Christian priests, Protestant and Catholic, absence of a priest,
clearly shows that the question of the presence of religion in these moments
seems to him highly significant. The only remark he adds is equally dis-
criminating and, in its very brevity, symptomatic; he notes in fact that]

> Rossel wanted to give the command to fire [you know that Rossel was a   *245*
> general of the Commune]. He was refused. He let his eyes be blindfolded.
> So here is the political death penalty reinstated. Crime. (258–59)

Thus, the reinstatement of the political death penalty is a crime, *the* crime:
"crime" is the last word in this passage. That the political death penalty has
been reinstated, at least de facto and implicitly, after having been abolished
during the Revolution of February 1848, is deduced by Hugo from the fact

---

7. This quotation comes in fact from the third part of Marx's *The Civil War in France*.
See Marx/Engels *Gesamtausgabe*, vol. 22 (Berlin: Dietz Verlag, 1984), p. 501; Marx, *The
Civil War in France,* trans. Friedrich Engels (Gloucester, UK: Dodo Press, n.d.), p. 41;
emphasis added.

that a general was not even permitted to give a military command to the soldiers who were taking aim at him. One did not want this execution to be a death on the battlefront or an event of military justice in wartime. One wanted to make of it a civilian execution for a political motive. A few days later, on December 2, 1871, twenty years after his banishment, Hugo writes:

> We are traversing a fatal crisis. After the invasion, reactionary terrorism. 1871 is another 1815, but worse.[8] After the massacres, now the political gallows is reinstated. What baleful revenants! [Like that of Marx, the text of Hugo is crawling with revenants—and here is the blood]. . . . Let us cry out: Amnesty! Amnesty! Enough blood! Enough victims! Let France finally be spared! It is she who is bleeding! . . . . Have pity! Pardon! Fraternity! Let us not be weary, let us begin again without ceasing.

[This "let us begin again without ceasing" is a sign both of the hope in the irreversibility of the movement toward abolition of the death penalty and the despair faced with the fact that this irreversible movement is both infinite, meaning interminable, and above all nonlinear, discontinuous, always marked by interruptions, regressions, reactions, setbacks, and we should heed this lesson.]

> Have pity! Pardon! Fraternity! Let us not be weary, let us begin again without ceasing. Let us ask for peace and give the alarm. Let us sound the tocsin of clemency. I notice that today is December 2. Twenty years ago, at this time, I was fighting against a crime; I was being hunted down and was warned that, if they caught me, I would be shot. All is well, let us fight.[9] (259–60)

There are several possible readings of these generous pages. One can read generously or not these somewhat, even very, narcissistic remarks, where Victor Hugo does not miss a chance to recall his past action, and that if these Communards have been shot, he very nearly was too twenty years earlier. He remarks the anniversary of this instant of his death when he was not shot either, as Rossel and the others were. One can also read the preceding words in a Christian fashion or not, either generous or reticent: "Have pity! Pardon! Fraternity!" In *Politics of Friendship* I tried to deconstruct without indulgence Hugo's French fraternalism (a fraternalism that is at the same time French, thus, also Christian and phallocentric).[10] At the time I had

---

8. [Translator's note]: That is, worse than the year that saw the defeat at Waterloo, the exile of Napoleon, and the restoration of the Bourbon monarchy.

9. [Translator's note]: Hugo went into exile after the coup d'état of Louis-Napoléon Bonaparte in 1851 on December 2, which is the date of this letter.

10. Derrida, *Politics of Friendship*, pp. 264–67.

not read, or reread, or I had forgotten (I don't know anymore — probably never read) the text of Marx that I have just read when I was looking for what Marx said about the death penalty and the abolition of the political death penalty during the French Revolution of 1848 (which thus fulfilled a certain wish of the Revolution of 1789 and which we have talked about more than once).

In *The Class Struggle in France, 1848–1850*, right before evoking the abolition of the political death penalty in February 1848 and before doing so in terms that suggest he smells an interested move on the part of the bourgeoisie, a class calculation, here is what he writes on the subject of fraternity. You are going to see that he has but little tolerance for and trust in this political philosophy of fraternity, and that he comes close to seeing in the abolition of the death penalty an ideological stratagem of the bourgeoisie. That is, a class interest, an episode in the class struggle. Whether the death penalty is maintained or abolished, one can always decipher in these two policies, according to Marxist logic, a class reflex or interest, the calculation of an economy, whether or not this calculation is conscious, and an economy that always puts in play, as its name indicates, the proper of property, capital, and labor. Moreover, whether or not one is Marxist, when we analyzed the persistence or the aggravation of the death penalty in the United States, and we remarked the indisputable fact that those sentenced to death are in a disproportionate manner, in a very large majority, black and unemployed, poor proletarians, who can deny that what we have here is a political justice as class justice, even if one includes in it many other overdetermining factors, such as the history of slavery, racism, and so forth? As for Marx, at the time he is writing this, he too on the subject of the Revolution of 1848, it is conversely the abolition of the death penalty that translates a calculable, calculated, calculating interest of the bourgeoisie. Here is what he writes in *The Class Struggles in France, (1848–1850)*. (Read and comment on Marx, *The Class Struggles in France*, 81–82–83)

247

> The Luxembourg Commission, this creation of the Paris workers, must be given the credit of having disclosed, from a Europe-wide tribune, the secret of the revolution of the nineteenth century: the emancipation of the proletariat. The *Moniteur* blushed when it had to propagate officially the "wild ravings" which up to that time had lain buried in the apocryphal writings of the socialists and reached the ear of the bourgeoisie only from time to time as remote, half-terrifying, half-ludicrous legends. Europe awoke astonished from its bourgeois doze. Therefore, in the minds of the proletarians, who confused the finance aristocracy with the bourgeoisie in general; in the imagination of the good old republicans who denied the very existence

of classes or, at most, admitted them as a result of the constitutional monarchy; in the hypocritical phrases of the factions of the bourgeoisie which
up to now has been excluded from power, the rule of the bourgeoisie was
abolished with the introduction of the republic. At that time all the royalists
were transformed into republicans and the millionaires of Paris into workers. The phrase which corresponded to this imaginary abolition of class relations was *fraternité*, universal fraternization and brotherhood. This pleasant
abstraction from class antagonisms, this sentimental reconciliation of contradictory class interests, this visionary elevation above class struggle, this
fraternité, was the real catchword of the February Revolution. The classes
were divided by a mere misunderstanding, and on February 24 Lamartine
christened the Provisional Government "A government that halts the terrible misunderstanding that exists between the different classes." The Paris
proletariat reveled in this magnanimous intoxication of fraternity.

    The Provisional Government, for its part, once it was compelled to pro-
claim the republic, did everything to make it acceptable to the bourgeoisie
and to the provinces. The bloody terror of the first French republic was
disavowed by the abolition of the death penalty for political offences; the
press was opened to all opinions — the army, the courts, the administration
remained with a few exceptions in the hands of their old dignitaries; none
of the July Monarchy's great offenders was held to account. The bourgeois
republicans of the National amused themselves by exchanging monarchist
names and costumes for old republican ones. To them the republic was only
a new ball dress for the old bourgeois society. The young republic sought its
chief merit in not frightening, but rather in constantly taking fright itself,
and in winning the right to life and disarming resistance by soft compliance
and non-resistance. At home to the privileged classes, abroad to the despotic
powers, it was loudly announced that the republic was of a peaceful nature.
Live and let live was its professed motto. (48–49)

    One is not obliged to agree with Marx, I was saying, but one can at least
learn this from him: any abolition of the death penalty must also answer to
a certain interest, to a sociopolitical situation, to a relation of forces, and to
a relation between the state and civil society, between such and such fractions of the civil society holding power in the state. (Calling these fractions
social "classes," whatever one understands by "class," is another problem,
an immense and complex problem that I leave aside for the moment.) For
example, some particular social peace, some particular moment of euphoria
or fraternization of the Revolution of February 1848, was in truth, in Marx's
view, nothing but a moment in the concealed civil war between the proletariat and the bourgeoisie, between antagonistic social forces. A moment of

the class struggle. And a few months later, the February republic that could only have been a bourgeois republic — obligated, under the direct pressure from the proletariat, to proclaim social institutions — well, a few months later, in June, the bourgeoisie transformed this February Revolution into the June Revolution, and that is how Marx analyzed its fraternalist symptoms, in the *Neue Rheinische Zeitung* of June 29, 1848. He quotes himself in *The Eighteenth Brumaire*[11] and as you are going to hear, the word "apparition" [*fantôme*] (which earlier I missed in my inventory in *Specters of Marx*) will be picked up again a few pages later by the phrase "resurrected specter" to designate the proletariat that, in June, was going to organize demonstrations and demand amnesty for certain debts from an implacable bourgeois National Assembly. The fraternalist euphoria of February, in the course of which the political death penalty was abolished, is in Marx's view but an episode and passing symptom of an ongoing civil war, and of a civil war as class struggle between labor and capital. Abolition served, at a precise and moreover ephemeral moment, the calculable interests of a hegemonic bourgeoisie. What confirms indisputably Marx's interpretation are, at least to a certain degree, episodes in the history of France like the Commune (concerning which Victor Hugo deplores that it reinstated the political death penalty at a moment when the bourgeoisie was very scared), then, much later, during and after the Occupation, during the purge, when, in a much more problematic fashion one can speak of a political death sentence — always during conflicts that are difficult to define as war, civil war, with betrayal to the enemy, and so forth. (Read and comment, 97–99)

> The immediate impression which the news of the June defeat made on us, the reader will allow us to describe in the words of the *Neue Rheinische Zeitung*: $\qquad$ 250
>
> "The last official remnant of the February Revolution, the Executive Committee, has melted away, like an apparition [*fantôme*], before the seriousness of events. The fireworks of Lamartine have turned into the war rockets of Cavaignac. *Fraternité*, the fraternity of antagonistic classes of which one exploits the other, this *fraternité*, proclaimed in February, written in capital letters on the brow of Paris, on every prison, on every barracks — its true, unadulterated, its prosaic expression, is civil war in its most fearful form, the war of labor and capital. This fraternity flamed in front of all the

---

11. Although Derrida writes *The Eighteenth Brumaire*, he takes the quotation from *The Class Struggles in France, (1848–1850)* (New York: International Publishers, n.d.). He makes this clear moreover during the session.

windows of Paris on the evening of June 25, when the Paris of the bourgeoisie was illuminated, whilst the Paris of the proletariat burnt, bled, moaned. Fraternity endured just as long as the interests of the bourgeoisie were in fraternity with the interests of the proletariat. . . . The February Revolution was the beautiful revolution, the revolution of universal sympathy, because the antagonisms, which had flared up in it against the monarchy, slumbered peacefully side by side, still undeveloped, because the social struggle which formed its background had won only a joyous existence, an existence of phrases, of words. The June revolution is the ugly revolution, the repulsive revolution, because things have taken the place of phrases, because the republic uncovered the head of the monster itself, by striking off the crown that shielded and concealed it. Order! was the battle cry of Guizot. Order! cried Sebastiani, the follower of Guizot, when Warsaw became Russian. Order! shouts Cavaignac, the brutal echo of the French National Assembly and of the republican bourgeoisie. Order! thundered his grape-shot, as it ripped up the body of the proletariat. None of the numerous revolutions of the French bourgeoisie since 1789 was an attack on order; for they allowed the rule of the class, they allowed the slavery of the workers, they allowed the bourgeois order to endure, however often the political form of this rule and of this slavery changed. June has attacked this order. Woe to June! (*Neue Rheinische Zeitung*, June 29, 1848)." (57–58)

251   These texts of Marx illustrate, in my view, at least two lessons that we should keep in mind. On the one hand — but I have already said this — the vigilant concern to interpret the legal, juridical, legislative phenomenon of the abolition of the death penalty on the basis of an analysis of the sociopolitical situation and social antagonisms that determine infrastructural conditions of security or insecurity for the property and life of the citizens who hold power. I believe that this principle of analysis is still valid, in principle, and on condition of being intelligently adjusted to the specificity of social, national, state, and geopolitical situations. I also believe that it is not out of pure rational and ethico-spiritual obedience to metaphysical principles that people were able to abolish the death penalty in Europe, today's European Union, to the point of making it a condition of entrance into Europe (Turkey, etc.), whereas this is not possible in other parts of the world, in particular in societies and nation-states that are apparently so close to Europe, by reason of their democratic, Christian, etc. credo, especially in the United States.

On the other hand, by contrast, I believe that Marx, as he does often, by reducing juridical or judicial phenomena so quickly and so brutally to ideological and superstructural effects of the class struggle, does not take into account their relative autonomy, their duration, and their own efficacy, the supplementary contradictions that they introduce into both institutional and social life. The relative autonomy of the juridical is also that of the parliament; the most striking example would be that of France in 1981, which, in order to get in step with both the European movement under way and the relatively independent reflection of certain conservative members, abolished the death penalty at a time when a referendum would have revealed that a majority of the French were against abolition. The determination of interest, of interests here, is not impossible, but it is difficult and abyssally overdetermined.[12]

Beyond the virulence of these pamphleteering moments that are part of the sociopolitical and juridical history of the death penalty, one can indeed ask oneself if abolitionism, as an apparently irreversible philosophical and juridico-political movement linked to an apparently natural law concept of human rights, is not a movement linked historically and essentially to the Enlightenment, and to the Enlightenment inasmuch as it is indissociable from a figure of the bourgeoisie that is marked, avowedly or not, by Christianity, by a certain contradictory Christianity. Such that the question of the death penalty could well be the best and most indispensable introduction to the question, what is Enlightenment? on the threshold of a reelaboration of this question, from top to bottom, in particular through a rereading of Kant's famous "Was ist Aufklärung?," of the question of the relations between religion and Aufklärung, les Lumières, Illuminismo, Enlightenment, of everything that divided the delta of Enlightenment between supporters and adversaries of the death penalty, even as one would not forget that the author of "Was ist Aufklärung?" was a firm adversary of Beccaria, a convinced proponent of the death penalty who nevertheless admitted that the age was not yet enlightened (*aufgeklärt*) but that it was on the way to enlightenment (*Aufklärung*) in the historical movement of a progress open to perfectibility. No doubt you remember: "Wenn denn nun gefragt wird: Leben wir jetzt in einem *aufgeklärten* Zeitalter? so ist die Antwort: Nein, aber wohl in einem Zeitalter der *Aufklärung* (If it is now asked whether we at present live in an *enlightened* age, the answer is: No, but we do live in an age of *enlightenment*)."[13] One would have to privilege this passage when

252

12. Here we delete a paragraph and a quotation, which Derrida himself deleted when he presented this seminar in English. In the French typescript, the paragraph is crossed out, and in the margin is written "Gustav Hugo." The deletion concerns a quotation from Marx who speaks of "Hugo," which Derrida realized after the fact referred to Gustav Hugo and not Victor Hugo.

13. Immanuel Kant, "Beantwortung der Frage: Was ist Aufklärung?," in *Qu'est-ce que les lumières?*," bilingual edition (Saint-Étienne: Publications de l'Université de Saint-

asking oneself whether or not this propagation, this progress of *Aufklärung* ought to be moving toward an abolition for which Kant was obviously not ready, which he even opposed in the name of human dignity (*Würde*). In concluding his text, as you know, Kant said that government had an interest in treating man, who is henceforth more than a machine, in a manner appropriate to his dignity. Each word matters for us in this concluding sentence. What is translated as "interest" when it says that the government has an interest in treating man, who is more, that is, something other than a machine, in a manner appropriate to his dignity, that is, has an interest in treating him beyond calculable interest, as means, and to treat him as an end in-itself beyond any market price and any pathological interest, what is translated as "interest," then, is *zuträglich*, useful, profitable: government must find it useful, profitable for itself, to treat man, who is henceforth more than a machine, in a manner appropriate to his dignity—which is thus not a price, which is a value beyond values and beyond *Marktpreis*. There is then, once again, an interest beyond interested interest; there is here an interest without interest, a disinterested interest of reason: "auf die Grundsätze der *Regierung*, die es ihr selbst zuträglich findet, den Menschen, der nun mehr *als Maschine ist*, seiner Würde gemäss zu handeln"("the principles of governments, which find that they themselves have an interest [that find it useful for themselves] in treating man, who is *more than a machine*, in a manner appropriate to his dignity") (60).[14]

A moment ago, I quoted the passage from Hugo ("Rossel wanted to give the command to fire. He was refused. He let his eyes be blindfolded. So here is the political death penalty reinstated. Crime") for its own historical interest but also because it responds at more than a twenty-year distance to that other declaration of 1850 in which, more <than> twenty years earlier, then, Hugo applauds precisely the abolition of the *political* death penalty by the provisional government on February 8, 1848. Since this text of Hugo's contains, but for the future, the same formula "pure and simple abolition of the death penalty" (September 15, 1848) that we already read in a declaration to <the> Constituent Assembly, since this text curiously

Étienne, 1991), p. 81; Kant, "An Answer to the Question: 'What Is Enlightenment?,'" in *Kant's Political Writings*, ed. Hans Reiss, trans. H. B. Nisbet (Cambridge: Cambridge University Press, 1970), p. 58; emphasis added by Derrida in the German quotation.

14. [Translator's note]: The translation has been modified following Derrida's commentary. In the edition here cited, the phrase in fact reads: "the principles of governments, which find that they can themselves profit by treating man, etc."

combines the motif of the philosophy of natural right and the inviolability   *254*
of human life with its Christian reference, which is just as essential, since it
associates French patriotism with the future of Europe, with what he often
calls for under the prophetic name of the United States of Europe, I believe
that we must read this declaration, but I want to put in place first a few
historical reminders. One must recall that although abolitionist discourses
proliferated in France during the nineteenth century, as they did moreover
in the United States—let us never forget this in spite of the dark picture of
the United States today (let us not forget that in 1840 the man who founded
the *New York Tribune* had initiated a true abolitionist movement and that
in 1845, thus before the French Revolution of 1848, the American Society
for the Abolition of the Death Penalty was founded. In 1846, Michigan
replaces the death penalty by life imprisonment with one exception, once
again, and the exception is precisely political treason. In 1852, the state of
Rhode Island goes further because it abolishes the death penalty even in
the case of treason, which Wisconsin will do a year later. This movement
will grow until the end of World War I: North Dakota abolishes the death
penalty in 1915; Maine abolishes it in 1876, reinstates it in 1883, abolishes
it again in 1887. Six states had abolished it totally by the end of the Great
War; others had reduced the sphere of its application, to which one must
add a whole history of the modes of execution, from hanging to the electric
chair, adopted in 1880 following a campaign organized by General Electric,
the "electric chair" already provoking protests, nevertheless, from Thomas
Edison among others—and the process is not altogether over.)[15]

Let us return to France. Although abolitionist discourses proliferated
in France during the nineteenth century, the fact remains that there are
numerous, as one says, "death-dealing [*morticoles*]" anti-abolitionists, all of
them conservative Christians, who maintain, as does for example Joseph de
Maistre in his *Soirées de Saint-Petersburg*, that the death penalty represents
a divine weapon granted by the sovereign God to the sovereign monarch to
fulfill a providential law. Thus, a divine law presides over the death penalty,   *255*
as Hugo will also say, quite to the contrary, but those are his words, that "divine law" commands abolition. With the single exception of Abbé Le Noir
in 1867, notes Jean Imbert in the book I have quoted, "the whole Catholic hierarchy recognizes the legitimacy of the death penalty used against a
criminal."[16] From Saint Thomas Aquinas until the first half of the twentieth
century, "theologians agree on this point: the state has the right of life and

15. The closing parenthesis has been added.
16. Imbert, *La peine de mort*, 84.

death over its citizens." It is in this context, in which the Catholic hierarchy did not waver on the death penalty during the whole century and beyond, that one must also interpret Hugo's reference to Christianity. Without being merely a rhetorical and opportunistic strategy, this Christian reference has also a strong meaning: to make apparent the contradiction in the Christian camp and in the argument of the Christian discourse. Divine law of abolitionism against divine law of the death penalty.

Initial timid steps forward: in 1832 under Louis-Philippe and no doubt at his suggestion, the death penalty is partially abolished in nine cases, including counterfeiting and aggravated burglary. In 1838, Lamartine, another poet, recommended abolition to the Chamber of Deputies. And ten years later, on February 28, 1848, two days after the republic was declared, the provisional government votes for the abolition of the death penalty in political matters, and does so with a declaration about which one must remark that it refers, I quote, to the "consecration of a philosophical truth" (Imbert, 85) and to the French model whose Revolution must have a value of worldwide philosophical exemplarity — France being the most philosophical nation in the world, it owes philosophy to the world; it has the responsibility and the duty, the debt of philosophy, not to invent it but to discover and consecrate philosophy for the world:

> The provisional government, convinced that greatness of soul is the su-
256   preme politics and that every revolution brought about by the French
> people owes to the world the consecration of one more philosophical truth,
> considering that there is no more sublime principle than the respect for hu-
> man life, decrees: the death penalty is abolished in political matters.[17]

You will have noticed right away the contrast and the contradiction between, on the one hand, the principled, absolutist, hyperbolic, *unconditional* character — which is marked by the words "sublime," "principle," "respect for human life" ("there is no more sublime principle than the respect for human life"), the sublime rising above every other law, like human dignity in Kant — and, on the other hand, the *conditional* limitation of an abolition restricted to the matter of politics, to political crimes. Only in the case of the political felony would the respect of human life be a law and a sublime law. It is this contradiction or this limitation, this *conditionality* that no doubt shocked Hugo when, during the vote on the Constitution, November 4, 1848, in the declaration we have read, he asked for the pure and simple abolition of the death penalty, and it was on this date that Hugo was not listened

17. Quoted in ibid., p. 85.

to when the decree of the provisional government was included, as article 5, in the Constitution. Hugo's *absolutist* and *unconditional* abolitionist proposal was rejected on that occasion, by 498 votes against 216.

The fact remains that this abolition of the death penalty for political felonies remained to be interpreted. For an entire century, debate to determine what was a political crime raged. It sometimes happened that crimes with a political motive were judged as common law crimes by reason of their so-called odious and cruel character. Next, it was necessary to determine the punishment reserved for political crimes, and most often it was the appeals court [la Cour de Cassation] that decided the matter, for example, by imposing the next lesser punishment in the case of political crime, namely, deportation (Hugo's case). In June 1850, a law replaced the death penalty by imprisonment in a fortified stronghold. On November 21, 1901, the last legislative measure by the parliament of the Third Republic (I cite this, thinking of the text by Kant we read two weeks ago): the death penalty was 257 eliminated for mothers guilty of infanticide (ratification of a de facto state of affairs).

On the question of the mother, the woman, and sexual difference in the face of the death penalty (and we noticed that in the modern texts of international declarations, it was recommended that the execution of pregnant women be excluded even where the death penalty was still in force—and everyone joined in this consensus—as if the point were to avoid the horror of this double penalty that would take an innocent life, and sacrifice one more life, a life to come in the womb of the guilty mother), on the question of sexual difference in the face of the death penalty, and of Hugo in the face of this immense and abyssal question, I will not enter into it, having elsewhere devoted some analyses to Hugo from this point of view in *Politics of Friendship*;[18] but instead of spending years, as one should, commenting on the surface and the undersides of the text I am going to read, I will limit myself out of economy to quoting it, before coming back to the text I have been announcing since the last session. Here it is, a message sent to newspapers, dated July 28, 1872:

> I point this out to the whole of the press.
> Not only the press that is republican, but the press that is liberal, not only the press that is liberal, but the press that is human.
> A frightening question is posed.
> A woman named . . . — What does the name matter? — A woman is condemned to death.

18. Derrida, *Politics of Friendship*, see below, p. 174, n. 10.

By whom?

By a criminal court? — That's very simple. Guillotine her.

No. By a war tribunal? — Well, shoot her.

For in fact, the war tribunal does not have the guillotine at its disposal.

Now, let us examine this.

Shoot a woman?

Shooting a man, that's understandable. Man to man, these things are done. It is in the order of things; not in the natural order but in the social order.

But shooting a woman!

Shooting her coldly, officially, according to the rules.

Can one imagine this?

Twelve men, twelve young men, yesterday peasants, today soldiers, yesterday innocent in their village, tomorrow perhaps sublime on the battlefield, twelve brave hearts, twelve young souls, twelve citizens like you and me, whose number comes up, chosen by chance, and there they are executioners.

Executioners of whom?

I am not accusing the law, I am not accusing the tribunal; the law is unconscious; the tribunal is honorable. I am merely stating the facts.

These twelve brave boys are led before a stake, to this stake someone is attached, and they are told: Shoot at it.

They look, and they see a woman.

They see a forehead that reminds them of their sister; they see a bosom that reminds them of their fiancée; they see a belly that reminds them of their mother.

And this forehead must be struck down; and this bosom must be pierced; and this belly must be riddled with bullets.

I say that this is terrible.

In this phrase, war tribunal, there is war; that is to say, death inflicted by man on man; there is not death inflicted by man on woman.

Let us not overthrow man's deep instincts. Leave our soldiers in peace. Let us not make them shoot women.

Agreed, they say. There is the guillotine.

This is serious.

Let us say it very clearly: the guillotine will not do it. The guillotine is a civilian and not a military official; it obeys red robes, not epaulettes. It is ready to kill, but correctly. It declares that this is not its purview.

Let us continue.

Who will pick up the corpse? Who will carry it away? Who will strip it? Who will describe limb to limb, upon a wound there, a fracture there, the passage of the law through this poor unfortunate body? Here there arises within us one knows not what formidable modesty, which is the greatest thing in the human conscience.

And if the wretched woman does not fall down dead, who will give what is called the coup de grâce? Imagine to yourself some man you are going to pull from the ranks, and to whom you say: she's still alive, finish her off. What crime has this man committed that he is forced to do that? By what right do you sentence another in addition to her who is sentenced? From then on how will he look upon his chassepot? What trust will this soldier be able to have in this rifle? Will he still believe, after it has blown out these brains, that it is good for freeing your Alsace and your Lorraine? Will the executioner be able to become a hero once again?

259

Awful dilemma. Monstrous alternative.

Shooting is legal, but impossible.

Guillotining is possible, but illegal.

Which one to choose then?

I am going to say something very shocking to you:

Grant pardon.[19]

This concern for the innocent child, a victim of what is most cruel in the cruelty of the death penalty, appeared moreover in the rest of the letter that has preoccupied us for the last two weeks and from which I excerpted the passage on natural law as something philosophical. Right after this passage, Hugo continues:

You are defending Maroteau, that young man who, a poet at seventeen, a patriot soldier at twenty, in the mournful spring of 1871, in a feverish state of mind, wrote down the nightmare of this fever, and today, if things are not put in order, for this fatal page he is going to be shot at age twenty-two, and die almost before having lived. A man condemned to death for a newspaper article: such a thing has never been seen before. You are pleading for the life of this condemned man.

As for me, I ask it for all of them. I plead for the life of Maroteau; I plead for the life of Rossel, for Ferré, for Lullier, for Crémieux; I plead for the life of those three unfortunate women, Marchais, Suétens, and Papavoine, even as I acknowledge that, in my feeble mind, it is proven that they wore red scarves, that Papavoine is a frightful name, and that they were seen on the barricades, so as to fight, according to their accusers, so as to tend to the wounded, according to them. One more thing has been proven to me, which is that one of them is a mother and that, faced with the death sentence, she said: *Fine, but who will feed my child?*

260

19. Hugo, *Écrits sur la peine de mort*, pp. 261–63.

I plead for this child's life.

Let me pause a moment.

Who will feed my child? The entire social wound is contained in this question. I know that I was ridiculous last week when, in the face of France's misfortunes, I asked for unity among the French, and that I am going to be ridiculous this week when I ask for the life of those condemned. I am resigned to it. Thus, here is a mother who is going to die, and here is a little child who is going to die as well, as a repercussion. Our justice has such successes. Is the mother guilty? Answer yes or no. Is the child? Just try to answer yes. (250–51)

And I come finally, to conclude today, to the previously announced text in which I will underline not only the teleo-theological reconciliation of the Enlightenment of reason or natural law with Christianity, the Christianity of the living and resurrected Christ, of the saved Christ in sum, of the redeemed and redeemer Christ, of the redemption, the simultaneous reconciliation in a Christian Europe of France and of Europe, of the marketplace of interest and of the non-marketplace, of the present and the promise, as "advance" in the sense both of progress and of loan, at the moment Hugo, then, applauds the abolition of the death penalty in political matters by the February Revolution even while he still hopes for the pure and simple abolition he calls for and that is still refused him. (For V. Hugo, when he applauds a conditional [political] abolition calls for an unconditional abolition in the double name of the divine law of Christ and of what he calls the "almightiness of logic.")

So, to conclude, I am going to underline and comment on several remarks in this declaration to the assembly. (Read and comment on *Écrits*, 85–88)

261   Gentlemen, during the days of February, days that have no comparison in history, there was one admirable day; it was the day when the people's sovereign voice that, through the confused rumbling [*rumeurs*] of the public square, was dictating the decrees of the provisional government [thus, a little like Marx on this point. Hugo says that the provisional government was obeying what he calls "rumeurs," that is, the demand of the sovereign voice of the people — the provisional government was writing at the dictation of the sovereign people], pronounced this great sentence [so it is the people who pronounced this great sentence, the government was but the people's secretary, the people are sovereign]: The death penalty is abolished in political matters! That day, all generous souls, all serious minds, were thrilled [he says that even though he has reservations about the political character of this abolition]. And, indeed, to see progress arise immediately,

arise calm and majestic from a still simmering revolution; to see rise up over the excited masses the living and crowned Christ [that is what happened, that is what Marx didn't like and probably Baudelaire didn't either]; to see, in the middle of this enormous collapse of human laws, the divine law break forth in all its splendor (*Bravo!*); to see the multitude behave like a wise man; to see all these passions, all these minds, all these souls, which the day before were still full of anger, all these mouths that had just torn open cartridges, to see them unite and combine into a single cry, the finest one that can be carried by the human voice: Clemency! this was, gentlemen [and here is the point I wanted especially to underline], for the philosopher, for the jurist, for the Christian man, for the politician, this was for France and for Europe a magnificent spectacle. The very ones whose interests, whose feelings, whose affections were trampled by the events of February, the very ones who trembled, the very ones who moaned, now applauded and acknowledged that revolutions can mix the good in with their most violent explosions, and that the marvelous thing about them is that they need but one sublime hour to erase all the terrible hours. (*Shouts on the right. Approval on the left*) [One would have to read this otherwise than I am doing: "they need but one sublime hour to erase all the terrible hours"; in other words, in revolution, in conflict, in the war of interests, which is not a beautiful thing, there is the majestic Christ who rises above the masses, and then the sublime, the divine law, one sublime hour.]

What is more, gentlemen, this sudden and shining, although partial triumph [I underscore that he does not renounce criticizing the limited and conditional character of what has just happened] of the dogma that prescribes the inviolability of human life did not surprise those who know the power of ideas [thus, this is the philosophical logic, philosophy, ideas, etc., Aufklärung, Enlightenment, and then Christ]. In ordinary times, in what are conventionally called times of peace, for lack of perceiving the profound movement happening under the apparent immobility on the surface, in those periods called peaceful periods, ideas are willingly scorned; it is in good taste to mock them. Dream, tirade, utopia! people cry. Only facts are taken into account, and the more material they are, the more they are esteemed. People pay attention only to businessmen, *practical* minds as one says in a certain jargon (*Hear, hear!*), and those positive men, who are, after all, but negative men. (*That's true!*)

But should a revolution break out, businessmen [you see how this intersects with Marx], clever men, who seemed to be giants, are now nothing but dwarves; any reality that is no longer proportional to the new events collapses and vanishes; material facts crumble and ideas grow to meet the sky. (*Agitation*).

It is thus, through this sudden force of *expansion* [I underscore this word expansion because what Marx said is that February — the Commune — was

262

a movement of expansion and not of repression. Here, it is February '48]
attained by ideas in revolutionary times, that this great thing was done, the
abolition of the death penalty in political matters.

Gentlemen, this great thing, this fertile decree that contains the seed
[*germe*: this is important, this metaphor of the seed; it goes together with
what I call teleology; it is the idea that progress is germinating, is irreversible, and that this organism is going to develop, not cease to develop. It is a
kind of teleological geneticism, organicism, in this vision of the irreversible
progress of the abolition of the death penalty. Which is a progress of life. It is
the right to life, and it is normal to describe the progress of the right to life as
an organic, genetic progress, in a metaphor of the seed and that contains the
seed] of a whole code, this progress, which was more than a progress, which
was a principle, the Constituent Assembly adopted it and consecrated it.
It placed the decree I would almost say at the summit of the Constitution
as a magnificent advance made by the spirit of the revolution to the spirit
of civilization [this word "advance" is magnificent, as always in Hugo, of
course, he knows how to write — OK. So the advance is, obviously, progress. It is seduction; revolution seduces civilization. What is one doing when
one seduces? One sweeps civilization along. The advance is credit; it makes
civilization a loan in advance. "It placed the decree I would almost say at
the summit of the Constitution as a magnificent advance made by the spirit
of the revolution to the spirit of civilization," and the abolition of the death
penalty is always placed on the side of civilization, civilization will progress
with the abolition of the death penalty. It is the revolution, it is the spirit
of the revolution that can make this advance to the spirit of civilization];
like a conquest, but especially like a promise [The advance is a promise. So
Hugo continues to plead so that . . . one more effort, gentlemen republicans,
Frenchmen, one more effort, you have abolished the political death penalty,
go further. There is here an advance and a promise]; like a kind of open
door that lets penetrate, in the midst of the obscure and incomplete progress
of the present, the serene light of the future.

And in fact, at a given time, the abolition of capital punishment in political matters must bring about and will necessarily bring about [here one
is going to see the formula that he takes up again elsewhere when he says
"I vote for pure and simple abolition"; it already appears in this speech], by
the almightiness of logic [this is not directly the revolution of Christ, it is
logic, an irresistible movement of reason, of logos. Implacably, it will take
however long it takes; reason will impose it, and between reason and life,
there is an alliance here. So, implacable necessity of logic. There is pathos,
feeling, heart, etc. In fact, what is almighty in the last instance is logic. No
proponent of the death penalty can be in agreement with himself logically,
can be in agreement with logic. There is no logic of the death penalty. Thus,
the almightiness of logic will end up triumphing. "And in fact, at a given

263

time, the abolition of capital punishment in political matters must bring about and will necessarily bring about by the almightiness of logic"], the pure and simple abolition of the death penalty! (*Yes, yes!*) (85–88)

[It was not yes! yes! at the moment; one will have to wait, yes! yes!; one will have to wait until 1981, that is, a century and a half for this yes! yes! to be consistent with the almightiness of the logic in question.]   *264*

February 23, 2000

The mechanism falls like a bolt of lightning, the head flies off, blood spurts out, the man is no more. (Reread).

We will read this statement again later. We will identify it and, beyond its signature, we will analyze it. We will analyze its *sense* [sens] and its *blood* [sang]. We will run a blood test on it—on the word *sang* [blood] and all the homonyms of *sans* [without], of death with and without the effusion of blood.

A number of recent signs these past two weeks, which come to us, of course, from the United States (you read the newspapers, there are so many of them, French and American, that I must give up trying to give a full account), this avalanche, this precipitation of signs, seems to confirm—and how not to celebrate this—the diagnosis or prognosis we have been giving here for months, which in truth organizes our very discourse, on the subject of the growing, accelerated, constantly intensified pressure, both internal and external, to urge the state, the States, if not toward the pure and simple abolition of the death penalty ("pure and simple," the words with which Hugo designated the unconditional abolition that he wished to see, beyond the political death penalty), at least toward a conditional transformation, a profound limitation in the law and in practice, in the *economy* of the death penalty.

Might there be an economy of the death penalty? we were asking ourselves last time.

266 And what could that mean?

If someone formulated the following sentence: "to abolish the death penalty is to economize on the death penalty," how would one interpret such a declaration? Or again if someone said, "the European Union has from now on 'classé,' ['closed the file on,' 'classified'] the death penalty, the United

States will do it one day, a day that is ever closer even if it's not going to happen tomorrow," how should one hear that?

To conclude the long trajectory that guided us in the interpretation of this economy last time, we read a certain text of Hugo's in which I underscored not only the teleo-theological reconciliation of the Enlightenment of reason or of natural law with Christianity, the Christianity of the living and resurrected Christ, of the saved Christ in sum, of Christ the redeemed and Christ the redeemer, of the redemption, the simultaneous reconciliation in a Christian Europe, of France and of Europe, of the marketplace of interest and of the non-marketplace, of the present and the promise, as an "advance" in the sense of both progress and loan, at the moment Hugo, then, salutes the abolition of the death penalty in political matters by the Revolution of February 1848 even while he still hopes for the pure and simple abolition he calls for and that is still refused him. (Since Victor Hugo, when he applauds a conditional [political] abolition, also calls for an unconditional abolition in the double name of the divine law of Christ and of what he calls the "almightiness of logic.")

Well, today I would like to propose we recognize a *turning point* that is also a return, an additional turn in the history of this economy of the death penalty.

This additional turn would also be a turn around the body, not only, not directly, the turn around the neck following the line of a decapitation or decollation (and no doubt you remember this terrible moment, shown in certain films, where the shirt collar is cut off around the neck of the condemned one so as to bare the nape that will be exposed just as it is, naked, to the blade of the guillotine); this additional turn would, then, also be a turn around the body, not only, not directly, the turn around the neck following the line of a decapitation or decollation, but a turn in the rhetoric of the body, the trope that causes blood to turn or circulate in this history, the symbol of blood, blood that flows, red blood, of the color of blood that exhibits, by pouring out, and lets one see the inside on the outside.

267

No history of the economy of the death penalty will be possible without a history of blood; and I would even say, without overdoing the homonymy, a history of the *sans sang*, the "without blood," of what progressively and always in memory of the blood of Christ—that is, in the experience and the general rhetoric of the Eucharist, of the transubstantiation that brings about the real presence of the blood of God or of the man who is the son of God in the wine, and his flesh in the host, the *sans du sang*, then—what must progressively absent itself, make its absence sensible, the virtue of its absence, and will endeavor to make the blood disappear, so that the stages toward abolition or the so-called pure and simple economy of the death penalty will be experiences of the bloodless, experiences of becoming bloodless, of reabsorption, drying up, or the disappearance by interiorization of blood, of the visibility of blood.

Whether or not this is a matter of an economy, merely of an economy, what has happened in the United States from the beginning, in the United States, that is, in the most Christian democracy in the world, is—from hanging to the electric chair, then to lethal injection, and, let us hope, beyond—the end of blood, if one can say that, in the administration of capital punishment. People no longer want to see blood flow; people no longer want to see flow the blood of men or the blood of Christ. Thus, if there is still killing, if that has any meaning, if death has any meaning (and we will come upon this problem again later on), then executing will mean killing without blood [*sans sang*], without a drop of blood.

What, then, is this additional turn, this too-much or this trope [*ce trop ou ce trope*] of blood that one must have done with?

What is blood?

Since we French have, ahead of all, the history, the memory, and the image of the guillotine in our heads [*en tête*], if I may say that, and before or behind our eyes, since, on the other hand, we are still going to be speaking of it a lot, both through Hugo as regards blood and through Camus, I must recall and specify something that is not well known, among the French and others, namely that the guillotine signaled or in any case was felt to be and was interpreted and justified as humane progress, progress in the sense of the human, a becoming-human of putting to death, and even, as Daniel Arasse puts it in his very valuable book, *La guillotine et l'imaginaire de la terreur*, to which I have already referred you, a "humanitarian machine."[1]

Before going further and insisting on this humanization, this humanism, this humanitarianism of the guillotine, I would be tempted to ask the following question: what is it that is proper to man; what is the history of what is proper to man that allows one to think this? What must be that which is called man so that at a moment of his history he comes to consider the guillotine as an advance in human progress, an advance in man's appropriation of his essence? And let us never forget that this moment of supposed humanization of the death penalty by the guillotine is not just any moment

1. Daniel Arasse, *La guillotine et l'imaginaire de la terreur* (Paris : Flammarion, 1987), p. 20.

268

in the history of humanity; it is the French Revolution, that is, among other things, the death[2] of the monarchy of divine right and the declaration of the rights of man. The guillotine, this humanitarian machine, is also not only in synchrony but in metaphysical system, if I may say that, with the Revolution and the Rights of Man. So I repeat my question: what must man be, what is proper to man, the right of man proper to what is proper to man, the history of the right of man proper to what is proper to man for this machine not only not to be the instrument of what has been called for fifty years a crime against humanity but to be interpreted as a machine that serves the dignity of man?

What must man be, what must man, the humanity of man have been, to have inscribed, incorporated as it were, the guillotine in the corpus of the rights of man? To have invented such a machine while interpreting it as a sign of man's love for man, man who is a man and not a wolf for man, human for man, humanitarian or even "philanthropic" — in a moment we will hear the guillotine qualified in these terms: as a visible manifestation of a *philanthropy*. Moreover, in one of his first texts against the death penalty, the guillotine, and Doctor Guillotin, Hugo says ironically in 1832, "Mr. Guillotin was a philanthropist" (36).

269

To give body to these questions, let us first recall certain facts and indications.

First of all, these facts, which might seem to be bio-graphical, to pertain to the bio-graphical history of an inventor of death who was also considered to be the hero of euthanasia, in sum. Who was Guillotin? Doctor Guillotin was a member of the Society of Jesus from 1756 to 1763 before studying medicine. It is thus a former Jesuit, someone who belonged to a corps, a corporation called the Society of Jesus, who invented the guillotine, but who invented it and proposed it in a law when he was already a doctor. We have here the society of the Society of Jesus and of the medical corporation at the origin of the "humanitarian machine," nicknamed, in the feminine, *la guillotine*. The word "machine" took hold very quickly in the vocabulary of the time so as to designate the passage, in effect, from instrument, tool, or manual weapon to the mechanics of a machine, that is, to an automatic, autonomous functioning, from which the hand of man, as it were, could seem to be starting to withdraw, to let itself be neutralized. As if, even though blood is not going to let itself be wiped away, dried up, erased, let its red color fade — far from that — as if, then, *l'arme blanche*[3] were in

---

2. "At least the apparent death," Derrida adds during the session.
3. [Translator's note]: Literally, "the white weapon," i.e., the knife.

the process of yielding to the red machine. But it is in order to rhyme, in a feminine rhyme then, with the word "machine" that Guillotin's child was called guillotine.

Speaking of filiation, of fathers, mothers, sons, and daughters (and we are going to talk about it a lot today), I must recall another legend. The story is told that the mother of Joseph Ignace Guillotin, born in Saintes in May 1738, was pregnant when, walking in the streets of Saintes, she was traumatized by the screams of a man who was being tortured on the wheel, and this traumatic shock is supposed to have precipitated the birth of Joseph Ignace (predestined names for a Jesuit). To establish once and for all the moral of this fable, people said, I quote, that Guillotin had "the executioner for a midwife" (qtd. in Arasse, 17).

So, that's it as concerns his birth.

At the time of the death of the Jesuit doctor, who passed away peacefully in his bed in 1814, his eulogy was delivered by one of his colleagues with a no less edifying name, a certain Doctor Bourru.[4] Bourru underscored the *philanthropic* character of the motion or the proposed law of the guillotine by Guillotin, even as he was already quite sensitive, despite his gruffness, to the vulgar and vulgarizing ambiguity that the vulgar would not fail to associate, quite unfairly, with this brilliant sign of love for mankind, with this philanthropic machine. Bourru said, in the presence of the intact cadaver of his colleague Guillotin:

> Unfortunately for our colleague, his philanthropic gesture, which was accepted and gave rise to an instrument to which the vulgar affixed his name, made him many enemies; for it is so true that it is difficult to do good for mankind without incurring some trouble for oneself. (Qtd. in Arasse, 18) [Comment][5]

To stay for a moment with this question of the name sullied by ambiguity, when a proper name becomes a common noun, which is already a machination, here the proper name becomes the common name of a machine; much later Hugo himself, discerning in his way between *discovery* and *invention*, writes: "There are some unfortunate men. Christopher Co-

4. [Translator's note]: The adjective *bourru* means rough or gruff; it also echos the term *bourreau*, hangman. See below, n. 12.

5. During the session Derrida adds: "So this began right away, right away one began to doubt the philanthropic character of this machine, and yet that was the intention, the will, the good will of the doctor. We are going to see why — I will explain — this anecdote, why it was in fact progress, it was conceived by the shrewdest thinkers of this time as progress. Political progress. We are going to come back to this."

lumbus cannot attach his name to his discovery; Guillotin cannot detach his from his invention."[6]

Once again, it is more than that; once again this witty mark of Hugo's ge- 271
nius says more than it means to say. For Columbus's *discovery*, which Hugo thinks he can oppose feature for feature to Guillotin's *invention*, was also the discovery of an America that will have been the last Christian country massively practicing the death penalty, a few centuries later, and Christopher Columbus is also a contemporary, not to say a symptom or a product, of a Spanish Inquisition that not only expelled, almost the same year, the Jews from Spain, but also condemned to death, in the name of Christ, in conditions I need not recall, and that have given the current pope the idea that, on this point as well, the church will perhaps one day have to examine its conscience and even ask for forgiveness. With this, we are at the most undecidable heart of our subject: Christ and the Christian church, the Christian church and the death penalty, political theology, outside of Christianity, and the death penalty.

To understand fully the guillotine, one must have a good grasp of the projected law with which Guillotin proposed to the Constituent Assembly a reform of the monarchical penal system. Guillotin's project is progressive in spirit, therefore inspired in a certain way by the Enlightenment, which as it is not in contradiction with Christianity, with a certain Christian humanism — and with the Jesuit origins of its author — leads one to think about the complexity of relations among Enlightenment, Aufklärung, and Christianity. The same might be said of Kant: an Enlightenment man if there ever was one, deeply Christian, and rigorous proponent of the death penalty in the name of ethical purity, of human dignity, of that ethics of which the Christian religion alone is in an essential way the religious representation (Christianity is the only intrinsically moral religion). *Progressive* in spirit, Guillotin's proposed law is also *individualist* (the punishment must be individual and have no repercussions on anyone in the family or immediate circle, or on another generation), *egalitarian* (all are equal before the law and the law's form of execution), and *mechanistic, machinistic.* And the three features of this progressivism go together (individualism, egalitarianism, and machinism or mechanism); for fundamentally only the machine, what Guillotin calls "simple mechanics," can make each and everyone equal before 272
the law (just as voting or the counting of votes must mechanically apply the same law for everyone; all votes, one vote per capita, are equal and add up

6. Victor Hugo, "Littérature et philosophie mêlées," quoted by Arasse, *La guillotine et l'imaginaire de la terreur*, p. 19.

in a homogeneous manner; no vote is worth more than any other. One vote
is worth one vote). Let me quickly read the six articles of this proposed law
to underscore this *individualistic, egalitarian, and mechanistic progressivism.*
(Read Arasse, 19–20)

> Article 1. Felonies of the same kind will be punished by the same kind
> of penalties, regardless of the rank and status of the guilty party [Thus,
> democracy].

> Article 2. Felonies and crimes being personal [individualism], the punish-
> ment of a guilty party and whatever defamatory sentences place no stain on
> his family [enormous progress]. The honor of those attached to him is in no
> way sullied and all will continue to be admissible to any kind of profession,
> employment, or honors.

> Article 3. No confiscations of the property of those sentenced can ever be
> decreed, in any case.

> Article 4. The body of the one punished will be turned over to his family if
> they so request. [Here too, this is progress: burial, the body at the disposal
> of the family.] In all cases, he will be allowed ordinary burial and there
> will be no mention in the burial record of the type of death. [All of this is
> progress, isn't it.]

> Article 5. No one may reproach a citizen with whatever punishment or
> defamatory sentences any of his relatives have received. Whoever dares to
> do so will be reprimanded by the judge.

> Article 6. In every case in which the law pronounces the death penalty
> against an accused, the punishment will be the same, whatever may be the
> nature of the felony of which he has been judged guilty [here is the egali-
> tarianism, only the guillotine can accomplish that]. The criminal will be
> decapitated; he will be so by the effect of simple mechanics.[7]

I leave you now to discover as you read Arasse's descriptions the
ancestors—all of them European and Christian—of the guillotine, machines that all have extraordinary names. It is a Dominican, Father Labat,
who analyzes the Mannaia in his *Voyage en Espagne et en Italie* (1730), the
Mannaia that, as a "very reliable machine," "does not prolong the suffering of the patient [!!! more and more, between the sinner and the patient,
the one sentenced to death will be caught between the two complicitous
scenes of Christ's Passion and the pathology of the soul or the body, between

273

7. Quoted in Arasse, *La guillotine et l'imaginaire de la terreur*, pp. 19–20; commentary
added by Derrida during the session has been inserted in brackets.

the priest and the physician] who, through the executioner's lack of skill, is sometimes subjected to several blows before having his head separated from his trunk" (qtd. in Arasse, 23).

There is also the "Maiden" (not the widow but the young girl or the   274
virgin) in Scotland, which we know of through the fascinated description of another churchman, Abbé La Porte (after Labat, La Porte, as if it were always clerics who devoted themselves to describing passionately, compulsively, minutely, scientifically, these death machines) and the English "Halifax Gibbet" and other examples in Holland and Germany. Always reserved for the aristocratic elite. As for the guillotine, it will be democratic and egalitarian. This will be the meaning of its invention, the spirit of its invention.

Before returning to Hugo, I would now like to retain three historical indications. One concerns precisely egalitarianism; the other concerns the lessening or softening of cruelty and its alleged end; the third, finally, the history of blood.

1. As for egalitarianism (penal egalitarianism, that of the equality of punishments, whose juridical concept is literally inherited from Beccaria during the French Revolution, as we will see), I will come back once again to what may be called the double conversion of Robespierre. His first conversion was the conversion to abolitionism, in 1791; the second was the conversion of the conversion, a reconversion to capital punishment in 1793, when he defends the death penalty by the blade on the pretext that it democratizes or equalizes punishment and appearance before the law in what is basically a history of the social classes. In an essay contest organized by the Academy of Metz, Robespierre writes: (Read comment on Arasse, p. 20)

> The wheel, the gibbet . . . dishonor the family of those who perish from this kind of punishment, but the blade that cuts off a guilty head does not debase the relatives of the criminal; it becomes almost a title of nobility for posterity. Would it not be possible to profit from this attitude of mind and to extend to all classes of citizens this latter form of punishing crimes? Let us erase a harmful distinction. . . . In place of a punishment that, to the shame inseparable from the torture, adds a character of disgrace proper to it, let us establish another kind of punishment to which the imagination is used to attaching a kind of brilliance, and from which it separates the idea of family dishonor. (Qtd. in Arasse, 20).

2. But already in 1777, Marat, the terrible Marat —*second indication*— had advocated a less cruel and even "gentle" [*douce*] capital punishment. Why did this softening [*adoucissement*] seem so urgent to him? (Read comment on Arasse, 21)

"Punishments [so it is a plan for criminal legislation; here too, Marat is responding to a contest organized by the Society of Citizens of Neuchâtel, and proposes a plan of criminal legislation, one of whose themes, I quote, aims "to reconcile gentleness with the certainty of punishment," gentleness, more cruel] must rarely be capital [the motif of the exception that we have spoken of a lot . . .]. Life is the only good in this world that has no equivalent; thus justice demands that the punishment for murder be capital. But how one puts to death must never be cruel [here one sees again the matrix of all the texts of modernity on "cruel and unusual punishment," all the texts after World War II: no torture, no cruel punishment], one must look rather in the direction of ignominy. Even in the gravest cases (liberticide, parricide, fratricide, the killing of a friend or benefactor), the apparatus of justice should be dreadful, but death should be gentle." [In other words, strange concept of gentleness, the torment must be terrible, spectacular, etc., but death must be gentle, the moment of death must be gentle. Arasse, who quotes this text, writes this:]

275   Terrifying apparatus / gentle death. Guillotin could think that his proposal went in the direction of these aspirations of the "intellectual" and "philosophical" milieu of the time: reduce punishments, while maintaining the value of example of the supreme punishment.

Today people often grant an exceptional place to the execution of Damiens in 1757: having slightly wounded Louis XV with a knife, he was condemned to be drawn and quartered, the punishment set aside for regicide. As is well known, it turned into a catastrophe: Damiens does not die, the horses cannot manage to dismember him, and the executioner must finally cut him up with a knife. This horror, it is true, was due in part to the almost excusable inexperience of the head executioner Charles Jean-Baptiste Sanson, his son Charles Henri, and of the numerous assistants he had called upon for such an exceptional case: drawing and quartering had no longer been practiced in Paris since Ravaillac[8] and thus the technique had not been handed down. . . . Meanwhile, the affair caused a scandal, to the point that in the autumn of 1758 the usher of the king's household, Mauriceau de La Motte, was hanged and his property confiscated for having, in this regard, "spoken against the government itself, against the King, and the ministers" and made posters about the execution of Damiens.[9]

3. *Third indication*, finally, which takes us back, via egalitarianism and the supposed end of cruelty, to the great hematographic, or even hemophilic

---

8. [Translator's note]: François Ravaillac, who assassinated Henri IV, was drawn and quartered in Paris on May 27, 1610.

9. Quoted in Arasse, *La guillotine et l'imaginaire de la terreur*, p. 21; commentary added by Derrida during the session has been inserted in brackets.

or hemophobic question, the limitless question of blood and of the blood of one's fellow man, to the equivocation of red blood that will be the revolutionary symbol (before being the flag of the Commune, or one-third of the French flag, the red flag, by decree of the Constituent Assembly, was to be flown each time that, in conformity with martial law [and red is a signal of war here], it was necessary to disperse a counterrevolutionary gathering, hence, no doubt, the constant association ever since of the red flag with rallying and revolutionary insurrection, up to the Commune and the 1917 revolution).[10]

With reference to what was said last time about the Revolution of 1848, I would point out that Marx ironically notes the ambiguity of red in *The Eighteenth Brumaire* when he names the "red specter" (*das "rote Gespenst"*) of the revolutionaries; the red specter conjured away by the counterrevolutionaries in 1848 who counter it not with the red Phrygian cap but the red pantaloons of the police force (*in roten Plumphosen*). There is also (if it interests you and if you want references, I talk about all this in *Specters of Marx*)[11] a newspaper titled *The Red Specter* that, during the 1848 revolution, after the June massacres apparently, evoked the specter of the dead proletarian revolutionaries, which means that red is the blood of the victims, those who died in the revolutionary fight — and in this sense it has positive connotations. Villiers de l'Isle Adam is also the author of a "Specter of the Red Death," which apparently is not the same thing as the death of the reds.

So, third indication, the guillotine that both allows one to avoid soaking one's hands in the blood of one's fellow men and that, by the same blow, puts an end to the *bourreau* who becomes an executioner, basically a civil servant.[12] The *bourreau* is repatriated into civil society; he becomes, in an egalitarian manner, a citizen like any other, a legal subject who will have the right to vote, the right to elect, and be elected. The guillotine is what will have been interpreted as this progress toward the end of cruelty, a bloody, sanguinary cruelty between fellow men and brothers, and the end of the *bourreau*. Guillotin's speech has been lost; all that remains is the proposed

276

10. The closing parenthesis has been added.

11. J. Derrida, *Spectres de Marx*, trans. Peggy Kamuf (New York: Routledge, 1994), p. 189.

12. [Translator's note]: The noun *bourreau*, ordinarily translated as executioner or hangman, is from the verb *bourrer*, to strike. In addition to designating the state-appointed executioner of death penalties, it has a more general extension: torturer, taskmaster, cruel or sadistic person. Before the Revolution, the *bourreau* and his family were social pariahs. For the reasons explained here by Derrida, the term will be left in French when the difference from "executioner" is pertinent.

legislation that I quoted earlier, but we still have the commentary on his speech that was published in the *Journal des États Généraux:*

> Mr. Guillotin dwelled at length on the tortures that place humanity below savage beasts; flaying, and so forth, I pass over them in silence. It is to be wished that even their names might soon be forgotten. He described the horror inspired by those known as *bourreaux.* Filled with the same feelings ... what especially overwhelmed my imagination is that there have been those capable of dishonoring man to the point of soaking their hands, in cold blood, in the blood of their fellow men, out of obedience. [That is the horror, that there are men capable in cold blood of soaking their hands in the blood of their fellow men. That is what the executioner of the guillotine puts an end to. The guillotine, the executioner, puts an end to the *bourreau.* Arasse, who is citing this text, comments: "This text is clear: the machine has the great merit of making an *unimaginable* being *imaginable*, of finally transforming the *bourreau* into an 'executioner.' In short, the guillotine also justifies that, along with actors and Jews, the only singular one and noun in this series, the *bourreau* becomes electable in 1790 by decree of the assembly: imaginable as a representative even." (Arasse, 22)][13]

277

As you know, in the inexhaustible symbolics of blood, from sacrificial blood or Christ's blood to the blood of filiation, and so on and so forth, there is always good blood and bad blood, and the two are often indiscernible. And often, within the same and unsurpassable sacrificial logic, good blood is supposed to redeem bad blood, to have the historical meaning of a redeeming expiation. I had first thought to analyze closely with you the logic, the rhetoric and the thematics, the philosophical and spiritual, religious semantics of blood and the color red in all Hugo's texts on the death penalty. I must forgo that because this hematochromatic corpus is too rich and would take us all year. And besides you can do this work by reading the volume of [Hugo's] *Writings on the Death Penalty.*

I will limit myself, therefore, to a few schematic and preliminary points of reference. I select them first of all from Hugo's earliest text, from 1832, which is the postponed preface, three years afterward, to his book *The Last Day of a Condemned Man.* Given the subject I am privileging, namely the question of blood, of good and bad blood as Christian ambiguity, or even as sacrificial logic that allows the redemption, through substitution, of the evil of bad blood by the sacrifice of good blood, I begin with the end where, announcing and welcoming the progress under way that must ineluctably

278

---

13. Derrida's comments during the session are inserted in brackets, along with the additional quotation provided during that commentary.

lead to the end of the death penalty, Hugo sees there in sum a triumph and victory of Christ, of the "gentle law of Christ" and of charity, and the sacrificial process will be signaled by a substitution, as you are going to hear, that of the cross for the gallows.

Just before this, Hugo was doing what we do today, but he is still more naïve and credulous than we pretend to be (for if we believe in the same movement, in the same abolitionist progress, we know now both that it will be long and interminable and <that it> will take on all sorts of new forms); Hugo was saying, then, that the end of the death penalty is imminent and ineluctable. He lists the signs of this and writes:

> Besides, let one make no mistake, this question of the death penalty is maturing every day. Before long, society as a whole will resolve it as we do.
> The most stubborn criminalists should beware: for a century the death penalty has been on the decrease [Let us not forget that we are in 1832; today it is more than 168 years since Hugo said that and when he says "for a century the death penalty has been on the decrease," this goes back almost thirty years before Beccaria, 1765, of whom he has already spoken in the same text and to which we will return]. It is becoming almost gentle [*douce*].

The word *douceur* here, that is, the inverse of cruelty, prepares what will be said two pages later, namely that "the gentle [*douce*] law of Christ will finally permeate the legal code and radiate out from there" (38) (comment with reference to the already explicated text: natural law and unwritten law against code, here natural law: law of Jesus.)[14]

> Sign of decrepitude. Sign of imminent death [the death penalty is going to die, agony; end; but thanks to Christ's Passion and the "gentle law of Christ"].
> Torture has vanished, the wheel has vanished. The gallows has vanished. It is a strange thing! The guillotine itself is progress.

279

14. Derrida adds during the session: "It is interesting, this sentence, because it means that the law of Christ, which Hugo seems too often to confuse with natural law, that is, with an unwritten law, an originary unwritten law, is going to permeate the legal code. It is going to irrigate the law, the written legislation. Little by little, Christ, the spirit, the soul, the gentle law, the gentleness of Christ, charity, the blood of Christ, is going to irrigate the legal code and transform legislative writing. So he is playing here natural law against written law while hoping, while even being sure that natural law — the heart, finally, Jesus is the heart, the blood is the heart — the heart is going to transform the written and positive, historical law. Little by little, the legal code, written law, historical law, will be irrigated, inspired, vivified, spiritualized, by gentleness, the gentle law of Christ."

202 ‡ EIGHTH SESSION, FEBRUARY 23, 2000

Here Victor Hugo waxes ironic; he begins a new paragraph and continues:

> Mr. Guillotin was a philanthropist.
>
> Yes, the horrible toothy and voracious Themis of Farinace and of Vouglans, of Delancre and of Isaac Loisel, of d'Oppède and of Machault [I assume these are names of *bourreaux*] is dying. She is wasting away. She is dying. (36)

Once again, the figure of abolition is that of a death of the death penalty, an end of the end, after a process of senescence, senility, debility. And this death of death, this agony of the guillotine, may go on, to be sure, but it will go to term, like an organism justly condemned. This rhetorical organicism, this diagnosis or prognosis in its medical figure that causes one to say here that the sentence of death is sentenced and later, I quote, that "all the symptoms are in our favor" (37), this clinical and teleo-pathological language is the reaffirmation of what Shelley (another adversary of the death penalty) calls in the title of his great poem "The Triumph of Life," by opposition to the classical, poetic, and pictorial figure of all the triumphs of death, a classical motif and well-known allegory, for it is in the name of what Hugo a hundred times calls "the inviolability of human life" that death is going to die. It is a principle of life that sentences the death sentence to death.

Before coming to the sign by which Hugo recognizes this imminent end, namely, the moving of the guillotine out of the center of Paris, I will open a parenthesis on the subject of this medical language and the blood lab in which Hugo treats this verdict of the death penalty in our society. In an extraordinary and very symptomatic passage from "Literature and Philosophy Combined," Hugo has to have it out with the Revolution, with Robespierre, and thus with the Terror. And thus with the guillotine. He is for the Revolution but against the Terror and against the guillotine. Against 93.[15] How is he going to pull this off? Well, by a staging that threads a long hemato-medico-surgical metaphor. He condemns the red of the Phrygian cap as well as the red of the blood of the guillotine. He rejects the argument of those who want to justify the Terror by speaking of a necessary amputation and comparing the guillotine to a surgeon's scalpel. Hugo will have none of this scalpel argument. Finally, indeed, in place of the operation of mutilation, he proposes the purification of blood, just as he proposes to substitute the doctor of internal medicine, in sum, for the surgeon. The words,

15. [Translator's note]: That is, 1793, the year of Louis XVI's execution, which signaled the beginning of the Terror.

which you are going to hear, "slow and gradual purification of the blood," in place of surgery, point clearly to the spiritualizing, interiorizing, sublating, redeeming, and fundamentally Christian economy that Hugo opposes both to the revolutionary Terror and to the guillotine. I am going to read the beginning and the end of this extract, for you will see how the humanities that must preside over this humanization of the law are Christian humanities and are opposed to both the Hebraic and the Roman. (Read and comment on *Écrits*, 39–40)

I am not one of your people wearing a red cap and stubbornly in favor of the guillotine.

For many dispassionate reasoners who theorize the Terror after the fact, 93 was a brutal but necessary amputation. Robespierre is a political Dupuytren.[16] What we call the guillotine is but a scalpel.

That may be. But from now on the ills of society must be treated not by the scalpel, but by the slow and gradual purification of the blood, by the cautious reabsorption of exuded humors, by healthy nutrition, by the exercise of one's strengths and faculties, by good diet. Let us no longer turn to the surgeon, but to the physician. . . .

Political rights, the functions of juror, voter, and national guard, obviously enter into the normal constitution of every member of the polity. Every man of the people is, a priori, a man of the polity.

However, political rights, also obviously, must slumber in the individual until the individual knows clearly what political rights are, what they mean, and what one does with them. To exercise one must understand. In good logic, the understanding of the thing must always precede action on the thing.

One must thus — and this point cannot be overemphasized — enlighten the people in order to be able to constitute it one day. And it is a sacred duty for those who govern to hasten to spread enlightenment among those benighted masses on which definitive law rests. Every honest tutor hurries the emancipation of his pupil. Multiply, then, the paths that lead to intelligence, knowledge, aptitude. The Chamber — I almost said the throne — must be the last step on a ladder of which the first step is a school.

And moreover, to instruct the people is to better them; to enlighten the people is to make them moral; to bring literacy to the people is to civilize them. All brutality melts away over the gentle fire of good daily reading. *Humaniores litterae*. One must make the people study their humanities.

Do not ask for rights for the people so long as the people are asking for heads. . . .

16. [Translator's note]: Guillaume Dupuytren (1777–1835) was a famous French anatomist and military surgeon.

282   The death penalty is departing from our customs. A little while longer
and Christian European civilization,[17] having developed more and more
in the direction that is properly its own, will let fall in ruins this old laby-
rinthine construction of bloody punishments, built of gallows, paved with
skulls, covered on every level with the bronze of Hebraic texts,[18] ironclad,
nailed, pieced together here and there with the rusted and formless debris
of Roman law; a veritable Babel of criminal procedure that speaks every
language except ours. (39–40)[19]

The sign by which Hugo recognizes this imminent end is first of all the
moving of the guillotine out of the center of Paris. This is an event that will
constantly hold Hugo's attention during this period and he comes back to it
often. The decision was made to move the guillotine, which Hugo also regularly calls the machine ("this hideous machine," "the infamous machine"
on the same page [37]: this means that, in an interesting complication, the
organism condemned to death, the sick organism destined to die after having exhibited so many symptoms of its illness, this living organism is not
living, has never been a living being but already a machine; what is dying
is not a living being but a mechanism, a machine of death, a dead machine
of death—and which was thus always already dead, mortal, dying, deadly
because it is a machine; and we will soon see that, on top of it all, this machine did not work well, it malfunctioned in a terrifying and barbaric way).
Thus, in a symptom of shame and disavowal, the decision has just been
made to move the hideous machine, away from the Place de la Grève, that
283   is, the Place de l'Hôtel de Ville, to the Saint Jacques gate.[20] Some forty pages
earlier Hugo pretended to address the machine and to say to it: "You are
leaving the Grève for the Saint Jacques gate, the crowd for solitude, daylight

17. During the session, Derrida adds: "And one must say that Hugo always says
'Christian European,' and that, if you read his texts on Europe, he was a prophet, of
extraordinary lucidity, as concerns the Christian Europe that is ours today. I know few
texts that are as lucid as concerns the Europe that is coming."

18. During the session, Derrida refers back to the seminar of the two preceding years,
"Perjury and Pardon" (1997–99): "Remember the texts of Hegel that we were reading
on forgiveness, the passage from the Hebraic to the Christic. Everything that is indicted
here is the Hebraic and the Roman, as opposed to the Christian."

19. During the session, Derrida adds: "If one wanted to read this text with ill will,
today, one could. 'A veritable Babel of criminal procedure that speaks every language
except ours,' thus that speaks Hebraic, Roman, but not French-Christian. Here is the
Christian Europe that is heralded."

20. [Translator's note]: One of the gates in the earliest fortifications of Paris. Where
it used to stand is near the Pantheon in the Fifth Arrondissement.

for twilight. You no longer do steadfastly what you do. You are hiding, I tell you" (30). This "You no longer do steadfastly what you do" is an allusion to a terrifying malfunction that Hugo describes in detail elsewhere (we will come back to it perhaps at the end of the session) when the guillotine is seen failing to deliver its blow and having doggedly to start over again ten times before finishing its job and finishing off the condemned one. The Place de la Grève, which Hugo names ten times to welcome the fact that the "infamous machine" has been moved away from it, one should know (you no doubt know this but I spell it out at least for foreigners and those French who are not lovers of the memory of Paris) that it was the Place de l'Hôtel de Ville, situated, therefore, on the bank of the Seine, that is, on the *grève*, a word that means ground formed by gravel on the bank of a river or the sea. One says *grève* or *grave* to designate these "banks" [*rives*]. Now, the Place de la Grève was for a long time the place of executions, even before the guillotine. People were drawn on the wheel and hanged in the Place de la Grève. One said "la Grève." But since it was also the place where people were hired, well, to be *en grève*, on strike,[21] was to find oneself without work at the Place de la Grève, while waiting for work or protesting against the lack of work. The word *grève* (as in *grève ouvrière, grève générale, grève révolutionnaire, gréviste*)[22] comes from there. So that, in a supplementary play or paradox, to move the guillotine away from the Place de la Grève, from "la Grève" as people said, signaled, according to Hugo, that the machine was doing its job badly, that one was hiding it by exiling it and that one day or other, it is as if it itself would have to be *en grève*, "on strike." *En grève* far from the Grève, *en grève* far from the Place de la Grève. The *grève* of the death penalty is signaled when the "hideous machine" is moved away from the Grève, from the central, visible place, from the heart and theater of Paris. From the Hôtel de Ville.[23]

All of this, then, would stem from that process of devisibilization, despectacularization, whose overdetermined complexity we underscored at the beginning of the seminar. Overdetermined because the spectacle will have continued; it still continues by becoming virtual. And even far from the Grève, the execution by guillotine remained a public spectacle until the

284

21. [Translator's note]: The phrase "on strike" is in English in the original.

22. [Translator's note]: That is, worker's strike, general strike, revolutionary strike, striker.

23. [Translator's note]: The Hôtel de Ville is the city hall and in Paris it and the large square surrounding it are indeed situated, as Derrida points out, on the right bank of the Seine in the center of the city.

middle of the twentieth century, until 1938 it seems to me. Children were taken to see the thing and one of you told me that his/her parents were brought to the spectacle by their own parents during their childhood.

And this is where blood appears in this passage, just as it flows everywhere on every page of these *Writings* of Hugo. What happens is also the end of the *bourreau* repudiated by his wife. For it is a procedure of repudiation between a woman and her husband, or man, or procurer, and it is the woman who repudiates the man, and one must also pay attention to Hugo's insistence on the feminine nature, on the femininity of this cruel machine, this guillotine daughter of the philanthropist Guillotin. It is an old woman, an old whore who is losing her teeth, who is no longer the "toothed and voracious Themis." She can no longer eat; she drinks. Hugo does not say "widow," as people will do later on in a slangy fashion, but "old blood swiller," old prostitute who, by leaving the Grève, the sidewalk of the Hôtel de Ville, repudiates her husband or her pimp, namely, the *bourreau*, the executioner. This is but the first appearance of woman in this session.

The expression "blood swiller" [*buveuse de sang*] deserves, it seems to me, a moment's pause. It means, of course, that she makes blood flow, that she demands and consumes blood, she is bloodthirsty and bloody and blood red, butcher red, like her wooden uprights.[24] But since she swills blood, she is
285 also a blotter [*buvard*] that makes blood disappear. She absorbs blood; she assimilates it and does not splatter, hence the progress people credit her with: she causes blood to flow, to be sure, but she economizes on it by drinking it, by making it disappear right away into herself, by swallowing it, by gulping it down, by no longer letting it appear so much on the outside, by minimizing it, by reducing it, by sparing it. She is hemophilic, but so hemophilic that she keeps the blood for herself, she keeps it to herself. She economizes blood. She manages to do this all by herself. Which allows her to repudiate the executioner. (Read and comment on 37)

> Here already the Grève does not want her anymore. The Grève is rehabilitating herself. The old blood swiller behaved well in July. From now on she

24. Derrida adds during the session: "These wooden uprights that Hugo abundantly describes elsewhere. Notably when he describes—I will not have time to analyze the text, but I refer to it in passing—an extraordinary page, the arrival in Algiers of the first guillotine soon after 1830. Then two marvelous pages where he describes the marvel that is Algiers upon the arrival of the boat, all the merchandise, the produce, and all of a sudden there is this object, no one knows what it is, and then they see the red wood, and then the first guillotine is delivered to Algiers. And the rhythm of the text, there, is absolutely extraordinary. You will find the page."

wants to lead a better life and remain worthy of her last beautiful act. She who had prostituted herself for more than three centuries to all the scaffolds, now is overcome with modesty. She is ashamed of her old profession. She wants to lose her sordid name. She repudiates her *bourreau*. She washes down her pavement.

At the present time, the death penalty is already outside of Paris. Now, let us say this clearly here, to leave Paris is to leave civilization.

All the symptoms are in our favor. It also seems to lose heart and become recalcitrant, this hideous machine, or rather this monster made of wood and iron that is to Guillotin what Galatea is to Pygmalion. Seen from a certain angle, the frightful executions that we detailed above are excellent signs. The guillotine is hesitating. It has begun to misfire. All the old scaffolding of the death penalty is becoming unhinged.

The infamous machine will leave France, we count on that, and God willing, it will leave limping for we will try to land some harsh blows on it.

Let it go seek hospitality elsewhere, from some barbaric people, not from Turkey, which is becoming civilized, not from the savages, who will not want it; but let it descend a few more steps on the ladder of civilization, let it go to Spain or Russia.

The social edifice of the past rested on three columns, the priest, the king, the executioner. (37)

At this point is laid out the most tenacious and the most profound logic, the trickiest as well, in what must indeed be called Hugo's *economy*, his own and the one of which he is the eloquent, ingenious, generous, eloquent [*sic*], and lively representative. For what moves away from the Place de la Grève, with the guillotine, in 1832 (date on which, as I recalled the last time, under Louis-Philippe and at his suggestion, the death penalty was abolished in nine cases including counterfeiting and aggravated burglary), what moves away from the Place de la Grève, with the guillotine, in 1832, is also the old society with its three pillars, its three columns, namely and I emphasize this, *the priest, the king, and the executioner* (and so the priest was part of the old edifice, and the church is an accomplice, like the king and the executioner, of the death penalty), but—and here is the economy that always proceeds by substitution—the distancing of the priest does not mean the disappearance of God or Christ any more than the disappearance of the king or the father means the disappearance of the fatherland. As for the disappearance of the executioner, well, even though things and the substitution are more enigmatic here, as you are going to hear, it does not signify the disappearance of order. This whole economy of substitution or this sublation (Christian *Aufhebung*, as always, that amounts to keeping what it loses) plays on, turns round, and this is not fortuitous, the little word *reste*

286

[remains]. There is what leaves, moves away, disappears (the guillotine, the death machine, and the columns of the old social order, the priest, the king, the executioner), but there is what remains and replaces or relieves, advantageously, what is lost. The difference marked by the executioner in the series "priest, king, executioner" does not count, finally; you are going to see that the executioner also is replaced by an order that *remains*. What counts is the remainder, what remains.

I continue reading. (Read and comment on 37–38)

> The social edifice of the past rested on three columns, the priest, the king, the executioner. Already a long time ago a voice said: *The gods are leaving!* Recently another voice was raised and cried out: *The kings are leaving!* It is now time that a third voice be raised and say: *The executioner is leaving!*
>
> Thus the old society will have fallen stone by stone; thus providence will have completed the collapse of the past.
>
> To those who regretted the gods, it was possible to say: God remains. To those who regret the kings, one can say: the fatherland remains. To those who would regret the executioner, there is nothing to say.
>
> And order will not disappear with the executioner; do not believe that at all. The vault of the future society will not collapse from not having this hideous keystone. Civilization is nothing other than a series of successive transformations. What then are you going to witness? The transformation of penality. The gentle law of Christ will finally permeate the legal code and radiate out from there. Crime will be regarded as an illness, and this illness will have its doctors who will replace your judges, its hospitals that will replace your penal colonies. Freedom and health will resemble each other. Balm and oil will be poured where one used to apply the iron and the fire.[25] This illness that used to be treated with anger will be treated with charity. It will be simple and sublime. The cross will be substituted for the gallows. That is all. (37–38)

We can already recognize in the logico-teleological structure of this argumentation a setting for a debate, no doubt a false debate, between those who, like Hugo, see in the death penalty a phenomenon that, however tied it may be to the church, cannot be abolished except through recourse to a natural law implicating both the existence of God and Christ's passion (the death

25. Derrida adds during the session: "In other words, alliance of the modern confusion between justice and medicine. To replace prisons by hospitals, to treat criminals, etc., a respectable and complex motif. Alliance between that motif, the medicalization of the criminal and the Christic motif, they are the same. Balm, unction, balm and oil, iron and flame. In other words, the medicalization *is* Christic. The medicalization of justice is done in the figure, history, narrative of Christ."

penalty is abolished in the name of Christ), and, on the other hand, those who, like Camus (we will hear from him later), think on the contrary that the abolitionist horizon is a horizon of atheistic humanism, immanentist humanism — given that one can accept the death penalty only by believing in divine justice in the beyond, a justice that renders the verdict of death reversible, not irreparable, relativizable, whereas in a world of man alone, without God, the death sentence, its merciless, implacable irreversibility, would no longer be tolerable. As incompatible as these two logics of abo-   *288*
litionism apparently are, the one conforming to a Christological transcendence and the other to an immanentist humanism, in truth if one reflects that, unlike Judaism and Islam, Christian monotheism is also a humanist immanentism, a belief in the mediation of God made man, precisely in the sacrifice of the Passion and in the Incarnation, the logic of the remainder that I just evoked reconciles the two apparently irreconcilable poles — and Camus's discourse, which we will come to, would be more Christian, more Christlike, than he thought.

Once again, we are treating what I call the Hugolian economy as an exemplary example of what it represents, which considerably exceeds the singular genius who represents it so well. It must be said, so as to try, as always, to be as just as possible, that even as he respects his own economy, Hugo does not fail, in turn, and on this date (1830–32, in the same text) — and this is still part of his economy — to analyze, we will say to "deconstruct," the interests of those in the Chamber who, at a given moment, were tempted to abolish the death penalty, but so as to save four of their own, four politicians, "four men of the world," says Hugo, "four proper gentlemen." Hugo is merciless in denouncing the *interest* — and as Marx would have done, as he did do much later — the *class* interest that dictated this attempt to put the death penalty in question; he calls it a "clumsy, awkward, almost hypocritical attempt and done in an interest other than the general interest" (13). Hugo had earlier declared that "if ever a revolution seemed to us worthy and capable of abolishing the death penalty, it was the July Revolution. It seems, indeed, that it was up to the most lenient popular movement of modern times to discard the barbaric penality of Louis XI, Richelieu, and Robespierre [in the same basket!] and to inscribe on the forehead of the law the inviolability of human life. The year 1830 was worthy of breaking the blade of 93" (12–13).

    When four politicians, men of the world, risk being sent to the guil-   *289*
lotine, the Chamber examines the possibility of an abolition of the death penalty. Even as he is pleased to see this hypothesis entertained, Hugo re-

grets that it is being done on this occasion and in this interest, which, as you will hear, he does not hesitate to call — as Marx will do more than twenty years later for the Revolution of 1848 and its abolition of the political death penalty — class justice. The satirical description that he gives of the situation, of the threads and strings of this social puppet, of the symbolic colors (for this text is a chromatics and one could read it simply from this point of view, the point of view of the spectrum of colors), all of this dismantles the social machination that is busy dismantling the machine of the guillotine, "Guillotin's mechanics," but in view of its own immediate interests. Hugo dismantles a dismantling; he dismantles the machination that wishes to dismantle the machine so as to save its neck, these necks rather than others. By dismantling this dismantling, by "deconstructing," if you will, an interested deconstruction, Hugo denounces what he calls an "alloy of egotism" and "fine social schemes." (Read and comment on 14–17)

> The good public, which understood nothing of the affair, had tears in their eyes.
> So what was at issue? Abolishing the death penalty?
> Yes and no.
> Here are the facts:
> Four men of the world, four proper gentlemen, men of the sort one might meet in a salon, and with whom one perhaps exchanged a few polite words; four of these men, I say, had attempted to pull off, in high political places, one of those bold moves that Bacon calls *crimes* and that Machiavelli calls *enterprises*. Well, crime or enterprise, the law, brutal for everyone, punishes it with death. And the four unfortunates were there, prisoners, captives of the law, guarded by three hundred tricolor cockades beneath the beautiful ogives of Vincennes. What to do and how to do it? You understand that it is impossible to send four men like you and me, four *men of the world*, in a tumbrel, tied up ignobly with heavy ropes, back to back together with that civil servant one must not even name, to the Grève? Maybe if there were a guillotine made of mahogany!
> Hey! We just have to abolish the death penalty!
> And thereupon, the Chamber got to work.
> Notice, gentlemen, that only yesterday you dismissed this abolition as utopia, theory, dream, madness, poetry. Notice that this is not the first time someone sought to call your attention to the tumbrel, the heavy ropes, and the horrible scarlet machine, and that it is strange how this hideous apparatus thus becomes so obvious to you all of a sudden.
> Bah! As if that were the issue! It is not because of you, the people, that we are abolishing the death penalty, but because of us, representatives who

290

might become ministers. We do not want Guillotin's mechanics to bite into the upper classes. We are breaking it. So much the better if that is best for everyone, but we were thinking only of ourselves. Ucalegon is burning. Let us put out the fire. Quick, let us get rid of the executioner, let us cross out the legal code.

And that is how an alloy of egotism alters and deforms the finest social schemes. That is the black vein in the white marble; it circulates everywhere and appears at any moment without warning beneath the chisel. Your statue has to be done over.

To be sure, it is not necessary for us to declare it here, we are not among those who were demanding the heads of the four ministers. . . . For, it must also be said that, in social crises, of all the scaffolds the political scaffold is the most abominable, the most baleful, the most poisonous, the one it is most necessary to rip out. This kind of guillotine takes root in the pavement and before long has sent up shoots all over the ground.

In revolutionary times, beware of the first head to fall. It gives the people an appetite.

We were thus personally in accord with those who wanted to spare the four ministers, and in accord on every score, for sentimental reasons as well as for political reasons. Simply, we would have preferred that the Chamber chose another occasion to propose the abolition of the death penalty. (14–17)

I owe you some justifications and explanations of the economy and strategy of my own reading and the discourse I am maintaining here. It is of course a compromise among several different, or even contradictory, imperatives. On the one hand, for example, I feel that one should analyze for itself, and almost ad infinitum, Hugo's writing, its logic, its rhetoric, even its poetics (for example its chromatics and its treatment of blood, and of red, etc.), but I should also, while analyzing the philosophico-religious economy of his argument, bring out through the exemplary text of Hugo something like a ground or a pedestal, the bases or the foundations, the alleged fundaments of the abolitionist discourse that, since the Enlightenment and a certain Christian inflection of the Enlightenment, for example, since Beccaria, have supported and support still today the logic of the abolitionist struggle. It is a matter, of course, of doing history, but while doing history, of bringing to light the powers and limits of the abolitionist discursive machine or architecture, of an abolitionist argument that is still in force today. The abolitionist discourse today, even if it lays claim to great timeless, ahistorical, or unconditional principles such as the right to life or human rights (whether natural rights or not) has a sedimented history, a European history, a history of Europe, of Christian Europe, that is getting itself ready or constructing

291

itself by means of the Enlightenment, revolutions, declarations of the rights of man, and so forth.

For example, Hugo's argument for the prosecution is grafted onto the event that was Beccaria's argument. Well, we must privilege in this economy the explicit references that Hugo repeatedly makes to Beccaria in his *Writings*. Obviously, Beccaria himself had his teachers who were the teachers of the Enlightenment. He explicitly lays claim to the legacy of d'Alembert, Montesquieu, Diderot, Helvétius, Buffon, Hume, d'Holbach and especially Rousseau, even if he does not mention the latter and sometimes takes a distance from him here or there. In turn, he is saluted and praised by Voltaire. Finally, the influence of Beccaria quickly spread in Europe and even in the United States where, already in 1777 (and one must underscore this to give a measure of the depth and length of this American history of abolitionism), *Of Crimes and Punishments* was published in Charleston. And, as Badinter points out in the preface to Beccaria that I have already quoted, the first work of Voltaire's to appear in the United States was his *Commentary* on Beccaria. Thomas Jefferson subscribed ardently to Beccaria's principles and took inspiration from them when drafting his famous proposed legislation on "the proportionality of crimes and punishments in cases of heretofore capital crimes." Ten years later, in Pennsylvania, the state where Mumia is today and has been for eighteen years on death row along with so many others, in Pennsylvania, which is today one of the most prominent "killing states" (to cite the title of a book edited by Austin Sarat: *The Killing State: Capital Punishment in Law, Politics, and Culture*),[26] well, in 1787, ten years after the translation of Beccaria in the United States, Pennsylvania was the site of a campaign for the abolition of the death penalty.

Hugo, beginning with this first text, cites Beccaria.[27] He does so in a singular manner and according to a strategy that deserves to be taken into account. I draw three features from it.

1. First of all, the autobiography of a young man not even thirty years old who presents modestly, in a preface, his book *The Last Day of a Condemned Man* as the work of a timid writer who is something like the son or grandson of Beccaria whose work he wishes merely to continue and extend. And this scene of autobiographical filiation, basically like that of a genealogical tree in the family of abolitionists, is remarkably well served

---

26. Austin Sarat, *The Killing State: Capital Punishment in Law, Politics, and Culture* (Oxford : Oxford University Press, 1999).

27. Hugo, *Écrits sur la peine de mort,* pp. 12, 20, 35.

by a metaphor of the tree, not only the genealogical tree but the tree that is to be cut down with a new hatchet blow, after the notch that Beccaria has made in it.

2. And this is the *second feature*: this tree that must be cut down is the death penalty; it is the tree that revolutions do not know how to cut down. Thus: critique of the limit of revolution. It does not uproot the sinister tree of the death penalty. Well, following the notch that grandfather Beccaria made in it, sixty-six years ago, I, the young Victor Hugo, his puny grandson, I am going to try to cut it down with a hatchet blow. It is true that in this genealogical tree, filiation does not stop at the grandfather. Grandfather Beccaria himself was engendered. This Italian ancestor was himself the son   *293* of a Frenchman, and this "generation" is a grafting of books. Hugo writes: "The *Treatise on Crimes* is grafted onto *The Spirit of the Laws*. Montesquieu engendered Beccaria" (35).

3. Finally, the *third feature* features Christianity. In the Christian filiation, in the filiation of Christ, son of God, first of all. The tree in question is also that of the old gallows erected for so many centuries "on Christendom"; this "on Christendom" means both, it seems to me, that the gallows in question was founded on Christendom and that, founded on Christendom, it has also betrayed, hidden, buried the Christian message. It was founded on Christendom against Christ, against the son of God. It has put Christ in the tomb and one must now resurrect him from there. And obviously the blood that flows in this page is also irrigated by the blood of the crucified. Here is the first reference to Beccaria in the work of the young Hugo. I read and comment on this page in conclusion, or almost, today. (Read and comment on 10–12)

> Three years ago, when this book appeared, a few people thought it worthwhile to challenge the source of the author's idea. Some supposed it to be an English book, others an American book. How odd the obsession with looking a thousand leagues distant for the origins of things, and to make the stream that washes your pavement flow from the sources of the Nile! Alas! There is in this neither English book, nor American book, nor Chinese book. The author took the idea for *The Last Day of a Condemned Man* not from a book — he does not have the habit of going so far to find his ideas — but where any of you can find it, where you did find it perhaps (for who has not done or dreamed in his mind *The Last Day of a Condemned Man?*), quite simply on the public square, on the Place de Grève. It was there that one day, passing by, he picked up this fatal idea that was lying lifeless in a puddle of blood beneath the red stumps of the guillotine.

Since then, each time that, at the mercy of the funereal Thursdays of the appeals court, one of those days arrived when the cry of a death sentence rings out in Paris, each time that the author heard beneath his windows those hoarse howls that draw a pack of spectators for the Grève, each time the painful idea came back to him, grabbed hold of him, filled his head with armed guards, executioners, and crowds, detailed to him hour by hour the last sufferings of the miserable one in agony — now someone is taking his confession, now they are cutting his hair, now his hands are being bound — summoned him, a poor poet, to recount all this to society, which goes about its business while this monstrous thing is being carried out, pressed him, urged him, shook him, tore his verses from his mind, if that is what he was in the midst of doing, and killed them when they were barely sketched, blocked all his work, put itself in the way of everything, took him over, obsessed him, besieged him. It was torture, torture that began with the day, and that lasted, like that of the miserable one who was being tortured at the same moment, until *four o'clock*. Only then, once the *ponens caput expiravit* cried out by the sinister voice of the clock, did the author breathe and find once more some freedom of mind. One day, finally — it was, he thinks, the day after the execution of Ulbach — he began to write this book. Since then he feels relieved. When one of these public crimes, which are called judicial executions, has been committed, his conscience has told him he was no longer in solidarity with it; he has no longer felt on his forehead that drop of blood that spurts from the Grève onto the head of all members of the social community.

All the same, that is not enough. To wash one's hands is good; to prevent blood from flowing would be better.

Thus, he can know of no higher, no holier, no more august aim than that one: to contribute to the abolition of the death penalty. Thus, it is from the bottom of his heart that he endorses the hopes and efforts of generous men from all nations who have been working for many years to bring down the sinister tree, the only tree that revolutions do not uproot. It is with joy that he comes in turn, puny one that he is, to deliver his hatchet blow and to enlarge as best he can the notch that Beccaria made, sixty-six years ago, in the old gallows erected for so many centuries on Christendom.

We just said that the scaffold is the only edifice that revolutions do not demolish. It is rare, in fact, that revolutions not be drunk on human blood and, given that they have come to prune, debranch, pollard[28] society, the death penalty is one of the billhooks they give up with the most difficulty. (10–12)

28. [Translator's note]: Hugo uses here three specifically horticultural terms, *émonder*, *ébrancher*, *étêter*, the last of which means literally to cut off the head (e.g., of a tree).

294

Finally, to conclude and complicate further or complete these scenes of   *295*
filiation between father and son, Christ, Montesquieu, Beccaria, Hugo, one
must return for a moment to woman, as we had begun to do the previous times, and earlier when we noted the feminization of the guillotine as
a toothless old prostitute who dismisses her pimp the *bourreau*. To refine
somewhat the analysis of Hugo's fraternalist phallogocentrism[29] that I concerned myself with elsewhere, I would like to read a long passage where
two allusions to woman in truth need no commentary today. They are sympathetic and compassionate, you will see. Hugo speaks well of women and
suffers for them. But you are going to hear the classical connotations of
this compassionate sympathy. And its place of inscription is a demonstration, a narration seeking to demonstrate with an example how the "blood
swiller," Doctor Guillotin's guillotine, functions badly, does not do the job
of the good machine it is supposed to be. The blood swiller does horrible
things, sometimes enough to make women shudder, sometimes even against
women. Since the painful scene I am going to read (children should be made
to leave the room and a white rectangle would be displayed on the television
screen, or something like that) will be relayed by analogous examples from
modern times in Camus, it deserves to be inscribed already in a series and a
law of the genre. (Read 22–25)

> One must cite here two or three examples of dreadful and ungodly execu-
> tions. One must try the nerves of the wives of the king's prosecutors. A
> woman is sometimes a conscience.
>
> In the Midi, toward the end of last September — we do not have present
> to mind the place, the day, or the name of the condemned man, but we will
> locate them again if anyone challenges the facts, and we think it was in Pam-
> iers; so, toward the end of September, someone comes to get a man in his
> prison cell, where he was calmly playing cards; he is told that he must die in
> two hours, which causes all his limbs to shake because he had been forgotten
> for six months and he was no longer reckoning with death;[30] he is shaved,
> sheared, tied up, confessed; then he is carted off between four armed guards   *296*
> and through the crowd to the place of execution. Up to this point nothing
> out of the ordinary. This is how it is done. Once arrived at the scaffold, he is
> taken from the priest by the executioner, who carries him off, ties him to the
> plank, *shoves him in the oven* — I am using here the slang phrase — and then
> releases the blade. The heavy iron triangle comes loose with difficulty, falls
> joltingly through its slots, and — here the horrible part begins — cuts into

29. During the session, Derrida adds: "French."
30. During the session, Derrida adds: "Think of Mumia's eighteen years."

the man without killing him. The man emits a ghastly cry. The executioner, disconcerted, raises the blade again and lets it fall once more. The blade bites into the neck of the patient a second time, but does not cut through. The patient screams, the crowd as well. The executioner hoists up the blade once again, hoping for better with the third blow. Not at all. The third blow causes a third stream of blood to spout from the nape of the condemned man, but does not make his head fall. Let us abbreviate things. The blade went up and fell down five times; five times it cut into the condemned one; five times the condemned one screamed beneath the blow and shook his living head while crying for mercy! Outraged, the people took stones and in their justice began to lapidate the miserable executioner. The executioner ran away beneath the guillotine and crouched behind the guards' horses. But you are not at the end. The tortured one, seeing himself alone on the scaffold, stood up on the plank, and there, standing, frightful, dripping with blood, holding up his half-severed head that hung on his shoulder, he cried out feebly for someone to come untie him. The crowd, full of pity, was on the point of forcing past the guards and coming to the aid of the wretched one who had undergone his death sentence five times. At that moment, a servant of the executioner, a young man of twenty, climbs up onto the scaffold, tells the patient to turn around so he can untie him, and taking advantage of the position of the dying man who gave himself up to the other trustingly, jumps on his back and sets about cutting painfully what remained of his neck with some sort of butcher's knife. This happened. This was seen. Yes. . . .

Here, nothing. The thing took place after July,[31] in a time of mild customs and progress, a year after the famous lamentation in the Chamber about the death penalty. Well, the event went absolutely unnoticed. The Paris newspapers published it as an anecdote. No one was investigated. It was learned only that the guillotine had been deliberately tampered with by someone *who wanted to harm the state's high executioner*. It was one of the servants of the executioner, dismissed by his master, who had played this trick on him to exact vengeance.

It was only a bit of mischief. Let us continue.

297 In Dijon, three months ago, a woman (a woman!) was led to the last torment. This time once again, Doctor Guillotin's blade did its job poorly. The head was not entirely severed. So, the executioner's assistants harnessed themselves to the woman's feet, and through the screams of the wretch and by dint of tugging and jerks, they separated her head from her body by tearing it off. (22–25).

I end on this example of the woman with a thought, in which I wanted you to join, for a sixty-two-year-old woman, in Texas, who is supposed to be

31. [Translator's note]: That is, after the Revolution of July 1830.

executed tomorrow[32] for having killed her fifth husband. She appealed for a pardon to the Texas governor, the candidate Bush who, in the middle of an electoral campaign, is certainly not going to weaken in the face of a Texas constituency that is fiercely in favor of the death penalty in the killing state[33] that has beaten every record in the United States for the last twenty-five years. It was possible to see this woman ask for a pardon on television, on international television, then, since one could see it on <channel> France 2 in France, which obviously is an absolutely unprecedented possibility or scene[34]—and which will certainly play its role in the abolition of the death penalty one day, even if this woman must die, alas, tomorrow.

32. During the session, Derrida explains: "It is Betty Lou Beets, you may have read this in the press, grandmother of nine, I quote the press: 'Raped at age five by an alcoholic father, married at fifteen, an abused wife throughout her life, sentenced to death for the murder of her fifth husband, an invalid, suffering from brain injuries, and who will be executed Thursday, February 24, 2000, if George Bush, governor of Texas, who has pardoned only one of the hundred and twenty of those sentenced to death during his tenure, refuses to let her live.' 'George Bush, governor of Texas, who has pardoned only one of the hundred and twenty of those sentenced to death during his tenure.'" Derrida is quoting an article by Christian Colombani that appeared in *Le Monde* on February 23, 2000.

33. [Translator's note]: The phrase "killing state" is in English in the original.

34. During the session, Derrida adds: "I point this out because Hugo said that the horror I have just read was barely mentioned in the press, and now there is a mutation, which is that a prisoner can ask for a pardon while being filmed and can see this image broadcast internationally. That is certainly not going to save her life; no one knows what is going to happen, tomorrow; everything is possible with Bush, but in any case, with this transformation of public space by international television, there is naturally a change of scene that explains many things."

March 1/8, 2000[1]

When to die finally?

Is it enough to say "I have to die" or "I will have to die" to be authorized to translate these utterances by "I am condemned to death"? According to the common sense of the language, the answer is *no*, obviously *not*. Even if one keeps, more or less as a metaphoric figure, the word "condemned," well, "I am condemned to die" does not signify, sensu stricto, "I am condemned to death." That is just good sense, common sense. I am, we are all here condemned to die, but the chances are few that any of us here will ever be condemned to death — especially in France and in Europe.

From "being condemned to die" to "being condemned to death," it is a matter, then, of passing over to another death, *perhaps. Perhaps.* I keep the "perhaps" in reserve. And I keep in reserve the decision as to which may appear preferable: to be condemned to death or to be condemned to die. If, for example, I was given the choice between being condemned to death at age seventy-five (guillotined) or being condemned to die at age seventy-four (in my bed), admit that the choice would be difficult. In order to pose seriously the same question of what may be intolerable about the death penalty, one must put oneself in another situation, the real situation, namely that, at the moment of execution, the condemned one knows in all certitude that without the execution he or she would live longer, be it only a year, a month, a day, a second. The alternative is terrible and infinite: I may deem it intolerable, and this is the case of the death penalty, to know that the hour of my death is fixed, by others, by a third party, at a certain day, a certain hour, a certain second, whereas if I am not condemned to death but only to die, this calculable knowledge is impossible. But conversely, I may deem it intoler-

---

1. We have preserved the dual dating found on Derrida's file and typescript even though the uninterrupted recording indicates that it was read in one session either on the first or the eighth of March.

able not to know the date, the place, and the hour of my death and thus I may dream of appropriating this knowledge, of having this knowledge at my disposal, at least phantasmatically, by getting myself condemned to death and thus by arriving in this fashion at some calculable certitude, some quasi-suicidal mastery of my death (one can thus imagine—and there are such stories—that some person contrives, or even asks, to be guillotined so as to secure this knowledge and this phantasmatic mastery, which one can believe finally to be precisely meta-phantasmatic, real, of the moment of death). By knowing at what hour, on what day I will die, I can tell myself the story of how death will not take me by surprise and will thus remain at my disposal, like a quasi-suicidal auto-affection—hence, I repeat, sometimes, and this can always be inferred in every case, the behavior of criminals or condemned ones who seem to do everything so as to give themselves this death [se donner cette mort], this phantasm of omnipotence over their own death, and so forth.

When does one die? How to die? Given that I have to die, how do I know, how do I determine what will happen to me under that name, under that intransitive verb, "to die," a verb that is more intransitive than any other even as it is always understood as the passage of a transition, a transiting, a perishing, and whose subject, the I, as such, is neither the agent nor the patient, even if it thinks it is committing suicide?

In all these questions on the "how" or the "when" of my death, the difficulty, and first of all the semantic difficulty, has at least as much to do with the *modality* (the "how," the "where," and especially the "when") as with the fact of my death, and with the possessive "my" at least as much as with "death."

But since what is called the condemnation to death decides above all, before even the technical modes of execution, as to the term, the moment, *301* the date, the hour, in truth the instant, well, the question, when? when will I have to die? holds or is granted a privilege that must be analyzed. Fundamentally, it is by answering the question, when? that one can divide, as with a knife blade, two deaths or two condemnations, the condemnation to die and the condemnation to death. The mortal that I am knows that he is condemned to die, but even if he is sick, incurable, or even in the throes of death, the mortal that I am does not know the moment, the date, the precise hour that he will die. He does not know, I do not know, and I will never know it in advance. And no one will know it in advance. This indetermination is an essential trait of my relation to death. It may be a little sooner, a little later, much sooner, much later, even if it cannot fail to happen. Whereas the one condemned to death—and this is the difference—can know, can think he knows, and in any case others know for him, in principle, by right, on which day, at which hour, or even at which instant death will befall him. In any case—and it is to this acute and as yet poorly thought-out point that I wanted to redirect all these questions, questions that themselves remain basically rather banal—in any case, the concept of the death penalty supposes that the state, the judges, society, the *bourreaux* and executioners, that is, third parties, have mastery over the time of life of the condemned one and thus know how to calculate and produce, in so-called objective time, the deadline to within a second. This knowledge, this mastery over the time of life and death, this mastering and calculating knowledge of the time of life of the subject is presupposed—note that I say presupposed—alleged, presumed in the very concept of the death penalty. Society, the state, its legal system, its justice, its judges and executioners, all these third parties are presumed to know, calculate, operate the time of death. Their knowledge of death is a presumed knowledge on the subject of time and of the coincidence between objective time and let us say the subjective time of the subject condemned to death and executed.

Let us keep these questions and suspicions waiting. What is certain, and trivial—and you will easily agree with me on this—is that if there is some torture, torturing, cruelty in the process of the condemnation to death, what is most cruel and the cruel itself, the crux [*croix*], is indeed, beyond everything, beyond the conditions of detention, for example, and so many other torments, the experience of time. One cannot think cruelty without time, the time given or the time taken, time that becomes the calculation of the other, time delivered up to the calculating decision of the other, sometimes another who is as anonymous as a state or a justice system, in truth and in the last instance, the calculating and exceptional decision of a great other in the figure of the prince, the president, the governor, that is, the sovereign holder of the right to pardon.

I do not need to underscore and describe here the dramaturgy that links the concept of time to that of the pardon. The pardon [*la grâce*] gives time, and the only "thing" that can be given graciously is time, that is to say, at once nothing and everything.

Even the so-called master of this calculation, that is, the prince, the governor, whoever holds the ultimate right of pardon, can suffer from it and here I think of the infinite indecency, the bottomless obscenity, of the governor and potential candidate for the presidency of the United States, Bush, Jr.,[2] who, with only one exception, I believe, has never pardoned anyone (more

302

2. [Translator's note]: That is, George W. Bush.

than 120 executions while he was governor, and he did not pardon the woman whom we were speaking of the other evening), this Bush, who is anything but burning or ardent with any fire whatsoever, and who dared to declare that the forty-five minutes of the execution of one of the 120 condemned ones he had not pardoned had been the worst in his life. And this man, if one may say that, perhaps hoped to garner more sympathy by making this declaration, unless once again he was only thinking of winning over a few more voters, like, one must admit, every candidate for the presidency of the United States. It is impossible for a candidate for the presidency of that great Christian country to take a position, during his campaign, against the death penalty, and thus to promise anything other than its maintenance. Things will change over there the day when — and it is not going to happen tomorrow — a candidate for president or for governor can dare to present himself or herself to the voters as an abolitionist. This time will certainly come, I am convinced of it, but, like death (and not like the death penalty that it will then be a matter of canceling), I do not know when.

The question remains, then: when? When will death come upon me? At what moment? In which sense am I condemned? Is it to die or to death that I am condemned? And why is it the question, when? that makes the difference between condemnation to death and condemnation to die?

The mechanism falls like a bolt of lightning, the head flies off, blood spurts out, the man is no more. (Reread)

I had announced that I would reread this sentence.[3] That we would attribute it and analyze its sense and its blood [*le sens et le sang*]. The redness. In truth, it is its time that one must analyze first. For it is, among other things, a sentence on time. Notice first the time or tense of its verbs. It is written in the present; it describes in the present, the present indicative, and all the verbs are *intransitive* ("The mechanism *falls* like a bolt of lightning, the head *flies off*, the blood *spurts out*, the man *is* no more"); it describes *intransitively in the present indicative the presence of a present*, of a present instant that does not last; but you notice right away that this present, notably the present of the verb "to be," the third person of the verb "to be" (for everything remains here in the third person: the subject of the utterance could not use any other person but the third person; he could not say, for example: I am no more, you singular are no more, you plural are no more; he must, in the third person, speak of what happens to one condemned to death, to a man as

3. See above, "Eighth Session, February 23, 2000," p. 190.

third man, as third party ["he, the man, is no more"]), you notice, then, right away that this present, notably the present of the verb "to be," in the third person of the verb "to be," describes by way of the negation affecting it (it is the only present indicative that forms a negative proposition) the instantaneous passage, without duration, from the presence to the non-presence of the subject, of the man: the man right away is no longer. It suffices that in an infinitesimal, inconsistent, inexistent instant, an instant without time, it suffices that on the point (*stigmē*: instant in Greek) or on the blade edge of an instant the "mechanism falls like a bolt of lightning" (and lightning here is what lasts no longer than a flash, but it is also what comes from on high and that, coming from on high — like the bolt of lightning that has always sig-

304   nified it — gathers in a flash without duration both God's verdict, the Last Judgment, and the act of punishment emanating, falling, striking down on the sinner, from the transcendence of the Most High — and the guillotine supplements here, replaces and represents the height of the Most High); it suffices that in an instant the mechanism, like a deus ex machina, falls like a bolt of lightning and the little "is," the presence of the "is," signifies no longer presence but the passage to nothingness, the transition without transition from being to nothingness: "the man is no longer."

It is truly the instant of death, but not the instant of my death, always the instant of the death of a third party, of the other who is not and will never be either me, or you, or us: "the man is no longer."

It is very well described; it is very well written, this operation, the motor of this four-stroke verbal machine, four present indicatives that are not only intransitive but extenuate any transition between the four moments of which the fourth nevertheless (it too in the present) signifies, without transition, the passage from being to nonbeing, more precisely to no-longer-being: "The mechanism falls like a bolt of lightning, the head flies off, blood spurts out, the man is no more."

Who is it who *writes* so well? Or who *speaks* so well, for the striking density, the impeccable economy of this four-verb sentence in the intransitive present indicative is due first of all to the rhetoric of an orator who knows how to count out the tempo, who knows how to count with time, and who lets his sentence fall, like a blade or a bolt of lightning, with the same rhythm as that of which it is speaking. This orator is none other than Doctor Guillotin himself. He was then presenting his invention to the Constituent Assembly. And although, as I said, his speech has been lost even as the proposed law I read last week was preserved, it happens that the sentence in four strokes minus one, so to speak ("The mechanism falls like a bolt of lightning, the head flies off, blood spurts out, the man is no more"), was quoted the next day in the *Journal des États Généraux*, which both praises and mocks the qualities of someone who speaks as an orator rather than a legislator. With the same stroke, if I may say that, this newspaper article, the very next day after the speech, institutes a law of the genre: by insinuating that a proposed law ought not to be a passage of poetico-rhetorical declamation, ought not to give in to pomposity or pathetic bombast, the *Journal* does indeed initiate the law of the satiric, comic, ironic genre that for the last two centuries has been deriding and denigrating Guillotin's guillotine, the machine said to be progressive, individualist, egalitarian, painless, anesthetizing, euthanizing, mechanical, and so forth. Before reading a few lines of this article, I would like at least to formulate the following question: how does it happen that an urge or a compulsion drives one to turn these tragic death machines (the guillotine and others, Old Sparky, for example) into targets of laughter, ridiculous figures, quasi persons appealing to *Witz*, to the *mot d'esprit*, to some joke,[4] or witticism in bad taste? And first of all, what is this compulsion to name them derisively, to give them a proper name, a name at once proper and common (Old Sparky, la Guillotine, The Widow, The Maiden, Mannaia, etc.?), the proper and common name of a figure that is more often than not feminine? Why, as we said, would this death machine resemble, for man, for the human and more often than not the masculine phantasm, a woman (virgin, mother, whore, or widow) who makes us laugh where she scares us, in whose face we sometimes laugh with nervous and anxious laughter, you remember, upon seeing in this woman a devourer, a swiller, with or without teeth?

I will not insist, you see very well, I suppose, in which direction these questions can orient their elaboration if not their answers. All I am suggesting is that this direction is perhaps not so foreign to the one that leads to the drives and compulsions that gave birth in the first place to these machines themselves, to their figuration, to the figuration of their figure, to their invention, and to their being put into operation. I read now the *Journal des États Généraux*:

> Mr. Guillotin described the mechanism; I will not follow him in all his details; depicting its effect, he forgot for a moment he was a legislator when, speaking as an orator, he said: "*The mechanism falls like a bolt of lightning, the*

4. [Translator's note]: "Joke" in English in the original.

306 *head flies off, blood spurts out, the man is no more.*" It is not in the penal code that such passages are permitted. (Qtd. in Arasse, 26).

"It is not in the penal code that such passages are permitted."

This latter remark goes so far as to issue a kind of prescription, with reference to a law, to a "one must," "one must not," "it must not be done," it is *not permitted* — and it is not permitted to speak in this fashion in a juridico-penal code. "It is not in the penal code that such passages are permitted."

Right away there were other parodies of the same speech by Guillotin on his daughter the guillotine. I will retain only two features for what matters to me here. The two features intersect inasmuch as they associate the instant of death, the death of the other, the claimed reduction to an utterly negligible lapse of time, to the trenchant extenuation of duration in the passage from the present to non-presence, from being to nonbeing; they associate all this with the misleading motif of a certainty without appeal, of an alleged indubitability of death, as indubitable as the cogito for the executed prisoner, of an efficacy such that the machine does not need to start over a second time (we have seen and will see again how misleading this certainty is). The first of these texts (mentioned by the Goncourt brothers in their *History of French Society during the Revolution*) plays on the theatrical metaphor and represents Guillotin as a stage director praising his spectacle from the angle of the head stagehand — inventor of the machine that is, you recall, progressive, egalitarian, individualist, and mechanistic:

307
> My dear brothers in the fatherland [!!! comment[5]], I have had so many patients die in my hands [the stage director is a doctor out of Molière] that I can boast of being one of the greatest experts on ways to depart this world. . . . With my stagehand, I have managed to invent the ravishing machine you see here. . . . Beneath the stage is a bird-organ set up to play very merry melodies, like this one [bird-organ (*serinette*) is the name of a small mechanical organ meant to *seriner*, that is, to instruct a bird, to teach it a melody]: *My good woman when I dance*, or this other one: *Adieu then French lady*; or else this one, *Good evening everyone, good evening everyone.* Having reached this point, the actor will place himself between the two columns, he will be asked to press his ear to this stylobate [an architectural term: foundation decorated with molding that supports a colonnade] on the pretext that he will be able to hear much better the ravishing sounds played by the

---

5. During the session, Derrida ironically adds: "It's off to a good start. So, it is in the name of republican and patriotic fraternity that he speaks. And it is brothers and not sisters. And it's a doctor who is speaking, don't forget that."

bird-organ; and his head will be so subtly severed that, still long after it has been separated, it itself will be in doubt. In order to convince it, applause must necessarily resound in the public square.[6]

What this derision, this parody, this caricature, gives one to think about is both the supposed subtle and the sudden ("so subtly severed"), the sharp edge of time that, canceling both time and suffering, leaves a doubt in the head of the condemned one as to the instant of its death even as the head will have been so subtly detached from the body. One could extend the serious-ness of this play by calling Descartes and the Cartesian cogito to the witness stand, and perhaps so as to evoke at least a certain Cartesianism of Guillotin and the guillotine: not only because of the mechanism and the individualism and the egalitarian universalism (equality before the penal law being, like common sense, a manner of attesting to the universal rationality of good sense, the most widely shared thing in the world), but also the philosophy of time that was Descartes's, namely, his instantaneism (time is constituted of simple, discontinuous, discrete, and undecomposable instants), but also the dualism of the soul and the body that leaves the essence of the thinking substance untouched by anything that may happen to the body and inacces-sible to any corporal accident, the complication arising (but I am not going to undertake a serious lecture on Descartes; I am contenting myself here with a Cartesian *doxa* or ideology) as to the place of the pineal gland: what happens to the pineal gland when the head is separated from the body in a splitting instant? What happens to the cogito? Well, the head all by itself has doubts, says the satirical text I have just quoted; it no longer knows if it has been separated, it will not know that the execution has taken place and that the instant of death is past until it hears the applause from the public square. It is the other who determines the instant of my death, never I.

 308

Later you will understand better why I insist on this time and this instant of death. Before explaining it, I will evoke one more parodic echo that, in the same satiric vein, allies the theme of the *Augenblick*, the instant as blink of an eye, *on the one hand*, and *on the other*, that of absolute non-cruelty, euthanasia, anesthesia, the "it goes so fast one does not even have the time to feel or suffer." For these two themes — instantaneity and anesthesia, the almost intemporal instantaneity and insensibility, non-pain, non-cruelty, even gentleness — are indissociable. Time is sensibility or receptivity, affec-tion (a major vein of philosophy from Kant to Heidegger, which I will not

6. Edmond and Jules de Goncourt, *Histoire de la société française pendant la Révolu-tion*, quoted in Arasse, *La guillotine et l'imaginaire de la terreur*, p. 26.

get into here); time is suffering; the time of execution is endurance, passion, the pathetic, pathological *paskhein* — which sometimes means not only "to undergo" but "to undergo a punishment," and the fact of passively undergoing can already be interpreted as the suffering of a punishment: sensibility is in itself a punishment. If you suppress time, you will suppress sensibility (*pathē* is sensibility, passivity but also suffering, pain), so that the guillotine, inasmuch as it is supposed to act instantaneously and suppress time, would be what relieves pain, what puts an end to pain: playing with it a little, one could say that it is a little like what is called in American English, speaking of analgesics, a "painkiller." The guillotine is not just a killer, it's a painkiller.[7] And it kills pain because in a certain way, reducing time to the nothing of an instant, to the nothing but an instant, it kills time.

309   Here, then, is the article that gathers together, as they must be, the argument of the instant, the blink of an eye (*Augenblick*), and that of anesthesia, an anesthesia that becomes euthanasia a little the way one transforms an absence of pain into a mild sensation, or even a sensation of pleasure. As if to die guillotined became, for lack of time, thanks to the abolition of time (as in Hegel's absolute knowledge where time is not merely sublated but suppressed — *Tilgen* and not *Aufheben*, at the end of *The Phenomenology of Spirit*, which comes after Christ's passion in a philosophy and a logic of absolute knowledge that is the truth of revealed religion), as if to die guillotined became, for lack of time, thanks to the abolition of time not merely painless but almost a pleasure [*jouissance*] or in any case the beginning of some pleasure. Pay attention to the tenses and modes of the verbs in these two sentences from the *Moniteur*, two weeks after Guillotin's speech:

> Gentlemen [says Guillotin's caricature], with my machine, I chop off your head in the blink of an eye and without your feeling the least pain from it. [And elsewhere]: The punishment I have invented is so gentle that one would not know what was happening if one were not expecting to die and that one would have imagined feeling nothing but a slight coolness on the neck. (Qtd. in Arasse, 26)

This expression, these words "slight coolness on the neck" were doubtless pronounced by Guillotin, since many traces of them can be found. One of these traces reappears in Camus's "Reflections on the Guillotine" — which we will talk about again later from another point of view, notably as regards the system of historical or philosophical interpretation proposed by

7. [Translator's note]: "Killer" and "painkiller" are in English in the original.

Camus, in this text published in 1957 in *La Nouvelle Revue Française* (no. 54–55), reprinted in *Reflexions sur la peine capitale* by Camus and Koestler (Calmann-Lévy, 1957). Today I will choose only two passages to support what we are examining. I pause on the *first passage*, at the opening of the article, for several reasons, as you will see, in particular because <it is about a> memory of Algeria, of the death penalty in Algeria (where Hugo, you recall, had described the arrival of the first guillotine, in two pages [53–54] that you will read and from which I recall merely the conclusion). (Read Hugo's *Écrits*, p. 54)   *310*

> The whole scene was grand, charming, and pure, yet it is not what a large group was looking at, a group of men, women, Arabs, Jews, Europeans, who had rushed there and were crowded around the steamship.
>
> Workers and sailors were coming and going from the ship to shore, unloading crates at which all the eyes of the crowd were staring. On the wharf, customs men were opening the crates and, through the planks of the gaping boxes, in the straw that was partly shoved aside, beneath the packing canvases, one could make out strange objects, two long joists painted red, a ladder painted red, a basket painted red, a heavy crosspiece painted red in which seemed to be encased on one of its sides a thick and enormous blade in the shape of a triangle.
>
> A spectacle that was in fact otherwise enticing than the palm tree, the aloe, the fig tree, and the lentisk, than the sun and the hills, than the sea and the sky: it was civilization arriving in Algiers in the form of a guillotine. (54)

I pause, then, on the *first passage*, at the opening of Camus's article, for several reasons, as you will see, and they are all, directly or not, reasons that I would call "genealogical" or to do with "filiations," once again, for you have already noticed, and again a moment ago, I insist on this, how difficult it was very often to separate *familial* dramaturgy, that is, also that of sexual differences (man/woman; father/son, mother/son; brother/brother,[8]   *311* etc.) in this question of the death penalty, and here I choose, I was saying, this first passage of "Reflections on the Guillotine" in particular because, as a memory of Algeria, of the death penalty in Algeria, it reminds us that the author of *The Stranger* is the author of a narrative that begins on a beach in Algeria with "Maman died today" and recounts the murder of an Arab followed by a trial and a sentencing to death, the sentencing of a murderer who does not even know why he killed other than because of the sun, the narrative being signed in the first person by a narrator who is thus writing between the moment he was sentenced to death and the mo-

8. Thus in the typescript.

ment of execution. The time of the narrative corresponds in the law to the imminence of a decapitation by the guillotine, after the death sentence, the sentence, says the text of the verdict read by the judge and quoted by the narrator, to have his "head cut off in the public square in the name of the French people."

> I didn't look in Marie's direction [with the exception of the mother who dies at the beginning of the book, and whom one may suppose was loved by her son, the only other name of a loved woman is Marie]. I didn't have time to because the presiding judge said to me in a bizarre formula that I was to have my head cut off in the public square in the name of the French people.[9]

A little further on, the condemned man, the stranger, Meursault, comes back to this formula and after having several times called it "mechanical" or a "mechanism" ("implacable mechanism," "I would be caught up in the machinery again," two pages later it is once again a question of the "smooth functioning of the machine"), he describes the disproportion, which he deems "ridiculous," between the verdict that had grounded this "arrogant certainty" of the mechanism and the "imperturbable march of events from the moment the verdict was announced" (103–5; Folio,165–69). And this absurd contingency, this cold and insignificant mechanism, this everyday banality, seems to him ultimately to deprive of any sense and seriousness what all the same is soon, "in the name of the French people," to deprive him seriously of his life:

312

> The fact that the sentence was read out at eight o'clock at night and not at five o'clock, the fact that it could have been an entirely different one, the fact that it was decided by men who change their underwear, the fact that it had been handed down in the name of some vague notion called the French (or German or Chinese) people — all of it seemed to me to deprive the decision of much of its seriousness. I was forced to admit, however, that from the moment it was made, its consequences became as real and as serious as the wall against which I pressed the length of my body. (104; Folio,167)

I will come back to the passage immediately following, you will understand why, but after having begun to read "Reflections on the Guillotine" (the two texts seeming to me, as I have just now noticed, profoundly con-

---

9. Albert Camus, *L'Étranger* (Paris: Gallimard, 1942 [1971]), p. 164; page numbers refer to the "Folio" edition of 1999 used by Derrida; *The Stranger*, trans. Matthew Ward (New York: Alfred A. Knopf, 1988), p. 102.

nected through a link that I don't know if Camus criticism has ever noticed, still less analyzed).

Opening a parenthesis here, I note this on the subject of the supposed difference between murder or the criminal putting to death, on the one hand, and the death penalty, on the other. We have already said what is essential here, at least so I hope, from the point of view of the concept and what precisely separates them irreducibly, by right. But if one steps back on this side of legal discourse or if, conversely, one puts in question again the difference between the discourse of law and its other, then things get complicated. Reread *The Stranger*, which I have just done for the first time in some fifty years. You will see that Meursault, the stranger condemned to death, can give no explanation, no justification, when he is pressed to explain why he killed the Arab. He speaks, in sum, of light and color; he says he doesn't know, that there was the sun, that the beach was red. For example, you remember: (Read and comment on *L'Étranger*, 104–6)

313

> The interrogation began. He started out by saying that people described me as a taciturn and withdrawn person and he wanted to know what I thought. I answered, "It's just that I never have much to say. So I keep quiet." He smiled the way he had the first time, agreed that that was the best reason of all, and added, "Besides, it's not at all important." Then he looked at me without saying anything, straightened up rather abruptly, and said very quickly, "What interests me is you." I didn't really understand what he meant by that, so I didn't respond. "There are one or two things," he added, "that I don't quite understand. I'm sure you'll help me clear them up." I said it was all pretty simple. He pressed me to go back over that day. I went back over what I had already told him: Raymond, the beach, the swim, the quarrel, then back to the beach, the little spring, the sun, and the five shots from the revolver. After each sentence he would say, "Fine, fine." When I got to the body lying there, he nodded and said, "Good." But I was tired of repeating the same story over and over. It seemed as if I had never talked so much in my life.
>
> After a short silence, he stood up and told me that he wanted to help me, that I interested him, and that, with God's help, he would do something for me. But first he wanted to ask me a few more questions. Without working up to it, he asked if I loved Maman. I said, "Yes, the same as anyone," and the clerk, who up to then had been typing steadily, must have hit the wrong key, because he lost his place and had to go back. Again, without any apparent logic, the magistrate then asked if I had fired all five shots at once. I thought for a minute and explained that at first I had fired a single

shot and then, a few seconds later, the other four. "Why did you pause between the first and second shot?" Once again I could see the red sand and feel the burning of the sun on my forehead. But this time I didn't answer. In the silence that followed, the magistrate seemed to be getting fidgety. He sat down, ran his fingers through his hair, put his elbows on his desk, and leaned toward me slightly with a strange look on his face. "Why, why did you shoot at a body that was on the ground?" Once again I didn't know how to answer. The magistrate ran his hands across his forehead and repeated his question with a slightly different tone in his voice. "Why? You must tell me. Why?" Still I didn't say anything. (64–65; Folio, 104–6)

314

The fact that the stranger has neither an explanation nor a justification to give for his act, paradoxically, clears him of guilt in a certain way. He did not mean, he did not intend, to kill or to harm. He does not know, he does not understand, why he killed. "Because the beach was red," declares the one of whom the prosecutor will nevertheless say that he is responsible and "knows the meaning of words" (96; Folio, 154). This phrase "because the beach was red," in its apparent nonchalance and its massive, opaque certainty, might remind me — if we were to pursue the spectrography of lethal red that we initiated the last time — this "because the beach was red" might remind me of the extraordinary thing Matisse once said: "Fauvism is when there is a lot of red." And fauvism, as you know, got its name because of the violence of the pure colors that painters like Matisse, Braque, Dufy used in the work of their so-called fauve period. Red is a violent color; it calls up murder or recalls murder; blood and the *corrida* are both examples and paradigms of it.

The stranger's murderous gesture was thus absurd or insignificant, indifferent, on the near or the far side of signifying language. Which leads one to think, *a contrario*, that whoever kills deliberately and while giving himself some reason or other, while giving meaning to his act, has already entered into a system of symbolic justification that, virtually, appeals to a code of law, to a universal law. If I know why I kill, I think I am right to kill and this reason that I give myself is a reason that one must be able to argue for rationally with the help of universalizable principles. I kill someone, and I know why, because I think that it is necessary, that it is just, that whoever found himself in my place would have to do the same, that the other is guilty toward me, has wronged me or will wrong me, and so forth. So, even if a court as such has not heard the case, I kill by condemning to death as regards universal

315

law, at least potentially. And therefore, given that the crime is meaningful, deliberate, calculated, premeditated, goal-oriented, it belongs to the order of penal justice and is no longer dissociable from a condemnation to death, from a properly penal act. At that point, the distinction between vengeance and justice becomes precarious. The only remaining difference separates merely two powers of condemnation and execution, an individual or familial or tribal power, on the one hand, and a state power, on the other. Among the numerous and decisive consequences to be drawn from this analysis, there is this one: on one side, vengeance is *already* a form of justice; justice is *still* a form of vengeance, and this allows both for the excesses of wild vengeance and self-defense and, conversely, on the other side, for the abolitionist discourse that holds the condemnation to death to be a barbaric murder. I close this parenthesis.

The author of *The Stranger*, his first great book, no doubt also motivated, like *The Myth of Sisyphus* and later like *The Rebel*, by a refusal of the death penalty, the author of *The Stranger* is also the author of the unfinished and posthumous novel *The First Man*, which is entirely governed by the genealogical motif and whose first part is titled "Search for the Father" and the second "The Son or the First Man." Working retrospectively as it were, and thus before coming back to "Reflections on the Guillotine" and to *The Stranger*, in the first part of *The First Man*, then, I cannot resist the desire urging me to point out to you and to read a page that both reminds me of names from my childhood and concerns some "bourreaux" (that is Camus's word), *bourreaux* of animals (for at the horizon of our seminar, obviously, there is the question of man's putting to death of animals and of whether one can speak of a death penalty inflicted by man on animals, or whether the death penalty is something proper to man, a putting to death only of man by man and not of one living being by another living being in general). Camus recounts how, as a child, he saw other children try literally to guillotine cats (he calls these children "bourreaux") and above all he remembers a mythical character, the name of a character that I myself knew in my Algerian childhood; he was nicknamed with the mythical name Galoufa (no doubt because the first person who fulfilled this function was so named). And this Galoufa was a municipal employee whose job it was to capture stray dogs and take them away. Camus describes very well, with faultless detail, all the operations of the said Galoufa, which I witnessed more than once in my childhood. (What's more, when one wanted to frighten disobedient children, one threatened to call Galoufa.) And what is remarkable in Camus's description, which runs for several pages that you can read without me (pages 140–43 in *The First Man* in the chapter "Search for the Father"), is that he borrows from the rhetorical code of the Terror (Camus speaks of

316

the "death tumbrel") and the code of executions or the eve of executions, strangling being one stage on the way to certain death. It is indeed a matter of arrest with torture and putting to death by a *bourreau*, but this time the victims are neither men nor cats but undomesticated dogs, stray dogs in the streets of Algiers. I excerpt a passage and I can assure you, my childhood memory can attest, that Camus's description is soberly and impeccably exact. (Read Camus's *Le premier homme*, 133–35)

And suddenly, at a word from the dogcatcher, the old Arab would pull back on the reins and the cart would stop. The dogcatcher had spotted one of his wretched victims digging feverishly in a garbage can, glancing back frantically at regular intervals, or else trotting rapidly along a wall with the hurried and anxious look of a malnourished dog. Galoufa then seized from the top of the cart a leather rod with a chain that ran through a ring down the handle. He moved toward the animal at the supple, rapid, and silent pace of a trapper, and when he had caught up with the beast, if it was not wearing the collar that proves membership in a good family, he would run at it, in a sudden burst of astonishing speed, and put his weapon around the dog's neck, so that it served as an iron and leather lasso. Suddenly strangled, the animal struggled wildly while making inarticulate groans. But the man quickly dragged [it] to the cart, opened one of the cage doors, lifted the dog, strangling it more and more, and shoved it into the cage, making sure to put the handle of his lasso through the bars. Once the dog was captured, he loosened the iron chain and freed the neck of the now imprisoned animal. At least that is how things happened when the dog was not under the protection of the neighborhood children. For they were all in league against Galoufa. They knew the captured dogs were taken to the municipal pound, kept for three days, after which, if no one claimed them, the animals were put to death. And if they had not known it, the pitiful spectacle of that death tumbrel returning after a fruitful journey, loaded with wretched animals of all colors and sizes, terrified behind their bars and leaving behind the vehicle a trail of cries and mortal howls, would have been enough to rouse the children's indignation. So, as soon as the prison van appeared in the area, the children would alert each other. They would scatter throughout the streets of the neighborhood, they too hunting down the dogs, but in order to chase them off to other parts of the city, far from the terrible lasso. If despite these precautions the dogcatcher found a stray dog in their presence, as happened several times to Pierre and Jacques, their tactics were always the same. Before the dogcatcher could get close enough to his quarry, Jacques and Pierre would start screaming "Galoufa! Galoufa!" in voices so piercing and so terrifying that the dog would flee as fast as he could and soon be out of reach. Now it was the children's turn to prove their skill as sprinters, for the unfortunate Galoufa, who was paid a bounty for each dog

317

he caught, was wild with anger, and he would chase them brandishing his leather rod.[10]

But this was only a preamble, if you still remember, to the evocation of *two* passages from Camus's "Reflections on the Guillotine." I directly connect the first evocation to, let us say, the guillotine and the father in Algiers, the other to the "slight coolness on the neck" that Guillotin speaks of and to the supposed instantaneousness of death beneath the cutting edge of the guillotine.

A. *The first passage* is in fact the opening of "Reflections on the Guillotine." Camus begins by recounting what happened to his father, in Algiers, when he insisted on witnessing a decapitation. His father, "a simple, upright man," he says, was an unthinking supporter of the death penalty; one day he wanted to witness a decapitation, but once back home, unable to speak, able only to reject, to vomit, he had manifestly changed his opinion without even having to explain it, without even being able to find words that would measure up to it, only a convulsive rejection by his whole body:

318

> Shortly before the war of 1914, a murderer whose crime was particularly repulsive (he had slaughtered a family of farmers, including the children) was condemned to death in Algiers. He was a farm worker who had killed in a bloodthirsty frenzy, but he had aggravated his case by robbing his victims. The affair created a great stir. It was generally thought that decapitation was too mild a punishment for such a monster. This was the opinion, I have been told, of my father, who was especially outraged by the murder of the children. One of the few things I know about him, in any case, is that he wanted to witness the execution, for the first time in his life. He got up in the dark to go to the place of execution, at the other end of town amid a great crowd of people. What he saw that morning he never told anyone. My mother relates merely that he came rushing home, his face distorted, refused to talk, lay down for a moment on the bed, and suddenly began to vomit. He had just discovered the reality hidden under the noble phrases with which it was masked. Instead of thinking of the slaughtered children, he could think of nothing but that quivering body that had just been dropped onto a plank to have its head cut off.
>
> One has to think this ritual act is horrible indeed if it manages to overcome the indignation of a simple, upright man and if a punishment he considered richly deserved had no other effect in the end than to turn his stomach. When the extreme penalty causes merely vomiting on the part of

10. Albert Camus, *Le premier homme* (Paris: Gallimard, 1994), pp. 133–35; *The First Man*, trans. David Hapgood (New York: Alfred A. Knopf, 1996), pp. 141–42.

the respectable citizen it is supposed to protect, it is difficult to maintain that it has the function, as it should, to bring more peace and order to the community. On the contrary, it is obviously no less repulsive than the crime, and this new murder, far from making amends for the harm done to the social body, adds a new stain to the first one. This is so obvious that no one dares speak directly of the ceremony.[11]

319

If we now read side by side these two texts that have such a different status and that were written and published fifteen years apart, *The Stranger*, a novelistic fiction, a literary work published during the Occupation, in 1942, and "Reflections on the Guillotine," a nonfictional philosophical essay or ethico-political manifesto published in 1957, well, between these two texts of heterogeneous status one finds odd intersections, and odd intersections with *The First Man*, whose status is somewhere between the other two, and one of whose chapters is titled "The Son" and the preceding one "Search for the Father." Thus, after the passage I read a moment ago in which the Stranger having been condemned to death ironizes in his way, in his neutral tone that is precisely a stranger to everything, unbelieving, atheistic, skeptical, nominalist, seeking in vain a meaning behind words and remarking the nonserious seriousness of "some vague notion called the French people" in the name of which he was going to die, right after this passage, in the following paragraph, it is now the son in him who speaks, the son whose mother is dead, which is what will have governed this whole story, and the son who recalls what his mother told him about a father he never knew. And here you will see, in the same testimony, the knotting of the threads of fiction and real autobiography, between Meursault and Camus. The son of the fiction and the son of the testimony are the same and say the same thing. They have the same father, whom they never knew and who had the same experience of a capital execution. (Read and comment on *L'Étranger*, 167–68)

> The fact that the sentence was read out at eight o'clock at night and not at five o'clock, the fact that it could have been an entirely different one, the fact that it was decided by men who change their underwear, the fact that it had been handed down in the name of some vague notion called the French (or German or Chinese) people—all of it seemed to me to deprive the decision of much of its seriousness. I was forced to admit, however, that from the

320

11. Albert Camus, "Réflexions sur la guillotine," in Camus, *Essais*, ed. R. Quilliot and L. Faucon (Paris: Gallimard, "Bibliothèque de la Pléiade," 1992), p. 1021; "Reflections on the Guillotine," in Camus, *Resistance, Rebellion, and Death*, trans. Justin O'Brien (New York: Vintage Books, 1974), p. 173.

moment it was made, its consequences became as real and as serious as the wall against which I pressed the length of my body.

At times like this I remembered a story Maman used to tell me about my father. I never knew him. Maybe the only thing I did know about the man was the story Maman would tell me back then: he'd gone to see a murderer be executed. The idea of going made him ill. But he went anyway, and when he came back, he spent half the morning throwing up. I felt disgusted by him at the time. But now I understood, it was perfectly natural. How had I not seen that nothing was more important than an execution and that, ultimately, it was the only thing that really interests a man! If I ever got out of this prison, I would go to see every execution. It was a mistake, I think, even to consider the possibility. Because at the thought that one fine morning I would find myself a free man standing behind a cordon of police—on the outside, as it were, at the thought of being the spectator who comes to watch and then can go and throw up afterward, a wave of poisoned joy rose up toward my heart. But it was not reasonable. It was a mistake to let myself speculate like this because the next minute I would get so frightfully cold that I would curl up under my blanket and I couldn't stop my teeth from chattering. (104–5)

B. But this is not the principal passage I wanted to highlight. So as to make our way toward the question of the time of death and to link it to both the invention of the virtuous guillotine (progressive, individualist, egalitarian, and mechanistic, thus gentle and free of cruelty, anesthetic or euthanistic) and the "slight coolness on the neck" it is supposed to procure, according to its inventor. Essentially Camus's text, basing itself on medical examinations, in 1956, intends to show that death by decapitation on the guillotine does not happen in a second or an instant, that it is a differentiated, slow process, the duration of which is difficult to measure and that it is accompanied by the most unspeakable and cruel suffering.

All I can do, since I do not wish to silence these pages, is to limit their length. Camus himself says: "I doubt that there are many readers who can read this dreadful report without blanching."

321

You will read for yourselves the rest of this page that I insist all the same on reading here. (Read and comment, 1027–28)

Instead of boasting, with the pretentious thoughtlessness characteristic of us, of having invented this swift and humane[12] method of killing those con-

12. Derrida reads here Camus's footnote that occurs at this point: "The condemned one, according to the optimistic Doctor Guillotin, ought to feel nothing. At most a 'slight coolness on the neck.'"

demned to death, we should print in thousands of copies, and read out in schools and universities, the eyewitness accounts and medical reports that describe the state of the body after execution. We recommend particularly the printing and distribution of a recent paper delivered to the Academy of Medicine by Doctors Piedelièvre and Fournier. These courageous physicians, invited in the interest of science to examine the bodies of the guillotined after execution, considered it their duty to sum up their dreadful observations: "If we may be permitted to give our opinion on this subject, such spectacles are frightfully painful. The blood gushes from the blood vessels at the rhythm of the severed carotid arteries, then it coagulates. The muscles contract and their fibrillation is stupefying: the intestines ripple and the heart produces irregular, incomplete, and fascinating movements. The mouth clenches at certain moments in a dreadful grimace. It is true that in the severed head the eyes are motionless with dilated pupils; fortunately they look at nothing, and although they have none of the cloudiness and opalescence of a cadaver, they have no motion: their clarity is a sign of life, but their fixed stare is deathly. All this can last several minutes, even hours in healthy subjects: death is not immediate. . . . Thus every vital element survives decapitation. The physician is left with the impression of a horrible experiment, a murderous vivisection, followed by a premature burial."

I doubt that there are many readers who can read this dreadful report without blanching. One may thus count on its exemplary power and its capacity to intimidate. Nothing prevents us from adding to it the reports of witnesses who confirm the doctors' observations. The tortured face of Charlotte Corday blushed, it is said, when it was slapped by the executioner. So no one will be shocked while listening to more recent observers. Here is how an executioner's assistant, who can hardly be suspected of sentimentalism or squeamishness, describes what he was obliged to witness: "It was a mad man in the throes of a true fit of *delirium tremens* that we threw under the blade. The head died right away. But the body literally leaped into the basket, straining against the cords. Twenty minutes later, at the cemetery, it was still quivering." The current chaplain of La Santé prison, Father Devoyod, who does not seem opposed to the death penalty, tells a far-reaching story in his book *Les Délinquants*, one which repeats the story of Languille, the condemned man whose decapitated head answered to the call of his name. (183–84)

We have asked ourselves, or we have pretended to ask directly in a classical philosophical form, the form of What is . . . ? a certain number of questions, such as: What is an exception? What is cruelty? What is blood? What is man? What is it that is proper to man or to the humanitarian? and so forth.

This was not just playing with what are called "rhetorical questions" in English, that is, simulacra of questions whose answer is known in advance, and inscribed in the very form of the question. But neither were they questions to which we expected an immediately satisfying or reassuring response. They were above all questions meant to show, with their own inadequation, the vertigo or the abyss of their own impossibility, the vertigo above or around their own impossibility, what makes them turn on themselves until they make the head turn, namely, that to articulate themselves, to take shape, they would have to pretend to know at least what they are talking about at the very moment they seem to be asking about it. And this vertigo is not only, I believe, the one that can be induced by the dizziness of a simple hermeneutic circle, even though there is indeed a sort of hermeneutic circle here that lets us suppose a pre-comprehension of that about which we are asking.

I believe on the subject of death, the question, what is death? — which is perhaps not preliminary to the question of death given or life taken[13] (by suicide: to take one's own life; by murder, to take someone else's life, or by capital punishment, a singular form of putting to death) — I believe on the subject of death, the question, what is death? cannot let its vertigo make the head spin in a simple hermeneutic circle that would give us some pre-comprehension of the meaning of the word "death," a supposed pre-comprehension on the basis of which the question and its elucidation would develop. At bottom, it is this pre-comprehension that is supposed, more or less explicitly, by all great thinking or philosophies of death (up to Heidegger or Lévinas, whatever may be the differences between them, and since I have explained myself on the subject elsewhere, in *The Gift of Death* and in *Aporias* notably, I am not going to approach the question of death again today along those wide angles:[14] I would like to attempt another gesture today starting from the question of the death penalty about which, strangely, these great thinkers of death never seriously spoke and which they no doubt held to be a circumscribable and relatively dependent, secondary question). Fundamentally, a blunt form of my question would be: is it necessary to think death first and then the death penalty as a question

323

13. [Translator's note]: The idiom *donner la mort* is used frequently in the rest of this session. Where possible or necessary, it has been rendered literally as "to give death" rather than the more idiomatic "to take a life" or "to kill."

14. Jacques Derrida, *Donner la mort* (Paris: Galilée, 1999), and *Apories* (Paris: Galilée, 1996); *The Gift of Death*, 2nd ed., trans. David Wills (Chicago: University of Chicago Press, 2007); and *Aporias*, trans. Thomas Dutoit (Stanford, CA: Stanford University Press, 1993).

derived from the first one, despite its importance? Is it necessary to think death before the death penalty? Or else, paradoxically, must one start out from the question of the death penalty, the apparently and falsely circumscribed question of the death penalty, in order to pose the question of death in general?

My hypothesis, today, is that all the alleged pre-comprehensions of the meaning of the word "death," like all the refined semantic or ontological analyses that purport to distinguish, for example, the dying (*Sterben*) of man or of *Dasein* (only *Dasein* dies, says Heidegger) from the objective forms of animal perishing or ending, of objective, social decease, and so forth (see Heidegger and *Aporias*), these refined semantico-ontological analyses must rely, even as they deny it, on so-called common sense, on the alleged objective and familiar knowledge, judged to be indubitable, of what separates a state of death from a state of life—a separation that is determined or registered or calculated by the other, by a third party—that is, of the supposed existence of an objectifiable instant that separates the living from the dying, be it of an ungraspable instant that is reduced to the blade of a knife or to the *stigmē* of a point. Without the supposed or supposedly possible knowledge of this clear-cut, sharp limit, there would be no philosophy or thinking of death that could claim to know what it is talking about and proceed "methodically," as once again Heidegger wishes to do (see *Aporias*). The simple idea of this limit between life and death organizes all these meditations, whether classic or less classic, even revolutionary, even those of a deconstruction, of a "destructio" in Luther's or in Heidegger's sense at least. Now the alleged access to this knowledge that is everywhere presupposed, at the very point where one claims to deconstruct every presupposition, organizes every calculation (I will call this *calculation*), everything that is calculable, in language, in the organization of the society of the living and the dead, and especially in the possibility of murder and the death penalty, of some taking of life or "giving death" that is distributed among crime, suicide, and execution, at that point of originarity where it is still difficult to discern them, to distinguish among them (for if, conceptually, there are those who indeed mean to distinguish the death penalty from vengeance and murder, this distinction will always remain problematic—that is our very subject here—and as problematic as the rigorous possibility of a suicide that is not a self-murder or a self-inflicted death penalty). This is to suggest that every imagined mastery of the sense of the word "death" in language, every calculation on this subject (and we are calculating all the time in order to speak and to count on some meaning-to-say, some intelligibility,

324

some translatability, some communication), every calculation on the subject, around or as a function of the word "death," every calculation of this type supposes the possibility of calculating and mastering the instant of death, and this calculating mastery can only be that of a subject presumed capable of giving death: in murder, suicide, or capital punishment, all three arising here from the same possibility. This is another way of saying—and ulti-   *325* mately it is rather simple—that the calculable credit we grant to the word "death" is indexed to a set of presuppositions, a network of presuppositions in which "capital punishment," the calculation of capital punishment, finds its place of inscription where it is indissociable from both murder and suicide.

Wherever at least the presumption of knowledge is lacking on the subject of this so-called objective limit, this end of life (which Heidegger would make us believe is not the *dying* proper to *Dasein*), wherever this mastering calculation would no longer be presumed accessible, possible, in our power, well then, one could no longer either speak of murder, suicide, and death penalty, or organize anything of the sort whatsoever in the law, in the legal code, in the social order, in its procedures and its techniques, and so forth.

Now, if there have been doubts for a long time about the objective determination of the state of death, if it has been known for a long time (these are the ABC's of anthropology) that the criteria of death differ from one society to another, sometimes from one state to another within the same confederation (for example, I believe this is the case in the United States), and especially from one moment to another in human history, which means that one does not die at the same moment, if I may say that, in different places (moreover, there would not be religions or differences of funeral rites or cultural difference in general without this trembling and this in-determination in the determination of the instant of death, in the delimitation of death, between the near side and the far side), well, if this has always been known and sensed, never more so than today has objective knowledge as to the delimitation of death, never has this supposedly objective knowledge, but always presupposed even by the most radical, the most critical, the most deconstructive phenomenologies or ontologies, never has this knowledge been as problematic, debatable, fragile, and deconstructible down to the minimal semantic kernel of the word "death." I already evoked (but I could have taken so many other examples and indications) a certain recent article from an American newspaper (whose reference I've lost and which was sent to me by my friend Richard Rand), an

article titled "What Is Death? Experts Wrestle with Legal Definitions and
Ethics,"[15] which reports the comments of a professor of psychiatry and biomedical ethics at Case Western Reserve University, who says: "I think we're
in a phase in which death is being deconstructed. The more we talk, the
more we write, the more we find the consensus defining death superficial
and fragile."[16]

Read here or later, if there's time, "What Is Death?," etc.[17]

To deconstruct death, then, that is the subject, while recalling that we do not
know what it is, if and when it happens, and to whom. Here is what is both
relatively incontestable and a task for every kind of vigilance in the world:
to be vigilant in deconstructing death, to keep one's eyes open to what this
word of death, this word "death" means, to what one wants to make it say or
make us say with it in more than one language. This is in fact a task of vigilance for the vigilant, for those who keep watch [veillent], who keep watch
over life, and yet here is a task of vigilance that sets one to dreaming. When
one loves keeping watch [la veille] and vigilance, when one loves period, one
may sleep perhaps, but one dreams.

Having stumbled on this American, and legitimate, use of the word
"deconstruction," where I had not expected it but where I had not expected
it even while always knowing that if there was one thing, one word to deconstruct, it is indeed what is called death, I nonetheless saw pass before
me, very quickly, a kind of angel, not an angel of death, not an announcer
or a messenger of death (an angel is a mailman, you know, a messenger,
the bearer of news, and the Gospel bears the good news, as its name indicates, but it is also the news of a death of God), not, then, my angel of death
but an angel who whispered to me while smiling or challenging me: hey,
at bottom that's the dream of deconstruction, a convulsive movement to
have done with death, to deconstruct death itself. Not to put into question
again the question, what is death? when and where does it take place? etc.

15. The reference to this article is given in an editors' note to Derrida, *The Beast
and the Sovereign II (2002–2003)*, ed. M. Lisse, M.-L. Mallet, and G. Michaud, trans.
G. Bennington (Chicago: University of Chicago Press, 2011), p. 162, which we reproduce here: "Karen Long, 'Oh, Death, Where Is Thy Starting?,'" *Baptist Standard: Insight
for Faithful Living* (November 3, 1999), http://www.baptiststandard.com/1999/11_3
/pages/death.html.

16. [Translator's note]: Derrida reads both the title of this article and the quote first
in English before translating them into French.

17. See below, p. 242, n. 19.

What comes afterward? and so forth. But to deconstruct death. Final period. And with the same blow, to come to blows with death and put it out of action. No less than that. Death to death. If death is not one, if there is nothing clearly identifiable and locatable beneath this word, if there is even more than one, if one can suffer a thousand deaths, for example through illness, love, or the illness of love, then death, death in the singular no longer exists. Why be anxious still? Stop taking seriously anxiety in the face of death—in the singular. Stop thinking of yourself as one condemned to death or the victim of a sentence of capital punishment. Your life is not a death row. That is perhaps what my angel might say to me. My angel, who is also my temptation. My angel is right, as always; it is necessary of course to deconstruct death and perhaps this is even the depth of the desire of what is called deconstruction. But the same guardian angel of deconstruction, or another guardian angel—for the problem of deconstruction is that it has more than one angel and that it is (this is its vigilance and its necessity) this knowledge of the multiplicity of angels—the same other angel of deconstruction just as implacably calls me back to order and says to me: you will not get off so easily. First of all, this "deconstruction of death," on the pretext of dissolving the unity or the identity or the gravity of death, must not serve to banalize or relativize the death penalty (as finally a whole Christian tradition has done, which uses an alibi of the beyond so as to deny the irreversible gravity of death and legitimize the death penalty, and thus demobilize abolitionism); it is not enough to deconstruct death, as it is necessary to do, and even if it is indeed necessary, it is not enough   *328* to deconstruct death, my other angel would continue, in order to assure one's salvation. It is not enough to deconstruct death even, as it is necessary to do, in order to survive or take out a life insurance policy. For neither does life come out unscathed by this deconstruction. Nothing comes out unscathed by this deconstruction. What, then, does "to come out" unscathed [*indemne*] mean?

The question of the death penalty is perhaps that of indemnity. What is the indemnity of the unscathed? In "Faith and Knowledge," I tried to articulate or elaborate this question of the unscathed [*l'indemne*], of the indemnity of the unscathed, of the safe and of salvation, of the saving-oneself, with that of the immunity of the immune, as the question of religion.[18] It is also, of course, the question of the death penalty.

---

18. Derrida, "Faith and Knowledge."

Read, if time permits, "What Is Death?," etc.[19]

19. At the end of the session, Derrida concludes with the following improvised reading, translation, and commentary: "That's it, I've finished but there are five minutes left and I still want to read you some passages of the article from which I excerpted the sentence 'I think we are in a phase when death is being deconstructed . . .' I translate quickly. 'Consider three cases: Teresa Hamilton falls into a severe diabetic coma and is diagnosed as brain-dead. Her family refuses to accept this and insists on taking her body home, on a ventilator. Despite a Florida law that states that people with dead brains are legally dead, and over the protests of doctors, the family gets its wish. Two students from Japan [second case] are shot in California and declared brain-dead. Hospital staff members take both off respirators without consulting their families in Japan where brain death is not recognized. The families are horrified.' There followed a debate: when? what are the criteria? 'Finally, a Hasidic boy [third case], Aaron Halberstam, is shot on the Brooklyn Bridge. He is diagnosed as brain-dead but his family, relying on rabbinical advice, doesn't accept their fifteen-year old as dead as long as a respirator can keep his body breathing. They turn to Genesis 7:22: "In whose nostrils was the breath of the spirit of life."' There is no brain death so long as he is there and can breathe. This is the criterion of respiration. 'A sympathetic doctor refuses to declare Aaron legally dead until his heart stops.' Third criterion, the heart. 'All these young people died in the spring of 1994, but the arguments framing their final hours show how hard the application of legal brain death can be. The diagnosis requires painstaking, repeated tests for the lack of spontaneous breathing and electrical activity in the brain. Nevertheless, some reject brain death for deeply held cultural or religious reasons. . . . Others, such as the Hamiltons, just can't believe that a loved one on medical machinery whose chest is rising and falling . . . can really be dead.' So the fiction makes it that they see he is breathing. For them, brain death is nothing at all. 'Among medical experts, the definition of death is so contentious that two international conferences have failed to resolve it. A third, scheduled for Cuba in February, has attracted a contingent from the Vatican and a presentation from controversial Yale ethicist Peter Singer.' So, in Cuba there will be people from the Vatican and then a very controversial professor of ethics at Yale, Peter Singer. 'He is the utilitarian philosopher who argues that human life is not sacred.' And then comes the quotation from another doctor, Stuart Youngner, '"I think we are in a phase in which death is being deconstructed," says Stuart Youngner, a professor of psychiatry and biomedical ethics at Case Western Reserve University.' Next, the whole article examines — I am not going to read it to you in entirety — all of the disputes, all of the reasons to dispute all the criteria of death. All the new <operations>, transplanted organs of course, grafts, all the techno-medical novelties make it that one knows less and less (1) when death has taken place; and (2) when it is, so to speak, irreversible. One can then say, according to which criteria, if the convention or the conventional fiction admits a certain criterion, for example brain death, then even according to this criterion, if one agrees on this criterion, it is not certain that one cannot recover from brain death. So, all of this naturally makes the concept of death, but not just the concept, the social, juridical application, etc., of the concept of death more than problematic, thus undergoing deconstruction. There it is."

March 15, 2000

Vertigos. To be seized by vertigo: the head that spins and the head that falls, separated, severed. The blade of the guillotine that severs the head — in one blow. The turn around the neck of decollation. Everything turns around what turns, thus, around vertigo, conversion, revolution, turns and re-turns, and turns that are not merely rhetorical, turns and turns of phrase given to the expression "condemnation to death" or "condemnation to die," the conventional if not arbitrary distinction that I proposed last time. Condemnation to death or condemnation to die, condemnation and revolution, revolution and religion, death penalty and faith, death penalty and belief, vertigo and conversion: these are the highs and the lows in which we have been trying to orient ourselves for some time and in which we are going to continue to climb up and down, to turn, to the point of vertigo, perhaps to the point of losing ourselves. The high and the low, the elevation and the hell of damnation, the damned of heaven and the damned of the earth, souls damned or condemned, all of this is asking us: what does it mean "to damn" and "to condemn"?

Death penalty and filiation, we often said and demonstrated.[1] And again the last time, with Camus, we analyzed, in more than one place, what *The First Man* calls, in its two parts, the "search for the father" and "the son."

We are going to speak a lot about religion, faith, or belief, once again. It would be flippant, therefore, in a seminar on the death penalty that is but a logical continuation of a seminar on pardon and perjury in the course of

---

1. A handwritten addition by Derrida in the margin of the typescript at this point: "Blood." During the session, Derrida develops the note: "The allusions to blood, the question of blood, were touching on blood, so to speak, in the proper sense, blood that flows, that is absorbed or that disappears with lethal injection [Eng.], apparently, or the blood of filiation, lineage. Blood is both the blood that flows beneath the axe or the guillotine, and the blood of genealogy. Of the father and of the son."

which, during the last two years, I alluded more than once to the church's acts of repentance and to the Holy Father's announced repentance on the subject of the Inquisition,[2] it would be flippant today not, dare I say, to evoke the event, both unheard-of and infinitely predictable, that three days ago saw a dying Pope, trembling but without fear, a Pope, the Holy Father who, in a Parkinsonian trembling, dares to commit the whole history of the Catholic church, the whole of its history, two thousand years of Christianity, in an act of repentance without precedent in the history of the church or any religious history or in any history, period[3] (if one excepts the gesture of Paul VI who in 1963 asked forgiveness for the division of the church).[4] Since over the past few years we have in a certain sense premeditated this event that we could see coming (I made allusion to it more than once), all the more so in that the pope had already formulated some ninety-four requests for forgiveness (the Jews, the Crusades, the Inquisition, forced conversions, Galileo, etc.), I will not comment on it at too much length. I will just highlight a few features, at least three, that concern our seminar.

333   1. This unheard-of inaugural gesture is theologico-political inasmuch as it in fact commits a church that is also a state, speaking through the mouth of someone who is also a head of state and who asks forgiveness for crimes with which a number of other Christian European states were associated (Spain for the Inquisition, the Americas and other states for slavery, so many other states for women and Jews who are once again put together in the same camp, if I may say that, etc.).

2. This Christian gesture is within the order of things despite its revolutionary character and the consequences it entails, which in my view are unlimited. This gesture simply conforms to a possibility that Christianity has always claimed it had in some way itself inaugurated and invented. Christianity is par excellence the religion that calls itself, that is the self-styled religion of a forgiveness of sins, which is its very essence and makes for its difference. Hegel is far from being the only one to say this (recall the texts we read in previous years on this subject). And this singularity of a

2. Seminar "Perjury and Pardon" (1997–1998), sessions 1, 2, and 4; and "Perjury and Pardon" (1998–1999), sessions 1 and 6.

3. Derrida is referring to John Paul II's homily on March 12, 2000, "Ash Wednesday 2000 Apologies," which was based on the research of the International Theological Commission, published in December 1999 under the title "Memory and Reconciliation: The Church and the Faults of the Past."

4. Pope Paul VI, in his opening speech to the second session of the Vatican II Council, September 29, 1963.

religion of forgiveness, if this claim is founded on a reading of the Gospels, is indissociable from the Passion, thus from the death of God, of the son of God, of God the Father made man as sacrifice and redemption of sins.[5] From a humanization of God. Now, if it is difficult to dissociate this idea of forgiveness from some death of God, as well as from his resurrection or redemption (that is, from what redeems a condemnation or a damnation), it is also difficult, for that very reason, not to hear in what happened three days ago a certain death knell of God on the basis of which everything has to begin again. Which is both a fathomless disaster and the hope of salvation for a certain Christianity (a Catholic Christianity, but which is militantly seeking an ecumenism that will perhaps find new momentum in this asked-for forgiveness). This indeed confirms what I had more than once ventured to say, namely, that this pope has sustained better than anyone the discourse of the death of God, that in this century there has been no better witness and orator and performer of the death of God the Father, a Christian theme par excellence, and that the "deconstruction of Christianity," to take up Nancy's expression, is the very thing, business, and initiative of Christianity. Naturally, by this deconstruction that overcomes itself as it is carried out, that sublates itself, one must understand a Christian deconstruction, that Lutheran *destructio* from which Heidegger no doubt inherited the word *Destruktion*. But one can, perhaps (nothing is less certain), think another deconstruction, a deconstruction without sublation of this deconstruction.[6] Leaving open this question, this immense question (namely, whether or not "to self-deconstruct" [*se déconstruire*] has to mean, in short, "to ask forgiveness" or to pass through the ordeal of forgiveness), and so as to refer to the difference here between the Catholic gesture and a Lutheran tradition, I refer you, for example, to what Luther says about condemnation and eternal damnation, for example in his "Sermon on Preparing to Die." (Quote Luther, 253–54)

334

> First, since death marks a farewell from this world and all its activities, it is necessary that a man regulate temporal goods properly or as he wishes to have them ordered. . . .
> Second, we must also take leave spiritually. That is, we must cheerfully and sincerely forgive, for God's sake, all men who have offended us. At the

5. During the session, Derrida adds: "Forgiveness has no meaning outside of this history of the son and the death of the son of God made man and sacrificing his son to redeem the sins of mankind."
6. During the session, Derrida spells out: "a radically non-Christian deconstruction."

same time we must also, for God's sake, earnestly seek the forgiveness of all the people whom we undoubtedly have greatly offended by setting them a bad example or by bestowing too few of the kindnesses demanded by the law of Christian brotherly love. This is necessary lest the soul remain burdened by its actions here on earth.

Third, since everyone must depart, we must turn our eyes to God, to whom the path of death leads and directs us. Here we find the beginning of the narrow gate and of the straight path to life. . . . Therefore, the death of the dear saints is called a new birth. . . .

335

Fourth, such preparation and readiness for this journey are accomplished first of all by providing ourselves with a sincere confession (of at least the greatest sins and those which by diligent search can be recalled by our memory), with the holy Christian sacrament of the holy and true body of Christ, and with the unction.[7]

3. Finally, the unheard-of and properly interruptive, ruptive gesture of this dying pope asking forgiveness at the microphone in front of all the televisions of the entire world, this gesture that is so novel, so audacious (which perhaps only someone dying, a dying pope,[8] a dying state, a dying church can permit itself), this very liberated gesture remains all the same both powerfully traditional (within the Christian order) and limited in many ways: it commits, at least nominally, only the Catholic church, it remains vague concerning many wrongs (and barely had the pope finished speaking before complaints and demands were voiced, about the Shoah and other details; not to mention the Protestants who protest the rehabilitation of indulgences even as forgiveness is being sought for the wars of religion, etc.); finally, since it is our subject, concerning the death penalty itself, which the Vatican has not yet formally condemned and which the Catholic church has never ceased to favor or approve throughout the same history, the forgiveness to be asked still has an intact future: there's a lot on the holy plate [*il y a du pain béni sur la planche*].[9] No doubt this will be the task of the next pope, if the papacy has a future, for it is for the history of the papacy itself that this pope asks forgiveness, as if the papacy itself were on its deathbed, henceforth

7. Martin Luther, "A Sermon on Preparing do Die," in *Martin Luther's Basic Theological Writings*, 2d ed., ed. Timothy F. Lull and William R. Russell (Minneapolis, MN: Fortress Press, 2005), pp. 418–19.

8. Added by hand in the margin of the typescript: "or Holy Father." During the session, Derrida often replaces "pope" by "Holy Father."

9. A sentence added by hand in the margin of the typescript reads: "The question of the death penalty, we will see, is that of <the> question of the father — thus of the pope."

condemned to die, if not condemned to death. To the Catholic church, as such, there remains the duty to think the death penalty.

The death penalty, where do you believe it comes from?   *336*

Even in cases where the death penalty is supposedly desired, beloved, chosen for oneself, even in cases where the death penalty might be obscurely, compulsively, irresistibly sought by the condemned one, by a criminal, or by two criminal associates, by a duo of criminals, two men, two women, a man, a woman, like Bonnie and Clyde in the movies (today we can no longer speak of crime and the death penalty without film and television; we have proof of this every day and it is an essential change in the given state of affairs)[10]

(speaking of the criminal duo, the alliance of criminals, recall that from the beginning of the seminar, both in the cases reported by Badinter, in *The Execution*, and in the case of *Dead Man Walking*, we were dealing with two criminal accomplices, linked by the same crime, and this only sharpened the question of a death and especially a death penalty that only ever kills one, singularly, irreplaceably: one cannot share the death penalty, even supposing, which is very improbable, that one could share a death, die together, desire to die together, two together, and yet that someone is each time, and once and for all, more than one in killing or more than one in dying, that too is an incontestable, undeniable state of affairs, however difficult it may be to integrate this into a calculation or an arithmetic, that is to say also, consequently, into a code of law: people are condemned to death always one by one [*un par un, une par une*], even if an entire group is executed by the same firing squad),

even in cases, then, where the death penalty might be obscurely, compulsively, irresistibly sought, desired—as desire itself—by the condemned one, by a criminal, or by two criminals associated by this strange alliance of the secret transgression that can be more sacred than that of a marriage

(and this desired death, desire itself, this death drive, if you wish to use that   *337* expression, is an abundant theme that we are not finished dealing with; even though it is not original, I will cite in this connection once again Camus who himself remarks what is too well known, in his "Reflections on the Guil-

10. The formatting of the next few pages follows that of the typescript. The sentence begun here ends below, p. 250.

lotine," so as to demonstrate the non-deterrent, non-exemplary character of the death penalty. "Man," Camus says,

> wants to live, but it is useless to hope that this desire will dictate all his actions. He also desires to be nothing, he wants the irreparable and death for its own sake. So it happens that the criminal wants not only the crime, but the suffering that goes with it, even and especially if this suffering is beyond measure [Comment at length: question of the beyond-measure. Measuring the beyond-measure, the incommensurable].[11] When this strange desire grows and takes command, the prospect of being put to death not only fails to stop the criminal, but probably further increases the vertigo [here is our first occurrence of the word "vertigo"] in which he loses himself. In a certain way, then, he kills in order to die [192]

And earlier, Camus remarks: "the murderer, most of the time, feels innocent when he kills. Every criminal acquits himself before the verdict" [191].[12]

338   And against those he nicknames "textbook psychologists," he recalls the death drive, which he designates, as was often done at the time, with the term "death instinct" (and thus in this we must hear, without too much artifice, the word *instant*, which we made our subject last week, together with *instinct*,[13] the death instinct seeking to reach that presumed indivisibility of a death from which I will not suffer because I take my own life, even as I keep it, as Blanchot says at the end of *The Instant of My Death*, "in abeyance,"

11. During the session, Derrida comments: "I will be tempted to place a lot of weight on this expression 'beyond measure' [*démesuré*] because in what we are talking about, the death penalty, it is a matter of an excessiveness [*démesure*], a penalty without proportion, without commensurability, without any possible relation that is proportional with the crime. With the death penalty, we touch on an alleged calculation that dares or alleges to incorporate the beyond-measure and the infinite and the incalculable into its calculation. If there is a scandal in all these penalties, in all these punishments, the unheard-of, unique scandal of the death penalty is precisely this excessiveness, the fact that it cannot be measured, 'commensured,' so to speak, with any crime. The death penalty dares to claim to measure the beyond-measure in some way."

12. During the session, Derrida adds: "In other words, the criminal, even though one often speaks, I said so the last time, of a vengeance irreducible to law, the criminal as speaking or reasoning being, the criminal has always at least the idea of doing justice and of referring to a universalizable law, and thus, he feels innocent, like a judge. The criminal operates like a judge. And thus he acquits himself. In what is called premeditated crime. In unpremeditated crime, there is no crime. When crime falls like rain on one's head, it is not crime. Premeditated crime, crime properly speaking, obviously, justifies *itself*. It bears within it a justification that acquits the criminal before the verdict."

13. [Translator's note]: In French, the pronunciations of *instant* and *instinct* are appreciably closer than they are in English.

[*en instance*]: "the death instinct," says Camus, "at certain moments calls for the destruction of oneself and of others. It is probable that the desire to kill often coincides with the desire to die or to annihilate oneself" [191]. A coincidence, then, that presupposes the gathering in the same instant, the identification in the same instance of the instant and the instinct of death. In a note he adds: "One can read every week in the papers of criminals who originally wavered between killing themselves and killing others" [ibid.]).[14]

The argument is both banal and very equivocal, very formidable in the consequences one may draw from it, those that Camus wants to draw from it: obviously these are, in the first place, consequences that would militate against the death penalty; but one might conclude, conversely — and this is what becomes terribly ambiguous — one might infer, rather boldly, that the suppression of the death penalty can frustrate these desires, prevent some from killing themselves by killing others as they might wish to do and thus create formidable turbulence in the economy of the drives or the psychic equilibrium of a social body: what indeed would a society be in which not only the death penalty is abolished, at least within national boundaries (not in war and here again the problem of civil war arises), but in which one could no longer either kill another or kill oneself by killing someone in oneself, and so forth? I leave this question suspended, but it is formidable, as you can easily imagine, and properly diabolical: it would be the question of an unforeseeable pathology of the social body provoked by the double disappearance of *both* the possibility of any murder *and* the possibility of any death penalty, as if the need for death and the death penalty were the response not only to a kind of external security, to the necessity of discouraging through example potential criminals, but to the necessity of securing for the social psyche a kind of internal health, by making sure it had its ration, its measure, its fill, its share of lethal sacrifice, as if a society, the health of a social or national psychic body, or even a human body in general, needed to have its share, its measure, its fill of murder or death penalty in order to survive),[15]

339

even in cases, then, I repeat, as I was saying, where the death sentence might be obscurely, compulsively, irresistibly sought, desired — as desire itself — by the condemned one, by a criminal, or by two criminals associated by that strange alliance of the secret transgression, which can be more

14. The closing parenthesis has been added.
15. The parenthesis on Camus, opened above on p. 247, closes here.

sacred than that of a religious marriage, well, the death penalty is always, by definition, death that comes from the other, given or decided by the other, be it the other within oneself. The possibility of the death penalty — this is too obvious but what we have here is an obscure obviousness that one must begin by recalling — the possibility, and note I say the *possibility*, of the death penalty begins where I am delivered into the power of the other, be it the power of the other in me. When does this begin? Does this begin? And does it end? To have done with it, one would have to have done with the other; and perhaps those who commit suicide, or those who run toward the condemnation to death as toward suicide want first of all to have done with the other, before finishing themselves off. Out of excess hatred or excess love.

Recall the question that resonated here during a past session and led us step by step toward that of a "deconstruction of death." This initial question was:

340 "When to die finally?"[16] (I was wondering if the pope asked himself or heard this question when he dared to ask forgiveness for centuries of Christianity.)

Upon rehearing it, upon letting resonate once again the echo of this atrocious and inevitable question ("When to die finally?"), a question that, as often happens when I speak, I listened to rather than saying or posing it last time, a question that, crossing my mind, imposed itself on me, as though dictated, even before I had to formulate it myself and decide on it, I remembered, then, upon saying "when to die finally?" "but, finally, when to die?" I recalled this strange coincidence, this bizarre synchrony, namely that the eighteenth century, what is called thus, the eighteenth century (what is the eighteenth century: well, it was both the century of Enlightenment, of the first abolitionist movements, and the century of the Revolution, the Terror, and the rights of man, etc.; we have talked a lot about all of this), well, setting out from this question, when to die finally? I recalled that the eighteenth century is at once all of that *plus* the century that is said to have seen the birth of what is called the happiness idea, the idea *of* happiness (the idea of a happiness that, fundamentally, is not only pleasure, joy, felicity, beatitude, that is not hedonist enjoyment, that is perhaps the *eudaimon*, with all the abyssal depth of this word — Heidegger devotes pages to it that one should read, but that one should read while recalling this, which Heidegger does not do: that the daimon, as we have read, speaks or abstains from speaking to Socrates at the moment of his condemnation to death — the happiness idea, thus the transformed inheritor of eudemonism, of the *demon* of eu-

16. See above, "Ninth Session. March 1/8, 2000, p. 218.

demonism, has a very singular history and belongs to a determined culture; it is in this sense that one says "happiness was a new idea in Europe,"[17] precisely in the eighteenth century), well, this eighteenth century that saw the birth of happiness, that is, the idea of happiness, since happiness is but an idea, to be happy with happiness is to believe in it; it is to believe, be able to believe in being happy, and to say so to oneself, just where this belief, like every belief, is a belief in the other, passing by way of language, that is, by way of sworn faith in the other or of the other, and thus a *belief of the other in oneself* [en soi] (belief of the other in oneself, a painfully equivocal expression since it designates at once that I believe the other, in the other, but that I believe him or believe in him only or first of all in me, or that there where I believe, it is the other in me who believes and not me, etc.), this century in which, they say, the idea of happiness was discovered, was also the one that invented the Terror and the guillotine, and reconverted to the most massive and mechanical death penalty people who, like Robespierre, had been abolitionists and had participated in essay contests in order to justify their position. As if the death penalty were always lying in wait for happiness.

If we suppose that someone could ever say "Now I am happy," would he or she conclude from that "now I can die," or even "now I must die" or on the contrary "I do not want to die," "moreover I now know that dying is impossible"? And can two people, more than one man or one woman, say and think this? These utterances always turn around the death penalty, that is, around a death that comes from the other, decided and calculated by the other, in the hands of the other.

I have no answer to this question, namely the question of a tragedy of happiness, of a tragic happiness, a damned or condemned happiness, a damnation of happiness (one can be damned to or by happiness — we will come back later to this lexicon, *damnum*, damned, condemned) and even if I had an answer, it's not certain that I would tell you. Moreover, it's like life, each has his or her own, for this question, and it is destined to remain secret. So I ask myself once again, as I did, I believe, during the seminar on the secret,[18] I ask myself what kind of seminar it might be in which the one who

17. This famous quotation from Saint-Just is drawn from "Report on Behalf of the Committee on Public Safety on the Mode of Execution of the Decree against the Enemies of the Revolution Presented to the National Convention on 13 Ventôse Year II." See Saint-Just, *Œuvres complètes*, ed. Anne Kupiec and Miguel Abensour (Paris: Gallimard, 2004).

18. Seminar "Répondre du secret" (1991–92), first session, November 13, 1991 ff.

342   takes the floor [*prend la parole*]—or the one who keeps the floor [*garde la parole*]—says to you: I am hiding something from you, I will not tell you the truth even if I know it. This would blow to pieces, deconstructed pieces, deconstructed like death itself, the idea and the conventional scene of everything called a "seminar"—to the extent that a seminar is obliged, as if by oath, to try to speak truly, to speak the true, to speak all possible truth. To link what I am saying to the question of the death penalty, that is, to link the hypothesis of a seminar that does not conform to the standard idea of the seminar, or even in general the almost mad force of a discourse that is inadmissible by academic or cultural or journalistic norms, a discourse, a manifestation of this counterculture that is so vitally, so urgently, needed today, especially when one reads the newspapers where, save for some thankful exceptions, one's only choice, roughly speaking and usually, is between news of executions in the United States and the advertising onslaught of political, literary, or philosophical mediocrity, an onslaught organized by a kind of culture mafia, well, I will ask myself if it makes sense to speak of a condemnation to death of something like culture. Or a language. Can one condemn to death something other than individual subjects, persons, legal subjects identifiable as such, individuals bearing a patronymic and obliged to appear before the law as individual subjects? Can one, other than by way of metaphor, condemn to death a language (languages are killed, in a thousand ways, I have no doubt on that score and there are hundreds of languages that have disappeared in colonial or commercial, capital, techno-capitalist capitalist [*sic*] violence in recent years)? Is it then a matter of condemnations to death sensu stricto? (It is still this question of semantics and rhetoric, which is not a rhetorical question,[19] which is not a simulacrum of a question because everything is at stake in it, this question, then, of the strict sense or the broad and metonymic sense of the expression "death penalty," "condemnation to death," that holds our attention and that will always come back as the most serious of questions: is it legitimate or not, is it necessary or forbidden to extend the expression "condemnation to death" beyond its strict legal sense and its juridico-statist field?)

343   I repeat my question, then: can one condemn to death an entity that is in some way anonymous, without individual patronymic? Can one condemn to death a culture, an institution, a nation, a group, an ethnic group? One can condemn someone to death, a person who has killed or participated in the murder of a nation, a community, an ethnic group (sooner or later we will return to the Nuremberg trials and the case of Eichmann in Jerusalem

19. [Translator's note]: "Rhetorical question" is in English in the original.

and to what Arendt says about it, in a certain mode at the end of a fictional indictment where she explains what should have been said and argued so as to justify Eichmann's hanging). But if one can call "death penalty" the penalty inflicted on someone who is guilty of a murder perpetrated against a culture, a nation, a community, can one condemn to death a community? Can genocide, for example, be presented, sensu stricto, as a condemnation to death? For there to be condemnation to death, and not just putting to death, crime, murder, or failure to come to the aid of a person in danger,[20] it is necessary at least, *in principle*, that there be, *at least*, precisely [*justement*] a system of justice, a code of law, a simulacrum at least, a scene of judgment. A genocide or the putting to death of a collective or anonymous entity (languages, institution, culture, community) does not therefore partake, sensu stricto, literally, of a logic or of the concept of condemnation to death. A question of structure and proportion. There must always be a judgment, a verdict, and the subject of it must be a personal, nameable subject, answerable to his or her name.

I return then to one of my initial questions: is it enough to say "I have to die" or "I will have to die," or even, another formula that I have glossed in the past, "I owe myself, we owe ourselves to death" to be authorized to translate these utterances by "I am condemned to death"?[21]

In the common meaning of the language, the answer is *no*, obviously *not*. Even if one keeps the word "condemned," more or less as a metaphorical figure, well, "I am condemned to die" does not mean, sensu stricto, "I am condemned to death." That is just good sense, common sense. I am, we are all here, man and woman alike, condemned to die, but the chances are slim that any of us here [*aucun de nous, aucune ici*] will ever be condemned to death — especially in France and in Europe.

First the "deconstruction of death" that we spoke of last time must not serve, on the pretext of dissolving the unity or the identity or the gravity of death, to banalize the death penalty, to relativize it (as ultimately a whole Christian tradition has done when it uses the alibi of the beyond to deny the irreversible gravity of death and to legitimize the death penalty, and thus demobilize abolitionism: from that point of view, Christianity has been a

344

20. [Translator's note]: Derrida is referring here to a specific provision in the French penal code that determines as a punishable crime the "willful failure to aid a person in danger."

21. See Derrida, *Demeure, Athènes* (Paris: Galilée, 2009); *Athens, Still Remains*, trans. Pascale-Anne Brault and Michael Naas (New York : Fordham University Press, 2010).

powerful "deconstruction of death"); it is not enough to deconstruct death, as it is necessary to do, and even if it is indeed necessary, it is not enough to deconstruct death, the one I was calling my other angel would continue, in order to assure one's salvation. It is not enough to deconstruct death itself, as it is necessary to do, in order to survive or take out a life insurance policy. For neither does life, we are saying, come out unscathed by this deconstruction.

Nothing comes out unscathed by this deconstruction.

What, then, does "to come out" *unscathed* [indemne] mean?

If the question of the death penalty is that of indemnity, it remains to be thought what *indemnity* means, that is, either *being-unscathed* [l'être-indemne] (that is, safe, sound, intact, virgin, unhurt, *heilig*, holy — I worked over all this in "Faith and Knowledge"[22]) or else *being-indemnified* [l'être indemnisé], that is, rendered once again unscathed, made unscathed, that is, paid, reimbursed by the payment of a compensation, redemption, by the payment of a debt. We will continue to interrogate this word and this logic of the *indemne*, of being-*indemne*, of being indemnified and of indemnity.

345   But since clearly indemnity signals toward an economy and an interest, I would like to return for a moment to the question of interest that has already interested us a lot. In answer to a question asked during the discussion, two weeks ago, on the subject of the interest there was in being an abolitionist, in militating for the abolition of the death penalty, and when I was asked if the abolitionist I would like to be must be as *disinterested* as the supporter of the death penalty in the Kantian logic of the categorical imperative (who in principle should not be driven by any interest, and we heard Nietzsche's protest on this subject), to this question I responded that I was not seeking to maintain a *disinterested* abolitionist discourse but to think *otherwise* the interest there could be in standing up against the death penalty and in universally abolishing the death penalty, an interest that was not only negative (as I said a little hastily the last time, while evoking especially, in a manner that risked being a little aestheticizing and aristocratic, my disgust with the death penalty, more precisely for death-dealing [*morticoles*] subjects, for the motivations and the gestures and the grimaces of the supporters, for the agents, the assistants, the ideologues of the death penalty, and the scene they act out). I would say then first, abruptly and directly, that, far from fleeing the accusation of Marx or Baudelaire, or even Victor Hugo, all three of whom, each in his own way, you recall, at a given moment suspected some fair-weather abolitionists of wanting first of all to save their necks, far from fleeing this accusation, I take this risk on myself — even while displacing it a little. And I say straight on: yes, I am against the death

22. Derrida, "Faith and Knowledge."

penalty because I want to save my neck, to save the life I love, what I love to live, what I love living. And when I say "I," of course, I mean "I," me, but also the "I," the "me," whoever says "I" in its place or in mine. That is my interest, the ultimate resource of my interest as of any possible interest in the end of the death penalty, every interest having finally to be a "my interest," we are going to see why, an interest so originary, so primordial that it risks being shared, in truth, by the supporters of the death penalty—and who will always tell you, moreover, that they are not for death, that they
do not love death, or killing, that like us they are for life ("but let messieurs 346
the murderers begin," they would say, as always, like Alphonse Karr, the pamphleteer to whom this joke is attributed); "it is in order to protect life, it is in the name of life," they would say, "that we urge, in certain cases, the death penalty against those who do not respect life"; so that in order to make the case for abolition against this argument, one must demonstrate that the death penalty is not the "best" means of protecting or affirming the primacy of life. Nonetheless, what I would like to clarify is the fact that the abolitionist struggle, without being either *disinterested*, in the sense of the Kantian categorical imperative, or *interested* in the sense of a calculating and hypocritical interest, unavowed and unavowable, of the particular interest that Marx, Baudelaire, and even Nietzsche, and even Hugo detected in certain others, in certain politicians or spokesmen for a social class or a part of a social class who were combatting the death penalty to save their skin, in short; well, neither disinterested nor interested in this sense, the abolitionist struggle, in my view, must still be driven; it cannot not be driven, motivated, justified by an interest, but by another interest, by another figure of interest that remains to be defined.

What does that mean? What interest? What is an interest here? I can believe in and affirm what is called life, what I call, what an "I" calls, life only by setting out from and within a "my life" even if this belief in "my life," the sense of "my life," originarily passes by way of the heart of the other. Even if my life drive [*pulsion*], my life pulse, is first of all confided to the heart of the other and would not survive the heart of the other. Consequently, in general, even before the question of the death penalty, I can put the living before the dead only on the basis of the affirmation and preference of my life, of my living present, right there where it receives its life from the heart of the other.[23] Even someone who commits suicide must accept this obvious

23. [Translator's note]: As rendered, this sentence covers over several translation problems. Here is the original: "Je ne peux faire passer le vivant avant le mort que depuis l'affirmation et la préférence de ma vie, de mon présent vivant, là même où il reçoit sa vie du coeur de l'autre."

fact. But that is not enough. It is still necessary to go from this originary and general preference of life by itself, for itself, from this self-preference of the living to the opposition to the death penalty; it is necessary to go from this quasi-tautological opposition of life to death to a more specific opposition:

347   no longer simply to the opposition to death but to the opposition to the death *penalty*. The point is that it belongs to life not necessarily to be immortal but to have a future, thus some life before it, some event to come only where death, the instant of death, is not calculable, is not the object of a calculable decision. Where the anticipation of my death becomes the anticipation of a calculable instant, there is no longer any future, there is thus no longer any event to come, nothing to come, no longer any other, even no more heart of the other, and so forth. So that where "my life," be it originarily granted by the heart of the other, is "my life," it must keep this relation to the coming of the other as coming of the to-come [*venue de l'à-venir*] in the opening of the incalculable and the undecidable. "My life," and especially my life insofar as it depends on the [*tient au*] heart of the other, cannot affirm itself and affirm its preference except over against this, which is not so much death as calculation and decision, the calculable decidability of what puts an end to it. At bottom, I would say by way of perhaps an excessive shortcut, that what we rebel against when we rebel against the death penalty is not death, or even the fact of killing, of taking a life; it is against the calculating decision, not so much the "you will die," a sentence that can refer to three or four deaths, three or four modalities of dying , three or four prescriptive or descriptive futures (1, you will die: in the future of so-called natural death, I know that you will end up dying; 2, you will die: murdered, I am going to kill you; or 3, you will die by your own doing by suicide; 4, you will die of capital punishment), not even the imperative "die" but the fourth "you will die," that of capital punishment, you will die on such and such a day, at such and such an hour, in that calculable place, and from blows delivered by several machines, the worst of which is perhaps neither the guillotine nor the syringe, but the clock and the anonymity of clockwork. Or of the calendar. The insult, the injury, the fundamental injustice done to the life in me, to the principle of life in me, is not death itself, from this point of view; it is rather the interruption of the principle of indetermination, the ending imposed on the opening of the incalculable chance whereby a living being has a relation to what comes, to the to-come and thus to some other as event, as guest, as *arrivant*. And the supreme form of the paradox, its philosophical

348   form, is that what is ended by the possibility of the death penalty is not the infinity of life or immortality, but on the contrary, the finitude of "my life." It is because my life is finite, "ended" in a certain sense, that I keep this relation to incalculability and undecidability as to the instant of my death. It is

because my life is finite, "finished" in a certain sense, that I do not know, and that I neither can nor want to know, when I am going to die. Only a living being as finite being can have a future, can be exposed to a future, to an incalculable and undecidable future that s/he does not have at his/her disposal like a master and that comes to him or to her from some other, from the heart of the other. So much so that when I say "my life," or even my "living present," here, I have already named the other in me, the other greater, younger, or older than me, the other of my sex or not, the other who none-theless lets me be me, the other whose heart is more interior to my heart than my heart itself, which means that I protect my heart, I protest in the name of my heart when I fight [*en me battant*] so that the heart of the other will continue to beat [*battre*] — in me before me, after me, or even without me. Where else would I find the strength and the drive and the interest to fight [*me battre*] and to struggle [*me débattre*], with my whole heart, with the beating [*battant*] of my heart against the death penalty? I can do it, me, as me, only thanks to the other, by the grace of the other heart that affirms life in me, by the grace of the other who appeals for grace and pardon or appeals the condemnation, and with an appeal to which I must respond, and that is what is called here, even before any correspondence, responsibility. It is my own interest, the interest of my life, of the heart of the other in me, that makes me responsible both for the other and before the other who is in front of me before me [*devant moi avant moi*]. Even when the other is beside me, or right up against me, or close to me, the other is first of all in front of me before me in me. And as I am in front of him, or her, he or she is also behind me, invisibly. In other words, I am *invested*: invested as one is by a force greater than oneself and that occupies you entirely by pre-occupying you, and *invested* as one is by a responsibility.

Given this, however paradoxical it may seem, the death penalty, as the only example of a death whose instant is calculable by a machine, by machines (not by someone, finally, as in a murder, but by all sorts of machines: the law, the penal code, the anonymous third party, the calendar, the clock, the guillotine or another apparatus), the machine of the death penalty deprives me of my own finitude; it exonerates me, even, of my experience of finitude. It is to some finitude that this madness of the death penalty claims to put an end[24] by putting an end, in a calculable fashion, to some life. Whence the seduction that it can exert over fascinated subjects, on the side

349

---

24. During the session, Derrida inserts the following remark, before taking up again the interrupted sentence from the beginning: "This is the infinite perversity, properly infinite and infinitizing, of the death penalty. It is this madness — to put an end to finitude."

of the condemning power but also sometimes on the side of the condemned. Fascinated by the power and by the calculation, fascinated by the end of finitude, in sum, by the end of this anxiety before the future that the calculating machine procures. The calculating decision, by putting an end to life, seems, paradoxically, to put an end to finitude; it affirms its power over time; it masters the future; it protects against the irruption of the other. In any case, it *seems* to do that, I say; it only seems to do that, for this calculation, this mastery, this decidability, remain phantasms. It would no doubt be possible to show that this is even the origin of phantasm in general.

And perhaps of what is called religion.

To be sure, an end will never put an end to finitude, for only a finite being can be condemned to death, but the finality of this end as damnation or condemnation to death, its paradoxical finality, is to produce the invincible illusion, the phantasm of this end of finitude, thus of the other side of an infinitization. And since this experience is constitutive of finitude, of mortality, since this phantasm is at work in us all the time, even outside any real scene of verdict and death penalty, since we "recount" this possibility to ourselves all the time, and a calculating decision on the subject of our death cherishes the dream of an infinitization and thus of an infinite survival assured by interruption itself, since we cannot keep ourselves from permanently playing out for ourselves the scene of the condemned one whom we potentially are, well, the fascination exerted by the real phenomena of death penalty and execution, this fascination of which we could give so many examples, has to do with its effect of truth or of acting out: we then see it <as> actually staged; we project it as one projects a film or as one projects a project; we see in projection actually enacted what we are dreaming of all the time — what we are dreaming of, that is, what in a certain way we desire, namely, to give ourselves death and to infinitize ourselves by giving ourselves death in a calculable, calculated, decidable fashion; and when I say "we," this means that in this dream we occupy, simultaneously or successively, all the positions, those of a judge, of judges, of the jury, of the executioner or the assistants, of the one condemned to death, of course, and the position of one's nearest and dearest, loved or hated, and that of the voyeuristic spectators who we are more than ever. And it is the force of this effect of phantasmatic truth that will probably remain forever invincible, thus guaranteeing forever, alas, a double survival, both the survival of the death penalty and the survival of the abolitionist protest.

This is one of the places of articulation with religion and with theology, with the theologico-political. For this phantasm of infinitization at the heart of finitude, of an infinitization of survival assured by calculation itself and

350

the cutting decision of the death penalty, this phantasm is one with God, with, if you prefer, the belief in God, the experience of God, the relation to God, faith or religion. This is another way of saying that as long as there is "God," belief in God, thus belief period, there will be some future for both the supporter of the death penalty and for his abolitionist opponent: both for the agent of the death penalty and for the militant abolitionist.[25] I will come back to this motif in a moment.

To account in a formalizable, calculable fashion for this terrifying solidarity, will one say that both of them redeem, supplement, or indemnify, compensate for or even recompense each other? This is perhaps the moment to return to the question: *What is an indemnity? And a damnation, a condemnation?*

Damnum, in Latin, is wrong, harm, damage, that which wrongs, but also by the same token, loss or fine or penalty: thus the wrong and what must be paid to repair the wrong, to remunerate, indemnify, redeem, and *damno* is to condemn. Even as I permit myself once again—on the questions of the unscathed [*l'indemne*], of indemnity, of the safe and the sound—to refer you to my text "Faith and Knowledge," I will also point out to you the paths followed by Benveniste in his *Indo-European Language and Society*. I will select, from the point of view of the interest that interests us here, certain remarks in the article "Gift and Exchange." For example, on the Germanic institution of the *ghilde* and of *Geld*, money, Benveniste notes *fra-gildan*, which means "to render, restitute," and he insists on the phenomena of fraternity as convivial communion. The origin of these economic groupings called *ghildes* are fraternities linked by a common interest, and the banquets, the *convivia*, the *ghilda*, are characteristic Germanic institutions in the course of which by "acquitting" (*guildan*) a duty of fraternity, one pays a bill, one acquits oneself of a debt, and the sum one must pay is money, *Geld*. Now, at this point, condensing a "long and complex" history, Benveniste recalls that the term *Geld* was connected first of all to a notion of a personal sort, to a *wergeld*, meaning the price of man (*Wer*: man). And this is the price paid to redeem a crime; it is a ransom. Evoking in sum a sort of crime and collective, familial, and national debt, which we should add to the genealogical file of filiation we have been regularly keeping here, Tacitus writes in *Germania* (chapter 21): "They are obliged to share the hostilities of the

25. During the session, Derrida adds this remark: "Unless one thinks, unless one changes this structure: that is what this seminar is about. The impossible task of this seminar is this: to break this alliance, this symmetry between abolitionism and anti-abolitionism where finally each of them needs the other."

260 ‡ TENTH SESSION, MARCH 15, 2000

352 father or their kinsmen as well as their friendships, but they are not prolonged indefinitely. Even homicide can be redeemed with heads of cattle
which are a benefit to the household."[26] This might lead one to think—I
note it although Benveniste does not say so—that payment by the sacrifice
of animals can also interrupt the process, the implacable concatenation of
inherited debts, of collective, familial, filial, tribal, or national guilt. In any
case, Benveniste notes, I quote:

> This *wergeld*, "compensation for murder by a certain payment," is equiva-
> lent to Gr. *tísis*; [which means *payment, remuneration, chastisement, punish-
> ment, vengeance*, but which can also mean *gift, returned or restituted present*,
> thus *restitution*]; it is [Benveniste concludes] one of the ancient aspects of
> the *geld*.
>   We are thus [continues Benveniste] on three lines of development: first
> *religious*, the sacrifice, a payment made to the divinity; secondly, *economic*,
> the fraternity of merchants, and thirdly *legal*, a compensation, a payment
> imposed in consequence of a crime, in order to redeem oneself. At the same
> time, it is a means of reconciliation. Once the crime is over and paid for,
> an alliance becomes established and we return to the notion of the guild.
> (60–61)

These fraternities are said to have the sense of both *group of close solidarity*
and a kind of *dining club*. The convivial group becomes an economic, utilitarian, and commercial association. And here Benveniste evokes a parallel
institution in another society, namely the *daps*, the banquet, a word whose
etymological network leads back, beyond Latin, to the Greek *daptō*, which
means first of all to devour, to consume, to eat in the case of wild beasts
but that gives us *dapnaō*, to spend, *dapanē*, expenditure, money expended,
dapanēma, expenditure, money spent (*dapanēria* is prodigality), *dapanēros*:
spendthrift, prodigal (these words occur in Plato and Aristotle). In some
languages, in Icelandic, *tafn* means "sacrificial animal, sacrificial food," and
353 in Armenian *tawn* means feast. I refer you to these pages for all the deriva-
tions and associations that Benveniste remarks. But he notes that these forms
all have an –n suffix and that through this formal link one can also connect
to it the Latin *dam-num* (*dap-nom*). Then, after a development on the pot-
latch and the rivalry of the agonistic bidding war, often in connection with
hospitality, Benveniste notes that if these archaic notions and terms tend to

26. Quoted in Émile Benveniste, *Vocabulaire des institutions indo-européennes*, vol. 1
(Paris: Minuit, 1969), p. 74; Benveniste, *Indo-European Language and Society*, trans. Elizabeth Palmer (Coral Gables, FL: University of Miami Press, 1973), p. 60.

get erased, in historical times there remains "*damnum* with the derived sense of 'injury sustained, what is taken away by forcible seizure.'" It is

> the expense to which one is condemned by circumstances or by certain legal stipulations. The peasant spirit and the legal exactitude of the Romans transformed the ancient conception: ostentatious expenditure became no more than a wasteful expenditure, what constitutes a loss. *Damnare* means to afflict a *damnum* on somebody, a curtailment of his resources; from this stems the legal notion of *damnare* "to condemn." (63)

Obviously, there remains to be derived the history of this curtailment [*retrenchement*] up to that curtailment of capital or of the head that is called capital punishment.

You would find the same logic and the same system of interpretation in the article "The Sacrifice" in the second volume of this work where Benveniste focuses on this notion of "expenditure," which he notes is not a "simple one" (485). For Benveniste, given the manifest connection between the forms of *dapanē* and *damnum,* it is a matter of seeing "the connection of sense that grounds it" (ibid.). *Damnum* means expense as attested to, for example, by texts of Plautus quoted by Benveniste who concludes that *damnare* means "to compel to spend," an expense considered as a "'sacrifice' of money." And Benveniste concludes: "Here we have the origin of the sense of *damnum* as 'damage': it is properly money given without any return. The fine is indeed money given for nothing. *Damnare* does not mean first of all to condemn in general, but to compel someone to spend money for nothing" (485–86). And this is how Benveniste associates the religious, the juridical, and the economic within the same sacrificial structure (the ritual feast of sacrifice). Whether or not one agrees with him when he interprets these philologico-semantico-institutional data or archives, one has to remark that the "for nothing," the excess of compelled expenditure that at once reimburses a debt, pays or recompenses, reimburses and in so doing pays more than is due, spends for nothing, this excess or this gap clearly marks the double law of homogeneity or of proportionality between the damage and the payment, on the one hand, but also the heterogeneity, the incommensurability of the punishment and the condemnation, on the other. The condemned or damned one pays what he owes but also does something altogether other and thus infinitely more than that, something more and other than acquit himself of a calculable debt. There is economy and aneconomy, unless it is a matter of reimbursement (indemnification) and interest as the incalculable surplus value of capital. And we can wonder where to situate capital pun-

354

ishment here, in this double logic or this double sense of interest. It is in this zone between the capital of capital punishment, or even of decapitation, and the capital of capitalism, of capitalization, that the relations are both necessary and murky, troubling, causing one's head to spin to the point of vertigo. Vertigo seizes hold of the calculating drive when capital or the interest of capital is no longer calculable and becomes virtually infinite, when death without return is a part of the market there where it cannot be part of the market, where it ought to remain incalculable.

Earlier I was suggesting that this was one of the places of articulation with religion and theology, with the theologico-political: the phantasm of infinitization at the heart of finitude, of an infinitization of survival assured by calculation itself and the cutting decision of the death penalty, a phantasm that is one with God, with, if you prefer, the belief in God, the experience of God, the relation to God, faith or religion. I added perhaps audaciously or imprudently that so long as there is "God," belief in God, thus belief period, there will be a future for the proponent of the death penalty and for its abolitionist opponent: both for the agent of the death penalty and for the militant abolitionist. Which would mean that the two apparently opposed interpretations, according to which, on the one hand (the typically Camusian thesis), the death penalty is an essentially religious thing and, in Europe, a Christian thing, that is to say, unable to survive for long in an atheistic society or as one so quickly and superficially says, a "secularized" society, and on the other hand (a typically Hugolian theme), the abolition of the death penalty is a lesson to be drawn from an authentic evangelical Christianity and from the death of Jesus on the cross, these two theses are perhaps obscurely more indissociable and complementary and allied than it appears, leaving then little chance for another path, precisely the one that we are seeking here.

Before coming to the pages in Camus that link the history of the death penalty to religion and notably to the history of the Catholic church, and before taking account of certain folds or certain complications in that thesis, I would like to reconstitute some of its premises in the age of Enlightenment and more precisely in Beccaria. The treatment of the religious and especially Christian dimension is formidably complex in Beccaria. From the beginning of his book, the accusation against priests and the church, an accusation launched in the name of the century's Enlightenment, can also be interpreted as the denunciation not of God or even of the Gospels but of those who — the priests, the church — have "sullied" (the term is Beccaria's) the

355

very object of their faith. For example, in chapter 5 titled "The Obscurity of the Laws," Beccaria begins by attacking both the interpretation of laws, which he calls an "evil" ("the interpretation of the laws is an evil,"[27] he says), and especially, in a gesture of critical and political emancipation that had become frequent at the time, he attacks the elite minority of priests and authorized interpreters, the *interpriesters* [interprêtres] one could say, who take advantage of the ignorance or the lack of education of the common people and capture, intercept, monopolize, capitalize power. The evil comes from the fact that the laws are written in a language that is foreign to ordinary people (in France, Latin, French, etc., a problem that is still with us), and they thus remain dependent on a handful of men, without the people being able "to judge for themselves what will become of their liberty or that of their fellows." Hence the project to write the law in a familiar language that, Beccaria says, "transforms a solemn and public book into one that is almost private and familiar." Thus, a project for the appropriation of the law, of the language of the legal code as democratic emancipation, as democratization:

> What must we think of mankind when we consider that such is the inveterate custom of a large part of cultured and enlightened Europe! The greater number of those who have access to and can understand the sacred code of the laws, the fewer crimes there will be, for there is no doubt that ignorance and uncertainty regarding punishments abet the persuasive power of the passions. (16)

A complex and tricky logic since, for one thing, it is going to link progress to a democratizing secularization, to the access for all or for the greatest number to the texts and the understanding of the laws, but of laws that nevertheless remain "sacred" (Beccaria speaks of the "*sacred* code of the laws" [ibid.]). For this progressivist emancipation, not only will one have to favor the written text, that is, the public character of the discourse of laws that will then represent the general will and not the particular interests of a class, of priests, or of interpreters ("One consequence of the foregoing reflections is that, without writing, a society will never achieve a fixed form of government in which power is a product of the whole rather than the parts and in which the laws—unalterable except by the general will—are not corrupted as they wade through the throng of private interests" [ibid.]), but for this very same reason, one must welcome the invention of the printing press that will have played a decisive role, through the reproduction, publication,

356

357

---

27. Beccaria, *On Crimes and Punishments, and Other Writings*, p. 16.

and distribution of texts, in this democratization. Nonetheless, this printing press (which at bottom will have indirectly supported the abolitionist movement, like the media and TV and the Internet today), this invention of print will have served the universalization and democratization of the texts of law, but — and here's the complication — the texts of law that, for a second time, and regularly, Beccaria calls "sacred" and not profane or secular. In other words, the movement of secularization or desacralization will remain in the service of an authentic sacredness of the law. (There is the same movement in Rousseau, as we confirmed with regard to *The Social Contract* and the idea of sovereignty — not by chance). And this equivocation characterizes the whole demonstration that forms the framework of this book, to the point of finally opposing not Enlightenment reason to faith or religion, but a bad appropriation or a corruption of the sacred texts by guilty priests or a church opposed to what should be the "Gospels' truth" and the "God of mercy" (17). To attest to this I call upon the conclusion to chapter 5 on the "Obscurity of the Laws." (Read Beccaria, 71–72)

> We see, therefore, how useful the printing press is, for it makes the public, not just a few individuals, the depositary of the sacred laws. And we can see how efficacious it has been in dispelling that dark spirit of cabal and intrigue, which vanishes when confronted with the enlightenment and the sciences, apparently despised but in reality feared by the followers of that spirit. This is why we observe in Europe a reduction in the atrocity of the crimes that made our forefathers grieve, becoming tyrants and slaves in turn. Anyone acquainted with the history of the past two or three centuries, as well as our own, will appreciate how the most pleasing virtues have sprung from the lap of luxury and easy living: humanity, benevolence, and tolerance of human error. He will see the effects of what is mistakenly called ancient simplicity and good faith: humanity grieving under implacable superstition; avarice, the ambition of the few stains the coffers of gold and thrones of kings with human blood; secret betrayals and public massacres; every nobleman a tyrant over the common people; preachers of the Gospels' truth soiling with blood the hands that daily touched the God of mercy — these are not the work of this enlightened century, which some call corrupt. (16–17)

358

This logic leads to or is deduced from a dissociation between human justice and divine justice, and in truth from what can be called a humanism of the law. Beccaria's definition of justice does not take into account only force and interest; it arises as if from a human source, radically distinguishing itself from divine justice, which is totally excluded on principle from the book

On Crimes and Punishments. This exclusion of divine justice does not mean that Beccaria does not believe in divine justice; simply, that it is of another order, inaccessible to men, and must be put in something like parentheses on methodological principle as it were. On methodological principle but also out of respect for divine justice, for its almightiness, but also and by the same token for its structure, namely, that in the unique case of God or the perfect, infinite Being, it is the same being that gives itself the right to be at once lawgiver and judge, which must be excluded by principle in any human law, a human law that is always defined by interest and common utility. It is moreover from the point of view of interest and common utility that Beccaria will define what provides the measure of punishments, which he will call "injury" caused to society. (Read Beccaria, 64–65, then 76–77)

> Note that the word *right* is not in contradiction with the word *force*; rather, the former is a modification of the latter, that is, the modification most useful to the greatest number. And by justice I mean nothing but the bond required to hold particular interests together, without which they would dissolve into the old state of unsociability; all punishments that exceed what is necessary to preserve this bond are unjust by their very nature. Care must be taken not to attribute to the word *justice* the notion that it is some real thing, such as a physical force or a living being. It is simply a human way of conceiving things, a way that infinitely influences the happiness of everyone. Much less am I referring to that other kind of justice, which emanates from God and is directly concerned with the punishments and rewards of life in the hereafter. (12)

359

> Finally, some have thought that the severity of the sin ought to be taken into account in the measurement of crimes. The fallaciousness of this opinion will be immediately clear to anyone who impartially examines the true relations among men and between men and God. The former relationships are based on equality. Out of the clash of passions and the opposition of interests, necessity alone gave rise to the idea of *common utility*, which is the foundation of human justice. The latter involves a relationship of dependence on a perfect Being and Creator, who has reserved to Himself alone the right to be lawgiver and judge at once, for only He can be both without any difficulty. If He has established eternal punishments for anyone who disobeys His omnipotence, what kind of insect will dare to supplement divine justice, or will wish to avenge the Being Who is sufficient unto Himself, upon Whom objects make no impression of pleasure or pain, and Who, alone among all beings, acts without being acted upon? The gravity of sins depends upon the inscrutable malice of the human heart, which finite beings cannot know except through revelation. How then can a norm

for punishing crimes be drawn from this? In such a case, men might punish when God forgives and forgive when God punishes. If men can run counter to the Almighty by offending Him, they can also do so when they administer punishments.

VIII. CLASSIFICATION OF CRIMES

We have seen what the true measure of crimes is, namely, *the injury caused to society.* (20)

And in chapter 39, in order to distinguish between crime and sin, between the crime of natural man and the sin of fallen man, Beccaria will further specify: "I am speaking only of the crimes that arise from human nature and from the social pact, and not of sins, whose punishments—even in this world—should be regulated by principles other than those of a limited philosophy" (77).

360   We will come later to the passages directly devoted to the death penalty, which will be criticized by Kant, whose objections to this utilitarian conception of law you can already imagine. What I limit myself to underscoring here is the ground on which there arises this first abolitionist discourse as properly juridical, philosophico-juridical discourse. This ground is not an atheistic or antireligious ground, or even perfectly secularized, but a ground of conventionalism and humanist utilitarianism from which one distinguishes and isolates the specificity of a human justice. And this ground is the one on which arises, less than two centuries later, Camus's "Reflections on the Guillotine" (1957).

There would be a thousand ways to approach this text, which I ask you once again to read since I will only be able to pick up a few threads from it. First of all, to continue with what I was saying about the difference between the death penalty and the other death as regards time, as regards a certain undecidability of the instant of my death that execution interrupts with a trenchant calculation, it so happens that Camus makes a certain remark as to what renders, in his view, the Greek culture of the death penalty, the hemlock in any case, the hemlock of Socrates with which we began, more "humane," and I underscore "humane." He claims that hemlock is more humane because the instant of death is almost chosen by the condemned one and because it is as if the choice of the moment, this relative freedom left to the condemned one, left him the choice between suicide and execution. And Camus then forms the hypothesis concerning what the justice of a death penalty would really be, outside of Greece, that is, in an Abrahamic world, what the justice of a death penalty would be that sought to retrieve *the equivalence*, the strict equivalence between two wrongs, in short, between the wrong, the harm caused and the damage paid in retribution, between the damage of the crime and the damage of the condemnation, between the crime and the punishment. Well, the death penalty would be just and "equivalent" only in the case where the criminal had warned his victim a long time in advance, had made him await his death on a certain day, at a certain hour, in certain conditions. Which, notes Camus, a little rashly perhaps, never happens. (Read Camus, "Réflexions," 1041)

> That day his being an object comes to an end. During the three quarters of *361*
> an hour separating him from the punishment, the certainty of a powerless
> death crushes everything; the animal, tied down and submissive, knows a
> hell that makes the hell he is threatened with seem laughable. The Greeks
> were, after all, more humane with their hemlock. They left a relative free-
> dom to those they condemned, the possibility of delaying or hastening the
> hour of their own deaths. They gave them a choice between suicide and
> execution. By contrast, in order to be doubly sure we carry out justice our-
> selves. But there could not truly be justice unless the condemned, after hav-
> ing made known his decision months in advance, had entered his victim's
> house, had bound him tightly, informed him that he would be put to death
> in an hour, and had finally used that hour to set up the apparatus of death.
> What criminal has ever reduced his victim to such a desperate and power-
> less condition?[28]

I leave you to read what follows so as to come to the conclusions of these "Reflections." They appear to be rather simple both in the objective they propose for the future and in the compromise that, in 1957, they propose for the present. Camus formulates the objective, the hope, for Europe, the unified Europe that is already on the march, a Europe that Camus knows is more Christian than Greek: "Because of what I have just said," he writes, "in the unified Europe of the future the solemn abolition of the death penalty ought to be the first article of the European Code we all hope for" (230).

But while waiting, in 1957, Camus recommends a *compromise* that concerns not the principle of the death penalty but the cruel, still too cruel, conditions of its application. He recommends then, while waiting and in truth to keep us waiting, to help the condemned one await death, an anesthesia or a euthanasia. I purposely choose and emphasize these two Greek words (*anaesthesia, euthanasia*) because, if a moment ago I alluded to Camus's praise for the Greek death penalty that gives the condemned one time, giving him as it were the freedom to decide the time and thus to give himself death rather than receive it, it is, in short, because in the very last conclu- *362*

28. Albert Camus, "Reflections on the Guillotine," p. 202.

sion of these "Reflections," the compromise — as you will hear, the word is Camus's — is a sort of return from Christianity to Greece, a return to a gentler, non-cruel death penalty, which would leave the prisoner the freedom to take himself across, gently, insensibly, from life to death, as if from waking to sleep. This absolute anesthetic would be left within reach of the condemned one. (Read "Réflexions," 1063–64)

> And if, really, public opinion and its representatives cannot give up this law of laziness that simply eliminates what it cannot reform, let us at least, while waiting for a new day of rebirth and truth, not make of it the "solemn slaughterhouse" that befouls our society. The death penalty as it is now applied, and however rarely it may be, is a revolting butchery, an outrage inflicted on the person and body of man. This truncation, that living and uprooted head, those long spurts of blood date from a barbarous period that thought to impress the masses with degrading spectacles. Today when this vile death is administered on the sly, what is the meaning of this torture? The truth is that in the nuclear age we kill as we did in the age of the spring balance. And there is not one man of normal sensitivity who, at the mere thought of such crude surgery, does not feel nauseated. If the French state is incapable of overcoming this habit and of giving Europe one of the remedies it needs, let it begin by reforming the manner of administering capital punishment. Science that serves to kill so many could at least serve to kill decently. An anaesthetic that would let the condemned slip from sleep[29] to death, which would be left within his reach for at least a day so he could take it freely, and which would be administered to him in another form if he were unwilling or weak of will, would assure elimination, if people insisted on it, but would bring a little decency to what is, today, but a sordid and obscene exhibition.
>
> I point to these compromises insofar as one must sometimes despair of seeing wisdom and true civilization influence those responsible for our future. For some men, more numerous than we think, it is physically unbearable to know what the death penalty really is and not to be able to prevent its application. In their own way, they also undergo this punishment, and without any justice. Society will lose nothing if the weight of the filthy images weighing on them is alleviated. But this itself, in the end, will be insufficient. There will be no lasting peace either in the heart of individuals or in social customs so long as death has not been outlawed. (233–34)

363

Next time we might ask ourselves what to think of this absolute anesthetic, if one may say that (death as an imperceptible slide toward sleep),

---

29. Derrida interrupts his reading of the quotation and adds: "This is finally lethal injection, where there is an anesthetic and then . . ."

and then we will analyze more closely what is finally the rather complex and problematic structure of Camus's argument concerning a death penalty linked not only to religion, to Christianity, but to the Catholic church and which ought not to survive in what he terms a "desacralized" society.

This is another way of returning to the Holy Father's recent declaration and the vertigo of eternal damnation. Since the Holy Father neither condemned the death penalty nor asked forgiveness for what is more than a sin of omission, if that is still a sin, we may wonder how long the death penalty will survive the Holy Father in the Catholic church and in Christianity in general, and how to measure the time of the Son's agony.

March 22, 2000

How to sur-vive? How to understand, in a sure enough way, the "sur" of survive? What is a sur-vival? And "The death penalty as theater of life,"[1] let us also say theater of sur-vival.

"To espouse," "to espouse at the cost of his or her life."

This is a quotation: "to espouse at the cost of his or her life." I am dramatizing this quotation, I am theatricalizing it a little by ripping it from its page: "to espouse at the cost of his or her life."

Later I will tell you where it comes from and from which body, from the body of which sentence I violently, or theatrically, extract it so as to let you see and hear it. "To espouse at the cost of his or her life." When I summon to appear on stage the body of this entire sentence, and the paragraph to which it belongs, you will see that it is a matter of an oath, a "beautiful oath," of sworn faith, therefore, that it is also a matter of religion, of circumcision and even of decircumcision. The text waiting to appear says in fact "decircumcise oneself." "To cause someone to espouse it at the cost of his or her life." I leave you to dream about this sentence fragment more or less painfully stolen from its integral body and I move on to a series of questions that you may, as you please, tie to it or untie from it.

Furthermore — before coming to these questions, since this sentence also speaks of cost and of the cost of life, besides all the other questions that one could turn loose on a "cost of life" or on what a life is *worth*, on what is *worth the trouble* [peine] of living, on what costs or what it costs, on life that, as one sometimes says, "has no price," but also on what is worth *more* than life, on the surplus value of life, on the "sur-viving" that would be ultra-life, more than life in life — I confirm that, here as everywhere, it is a matter

---

1. Derrida is referring to the title of a presentation on Burke and Schiller that a student was going to give at the end of this session.

once again, once and for all, *of interest*, of that interest that we have been speaking of since the opening of the seminar, and therefore of cost, of surplus value, and of the priceless, and I thus recall that Kant, precisely, when he opposes Beccaria and the abolitionist logic that was coming to light in his time, in that time of Enlightenment that was also his time, Kant always says that the categorical imperative, like human dignity (*Würde*), is without price and thus not negotiable by any calculation of interest; and he says precisely the same thing on the subject of the death penalty and of the justice that commands imperatively that one sentence to death without considering any benefit, without calculating any interest, without social or political goal, without any concern for setting an example or deterrence, without phenomenal calculation, without evaluation of price and cost. Thereby he means to disqualify in advance the two adversaries, the two parties in dispute, both those who are for the death penalty on the pretext that it is useful to society, to its security, its peace, and so forth, and the abolitionists who contest this calculation, who deny that the cruelty of the death penalty serves as an example and has any deterrent effect whatsoever. All this, says Kant, subjects the principle of justice, from both sides in short, to a calculation of interest and thus to the evaluation of a price. But justice must remain not pricey but priceless, transcendent in relation to any calculating operation, to any interest, or even to the price of life, at the cost of one's life. Justice is above life, beyond life or the life drive, in a sur-viving of which the *sur*, the transcendence of the "sur" — if it is a transcendence — remains to be interpreted.

I am going to read and comment on in succession two passages from Kant that immediately precede his refutation of Beccaria, which we will read on its own only next year. The argumentation developed in these two passages will allow us, I hope, to shed light on the conclusion according to which, I quote, "justice ceases to be justice if it can be bought for any price whatsoever (*denn die Gerechtigkeit hört auf eine zu sein, wenn sie sich für irgend einen Preis weggiebt*)." (Read and comment on Kant) 367

> If, however, [the criminal] has committed murder he must *die*. Here there is no substitute [*Surrogat*] that will satisfy justice. There is no *similarity* between life, however wretched it may be, and death, hence no likeness between the crime and the retribution unless death is judicially carried out upon the wrongdoer, although it must still be freed from any mistreatment that could make the humanity in the person suffering it into something abominable.–Even if a civil society were to be dissolved by the consent of all its members (e.g., if a people inhabiting an island decided to separate and disperse throughout the world), the last murderer remaining in prison would first have to be executed, so that each has done to him what his deeds

deserve and blood guilt does not cling to the people for not having insisted upon this punishment; for otherwise the people can be regarded as collaborators in this public violation of justice.

This fitting of punishment to the crime, which can occur only by a judge imposing the death sentence in accordance with the strict law of retribution, is shown by the fact that only by this is a sentence of death pronounced on every criminal in proportion to his *inner wickedness* (even when the crime is not murder but another crime against the state that can be paid for only by death).–Suppose that some (such as Balmerino and others) who took part in the recent Scottish rebellion believed that by their uprising they were only performing a duty they owed the House of Stuart, while others on the contrary were out for their private interests; and suppose that the judgment pronounced by the highest court had been that each is free to make the choice between death and convict labor. I say that in this case the man of honor would choose death, and the scoundrel convict labor. This comes along with the nature of the human mind; for the man of honor is acquainted with something that he values even more highly than life, namely *honor*, while the scoundrel considers it better to live in shame than not at all (*animam praeferre pudori*. Juvenal). Since the man of honor is undeniably less deserving of punishment than the other, both would be punished quite proportionately if all alike were sentenced to death; the man of honor would be punished mildly in terms of his sensibilities and the scoundrel severely in terms of his. On the other hand, if both were sentenced to convict labor the man of honor would be punished too severely and the other too mildly for his vile action. And so here too, when sentence is pronounced on a number of criminals united in a plot, the best equalizer before public justice is *death*.[2]

Punishment by a court (*poena forensis*) — that is distinct from *natural punishment* (*poena naturalis*), in which vice punishes itself and which the legislator does not take into account — can never be inflicted merely as a means to promote some other good for the criminal himself or for civil society. It must always be inflicted upon him only *because he has committed a crime*. For a human being can never be treated merely as a means to the purposes of another or be put among the objects of rights to things: his innate personality protects him from this, even though he can be condemned to lose his civil personality. He must previously have been found *punishable* before any thought can be given to drawing from his punishment something of use for himself or his fellow citizens. The law of punishment is a categorical imperative, and woe to him who crawls through the windings of eu-

2. Kant, "The Doctrine of Right," pp. 106–7.

daemonism in order to discover something that releases the criminal from punishment or even reduces its amount by the advantage it promises, in accordance with the pharisaical saying: "It is better for *one* man to die than for an entire people to perish." For if justice goes, there is no longer any value in human beings' living on earth.—What, therefore, should one think of the proposal to preserve the life of a criminal sentenced to death if he agrees to let dangerous experiments be made on him and is lucky enough to survive them, so that in this way physicians learn something new of benefit to the commonwealth? A court would reject with contempt such a proposal from a medical college, for justice ceases to be justice if it can be bought for any price whatsoever. (105)

369

Legal execution of the guilty, Kant is thus saying, death freed from any mistreatment (*von aller Misshandlung*) that could debase the humanity in the person of the sufferer (*die Menschheit in der leidenden Person zum Scheusal machen könnte*), from any mistreatment that could transform the condemned sufferer, the suffering person into an object of horror or a theatrical monstrosity.

(Notice that the conditions imposed or recalled, the norms prescribed by Kant for condemnation, for its motivations, and its execution, might well render in fact impossible, forever impracticable, both the condemnation to death and especially its execution. In this sense, the absolutely rigorous and inflexible supporter of the death penalty that Kant is would be *in fact* a de facto abolitionist. De jure, he is for the death penalty and de facto against it, relaunching thereby the whole question of this opposition of fact and right. This is a paradox that we will explore later. For how is one to prevent the calculation of interest from ever sliding into a condemnation to death? And especially, how is one to avoid the suffering and the spectacle of suffering in the execution, even the most discrete or the most anesthetic?)

Whence, once again, the question of anesthesia, which—after this first incursion into a certain theater of the "cost of life" and thus of "sur-viving"—we must approach once more, letting wait a little longer, in cold blood, the supplementary inquiry called up by what one should, then, "espouse at the cost of one's life."

Can one desire—what is really called desire—anesthesia? And desire to lose all sensation? This question might merge into that of suicide, but let us not go too quickly. It might also, in Kantian language, name the almost

370   sublime desire to escape from the realm of sensibility or imagination, from space and time, that is to say, from the realm of phenomenality, that is to say, of the pathological, of affect, of receptivity, that is to say, of the empirical. A certain insensitivity, a certain anesthesia would be the condition of access to a pure, intelligible, and transphenomenal justice, sur-viving beyond life. What is an anesthetic when seen from the promise of death? Of course, good sense and experience teach us that sometimes, and sometimes in an absolutely urgent, painful manner, we *need* an anesthetic, and we have recourse to it. But can one desire, what is really called *desire*, an anesthetic, and in this regard, is what people call death one kind of suffering among others, an example of pain that calls for an analgesic or else something altogether other, in terms of which the question of analgesics or anesthesia would have to be revised from top to bottom?

    The last time, and in the final moment, we were preparing to ask ourselves what to think about a certain absolute anesthetic, if one may say that, death as the unfelt slipping into sleep or more precisely, as Camus said in 1957 in his proposal for a provisional "compromise" with the death penalty, an "anaesthetic that would let the condemned slip from sleep to death, which would be left within his reach for at least a day so he could take it freely" — Camus indeed says "freely," as if the condemned had to choose the ultimate moment of death, as if he were left the freedom to imitate suicide, in some way, the freedom to give himself the illusion that he was the master of his death, master, as poet, to transfigure his execution into suicide; and Camus is the one who wrote, at the beginning of *The Myth of Sisyphus*, in 1942 (which is not just any date): "There is but one truly serious philosophical problem, and that is suicide,"[3] suicide, thus the possibility of giving oneself death by rising above life, through a sur-viving that would no longer belong to life, by ceasing to make of life, of "my life," of the[4] "my life" the absolute price, the without-price, the exorbitantly priced above which

371   nothing has value, not even a sur-viving, a question that Montaigne — from which I am returning and toward whom I will return — already answered in a very resolute manner by saying that since death is still death, whether one gives it to oneself or receives it, it is still better to give it to oneself:

> It comes to the same thing if a man puts an end to himself [*se donne sa fin*] or passively suffers it; whether he runs to meet his last day or awaits it; wherever it comes from [this day, then, the day of death], it is always his; wher-

---

    3. Albert Camus, *Le mythe de Sisyphe*, in *Essais*, p. 99; *The Myth of Sisyphus* (New York: Vintage, 1991), p. 3.
    4. As such in the typescript.

ever the thread [*filet*] may break, the whole thread is broken, the spindle is at an end. The fairest death is the one that is most willed.[5]

I confess that I am fascinated by this figure that I am not sure I understand, the figure of death as a thread or a net that breaks, "wherever the thread may break," he says.[6] I do not know what Montaigne means, of which thread [*fil*] of life, which trickle [*filet*] of blood, which fishing or circus net [*filet*] he is thinking, but since we are in the theater or at the cinema, I imagine a trapeze artist who spends his life throwing himself like a madman from one trapeze to another while relying on a net, whether real or not, on a phantasm of a net in which he has the strength or the weakness to believe; it's his opinion. He believes in this net, and he dies on the day the net breaks, and then it's a fall without a net, willed death, the beautiful death that Montaigne then speaks of. This death would thus be that of a trapeze artist who decides himself to put an end to the net or to the belief in this imaginary or phantasmatic net that was his life insurance, allowing him to live and survive as a tireless trapeze artist.[7]

We had promised ourselves that we would analyze more closely what is finally the rather complex and problematic structure of Camus's argument concerning a death penalty that he claims is linked not only to religion, to Christianity, but to the Catholic church, and that ought not to survive in what he terms a "desacralized" society. The question that always necessarily returns, and it will return today, is how to understand the meaning of sacred, or holy, or unscathed, safe, intact, *heilig*, and so forth. *Der Gesestzgeber ist heilig*, the legislator is holy or sacred, says Kant when he pleads against Beccaria for the maintenance of the death penalty and the penal law in general as categorical imperative, that is, as the only means to treat man, here the criminal, in a worthy manner, as an end in himself and not as a means, a logic that is loaded with consequences since it dismisses a priori, as we have just seen, all debates on the subject of utility or nonutility of the death pen- 372

5. Michel de Montaigne, "Coustume de l'isle de Cea," in *Essais*, livre 2, ch. 3, ed. Albert Thibaudet (Paris: Gallimard, "Bibliothèque de la Pléiade, 1934), p. 386; "A Custom of the Isle of Cea," *Essays*, book 2, chap. 3, trans. and ed. M. A. Screech (London and New York: Allen Lane, Penguin Press, 1991), p. 393.

6. [Translator's note]: The word *filet* can mean trickle, thread, thin line, and in this sense may be interchangeable with *fil*. But a *filet* can also be a net, like a fisherman's net or, as here, a safety net for a trapeze artist.

7. Added by hand on the typescript and read during the session: "Only a grace, a gracious grace granted, can save him then and let him survive. For we are speaking, here, in this seminar on pardon and perjury and death penalty, only of grace and passion. And of their Christian register or not."

alty, of an exemplarity or an empirical finality, of any interest whatsoever in the death penalty. We will return to this, as I've said, but no doubt next year, if life is granted us, and if some net protects us.

This was another way, we were saying, of returning to the Holy Father's recent declaration and to the vertigo of eternal damnation. Since the Holy Father neither condemned the death penalty[8] nor asked forgiveness for what is more than a sin of omission, if it is still a sin, we may wonder, we were saying, how long the death penalty will survive the Holy Father in the Catholic church and in Christianity in general, and how to measure the time of the Son's agony. Always the question of *survival*, then, and of the blood in filiation.

The time of the agony of the Son of God, then, and the absolute anesthetic. And what if religion, even before being defined <as> "the opium of the people," had been the anesthetic, the analgesic drug meant to make death pass, to appease, attenuate, deny, forget, distract from the pain linked to death, but also by the same token to make the death penalty pass for something less serious than it appears, a sleep or a transition, in short, to the beyond, to a survival in the beyond, the system of Christian justification of the death penalty playing the role of anesthetic, the priests and the confessors ritually assigned to the last scene confirming that they are there to alleviate a temporary suffering and to promise heaven, another survival, and so forth? You know that there are those condemned to death—we evoked some examples, I believe, along with Genet—who refuse the religious anesthetic and confession and the promise of survival. Well, Montaigne, whose tower I was lucky enough to visit last week, Montaigne, whose wily and enigmatic hand-to-hand combat with Christianity, or even with the Marrano Judaism that haunted his filiation on the side of his mother, would deserve more than one seminar, Montaigne, who died a Christian death in his bed in his fifties, rather old for the time, to be sure, but like a teenager for our time, and deprived of so many other lives to come beyond his fifties (I was deeply pained for him, who died so young, in short, I felt a great wave of inner compassion for him while meditating a few days ago next to what he no doubt loved the most—well, now I've a mind to read you a passage from "On Age," in chapter 57 of book 1).[9]

> I cannot accept the way we determine the span of our lives. I note that wise men shorten it considerably compared to common opinion. "What!"

8. During the session, Derrida specifies: "last week."

9. One might expect this parenthesis to close after the quotation from Montaigne, since the sentence begun before it continues beyond the quotation.

said Cato the Younger to those who wanted to prevent him killing himself: "Am I still at the age when you can accuse me of abandoning life too soon?" Yet he was only forty-eight. He reckoned, considering how few men reach it, that his age was fully mature and well advanced. And those who keep themselves going with the thought that some span of life or other which they call "natural" promises them a few years more could only do so provided that there was some privilege exempting them from those innumerable accidents—which each one of us comes up against and is subject to by nature—that can interrupt the course of life they promise themselves. What madness it is to expect to die of that failing of our powers brought on by extreme old age and to make that the target for our life to reach when it is the least usual, the rarest kind of death. We call that death, alone, a natural death, as if it were unnatural to find a man breaking his neck in a fall, engulfed in a shipwreck, surprised by plague or pleurisy, and as though our normal condition did not expose us to all of those harms. Let us not beguile ourselves with such fine words: perhaps we ought, rather, to call natural anything which is generic, common to all and universal. Dying of old age is a rare death, unique and out of the normal order and therefore less natural than the others. It is the last, the uttermost way of dying; the farther it is from us, the less we can hope to reach it; it is indeed the limit beyond which we shall not go and which has been prescribed by Nature's law as never to be crossed; but it is a very rare privilege of hers to make us last until then. It is an exemption which she grants as an individual favor to one man in the space of two or three centuries, freeing him from the burden of those obstacles and difficulties which she strews along the course of that long progress. (366–67)

374

Montaigne, who kept a prayer stool in his bedroom, above a chapel to which he was connected by a staircase he had built into the stone and through which, when he was ill, he could hear the chanting of the mass rising up toward him (today the chant or the song, if not the song of songs, would reach him by way of telephone, or even a telephone that would keep a recording of the live voice—as on a cell phone), well, Montaigne recounts in book 1, chapter 14 ("That the taste of good and evil things depends in large part on the opinion we have of them"), that a certain condemned man refused confession as a fraud or a trap by which he did not want to let himself be taken in, numbed, distracted, desensitized, anesthetized, signaling thereby that he preferred to love life, to live while loving, and to die while loving, to die while loving life, to die alive, in short, to die in his lifetime (as Hélène Cixous says, in *Or*, about her father),[10] to die in his lifetime, to die while

10. Hélène Cixous, *Or, les lettres de mon père* (Paris: Éditions Des femmes, 1997).

preferring life, or even to die from loving life rather than to let himself be diverted from it by the analgesic trap of confession. This man condemned to death, notes Montaigne, I quote, "answered his confessor, who promised him that he would sup that day at table with Our Lord [thus with the Son of God]: 'You go instead; as for me, I'm fasting'" (54).

This passage (since I'm at Montaigne,[11] I'm going to stay a while) confirms the idea that abolitionism, the idea that the death penalty was a problem, had not emerged at the time (it will await the Enlightenment, and once again this gives us access to a problem if not a definition as to the essence of the Lumières, or the Aufklärung, or the Enlightenment or the Illuminismo: the essence of the light common to all these enlightenings, the essence of this *aube* [dawn],[12] would it not be the twilight of capital punishment, the doubly crepuscular moment in which one begins to think the death penalty, starting from its end, starting from the possibility of its end, starting from the possibility of an end that breaks like day, and already begins to condemn the condemnation to death? The age of Enlightenment would be like the rising, the sunrise, the east or the yeast [*le levant ou le levain*] of a form of speech diagnosing, prognosticating: the condemnation to death is condemned, in the long run [*à échéance*]), so this passage from Montaigne, at a moment when the idea of sentencing to death the death sentence had not really begun to surface, explains to us, through a series of examples and quotations à la Montaigne, all the reasons men and women and children have had to prefer something else to life and have signaled this by the way they have accepted death, or even, most often preferred the death sentence and execution, all of this signaling that there was something worth more than life, which was above life, like a sur-vival that would be something other and better than life, a sur-vival that would not necessarily be a life prolonged in another way or in another world, but a survival without life [*une survie sans vie*], which would thus respond, correspond to something else (but what? but who?), to something or to someone that would be worthy of "causing one to espouse it at the cost of his or her life."

In the long fragments I am going to quote, which can very well dispense with any commentary since the thinking is, I think, very clear, I will nonetheless underscore two words or two concepts that might risk, on first hearing, not receiving all the emphasis I would like to give them. There is

11. [Translator's note]: Derrida's phrasing here recalls that the writer's name is also the name of the family's estate, the Château de Montaigne.

12. [Translator's note]: "Dawn" is in English in the original.

first of all the word or concept of "force," the word *forte* [strong, powerful]: what allows one to rise above life, sur-viving beyond the livingness [*vivance*] of life, and to "cause one to espouse it at the cost of his or her life," is a rather strong force, and although it is the force of an opinion ("Any opinion is strong enough to cause someone to espouse it at the cost of his or her life"), let us not forget that the word and the concept of "opinion" have themselves a great force here: "to opine" means *to say yes,* to judge by *saying yes,* by affirming, by believing as well, by believing in it while believing, while believing in it, to opine, thus, as a believer. To opine means here *I believe, I believe you, I want to believe in you, I believe I believe in you,* wanting to believe and believing one believes coming down to the same thing here or pulling each other along in the same momentum or the same movement of a flying trapeze, here at the cost of life, the trapeze flying here on the force of what one would have to espouse at the cost of one's life. Opinion here has the force of an act of faith that says *yes,* and it is the force of this force, when "opinion is strong enough [*assez forte*]," it is the force of this force that exceeds life, that causes one to espouse it at the cost of one's life, that amounts to sacrificing life to its force, to the force or the intensity of its *yes,* to its act of faith or love, to its belief, its will, its desire to believe, its believing in believing.

Hence the second word and the second concept that I wanted to emphasize in the passage I am going to read, that of "religion." The example par excellence, in truth the essence of this force of "opinion strong enough to cause someone to espouse it at the cost of his or her life," of this sworn faith or this belief, is what is called religion, the religious, religiosity. And Montaigne is speaking thus of *all* religions, not only the Christian religion ("This is an example," he says, "of which no religion is incapable")[13]—every religion is capable, because it is the essence of religion; every religion is capable of preferring something else to life, at the cost of life. In other words, religion is or grants the surviving of survival. So that this discourse and this doxography of *doxai,* of opinions strong enough to rise above life, be it in the condemnation to death, this doxographic discourse on *doxa,* this collection of opinions on the essence of opinion, of opining, of saying yes, is a thesis, in short, or at least a hypothesis of Montaigne's on the essence of the religious: the religious of religion is always the acceptance of sacrificial death and the death penalty, in the shadow of a sur-viving that supposedly is worth more than life.

377

13. The closing parenthesis has been added.

Let me now read and comment on a few of these passages. (Read and comment on Montaigne, pp. 103, 104, 105)

How many of the common people do we see who, when led toward their death, and not merely death, but one mixed with disgrace and sometimes grievous torments, show such assurance (some out of stubbornness, others out of natural simplicity) that we may perceive no change in their ordinary behavior: they settle their family affairs and commend themselves to their friends, singing, preaching, and addressing the crowd—indeed even including a few jests and drinking the health of their acquaintances every bit as well as Socrates did. One fellow as he was led to the gallows asked that they avoid a certain street, for he risked being arrested there by a tradesman for an old debt. Another asked the hangman not to touch his throat for fear that he would break out laughing since he was so ticklish. Another, whose confessor was promising him he would sup that day at the table of Our Lord, answered: "You go instead; as for me, I'm fasting." Another, who asked for a drink and the hangman having drunk of it first, said he didn't want to drink after him for fear of catching the pox. Everyone has heard tell the tale of the man from Picardy who was on the stairs when they showed him a young woman; if he agreed to marry her, his life would be saved (as our laws sometimes allows); he studied her a moment, and having noticed she limped, said: "Run up the noose: she's lame." And a similar story is told of a man in Denmark, who was condemned to be beheaded: he was on the scaffold when he was presented with similar terms, which he refused because the girl they offered him had sagging jowls and her nose was too pointed. A man-servant in Toulouse was accused of heresy and for sole justification of his belief he referred to that of his master, a young student in jail with him: he preferred to die rather than let himself be persuaded that his master could be mistaken. We read that when Louis XI took the city of Arras, there were many of its citizens who let themselves be hanged rather than cry "Long live the King."

Even today in the kingdom of Narsinga, the wives of their priests are buried alive with their dead husbands. All other wives are burned alive at their husbands' funerals not merely with constancy but with gaiety. And when they cremate the body of their dead king, all his wives and concubines, his favorites and a multitude of dignitaries and servants of every kind trip so lightly towards the pyre to cast themselves into it that they apparently deem it an honor to be his companions in death. . . . (53–54)

Any opinion is strong enough to cause someone to espouse it at the cost of his or her life. The first article in that fair oath that Greece swore and kept in the war against the Medes was that every man would rather exchange life for death than Persian laws for their own. In the wars of the Turks and the Greeks, how many men can be seen accepting the cruelest of deaths rather than decircumcise themselves in order to be baptized? This is an example that no religion is incapable of. (54–55)

Since last week, I have been meditating, if one may call it meditating, on this strange hypothesis of a compromise with the death penalty: an anesthetic meant to act imperceptibly, to desensitize imperceptibly, and that would be for one day, one single day, at the disposal of the condemned man, free (Camus does indeed say "freely"), free to use it as he wished at the moment he wished. Interrogating all the terms of this hypothetical compromise, one wonders about this time calculation: one day (why one day, only one day or one whole day that can look like an eternity, an eternity of bliss or suffering or painful bliss? Or why only a day: for whoever loves life, as one says, and remains attached to that right to life about which Camus, we will come back to this, says, like Hugo, that it is a "natural right,"[14] for whoever loves life, or loves living or lives to love, for whoever loves what life gives one to love, a day can be an incalculable eternity of suffering or bliss, or suffering in bliss, too much or too little, too much and too little, infinitely too much in the separation, infinitely too little in the bliss),[15] and before looking to this or that anesthetic or tranquilizer, sleeping pill or "painkiller," to some all-powerful Lexomil[16] that would dispense death like sleep, that would let death surprise us, as they say, in our sleep, it would first be necessary to find an anesthetic that would desensitize one not only to pain but to time itself, that is to say, to sensibility itself, or even to the form of sensibility, as Kant says of time ("form of the sensibility of internal objects and of objects in general"), there where suffering has to do with the time that must be calculated, the time that separates, that separates one instant from another or that separates one from another in general, the time that spaces, the spacing of time that must be endured in the calculation of the incalculable, a minute, a day, weeks, and so forth. I must say that the "compromise" proposed in conclusion by Camus, so as to make, he says, the death penalty or its application more decent, this compromise seems to me both serious and quite flimsy. It is serious because it points indeed to an empirical path for alleviating or humanizing things (and let us not forget that Camus had in mind the guillotine, that his text is titled "Reflections on the Guillotine"), but it finally anticipates a certain way in which the death-dealing American states could reinstate the death penalty after the 1972 Supreme Court decision, "lethal injection" with an initial anesthetic meant to remove the act

14. Camus, "Reflections on the Guillotine," p. 221.
15. The closing parenthesis has been added.
16. [Translator's note]: The brand name of a tranquilizer in wide use in France.

of putting to death from the constitutional concept of "cruel and unusual punishment"—which means that this anesthesial compromise can just as well confirm and legitimize and authorize the survival of the death penalty at the very moment this compromise attenuates the suffering it causes or even promises survival tout court.

Anesthesia and religion, then, there is the program.

Without knowing where this seminar is going, one can presume it will always be vain to conclude that the universal abolition of the death penalty, if it comes about one day, means the effective end of any death penalty, as vain as it is to believe that the vegetarian effectively abstains from eating, in reality or symbolically, living flesh, or even from participating in any cannibalism. How can one love a living being without being tempted to take it within oneself? Love and Eucharist. Transubstantiation. Eat me, this is my body, *hoc est corpus meum, touto estin to sōma mou*. Keep it in memory of me. Which also means, in the mouth of the Son, eat me, keep me, I am leaving (or I am dying provisionally), I sur-vive, that is to say, I am going to come back; I am coming back right away; time does not count, but on the condition that, as living beings, you eat while waiting, that you have the cold-blooded composure [*le sang froid*] to eat well, to eat me, that is, to eat for me, since one very well has to eat well, as the other says, while waiting for me, you must assimilate my blood or the blood for me, but without me, like a slow sugar.[17] Sense me–sans me [*Sens moi–sans moi*]. Cannibalism and the food of carnivores will always survive the literal end of human sacrifices or vegetarianism, just as crime and the death penalty will always survive the suppression of the death penalty. Even when the death penalty will have been abolished, when it will have been purely and simply, absolutely and unconditionally, abolished on earth, it will survive; there will still be some death penalty. Other figures will be found for it; other figures will be invented for it, other turns in the condemnation to death, and it is this rhetoric beyond rhetoric that we are taking seriously here. We are taking seriously here all that is condemned, whether it be a life or a door or a window[18]—or whatever or whoever it may be whose end would be promised, announced, prognosticated, decreed, signed like a verdict.

Let us harbor no illusion on this subject: even when it will have been

17. [Translator's note]: That is, *sucre lent*, which is more commonly called a complex carbohydrate in English.

18. [Translator's note]: In French, a door or window that is boarded up or filled in is said to have been condemned.

abolished, the death penalty will survive; it will have other lives in front of it, and other lives to sink its teeth into.

But nursing no illusion on this subject must not prevent us — on the contrary, this is courage and composure [*le sang-froid*] — from being militant, from organizing with cool heads [*de sang-froid*], to militate, while waiting, for what is called the abolition of the death penalty, and thus for life, for survival, in the priceless interest of life, to save what is left of life. Whether or not the corpus here is that of Jesus Christ, whether or not the blood, wine, or slow sugar of life comes to us from the Gospels, the Song of Songs, and from what they teach us about love as love of life, of my life, of the "my life," is at bottom, perhaps, somewhat secondary in my view. Let us say with a cool head [*de sang-froid*] that the Passion of the Son of God is but an example. An example of passion. Now, that the forceful *opinion* of some holds it to be the best example given, the exemplary example of the gift or forgiveness of love, of passion and of grace in general, which must put an end to the death penalty, thus put an end to the church, at least to that church which has supported it and has not yet asked forgiveness for that fact, this is no doubt an interesting problem, and we pose it, we envision it in fact, but let us be content to say here that the Son of God is but an *example*, or else a copy [*un exemplaire*] for us — and before this abyss of what is meant by *exemplarity* or "imitation of J. C.," before this abyss as before every other abyss, let us keep our composure [*sang froid*]. Love itself has need of it, of this granted grace, in order to save itself, to attempt forever to come through safe and sound. It must keep watch [*veiller*], it must mount sur-veillance over survival; it must keep watch to organize, work, and militate with a cool head, but it must never cease appealing to the chance of a pardon issued, of grace granted.

381

GEOFFREY BENNINGTON
teaches literature and French philosophy at Emory University.

MARC CRÉPON
is director of research at the Centre National de Recherche Scientifique
and chairs the Department of Philosophy at the École Normale
Supérieure (Paris).

THOMAS DUTOIT
is professor of English at the Université de Lille 3.

PEGGY KAMUF
is professor of French and comparative literature
at the University of Southern California.